Rock & Roll

IN HISTORICAL PERSPECTIVE

Customized version of
History of Rock and Roll, 4th Edition
by Thomas E. Larson
Designed specifically for
Steven Maxwell at Kansas State University

Steven Maxwell

Kendall Hunt
publishing company

Kendall Hunt
publishing company
www.kendallhunt.com
Send all inquiries to:
4050 Westmark Drive
Dubuque, IA 52004-1840

Copyright © 2015 by Kendall Hunt Publishing Company

ISBN 978-1-4652-7814-2

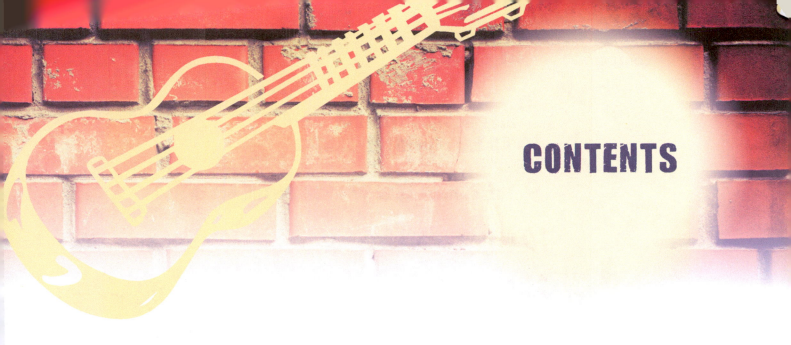

CONTENTS

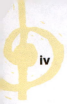

HISTORICAL INTERLUDE: 1920s–1940s

Before There Was Rock

Although many list the birth year of rock and roll as 1955, rock and roll did not just pop up overnight. It took years for the different styles of music in the United States to meld together and create this new, popular music. There was a perfect balance of musicians and history that created a "perfect storm" to set up the tidal wave of rock and roll in the 1950s.

In 1953 only 10% of music considered to be rock and roll was able to make on the pop charts. By 1945 that percentage grew to 25%, and by 1958, 95% of rock and roll music was being played on pop radio and was on the pop charts.

In order to understand how these events occurred, we must take a look at not only the musicians who were producing the music, but also what was happening historically in the United States. We need to begin before the 1950s in order to understand how the ground swell of rock and roll was able to become a tidal wave by 1955.

1920s

The 1920s were a time of both highs and lows in the United States. World War I came to a conclusion two years before the decade began but in many ways shaped the mind-set for many Americans. World War I was one of the bloodiest wars in the history of man. The technological advances in warfare grew tremendously throughout the campaign beginning with soldiers riding at each other on horse back with sabers drawn and single fire weapons, and finally ending with tanks, poisonous gas, and advanced air assaults.

As soldiers returned from the war, they tried to return to there regular lives even after witnessing this horrific devastation. Many art forms, including music, were heavily influenced by this mentality. The grotesque and the playful became the center of the many art mediums including music.

The 1920s, often referred to as "The roaring Twenties," was also the beginning of an unprecedented economic raise in the United States. The total wealth of the United States would more than double from 1920 to 1929. This wealth would create a new push for material goods including refrigerators, appliances, and cars. Radio would also become the exceptionally popular as well with stations able to broadcast "coast-to-coast" by 1928.

Jazz would become one of the most popular forms of music during the 1920s particularly with the young "new-money" up and comers. Its angular, sharp and bouncy style created a sense of freedom and the feeling of letting loose. Not unlike rock and roll in the 1950s, a conflict arose with those falling in love with the new music and those disturbed by it. By the 1930s jazz would become a radio staple and would usher in a new sound to pop music, big band.

1930s

Black Tuesday, or the stock market crash of 1929, brought the Roaring Twenties to a screeching halt. This, the worst stock market crash in US history, brought over ten years of economic and psychological depression to the United States

and the world, Nearly one quarter of all Americans were out of work, more than 26,000 businesses failed, and many families were force to move into shantytowns during this time, which is known as the Great Depression.

Although there was little money to spare, listening to the radio was free and became one of the most popular pastimes in the United States. Sports programs as well as entertainment shows, such as *Amos and Andy*, filled the air and became wildly popular. Music also filled this entertainment medium. Swing and big band music flew to the top of the charts and big band leaders such as Benny Goodman, Tommy and Jimmy Dorset, and Fletcher Henderson, became household names. Radio programs offered listeners a distraction from the difficult times in which they were living.

In 1932 Franklin Delano Roosevelt was elected president and implemented what he called "The New Deal," which used federal funding to employ many Americans. Although economic recovery did not happen overnight, it would begin the swing back to stability. In December of 1941, the Japanese bombed Pearl Harbor, which drew the United States into the Second World War. The war efforts helped stimulate the American economy throughout the beginning of the 1940s, bringing the Great Depression to an end.

1940s

World War II heavily influenced the first half of 1940s. Although the conflict had been going on since the late 1930s, the United States did not join the war until after the bombing of Pearl Harbor in 1941. With political pressure mounting in Congress for the United States to discontinue its strict neutrality dealing with world conflicts, the first peacetime draft was imposed in the United States in 1940.

As production of materials grew to outfit the United States in the war, so too grew the economy and jobs. The unemployment rates dropped significantly and by the end of the 1940s the United States had returned to a stable economy.

The GI Bill was introduced after the war to give members of the military financial assistance to attend college, get a low-rate mortgage and to receive low cost loans to start their own businesses. Many members of the military took advantage of this and either started their own companies or went to college. This instigated the raise of the middle class and allowed many to increase their income considerably. Eventually, this would generate numerous single-income families in the 1950s, creating opportunities for children to have allowances and to spend their own money. This, of course, would include purchasing rock and roll records!

1

THE ROOTS OF ROCK AND ROLL

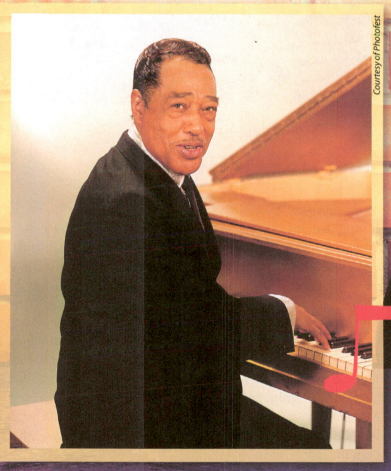

Courtesy of Photofest

"It's like an act of murder; you play with intent to commit something."

— *Duke Ellington on Jazz*

KEY TERMS

Tin Pan Alley
The Swing Era
Race music
Hillbilly music
Cover
Acoustical/electrical
    process
Album
Single
Major labels
Independent labels
Billboard magazine
Record Industry
    Association of
    America (RIAA)

Gold, platinum and
    diamond records
Disc jockey (DJ)
*The Moondog House
    Rock and Roll Party*
Top 40
Blues
Work song, shout, and
    field holler
Mississippi Delta
Country blues
AAB lyric form
Classic blues
Jazz
Black Gospel

Melisma
Rhythm and Blues
Doo-wop
British folk tradition
Bristol sessions
Grand Ole Opry
Cowboy songs
Western swing
Bluegrass
Honky tonk

KEY FIGURES

Bing Crosby
Frank Sinatra
Benny Goodman
Pat Boone
Alan Freed
Moondog
Todd Storz

Robert Johnson
Thomas Dorsey
Louis Jordan and His
    Tympany Five
Frankie Lymon and the
    Teenagers
Ralph Peer

The Carter Family
Jimmie Rodgers
Bill Monroe
Lester Flatt/Earl Scruggs
Hank Williams

ROCK AND ROLL: THE MUSIC THAT CHANGED THE WORLD

When rock and roll exploded onto the American landscape in the mid-1950s, it marked nothing less than a defining moment in history. In many ways its birth was a manifestation of a seismic shift that was already taking place in our cultural fabric: from an elitist to a working class ethos; from an adult oriented society to one that glorified youth; and from one where art was defined by European standards to one where it was defined in purely American terms. Rock and roll was purely American, as were all of its musical ancestors, which included the blues, jazz, Rhythm and Blues, gospel, hillbilly, country, bluegrass and honky tonk. And like America, rock and roll didn't sit still for long; it very quickly began to evolve as it embraced a wide variety of influences that ranged from new technologies to interpretations by British imitators. As a result, within just a few years there were a plethora of styles—folk rock, soul, psychedelic, hard rock, art rock, etc.—that all fit under the rock umbrella.

The emergence of rock and roll also signaled a major shift in the nature of our popular music. Unlike the pop music of the first half of the 20th century, which was largely conceived by an industry based in New York City and watered down to appeal to the largest audience possible—in other words, white, middle-class adults—rock and roll was from the South and middle states, and was decidedly more rural, more lower class, more dynamic, more African American, and more youth oriented. Unlike the music of Tin Pan Alley, rock incubated in the streets in a grassroots fashion, so it had a mind of its own and would not easily take orders from anyone. Rock's sense of independence has remained intact—even today it continues to demonstrate a remarkable virus-like resistance to the constant meddling by the pop music industry. This is in fact one of the central themes that runs through the music's history: every time the corporate types appear to have harnessed the music for their own self-interest, rock seems to somehow wriggle free and reinvent itself. Like the musicians who create it, rock in this sense is rebellious and self-determined, resentful of authority, and defies subordination.

But above all, rock and roll, simply stated, is, always has been and always will be, the music of youth and all that goes with it. During the mid-1950s, it exploded onto the American cultural landscape through the insistence of small independent record labels, renegade radio DJs and a teen audience that wouldn't take the watered down industry product any more. For the first time in history, the music of the underprivileged and disaffected, the angry and unruly, the idealistic and discontented would emerge as America's most popular music. As rock and roll took its place on center stage, it changed our society, and in turn reflected those changes within itself.

Chapters 2–13 of this text chronicle the history of the music and the important events and personalities that shaped it. But before we get there, let's take a look at the American music scene in the first half of the 20th century and see how the groundwork was laid for the rock and roll revolution.

THE EARLY YEARS OF AMERICAN POP MUSIC

Tin Pan Alley

America's pop music industry was created in the late 1800s when the publishers and songwriters of **Tin Pan Alley** began to supply vaudeville and Broadway shows with popular songs. These songs were also made available in written form to the general public through the sale of sheet music. Tin Pan Alley was originally an actual place, on 28th Street between Broadway and 6th Avenue in New York, where many of the earliest publishing companies set up shop. Although most eventually moved uptown, the name stuck and today is generally used to describe the music publishing industry as it operated in the first half of the 20th century. The music of the Tin Pan Alley composers defined much of our popular song catalogue of the era, and was eventually used not only for theatrical shows but also for popular songs, Hollywood movies, and jazz standards. Among the greatest Tin Pan Alley composers were Irving Berlin ("God Bless America," "White Christmas"); George and Ira Gershwin ("I Got Rhythm," "'S Wonderful"); Richard Rodgers, teaming with lyricists Lorenz Hart ("My Funny Valentine") and Oscar Hammerstein II (Broadway musicals *South Pacific, Oklahoma, The Sound of Music*); and Cole Porter ("I've Got You Under My Skin").

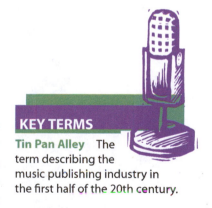

KEY TERMS

Tin Pan Alley The term describing the music publishing industry in the first half of the 20th century.

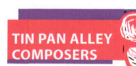

TIN PAN ALLEY COMPOSERS

- Irving Berlin
- George and Ira Gershwin
- Richard Rodgers
- Lorenz Hart
- Oscar Hammerstein II
- Cole Porter

The First Pop Singers

One of the first important pop singers in 20th century America was Al Jolson who, singing in blackface as minstrel singers had done in the mid-1800s, became Broadway's biggest star in the early 1900s. In 1927 Jolson also starred in the first successful talking picture, *The Jazz Singer*. As recordings and radio began to replace sheet music as the most popular medium for the distribution of pop music, the first true pop singers, known as crooners emerged. Rudy Vallee, who used a megaphone to project his voice (before amplification was used) became one of the first entertainers to effectively use radio to reach stardom in the 1920s. **Bing Crosby** became the most influential crooner with his easy-going charm and witty style of singing ballads. Starting his career in 1926 making records with the Paul Whiteman Orchestra (with whom he had his first #1 hit in 1928 with "Ol' Man River"), Crosby began working in network radio and film in 1931, and eventually starred in more than 60 movies before his death in 1977. His recording of "White Christmas" from the 1942 movie *Holiday Inn* rose to the #1 spot on the charts, won a Grammy Award for best song of 1942, and eventually sold over 30 million copies, making it the best-selling vinyl single in history. (Elton John's "Candle in the Wind" broke this record in 1997 with nearly 40 million copies sold in CD single format.)

The first pop singer to create a unique personal style and image was **Frank Sinatra**. Influenced by jazz singers Louis Armstrong and Billie Holiday, Sinatra took liberties with melodies and interpreted songs in his own way. Starting as a big band singer with the Tommy Dorsey Orchestra, Sinatra became a solo artist and film star in the 1950s with a tough-guy attitude and good looks that made him popular among both male and female fans. Although he condemned rock and roll at first, Sinatra's off-screen public macho posturing, womanizing, and associations with shadowy figures in fact became a sort of blueprint for many rock stars that followed him. He also spawned a generation of dark and handsome Italian singers such as Dean Martin, Tony Bennett, and Vic Damone that also had considerable pop success.

TRIVIA NOTE

Frank Sinatra was the first pop singer to create a unique personal style and image.

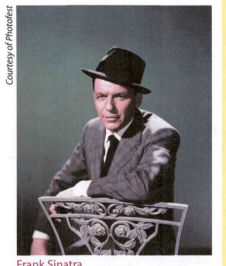

Courtesy of Photofest

Frank Sinatra

SINATRA ON ROCK AND ROLL

Frank Sinatra, who was the object of shrieking female fans in the 1940s, originally dismissed rock and roll, commenting that "It is sung, played, and written for the most part by cretinous goons, and by means of its almost imbecilic reiteration and sly, lewd, in plain fact dirty, lyrics it manages to be the martial music of every side-burned delinquent on the face of the earth." However, his tune quickly changed, and by 1960 he cohosted a network TV special with Elvis Presley on which the two sang each other's signature songs, "Love Me Tender" and "Witchcraft."

The Swing Era

During the **Swing Era** (1935–1946), big band jazz (now referred to as swing) became the dominant form of pop music. Swing brought the recording industry back to life after it was almost killed by the Depression. It helped the country get through WWII, as many of the biggest Swing Era hits were sentimental in nature and reflected the mood of anxiety that accompanied the war. Swing also firmly established itself as music to dance to, and spawned dozens of dance fads such as the Fox Trot, Lindy Hop, Jitterbug, and Rumba. The term "swing" was used as a marketing ploy to overcome the negative connotations that still persisted about jazz in the 1930s. During the early years of the Swing Era, most of the hit records were of original material written and arranged by the bands themselves. Later, as swing became more popular, most of the hits were novelty, sing-along, and sentimental songs written by Tin Pan Alley professionals that featured the band vocalists. It was in this way that the careers of Frank Sinatra, Doris Day, Peggy Lee, and others were launched.

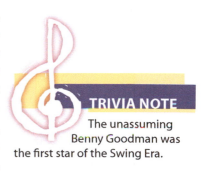

KEY TERMS

Swing Era   The name given to the period from 1935–1946 when big band jazz was the most popular music in America.

The first star of the Swing Era was the unassuming **Benny Goodman**, whose meteoric rise to fame started at the Palomar Ballroom in Los Angeles on August 21, 1935. Hundreds of teens showed up that night to hear and dance to the music they had been hearing on the NBC network radio program *Let's Dance*. One secret of Goodman's success was the arrangements he had bought from black musicians such as Fletcher Henderson and Don Redman that up to that point had rarely been heard outside of Harlem. By virtue of being white, Goodman was able to bring the music of African American culture to the mass white audience, in much the same way that Elvis Presley would do 20 years later. In his wake, hundreds of other bands that looked like Goodman's and sounded like pale imitations of the Harlem musicians who created the music provided the country with the soundtrack to an era.

TRIVIA NOTE

The unassuming Benny Goodman was the first star of the Swing Era.

The Post-War Transitional Years

From 1946 to 1954, the years between the Swing Era and the early years of rock and roll, the pop music business was in a state of transition. Although the major record labels continued to successfully promote mainstream pop artists such as Sinatra and Patti Page, **race music** (later known as Rhythm and Blues) and **hillbilly music** (later called Country Western) were becoming increasingly popular among a growing, albeit segmented audience. Around this same time, a number of small, independent record labels emerged that specialized in making race and hillbilly records. In spite of the fact that by 1952 there were around 100 independents, their mark on the industry was still negligible—only five of the more than 150 singles that became million sellers during this period came from independent labels.

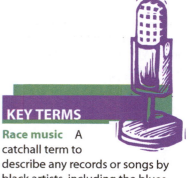

KEY TERMS

Race music   A catchall term to describe any records or songs by black artists, including the blues and what would later be known as Rhythm and Blues.

Hillbilly music   The traditional old time music of the rural southern United States, with origins in English folk music. Hillbilly music is the foundation of modern country music.

Cover   A new recording of a charting song that seeks to 'cover' up the original song.

On the rare occasion that an R&B or country record did break through and become a hit, the strategy that major labels often employed was to quickly record a cover version by a pop singer who had a broad commercial appeal. **Covers** were usually stripped of anything that might be offensive to any segment of record buyers, such as any traces of ethnic vocal delivery or off-color lyrics. As a result, most covers ended up sounding sanitized and antiseptic, even laughable. The poster child for this tactic could have been **Pat Boone**, whose watered-down covers of Fats Domino's "Ain't That a Shame" in 1955 and Little Richard's "Tutti Frutti" in 1956 both outsold the original versions.

Covers were an effective strategy for the 1946–1954 period, and as a result were an obstacle to commercial success for many R&B and country artists and their independent labels. However, once white teenagers started demanding the real thing, covers were no longer an effective marketing approach.

THE RECORD INDUSTRY

Record Sales: 1920–1954

Although Victrola phonograph players had been around since the early 1900s, it took several years before they became popular with consumers and there were any significant record sales. Before 1920, two of the most popular artists were opera singer Enrico Caruso and concert bandleader John Phillip Sousa (composer of "The Stars and Stripes Forever"). The first jazz recording, "Livery Stable Blues" made in 1917 by the Original Dixieland Jass Band was one of the first records to sell over one million copies. Throughout the 1920s, record sales were generally strong, hovering around $100 million a year. However, when radio first became popular in the mid-1920s and the Great Depression hit in 1929, record sales went into a tailspin, dropping to $6 million almost immediately, causing most of the smaller labels to go out of business.

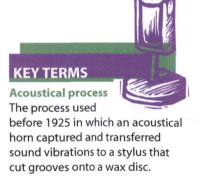

KEY TERMS

Acoustical process
The process used before 1925 in which an acoustical horn captured and transferred sound vibrations to a stylus that cut grooves onto a wax disc.

Helped by the popularity of crooners like Bing Crosby and the big band music of the Swing Era, record sales rebounded throughout the 1930s and 1940s. By 1945, sales were back up to $109 million; after wartime restrictions on shellac were lifted, sales soared to $218 million in 1946 where they leveled off for the next eight years. Helping the recovery was the introduction of the Duo Jr. in 1932, the first affordable and portable electric turntable, which sold for $16.50. By 1934 jukeboxes began popping up in thousands of restaurants and nightclubs around the country, which in some years accounted for as much as 40 percent of all record sales. The mid-1920s saw a dramatic improvement in the technology used to make recordings. Before 1925, recordings were made using the **acoustical process**, in which an acoustical horn captured the sound of the musicians huddled in front of it and transferred the sound vibrations

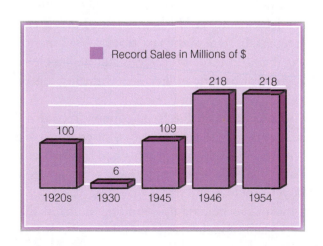

- Columbia—founded in 1885 in New York
- RCA Victor—1901, New York
- Decca—1934, New York
- Capitol—1942, Los Angeles
- Mercury—1946, Chicago
- MGM—1946, Hollywood

to a stylus that cut grooves onto a wax disc. Because the shellac records that resulted spun at 78 rpm, only three minutes of music could be recorded on a side. Because of the poor frequency response of the process, records also sounded tinny. In 1925, the **electrical process** was introduced, where microphones were used to convert the sound waves into an electrical signal, greatly improving sound quality.

After World War II, magnetic tape was increasingly used to record master tapes from which records were pressed. Among the many advantages of tape recording over disc recording is the ability to edit the master tape. An engineer could now construct a new version of a song by splicing two or more separate takes (or versions) together, eliminating any mistakes that may have been present in the original takes. This was a giant leap forward for recording artists, who previously had to strive for cutting a perfect take to disc, or settle for an imperfect one. Tape is also cheap, and can be reused many times, allowing an engineer to simply record over a bad take to further cut costs. It also allowed for longer songs to be recorded, as tape reels could hold up to 30 minutes of music, eliminating the 3-minute limit of the 78-rpm disc.

The post-war years also saw dramatic changes in the way recordings were manufactured and sold to consumers. In 1948, Columbia introduced the 12-inch 33-1/3 rpm LP (long-playing) **album** format. In addition to an increased playing time of 23 minutes of music per side, LPs were made of vinylite (vinyl), which offered superior fidelity and made the records less breakable and easier to distribute. The next year, RCA Victor introduced a rival format, the 7-inch 45 rpm **single** format, also on vinyl (later on polystyrene). RCA also introduced a low-cost portable turntable that included an attachment enabling several 45s to be stacked, allowing the listener a sequence of uninterrupted songs to play. Within a few years most record labels were releasing product on both formats. LPs became the choice of adults, who bought console hi-fi systems and placed

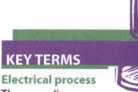

KEY TERMS

Electrical process
The recording process in which microphones are used to convert sound waves into an electrical signal.

Album   The 33-1/3 rpm 12" LP (long playing) format introduced by Columbia Records in 1948.

Single   The 45 rpm 7" format introduced in 1949 by RCA Victor.

- King—founded in 1945 in Cincinnati by Syd Nathan
- Specialty—1945, Los Angeles by Art Rupe
- Modern—1945, Los Angeles by Jules and Saul Bihari
- Imperial—1945, Los Angeles by Lew Chudd
- Chess—1947, Chicago by Phil and Leonard Chess (originally named Aristocrat)
- Atlantic—1948, New York by Ahmet Ertigan and Herb Abramson
- Duke/Peacock—1949, Houston by Don Robey
- Sun—1953, Memphis by Sam Phillips

them in the living room along with the TV set. The cheaper 45s became more popular with teens, who were able to buy the latest hit single and play them in their bedrooms on their portable players. In 1958, the world standard for stereo was established and the first stereo LPs were sold soon after.

Record Labels: The Majors and the Independents

Over the early years of the 20th century, the largest corporate record labels (known simply as the **major labels**) had built up well-established distribution networks and alliances with radio stations, record stores and jukebox operators to distribute and promote their product. By virtue of their nearly total control of the marketplace in the pre-rock and roll era, the majors (of which there were six) were able to prevent most records that they did not distribute from making an impact on the national charts. Even though most majors had a few R&B and country artists on their rosters, these singers were considered to have a specialty market outside the mainstream, and as a result were not marketed as heavily. Thus, when Mercury Records decided to release "Tennessee Waltz" in 1950, it was given to pop singer Patti Page rather than a country singer who might have been a better fit for the song. Even though Page's record became a #1 hit, for the most part the majors simply ignored R&B and country. This provided an opening for smaller, **independent labels**, or "indies" to find a niche in the market, and by the mid-1950s there were more than 100 of them scattered around the country. It was these indie labels that played an important role in fueling the growth of R&B and country music in the post-war years.

The typical major was headquartered in New York, Chicago, or Los Angeles with a team of producers, talent scouts, A&R (artist & repertoire) staff, song pluggers and advance men. Professional composers, arrangers, and recording studios were also utilized to carefully craft the product to standards that would appeal to the widest possible audience to maximize sale potential. Independent labels, on the other hand, could be found in any town, and might be operating out of the back room of a store, a basement, garage, or even the trunk of a car. The small staff (often less than five, usually just one or two) handled all details, from finding the talent to distributing the records in stores and meeting with disc jockeys to get airplay. Although some indies had their own small studios, storage rooms or garages were often used as makeshift studios. With their low overhead and constant struggle for survival, indies were more willing to take risks and quickly change business tactics to keep up with emerging industry trends.

Despite their competitive disadvantages, the indie labels were perfectly positioned to grab a larger share of the record market as a growing number of white teenagers started to turn away from major label pop to listen to R&B. But to connect with this new audience, they needed some help along the way, which they got from a group of renegade radio disc jockeys (more on that in a moment).

Hot 100s and Gold Records

The most reliable source for charting record sales throughout the Rock Era has been *Billboard* **magazine**. First published in 1894, *Billboard* began charting songs in 1940. In 1942 the magazine began to track the emerging country

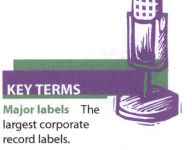

KEY TERMS

Major labels   The largest corporate record labels.

Independent labels   The small startup labels that began emerging in large numbers in the 1940s and 1950s.

Billboard **magazine**   The industry magazine that charts record sales.

and R&B styles under a single category "Western and Race," but eventually split them into two separate charts, "Country and Western" and "Rhythm and Blues" in 1949. From 1955 until 1958, it published a number of separate charts, including the Top 100, Best Sellers in Stores, Most Played in Jukeboxes, and Most Played by Disc Jockeys, all of which were merged into the new Hot 100 in 1958. The chart listings used in this book for singles are from the Hot 100 (or the Top 100 chart that preceded it), unless otherwise noted.

The RIAA (**Recording Industry Association of America**, the trade group representing the record industry) was founded in 1952 and began certifying singles with sales of one million units as gold and in 1958 certifying two million units as platinum. In 1989 these standards were lowered to 500,000 and one million respectively, making it much easier for a single to achieve gold status. The gold standard for albums was set in 1958 at 500,000; starting in 1976 albums with sales of one million were designated as platinum. In 1999 the RIAA also established the diamond certification for albums with sales of 10 million. As of this writing, 110 albums have achieved diamond status. In the early 2000s, the RIAA filed a number of lawsuits against file sharing sites such as Napster and the users of such sites on behalf of the recording industry. This controversial maneuver, which ultimately became a losing cause for the RIAA, is discussed at length in Chapter 13.

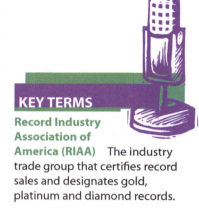

KEY TERMS

Record Industry Association of America (RIAA)   The industry trade group that certifies record sales and designates gold, platinum and diamond records.

GOLD, PLATINUM AND DIAMOND

Although the Beatles and Elvis Presley are the all-time runaway record sales leaders, the 1970s pop/country group the Eagles certainly deserve credit for their own sales achievements. Because the 1976 platinum distinction for album sales of one million units was not applied retroactively, the first album to achieve this status was Eagles/ Their Greatest Hits: 1971–1975, which achieved platinum status on February 24, 1976, just weeks after its release. Today the album holds the distinction of being the third best selling LP in U.S. history with sales of 29 million (and more than 40 million worldwide). The Eagles currently have eight albums listed in the top 100 selling albums of all time (U.S.), three of which have achieved diamond status. In all, 16 Eagles LPs have achieved platinum or multi-platinum status.

RADIO

The Birth of Radio and Important Early DJs

The first commercial radio station in America, KDKA in Pittsburgh, began broadcasting in 1920. Throughout the early 1920s, radio experienced explosive growth: by 1924 there were nearly 600 commercial stations broadcasting and three million receivers in homes. In the late 1920s, NBC and CBS established radio networks that provided programming to affiliate stations throughout the country. However, in the late 1940s and early 1950s, as television appeared on the scene many analysts were predicting radio's demise. Radio stations up to this point had programmed a variety of material, including live music, drama, variety

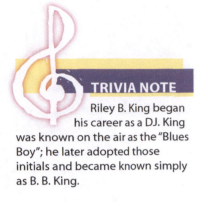

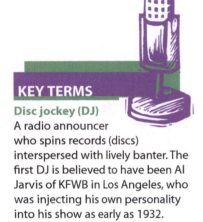

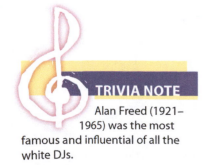

shows, sporting events, and news. With TV's dramatic growth in popularity, radio stations in the 1950s began concentrating their efforts on playing music and emphasizing local programming rather than relying on the network feed. These trends led to the rise in popularity of the local **disc jockey** or **DJ**. DJs often had complete control of the style of their show and the records that they played. After a time, it was not enough just to have a unique show, and many DJs started developing flamboyant and eccentric on-air personalities. They became showmen; in fact, several early rock and roll artists actually began their careers as DJs, including one at WDIA in Memphis named Riley B. King. King was known on the air as the "Blues Boy"; he later adopted those initials and became known simply as B. B. King.

Like the nation itself, in the late 1940s and early 1950s radio was segregated: a small number of black stations programmed jazz and R&B to black audiences, while white stations played pop and country for white audiences. However, R&B was becoming increasingly popular during the 1946–54 transitional period with white teenagers, who responded to the way the music was more emotional and viscerally exciting than conventional pop. To get their R&B fix, these teens began tuning in to black stations such as WDIA ("America's Only 50,000 Watt Negro Radio Station"), WERD in Atlanta, and KXLW in St. Louis. Among the most popular black DJs in R&B radio were "Yo' Ol' Swingmaster" Al Benson in Chicago, "Jockey Jack" Gibson in Atlanta, Tommy "Dr. Jive" Smalls in New York, and "Professor Bop" in Shreveport.

As the audience for R&B grew, the more attentive white DJs picked up on the trend and also began to play R&B records. Early white DJs who programmed R&B included Hunter Hancock (*Huntin' with Hunter*) at KFVD and KGFJ in Los Angeles, George "Cat Man" Stiles at WNJR in Newark, George "Hound Dog" Lorenz at WKBW in Buffalo, and "Symphony Sid" Torin at WBMS in Boston and later WOV in New York. By connecting the rapidly expanding needs of the teenage nation with R&B and rock and roll records, these renegade DJs, both black and white, essentially saved radio from television's onslaught. For all its strengths as a medium for family entertainment, TV could not connect with the young in the same direct way that radio could. By playing rock and roll records (which was also—conveniently—cheap programming), radio could pinpoint its audience with deadly accuracy. It was also portable: teens could listen at home or after school on the newly introduced transistor radio, or in their cars while cruising at night.

Alan Freed

The most famous and influential of all the white DJs was Alan Freed (1921–1965). Freed was a former jazz musician from Pennsylvania who was entrepreneurial, flamboyant, a hard worker, and a hard drinker. In June 1951 he took over the late-night Record Rendezvous show on Cleveland station WJW and turned it into an R&B program after seeing first-hand how white teenagers enthusiastically bought R&B records at a local store. Freed, who often drank while on the air, developed a wacky personality and renamed the show *The Moondog House Rock and Roll Party* (he sometimes howled like a dog during the show opening). Encouraged by the program's popularity, Freed's next move was to promote a dance that featured the same artists whose records he played. The Moondog Coronation Ball was set for the 10,000-seat Cleveland Arena in March 1952, but a near riot ensued as an overflow crowd of over 21,000 tried to get in, forcing the cancellation of the show. Later concert attempts proved successful however, and Freed's growing popularity led to his being hired by WINS in New York in September 1954. Freed named his new program The Rock and Roll Show, and began calling himself "Mr. Rock and Roll". Ratings for WINS soared, and Freed became immensely popular; however, he also became an easy target for a growing backlash against rock and roll by conservative and religious groups. Freed eventually became the focus of a congressional investigation into the music business in 1959 that ultimately ended his career (more on that in Chapter 3).

MOONDOG

When Alan Freed moved to WINS in 1954, he was forced to change the name of his show from *The Moondog House Rock and Roll Party* to *The Rock and Roll Show* by a blind street musician who dressed up in a Viking costume. Thomas Louis Hardin claimed that he had in fact used the name Moondog for many years, and that by using the name for his radio show, Freed was infringing on Hardin's right to make a living. After Hardin filed suit, Judge Carroll Walter awarded him $7,500 and forbade Freed from using the name Moondog. Although Alan Freed did not coin the term Rock and Roll (it was a black euphemism for sex that had been around for at least 30 years), he undoubtedly helped connect the label to the music for an ever-widening audience.

Top 40

Just as DJs such as Alan Freed were playing important roles in the incubation of rock and roll, a new radio format was emerging that would ultimately undermine their influence. **Top 40** was the brainchild of **Todd Storz**, the owner of a small group of radio stations, including ratings cellar-dweller KOWH in Omaha. While at a tavern located across the street from the station one night in 1955 (although some say the year was 1953), Storz and his companions noticed that patrons were plugging the jukebox to play the same songs over and over, and when the bar closed, the waitresses took their tip money and played those songs again. Storz and his program director wrote down the names of the top songs and began playing them throughout the day on KOWH, eliminating the classical, country, and other programs the station had been playing. Within two years, KOWH went from last to first in the Omaha market, and Storz was able to buy other stations in New Orleans, Kansas City, Minneapolis, and Miami, which he formatted in the same way. Top 40 was popular with listeners because they knew that they were never more than a few minutes away from hearing their favorite song played, and it quickly spread throughout the industry. Ultimately the Top 40 format had a homogenizing effect on radio, limiting playlists all over America to mainstream pop singles. And, of course, it further diminished the power of the DJ, who in the end was shut out from selecting the songs that he played on his show.

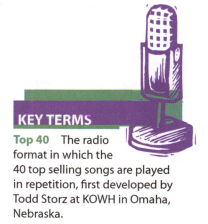

KEY TERMS

Top 40 The radio format in which the 40 top selling songs are played in repetition, first developed by Todd Storz at KOWH in Omaha, Nebraska.

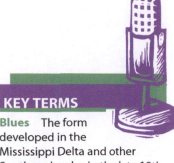

KEY TERMS

Blues   The form developed in the Mississippi Delta and other Southern locales in the late 19th century that incorporates a 12-bar verse, AAB lyric form, and tonalities from the blues scale.

Work songs, shouts, and field hollers   African song forms used to accompany work and other aspects of everyday life that were adapted by slaves on plantations and Southern work camps.

Mississippi Delta   The 250 mile long area of Mississippi stretching from Memphis south to Vicksburg that is widely believed to be the birthplace of the blues.

Country blues   The earliest form of the blues, performed by solo male singers accompanying themselves on guitar.

AAB lyric form   The format of most blues poetry, in which each verse is comprised of three lines, the second of which is a repeat of the first.

THE BLACK ROOTS OF ROCK AND ROLL

The Blues

The **blues** is a uniquely American musical form, born in the Southern middle states sometime between the years 1880 and 1900. It evolved from the **work songs, shouts, and field hollers** sung by slaves in plantation fields and prison camps. Songs sung to accompany various daily jobs and duties were a functional part of everyday life in Africa and a celebration of doing work to improve the quality of one's life. In the New World however, the very nature of the work song began to change, as the singer was no longer doing work for himself but for someone else—and the work no longer improved his quality of life. Over time, the songs sung in the fields therefore became personal expressions of pain and oppression. Singing work songs and field hollers became a catharsis for feelings of lost love, sexual frustration, poverty, jealousy, and hard times. It is from this context that the blues evolved.

After the Civil War, thousands of freed slaves began traveling through the South, looking for work, armed with no job skills to speak of other than as a common laborer. Once Reconstruction ended, life became increasingly bleak for many of them, as newly enacted Jim Crow laws and racial oppression became as commonplace as the hard work and poverty. Singing in work camps, street corners, and juke joints for food and tips was one of the few professions available to a black man in which he wasn't directly working for the white man (preaching was another, and in fact many of the first blues singers were former preachers). Today many scholars speculate that the blues incubated in the **Mississippi Delta**, a 250-mile oval of land stretching south from Memphis, Tennessee, to Vicksburg, Mississippi.

CHARACTERISTICS OF THE BLUES

1. 12-bar musical form
2. Three-phrase AAB lyrical form
3. Emotional, personal lyrics convey feelings of lust, lost love, jealousy, suffering, hard times, etc.

THE FIRST BLUES SINGERS

The first blues performers were solo singers who accompanied themselves on the guitar in a rambling and spontaneous fashion that became known as **country blues**. These performers worked out the basic standard blues formula: a three-phrase **AAB lyric form** of 12-bar length, with each phrase answered by the guitar in a call-and-response fashion. This evolution occurred in the backwoods away from almost everyone who might have been interested, and before there were any recording devices, so documentation of exactly how it happened is scarce. One of the first to archive the blues was W. C. Handy, a bandleader and former schoolteacher from Alabama who in 1903 heard a man playing and singing at the train station in Tutwiler, Mississippi. In his autobiography Handy wrote: "As he played, he pressed a knife on the strings of the guitar in a manner popularized by Hawaiian guitarists who used steel bars. 'Goin' where the Southern cross' the Dog'. The singer repeated the line three times, accompanying himself on the guitar with the weirdest music I had ever heard. The tune stayed in my mind." Realizing the commercial potential of this new music, Handy became the first to publish blues songs, including "Memphis Blues" in 1912 and "St. Louis Blues" in 1914. Both were huge hits through the sale of sheet music, and earned Handy the title "Father of the Blues." The blues sold on sheet music remained popular until 1917 when the first jazz recording started the jazz craze, and consumers began to buy more records.

THE FIRST BLUES RECORDINGS

The blues remained popular throughout the 1920s with the first commercially sold blues recordings by what became known as the **classic blues** singers. When "Crazy Blues" by Mamie Smith sold one million copies within a year of its 1920 release, record companies realized that there was a huge untapped black consumer market. Most of the classic blues recordings were released on small independent labels such as Vocalion, Black Swan, and Okeh that specialized in race music, a market that the major labels were largely unwilling to pursue. Although many of these female singers were merely singing pop tunes with a tragic delivery (and nearly all the records had the word "blues" in the title), some of them such as Bessie Smith (the "Empress of the Blues") and Ethel Waters were outstanding blues singers. In 1929, the Depression almost killed the record industry, and did manage to finish off the classic blues era.

It wasn't until 1925 that the first country blues singers began to record. It was that year that Blind Lemon Jefferson recorded "Black Snake Moan" in Chicago, after having worked his way north through the Mississippi Delta from his native Texas. Another Texan, Huddie Ledbetter, better known as Leadbelly, surfaced in the 1940s New York City folk scene with Woody Guthrie and Pete Seeger after several troublesome years in and out of prison. But the most spine-tingling blues performances came from the haunting vocals and bottleneck guitars of the Delta bluesmen, such as Charley Patton, Willie Brown, Son House, and **Robert Johnson**. Although Johnson only recorded 29 sides during his life, his songs are among the most influential in American history, including "Love in Vain," "Cross Road Blues," "Sweet Home Chicago," and "I Believe I'll Dust My Broom." Johnson's singing and guitar playing on these recordings is riveting even today. Unfortunately, his mythic life ended before he achieved any real national attention when a jealous husband poisoned him at a juke joint outside of Greenwood, Mississippi in 1938.

TRIVIA NOTE
In 1929, the Depression almost killed the record industry, and did manage to finish off the classic blues era.

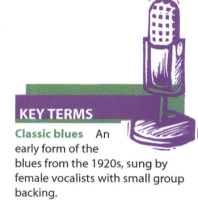

KEY TERMS

Classic blues   An early form of the blues from the 1920s, sung by female vocalists with small group backing.

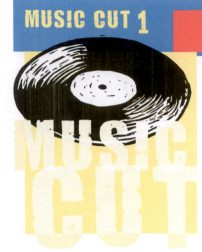

MUSIC CUT 1

"CROSS ROAD BLUES" (ROBERT JOHNSON)— ROBERT JOHNSON

Personnel: Robert Johnson: guitar, vocals. Recorded on November 27, 1936 in the Gunter Hotel, San Antonio, TX; produced by Don Law and Art Satherley.

When Robert Johnson recorded "Cross Road Blues" in a makeshift studio at the Gunter Hotel in San Antonio, he had already recorded 11 of the 16 songs that would come from the three sessions held during the week of November 22, 1936, including the classics "Sweet Home Chicago" and "Terraplane Blues." These sessions, along with a second round of sessions held on June 19 and 20, 1937 (which produced 13 more songs), produced what are arguably the most defining and influential blues recordings in history. With his haunting vocals and use of a bottleneck slide on the guitar, Johnson helps define the sound of Delta blues. The influence of Johnson's recording of "Cross Road Blues" can be found in the recordings of other artists who have covered it, which includes Cream, the Doors and Van Halen.

Jazz

An improvisational art form of individual expression, **jazz** developed as a parallel universe alongside the blues throughout the first half of the 20th century. Originally evolving as an ensemble form in New Orleans and other Southern locales around the turn of the century, like the blues it worked its way north to Chicago around 1920. It was in the 1920s that its first true innovator, trumpeter Louis Armstrong, revolutionized jazz by turning it into a soloist's art form simply on the strength and drama of his virtuoso improvisations. The 65 sides that he recorded for Okeh as the leader of the Hot Five and Hot Seven between 1925 and 1928 are among the most important artifacts of American music. By the 1930s, the center of the jazz world had moved to New York, where composers and arrangers such as Fletcher Henderson and Duke Ellington helped develop the jazz big band that was to become the standard ensemble of the Swing Era. At the same time, bandleaders in Kansas City like Count Basie were developing an exciting riff-based boogie style that would further invigorate swing music with the blues.

KEY TERMS

Jazz   The music of individual expression whose main characteristics are improvisation and swing rhythm.

DELTA BLUESMEN

- Charley Patton
- Willie Brown
- Son House
- Robert Johnson

- Alto saxophonist Charlie Parker
- Trumpeter Dizzy Gillespie
- Pianist Thelonious Monk

BEBOP'S ARCHITECTS

During the Swing Era, jazz became America's pop music, and music industry manipulation caused creative innovation and musical integrity to suffer. But jazz began to reinvent itself around 1940 in the late-night jam sessions at tiny nightclubs in Harlem such as Minton's Playhouse. Modern jazz, or bebop, was created by a small group of young musical revolutionaries in search of more stimulating musical expression. Bebop's architects were some of the most gifted musical talents America has ever produced, including alto saxophonist Charlie Parker, trumpeter Dizzy Gillespie and pianist Thelonious Monk. Although bebop infused a fresh new vitality into jazz, it also made it impossible for most people to dance or even listen to. In the post-bebop era, jazz musicians began to experiment with different stylistic approaches, including cool jazz, hard bop, and free jazz. In 1969 trumpeter Miles Davis, who had often been at the forefront of innovation throughout his music career, fused rock and jazz together with his seminal album *Bitches Brew*. Jazz continues to incorporate influences from rock and its offshoots to this day.

Black Gospel

Gospel emerged as a style in the early 1930s from the traditional spirituals that had been a part of black religious culture since the days of slavery. The man most responsible for commercializing gospel music was **Thomas Dorsey**, who is often called the "Father of Gospel Music." Ironically, before turning his attention to religious music, Dorsey was known as "Georgia Tom," the piano-playing half (along with guitarist Tampa Red) of the Hokum Brothers. Their hit recording "It's Tight Like That" from 1928 contained lewd, off-color, humorous lyrics that presaged similar songs by Louis Jordan, Little Richard, and Chuck Berry. In the 1930s Dorsey started writing songs of good news and salvation with blues-influenced melodies and rhythms that eventually became popular at church services in the black community. Among his many gospel standards are "Take My Hand, Precious Lord," written in 1932. Later gospel stars include Sister Rosetta Tharpe and Mahalia Jackson.

Gospel's influence on American popular music is immense. The **melismatic** singing of gospel can be heard throughout the entire history of rock music. Gospel backup bands often used the Hammond B3 organ, which became one of the most popular instruments in rock in the 1960s and 1970s. Typically performing in church accompanied by large choirs, the male gospel quartets that started to become popular in the 1930s were ancestors to doo-wop groups in the 1950s. Many of the early crossover R&B stars of the 1950s had gospel roots, including Little Richard and Sam Cooke, whose career took off when he joined the venerable gospel group the Soul Stirrers. Gospel is also one of the foundational

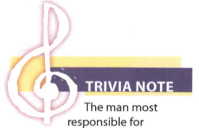

TRIVIA NOTE

The man most responsible for commercializing gospel music was Thomas Dorsey, who is often called the "Father of Gospel Music."

KEY TERMS

Gospel Highly emotional evangelical vocal music that emerged from spirituals and was highly influential to Rhythm and Blues.

Melisma The singing embellishment of a single syllable into several notes.

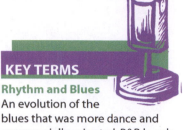

Rhythm and Blues
An evolution of the blues that was more dance and commercially oriented. R&B bands often included electric instruments such as guitars, bass guitars and organs, vocalists and a horn section, often with a honking tenor saxophone soloist.

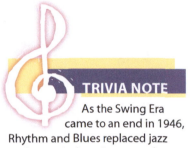

TRIVIA NOTE

As the Swing Era came to an end in 1946, Rhythm and Blues replaced jazz as the music America wanted to dance to.

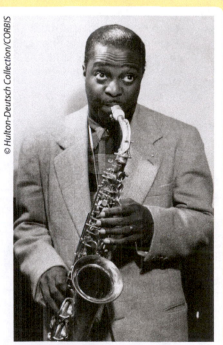

Louis Jordan, leader of the popular Tympany Five.

blocks of soul music, and its influence can be heard in the voice of the first soul singer, Ray Charles, and in every 1960s soul singer from James Brown to Otis Redding and Aretha Franklin.

Rhythm and Blues

In the 1940s, blues musicians in Chicago began amplifying themselves in order to be heard over the din of the crowded clubs in the city's South Side. Once the blues went electric, it was a natural progression to speed it up, put in a heavier beat and make it more danceable. Although the term **Rhythm and Blues** wasn't coined until 1949 (by Jerry Wexler of *Billboard* magazine), the style was developed in the 1940s out of jazz and blues roots. As the Swing Era came to an end in 1946, Rhythm and Blues, with its boogie-woogie bass lines and honking tenor sax solos, increasingly replaced jazz as the music America wanted to dance to. Jazz veteran Lionel Hampton had one of the first R&B hits in 1942 with "Flying Home," and the biggest R&B hit of 1946, "Hey! Ba-Ba-Re-Bop." Omaha native Wynonie Harris had the #1 R&B hit of 1947 with "Good Rocking Tonight," a song that Elvis Presley would later cover. Joe Turner's 1954 hit recording of "Shake, Rattle and Roll" was also covered by Presley and Bill Haley.

R&B styles ranged from the raunchy to the polished. On one end of the spectrum were the down-and-dirty bar bands that emerged from the urban blues of Chicago's South Side. The most prominent Chicago R&B performers were Muddy Waters, harmonica players Little Walter and Sonny Boy Williamson, guitarists Elmore James and John Lee Hooker, bassist and composer Willie Dixon, and singer Chester Burnett, better known as Howlin' Wolf. These performers all recorded at Chess Records, where they were closely linked to the soon-to-emerge rock-and-roll styles of Bo Diddley and Chuck Berry. They were also highly inspirational to a number of rock bands in the 1960s, including the Rolling Stones and Cream. (One of Waters' more influential records was 1950's "Rolling Stone," which provided the English band with their name.)

Jump bands, which usually included a small horn section along with the rhythm section and vocalist, played a smoother, more jazz-influenced type of R&B. Popular jump bands of this era included those of Johnny Otis, Louis Prima, and **Louis Jordan**. As leader of the **Tympany Five**, Jordan scored an unbelievable 18 #1 and 54 Top 10 records on the R&B charts in the 1940s. He still holds the record for the total number of weeks at #1 on the R&B charts—113 (Stevie Wonder is second with 70). Jordan sang songs that often contained street-smart jive and humor, such as "Open the Door, Richard" and "Saturday Night Fish Fry." His biggest hits included "Choo Choo Ch'Boogie," "Caldonia," and "Ain't Nobody Here But Us Chickens." Jordan also made innovative short movies of the Tympany Five in performance that were shown between feature films at theaters—predecessors to the contemporary music video.

Rhythm and Blues would become one of the most prevailing influences in popular music in the last half of the 20th century. In the mid-1950s its most commercially successful practitioners would play

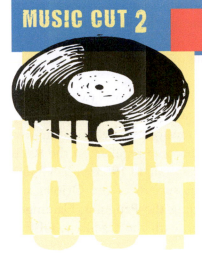

MUSIC CUT 2

"CHOO CHOO CH' BOOGIE" (VAUGHN HORTON/DENVER DARLING/ MILT GABLER)—LOUIS JORDAN AND HIS TYMPANY FIVE

Personnel: Louis Jordan: alto sax, vocals; Aaron Izenhall: trumpet; Josh Jackson: tenor sax; Bill Davis: piano; Carl Hogan: guitar; Po Simpkins: bass; Eddie Byrd: drums. Recorded January 23, 1946 in New York City; produced by Milt Gabler. Released 1946 on Decca; 18 weeks on the charts, peaking at #1 R&B, #4 pop.

"Choo Choo Ch' Boogie" is a great example of the kind of R&B that made Louis Jordan the most popular black recording artist in the 1940s. Jordan's group the Tympany Five, a so-called jump band, played a smooth, jazz-influenced type of R&B that prominently featured riffing horns and a driving rhythm section. In addition to being a fine vocalist who could deliver his often-humorous lyrics with a clear, smooth enunciation, Jordan was also a first rate alto saxophonist who had worked in the legendary Chick Webb Orchestra at the Savoy Ballroom in Harlem before going out on his own.

important roles in shaping the sound of early rock and roll. The lives and music of these men, Bo Diddley, Chuck Berry, Little Richard, Fats Domino and others, will be discussed in the next chapter.

PROMINENT CHICAGO R&B PERFORMERS

- Muddy Waters
- Little Walter
- Sonny Boy Williamson
- Elmore James
- John Lee Hooker
- Willie Dixon
- Howlin' Wolf

Doo-Wop

In terms of record sales, **doo-wop** was the most popular black music style in the 1950s. Its origins go back as far as the 1930s and the popularity of male gospel quartets and commercial vocal groups such as the Mills Brothers and the Ink Spots. The Mills Brothers (who were in fact four brothers from Ohio) prided themselves in creating a tightly woven cross between jazz and barbershop vocal harmonies with only guitar accompaniment. The Ink Spots were also influential to doo-wop, featuring lead vocalist Bill Kenny singing in a melismatic, gospel-inspired high tenor voice that became a staple of doo-wop. Both groups were immensely popular throughout the 1930s and 1940s.

THE EARLIEST DOO-WOP GROUPS

During the late 1940s and early 1950s, it became fashionable for amateur teen-age vocal groups to perform a cappella on street corners and on the stoops of apartment buildings, especially in New York. This was usually just for fun, although the possibility of being discovered by a talent scout was never far from anyone's thoughts. The first of these groups to hit it big was the Ravens with their 1947 hits "Write Me a Letter" and "Old Man River." The latter record,

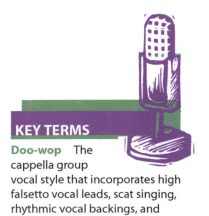

KEY TERMS

Doo-wop The cappella group vocal style that incorporates high falsetto vocal leads, scat singing, rhythmic vocal backings, and sometimes lead vocals or spoken verse by the bass singer.

which sold two million copies, was unusual in that bass singer Warren Suttles sang the vocal lead. This technique was to become one of the signature characteristics of the doo-wop genre. The Ravens also featured choreography in their shows—another first that was to become a staple of later soul acts such as the Temptations and the Supremes.

Other groups started to copy these innovations. The Orioles (who, like the baseball team, were from Baltimore) first pop hit was "It's Too Soon to Know," which hit the Top 20 in 1948. The song's huge crossover appeal was unprecedented for a race record and helped the group become regulars on the R&B charts over the next few years. Their biggest success came in 1953 with "Crying in the Chapel," which climbed to #11. With the success of the Orioles and the Ravens, other "bird" groups appeared, including the Penguins, Flamingos, and Swallows. Later "car" names became popular, with the Cadillacs, T-Birds, Fleetwoods, and Imperials, to name just a few.

Another doo-wop group that achieved notoriety of sorts was Hank Ballard and the Midnighters. In 1954 they had a series of "Annie" records ("Work with Me Annie," "Annie Had a Baby," and "Annie's Aunt Fanny") that sold over a million copies each despite being widely banned from radio play. Each song contained sexually suggestive lyrics—the "work" in the first hit was a thinly disguised metaphor for sex—that were as funny as they were risqué. Ballard also wrote "The Twist" in 1958, which became a #1 hit for Chubby Checker in 1960 and spawned the dance craze of the same name. In the context of the "Annie" records, one should reconsider what Ballard was writing about in the first line of "The Twist": "Well come on baby, *let's do the twist.*" Perhaps it wasn't dancing he was singing about.

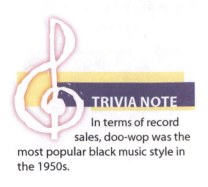

TRIVIA NOTE

In terms of record sales, doo-wop was the most popular black music style in the 1950s.

A PARTIAL LIST OF DOO-WOP GROUPS FROM THE 1950s

Bird Groups:	Car Groups:
Ravens	Cadillacs
Orioles	T-Birds
Penguins	Imperials
Flamingos	Fleetwoods
Swallows	Corvairs
Bluebirds	Galaxies
Crows	El Dorados
Robins	Impalas

THE INDUSTRY MOVES IN

Although doo-wop originated as an a cappella style, recordings were most often made using instrumental accompaniment, as record labels tried to maximize the commercial appeal of the records and make them more danceable. Many labels also took advantage of the street singers, who most often had no business skills and were just happy to get a record contract. The classic example of this type of exploitation is the story of **Frankie Lymon and the Teenagers**, who rose to fame in 1956 with "Why Do Fools Fall in Love" (#6) when Lymon was only 13 years old. Producer George Goldner paid Lymon a stipend of $25 a week with

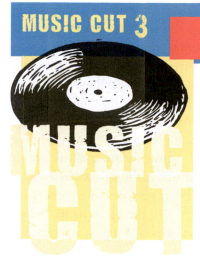

MUSIC CUT 3

"WHY DO FOOLS FALL IN LOVE" (FRANKIE LYMON/MORRIS LEVY)— FRANKIE LYMON AND THE TEENAGERS

Personnel: Frankie Lymon, Jimmy Merchant, Sherman Garnes, Herman Santiago, Joe Negroni: vocals; Jimmy Wright: tenor sax; Jimmy Shirley: guitar; Al Hall: bass; Gene Brooks: drums. Recorded 1955 at Bell Sound Studios, New York, NY; produced by George Goldner. Released January 1956 on Gee; 21 weeks on the charts, peaking at #6.

The Teenagers, made up of five school buddies from New York, were the quintessential "unknowns discovered singing on the street corner" doo-wop group. After another singer named Richard Barrett discovered them in 1955, the group signed with George Goldner's Gee records. At their first recording session, they performed "Why Do Fools Fall in Love," a song that Teenagers Herman Santiago and Jimmy Merchant co-wrote. However, Santiago, who was supposed to sing lead, had a cold, and the job was handed to Lymon. Subsequently he and producer Goldman were given writing credits for the song (this was later overturned by a federal judge in the early 1990s). The song has been a Hot 100 hit four times, most recently in 1981 with Diana Ross's version.

the rest of his earnings going into a "trust fund." When Lymon's voice changed a few years later and his career went in decline, he discovered that there was in fact no trust fund. He turned to heroin and died from an overdose at 26. Many other doo-wop groups were "one hit wonders," as bad business deals, competing cover versions, and instability of the small independent labels took their toll. One of the best examples of the one hit wonder was the Chords, whose only hit "Sh-Boom" in 1953 was quickly buried by the Crewcuts' cover.

One fledgling record company, Atlantic Records, had unusual success with doo-wop. Although its primary focus was on jazz when it was founded in 1947, Atlantic signed Clyde McPhatter of the Dominos in 1953 and built a new group, the Drifters, around him. They were an instant smash, with five hits that went to #1 or #2 on the R&B charts within the next two years. McPhatter was drafted into the military in 1955, and was replaced by a succession of lead singers until Ben E. King took over in 1958. At around the same time, the young songwriting duo of Jerry Leiber and Mike Stoller were assigned to the group, and their first production, "There Goes My Baby" went to #2 pop and stayed on the charts for fourteen weeks. Between 1957 and 1959, Leiber and Stoller also wrote five Top 10 hits for another doo-wop group, the Coasters.

THE WHITE ROOTS OF ROCK AND ROLL

Traditional Rural Music

Traditional rural music in America evolved primarily from the folk music brought to the New World by British immigrants. The Appalachian region of Tennessee, Kentucky, Virginia, and West Virginia were particularly fertile areas for the survival of this music tradition, as the rural and isolated mountainous settings hampered contact with the changing outside world. By the early 20th century, city dwellers began to mockingly call the poor white inhabitants of this region "hillbillies," and the simple folk music they played **hillbilly music.**

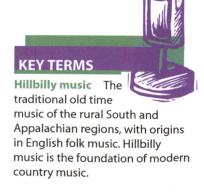

KEY TERMS

Hillbilly music The traditional old time music of the rural South and Appalachian regions, with origins in English folk music. Hillbilly music is the foundation of modern country music.

The **British folk tradition** included ballads, which typically tell a story, some of them epic tales; lyric songs, which are often songs of love; and work songs. Unlike African work songs, British work songs often came in the form of sea chanteys, railroad songs, and lumber songs. At first, folk music in America was simply sung verbatim by the new colonists as it had been in England; over time songs often underwent subtle changes as their original meanings and purposes were forgotten and singers adapted them to their new environment. New songs in the same tradition were also written. A good example of a traditional English ballad that survived in America is "Barbara Allen," a timeless song about young lovers and death believed to be from the 17th century. Although it has evolved over the years, it is still a folk standard that has been performed by everyone from Joan Baez to the Everly Brothers to Bob Dylan. On the other hand, "Sweet Betsy from Pike," written around 1870 using a traditional English melody, is a uniquely American song about the hard journey West, with lyrics that invoke the imagery of the Platte River, Salt Lake City, and California.

Unlike blues and country musicians who eventually embraced the use of electric instruments, rural and folk musicians continued to use the traditional acoustic instruments from the past, such as the fiddle, acoustic guitar, and banjo. After 1900 other acoustic instruments such as the mandolin, string bass, autoharp, and Hawaiian steel guitar were also often included. To this day, many folk musicians typically use only these traditional instruments in their performances.

THE FIRST COUNTRY RECORDINGS

Traditional rural music was first recorded in 1923 when Okeh Records recorded Atlanta favorite Fiddlin' John Carson at a local radio station. The records sold surprisingly well throughout the region, much to the amazement of company officials. Sensing a business opportunity, **Ralph Peer** of Victor Records went on a talent hunt for other rural musicians in August of 1927. Setting up his primitive mobile recording equipment in a warehouse in Bristol, Tennessee, and offering $50 per song to anyone who would audition, Peer struck gold. Among the many that came down from the hills to record at the **Bristol Sessions**, as they became known, were both the Carter Family and Jimmie Rodgers, who would become the first commercially successful and important performers of country music, as it was starting to be labeled by the late 1920s.

The **Carter Family**, led by A. P. Carter, his wife Sara, and their sister-in-law Maybelle, had learned hundreds of traditional songs and performed them putting emphasis on their strong vocals and a revolutionary flat picking guitar style that is still commonly used by folk guitarists. **Jimmie Rodgers**, known alternately as the "Father of Country Music," "America's Blue Yodeler," and the "Singing Brakeman," was indeed a railroad worker until his poor health forced him to quit and concentrate on music. Between 1927 and 1933 when he died from tuberculosis, Rodgers recorded over 100 songs, sold millions of records, and became the first nationally known country star. His song topics and vocal style (which included blues inflections and his signature yodeling) set the mold for later stars such as Ernest Tubb and Hank Williams. As one of the three original inductees into the Country Music Hall of Fame, Rodgers's plaque identifies him as "the man who started it all."

KEY TERMS

British folk tradition
The traditional folk music, including ballads, lyric songs and work songs, of the British Isles. British immigrants brought these songs to the New World.

Bristol Sessions   The first important country music recordings made in Bristol, Tennessee in 1927 by Ralph Peer. Among the artists that Peer recorded were Jimmie Rodgers and the Carter Family.

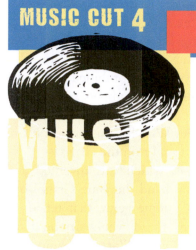

MUSIC CUT 4

"BLUE YODEL #1 (T FOR TEXAS)" (JIMMIE RODGERS)— JIMMIE RODGERS

Personnel: Jimmie Rodgers: guitar, vocals. Recorded on November 30, 1927 at RCA Victor Studio 1, Camden, NJ; produced by Ralph Peer. Released February 3, 1928.

"Blue Yodel #1 (T for Texas)" was recorded in the RCA Victor Studio 1, the former Trinity Baptist Church in Camden, New Jersey. It was Rodgers's second session for the label and its producer Ralph Peer (the first being the famous August 4, 1927 session in Bristol, Tennessee), and the one that made him a star. Rodgers originally called his song "T for Texas," but Peer, impressed by the "oh-de-lay" yodels at the end of each verse, renamed it "Blue Yodel." It became a smash that ended up selling approximately one million copies, and instantly made Rodgers a household name. Rodgers became known as "America's Blue Yodeler," and went on to record ten more "Blue Yodels." His use of both blue-infused melodies and yodels made him a major influence to both the black and white vocalists of his day.

NASHVILLE AND THE GRAND OLE OPRY

Radio played an important role in popularizing country music. In 1923, the first "barn dance" program was broadcast on station WBAP in Dallas, featuring live performances by country artists. Other shows soon followed: in 1924, Chicago's WLS premiered its National Barn Dance program, and on November 28, 1925, the WSM Barn Dance began broadcasting in Nashville. In 1927, WSM (which still resides at 650 Hz on the dial) changed the name of the program to the **Grand Ole Opry** and with the station's clear channel designation, the Opry became the most widely heard and influential radio show of its kind. Other "barn dance" programs included the Louisiana Hayride on KWKH in Shreveport, Louisiana, the Midwestern Hayride on WLW in Cincinnati, and the Big D Jamboree on KRLD in Dallas.

Today, the Grand Ole Opry is the longest continuously running radio program in the United States. It has influenced the course of country music by putting an emphasis on programming pop-oriented and crooning country singers (and forbidding drums for many years). Careers were often made by a successful debut there. Because the Opry was a live broadcast, performers had to maintain a presence in Nashville at least one day each week, and throughout the 1940s and 1950s, many moved there permanently. Songwriters, publishers, recording studios, and all the major record labels soon followed, and by the early 1950s, Nashville became the capital of the country music industry—in large part because of the Grand Ole Opry.

Cowboy Music, Western Swing, and Bluegrass

Around the same time that radio was starting to make country music more accessible, Hollywood filmmakers were popularizing **cowboy songs** in Westerns, and stars such as Gene Autry ("The Singing Cowboy") and Roy Rogers rose to fame. Cowboy songs were dressed up and orchestrated to give them a smoother and more commercial sound; the singing cowboys themselves were also dressed up in hats, boots, and ties to elevate them from the older and undesirable hillbilly

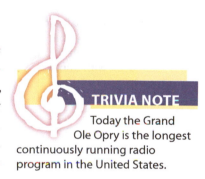

TRIVIA NOTE

Today the Grand Ole Opry is the longest continuously running radio program in the United States.

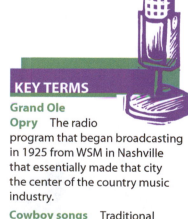

KEY TERMS

Grand Ole Opry   The radio program that began broadcasting in 1925 from WSM in Nashville that essentially made that city the center of the country music industry.

Cowboy songs   Traditional country and hillbilly songs used in Hollywood films that were orchestrated to create a more commercial pop sound.

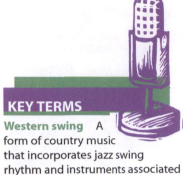

KEY TERMS

Western swing   A form of country music that incorporates jazz swing rhythm and instruments associated with a jazz swing band.

Bluegrass   A fast paced, acoustic music that incorporated virtuoso improvised solos similar to those found in jazz.

Honky-tonk   A country-oriented predecessor to rock and roll that used a rhythm section, electric guitar, and electric pedal steel guitar to create a louder and hard driving sound. Honky tonk lyrics often dealt with drinking, cheating, etc.

image. Cowboy songs helped pave the way for other commercialized offshoots of country to emerge that would reinvent the genre. One of these was **Western swing**, which became popular during the Swing Era and whose biggest star was Texas fiddler Bob Wills. Wills began broadcasting on station KVOO in Tulsa, Oklahoma in 1934 with his band the Texas Playboys, which combined traditional country instruments with those found in a swing big band: trumpets, saxophones, and drums. Despite their tendencies toward jazz, the Playboys wore the traditional country attire of cowboy hats, boots, and string ties. Wills had his biggest hit in 1940 with "New San Antonio Rose," which went to #11 on the charts.

Another stylistic development was **bluegrass**, which was invented and named by mandolin player **Bill Monroe**. With his band the Blue Grass Boys, which he formed in 1938, Monroe developed a unique genre that relied on faster tempos and jazz-like virtuoso solos that were spread evenly among mandolin, fiddle, and guitar. When guitarist and vocalist **Lester Flatt** and banjo wizard **Earl Scruggs** joined the band in 1944, the Blue Grass Boys were in their prime. Scruggs did nothing less than reinvent banjo playing with his amazing fast picking style. Flatt and Scruggs left in 1948 (due to Monroe's stubbornness and difficult personality) and started their own band, which in time became more popular than Monroe's.

Honky-Tonk

Honky-tonk grew out of the bars and roadhouses (called "honky-tonks") of Texas and the South, where the patrons were rough and rowdy and hard drinkers. The music is characterized by songs of drinkin' and cheatin', loves gained and lost. To be heard above the din of the crowded saloons, the honky-tonkers developed a louder, driving sound by adding drums, electric guitar, and electric pedal steel guitar that modernized country music and inched it closer in sound to the first rock-and-roll style, rockabilly. The first honky-tonk artist was Ernest Tubb, who with his Texas Troubadours had been touring constantly and performing on radio since the early 1930s, achieving national celebrity in the 1940s with movie roles and Opry appearances. Another honky-tonk artist, Texas-born

MUSIC CUT 5

"YOUR CHEATIN' HEART" (HANK WILLIAMS/FRED ROSE)— HANK WILLIAMS

Personnel: Hank Williams: guitar, vocal; other musicians unidentified. Recorded September 23, 1952 at Castle Studios, Nashville, TN; produced by Fred Rose. Released January 1953 on MGM; a #1 hit on the country charts.

"Your Cheatin' Heart," the song that is often called the song that defines country music—and honky tonk—was recorded at Hank Williams's last recording session. According to legend, Williams, who had just separated from his first wife Audrey, wrote the song while driving around with the woman who would become his second wife, Billie Jean Williams. After Billie Jean wrote down the lyrics, Hank took them to Nashville songwriter Fred Rose, who edited them and produced the final version of the song. After recording the song, Williams told a friend, "It's the best heart song I ever wrote."

William "Lefty" Frizzell, is widely credited with creating a smoother singing style that became the blueprint for modern country singers. He was a regular on the country charts throughout the 1950s and early 1960s.

Although his recording career lasted only six years (1946–1952), the man who most personified honky-tonk was undoubtedly **Hank Williams**, the "Hillbilly Shakespeare." Williams was a master poet with a knack for catchy melodies who wrote some of the most enduring tunes in country music history, including "Hey Good Lookin'," "Jambalaya," "Cold, Cold Heart," and "Your Cheatin' Heart." Williams became so popular in the late 1940s and early 1950s that he had 11 records that sold a million copies or more, and his concerts often resembled the near riots that Elvis Presley would incite a few years later. Unfortunately, his growing drinking problem paralleled that of his rising fame, and his life began to fall apart. He died of alcohol intoxication in the back seat of a car on the way to a gig on January 1, 1953. The last single released in his lifetime was his prophetic composition "I'll Never Get Out of This World Alive."

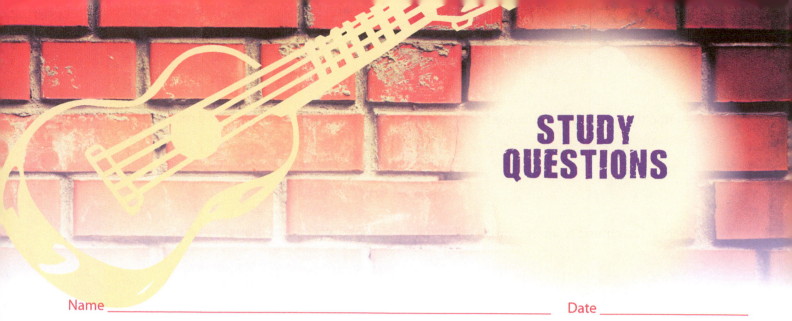

Name _____ Date _____

1. Describe Frank Sinatra's relationship to rock and roll, both his reaction to it and his influence on it.

2. Describe how technology changed the way music was recorded and packaged in the years leading up to 1954.

3. What were some differences between the major and independent labels, both in how they operated and what kind of music they specialized in?

4. What role did radio play in the explosion of rock and roll, and who were the important personalities?

5. Describe how the blues evolved from its beginning until the 1940s.

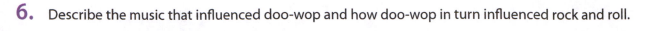

6. Describe the music that influenced doo-wop and how doo-wop in turn influenced rock and roll.

7. Describe how music from the British folk tradition changed after it was brought to America.

8. Describe how Nashville became such an important music center.

9. What were the musical influences on Western swing and how did they manifest themselves?

10. Why is honky tonk music so important to early rock and roll?

HISTORICAL INTERLUDE: 1950s

Happy Days!

The 1950s were a time of booms and social contradictions. The booms include the baby boom, the booming economy, and the booming suburbs. With the GI Bill in place in the early 1950s, many Americans received a college education and began working at higher paying jobs. This allowed for the growth of single-income families in which the father would work a job while the mother would stay at home and raise the kids. Many couples were eager to have children as they felt the world was now peaceful and children could be raised to face a positive future.

At the same time, suburbs were booming as the GI Bill allowed for extremely low mortgage rates. Families could purchase a house in the suburbs just outside of the city for the same or less money than renting in an apartment in the city. The idea of a "return to normalcy" after the war permeated the air, and families wanted to raise their children in an environment where the kids did not need to have as much responsibility. PTAs were first formed and many kids were given an allowance.

The economy boomed as new homes were built and appliances were created that made the daily lives of housewives easier. The highway systems were created and expanded, and automobiles became even more important for commuting from the suburbs to work.

Although this time of peace and prosperity created a sense of calm, many contradictions occurred including the fear of Communism, a focus on sexuality, and the civil rights movement. A rising fear of Communism arose as Senator Joseph McCarthy headed a senatorial committee to find Communists in the United States. Communists were suspected among politicians, labor unions, and creative people. Many involved in the entertainment industry including most folk artists and many composers were politically blacklisted and were not allowed to be employed. Even Aaron Copland, one of the United States' greatest composers, was blacklisted during the Communist witch hunt.

Previously taboo sexuality made it into the popular culture in the 1950s. Marilyn Monroe became one of the most popular movie stars by overtly displaying her sexuality on film and even posing nude for a popular calendar. In 1953 Hugh Hefner introduced the magazine *Playboy* to the United States.

The civil right movement became a leading political issue. By the 1960s, civil rights was one of the major subjects of many musicians music, particularly folk artists such as Bob Dylan and Joan Baez. The subject of race would be at the center of the birth of rock and roll, and young, white teenagers were falling in love with music their parents considered to be too controversial.

2

THE ROCK AND ROLL EXPLOSION

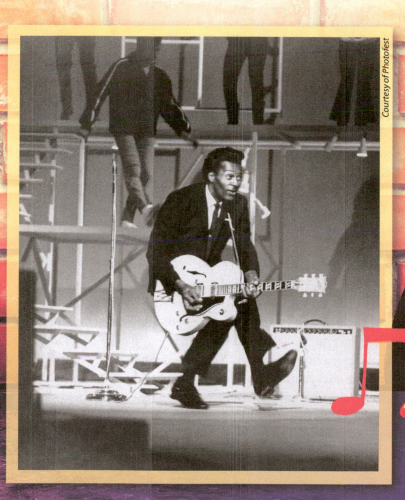

Courtesy of Photofest

"I wrote about cars because half the people had cars, or wanted them. I wrote about love, because everyone wants that. I wrote songs white people could buy, because that's nine pennies out of every dime. That was my goal: to look at my bankbook and see a million dollars there."

—*Chuck Berry*

KEY TERMS

Blackboard Jungle	Crossover	Bo Diddley rhythm
Sun Records	J&M Recording Studio	Nor Va Jak Studio
Tape-delay echo	Stop time	
Rockabilly	Chess Records	

KEY FIGURES

Bill Haley	Fats Domino	Roy Orbison
Sam Phillips	Little Richard	Carl Perkins
Elvis Presley	Willie Dixon	Jerry Lee Lewis
Colonel Tom Parker	Bo Diddley	Buddy Holly
Dave Bartholomew	Chuck Berry	Norman Petty

POST-WAR AMERICA

Change and Prosperity

In the years after World War II, America found itself in a state of peace and prosperity for the first time since the late 1920s. Economic good times meant a dramatic expansion of the middle class. Household items and consumer goods like refrigerators and televisions changed from being luxuries to necessities: between the mid-1940s and the mid-1950s, the number of TV sets in the United States increased from less than 10,000 to 50 million. Technological and scientific change was progressing at a stunning pace; computers, although new at the time, were becoming faster and more portable. Medicine brought us the polio vaccine, and electrical engineering made the introduction of the transistor radio possible. Research into the safe use of nuclear power was underway, resulting in the first commercial plant in 1957. When the Soviet Union sent Sputnik into orbit that same year, the world was ushered into a futuristic "space age" where space travel to space colonies was envisioned.

One of the biggest changes in our society was the increasing dependence on the automobile. By the mid-1950s there were nearly 70 million privately owned cars in America, and they began to change our lifestyles in profound ways. Suburban living became possible—and popular—as a way to attain the American dream of owning a home. Shopping centers sprang up, interstate highways were built, and families took more and more road trips and vacations. Disneyland opened, as did the first Holiday Inn and the first McDonald's, all of which catered to our new and fast-paced mobile life. Cars became a national obsession: faster, bigger, and shinier appealed to everyone, most of all teenagers.

Teenagers

Ah yes, teenagers—the word had been around since the 1940s, but teens in the 1950s were a different breed than any that preceded them. They were the first in American history that didn't have to work to help support the family—they could now take after-school jobs to earn and spend their own money. Add to this the advent of modern mass marketing on television and radio, and teens became a consumer entity with unprecedented buying power. They began to develop their own cultural values, social arrangements, fashions, and awareness of the world around them. Teenagers had become a class all unto themselves.

Parents were not oblivious to all this and many were none too happy, either. In an era where anxiety about The Bomb, Communism, and the Red Scare already had many adults feeling that they were heading straight for the Apocalypse, there was a growing concern that teenagers might get them there even sooner. With their new class status and independence, adults sensed that teens were flouting authority. Many were critical of a generation that had too much money and too much free time—teens had it too easy. Adults pointed to the growing problems of juvenile delinquency (although statistically there was no increase over previous years) and sexual permissiveness as the basis for their distrust. There seemed to be bored teenagers hanging out everywhere, just waiting to get themselves into trouble. The growing disapproval of adults only served to fuel any rebellious feelings that already existed in teens. Welcome to the Generation Gap.

Disconnect

In fact, a lot of teens were bored. There were strong feelings of disconnect for many: from parents, from authority, from each other. Television and suburbia fueled this isolation and loneliness, as did the usual problem of parents who didn't listen or understand. Cars with radios became essential to stay connected. Many teens looked to new role models who characterized their same feelings of alienation, such as the sarcastic and cynical antihero Holden Caulfield from J. D. Salinger's *Catcher in the Rye.* They also identified with young charismatic movie stars such as Marlon Brando and James Dean, who wore leather jackets, sullen looks and sneers while playing troubled youth in popular films such as 1954's *The Wild One,* starring Brando. Dean's portrayal of Jim Stark in *Rebel Without a Cause* (released in 1955) made him a cult hero, and his death in a fiery auto accident before the movie even opened made him a legend. *Rebel* was one of the first movies to explore themes of alienation and despair from the vantagepoint of the teen rather than the adult. Many teens identified with Jim Stark, including a young wannabe singer living in Memphis named Elvis Presley.

As the 1950s unfolded, a new teenage nation had arrived. All it needed was its own music.

THE FIRST SOUNDS

Bill Haley

As discussed in Chapter 1, observant white DJs around the country such as Alan Freed were tapping into this teen yearning and beginning to program R&B on their shows. Record distributors also caught wind about what was going on, and started putting R&B records in jukeboxes, giving teens even more access to the music. White bands started to respond to the demand for the music by including a few R&B-type songs into their repertoire. One of these was a country group called the Saddlemen, led by guitarist/vocalist Bill Haley (1925–1981).

TRIVIA NOTE

When Bill Haley and His Comets' "Crazy Man Crazy" hit #15 on the pop charts in 1953, they became the first white band to hit the Top 20 with an R&B song.

In 1951 the Saddlemen had recorded a cover of Jackie Brenston's "Rocket 88," giving it a slightly more country feel than the original. One of their next records was "Rock the Joint," which attracted the attention of Alan Freed, who started giving the song airplay. By 1952, with their popularity growing, Haley and the band (who were now all in their late 20s and early 30s, playing for teenagers at school dances) decided to scrap the cowboy image and adopt a wilder R&B-styled stage act. They also changed their name to Bill Haley and His Comets (a play on the Halley's Comet theme). When "Crazy Man Crazy," a Haley original whose inspiration came from hearing teens talk at a dance hit #15 on the pop charts in 1953, they became the first white band to hit the Top 20 with an R&B song. After signing with Decca Records in 1954, Haley recorded a cover of Joe Turner's "Shake, Rattle and Roll" (with cleaned-up lyrics) that went to #7 in late 1954 and early 1955 and sold over a million copies.

The First Rock and Roll Band

But Haley's biggest hit was yet to come. On April 12, 1954, the Comets recorded "Rock Around the Clock," which hit #23 and sold 75,000 copies before dropping off the charts. However, the song breathed new life when it was placed over the opening credits to the hit film ***Blackboard Jungle***. Decca re-released "Rock Around the Clock" and in May 1955 it shot up to #1 where it stayed for eight weeks, eventually selling over 20 million copies. Haley went on to score two more Top 10 hits, "Burn That Candle" (#9) in late 1955 and "See You Later, Alligator" (#6) in early 1956. The band appeared on national television, and was featured in the fictionalized teen film *Rock Around the Clock*. For a short while, they were not just the most popular white rock and roll band in the world, they were the *only* one.

Unfortunately Haley was soon swept aside by Elvis Presley, who scored his first national hit in March 1956 ("Heartbreak Hotel"). Presley was ten years younger, leaner, surlier, and more aggressively sexual than the rather pudgy and balding Haley. Nonetheless, Haley's calculated fusion of country and R&B was the same formula that Presley and many other early rock and roll stars would use. While Haley's music is often categorized with Presley and the other Sun Studio artists as rockabilly, his sound was slightly different than the sound heard on the earliest Sun records. The Comets included saxophone and drums, instruments that were often used in R&B groups but not present in the early Sun recordings. Haley also used group vocal chants, a technique often used by western swing bands but not typically used at Sun, where there was usually only one vocalist. Regardless, Bill Haley played an important role in pushing rock and roll up a notch in popularity.

The Indies Take Over

Even though Bill Haley was signed to one of the industry majors (Decca), the prevailing industry thought was that rock and roll was a fad that would quickly burn itself out. In fact, Haley and Elvis Presley (RCA) were the only important rock and roll stars of the 1950s that were signed to major labels. By ignoring rock and roll, the majors inadvertently opened the door for the independent labels, which were quick to grab control of the new market. Sales figures con-

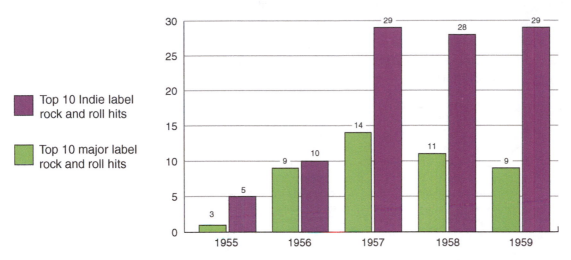

Top 10 Rock and Roll Hits from 1955–1959

firm this, as the following chart of *Billboard's* Top 10 rock and roll hits from 1955 to 1959 shows:

These impressive gains were made in a five-year period (1954–1959) where total record sales nearly tripled, from $213 million to $613 million. One of the more aggressive independent labels was Memphis-based **Sun Records**, owned by Sam Phillips.

Sun Records and Sam Phillips

Sam Phillips (1923–2003) was a true musical visionary, and tremendously important to the birth of rock and roll. He started his career as a DJ, but in early 1950 the allure of R&B enticed him to open the Memphis Recording Service in the vacant radiator shop at 706 Union Avenue. He had a great ear and an even better nose for talent, which the Memphis area, strategically located at the northernmost edge of the Mississippi Delta, was loaded with. Although anyone could plunk down $2 and make a record at the studio (which helped pay the rent in the early days), Phillips's primary interest was in making authentic recordings of the many blues and R&B singers in the area. One of his early recordings was 1951's "Rocket 88" by Jackie Brenston and His Delta Cats, which, because of its theme (a hot Oldsmobile sports car with hints of sexual innuendo), its boogie beat and distorted guitar is regarded by many to be the first rock and roll record. Initially, Phillips recorded singers such as Howlin' Wolf, B. B. King, Harmonica Frank Floyd, Sleepy John Estes, and Elmore James and leased the master tapes to Chess and Modern. In March 1952 he started his own label, Sun Records.

Phillips worked like a maniac to get his label off the ground. He not only owned the company, he served as engineer, producer, talent scout, and advance

TRIVIA NOTE

"My feeling was that there was more talent, innately natural, in the people that I wanted to work with—Southern black, Southern country white— than there was in the people who wrote the arrangements."

—Sam Phillips

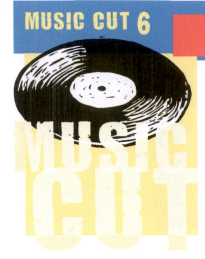

MUSIC CUT 6

"ROCKET 88" (JACKIE BRENSTON)—JACKIE BRENSTON AND HIS DELTA CATS

Personnel: Jackie Brenston: vocal, baritone sax; Raymond Hill: tenor sax; Ike Turner: piano; Willie Kizart: guitar; Jesse Knight: bass; Willie Sims: drums. Recorded March 3, 1951 at Memphis Recording Service, Memphis, TN; produced by Sam Phillips. Released April 1951 on Chess; peaking at #1 on the R&B charts.

"Rocket 88" was recorded at the Memphis Recording Service (later known as Sun Studio) on March 3, 1951, was released as Chess single #1458 and reached #1 on the R&B charts in April. Although Jackie Brenston is officially listed as the leader, it was really Ike Turner who led the Delta Cats. Hailing from Clarksdale, Mississippi, the group ran into trouble on the one-hour drive north to Memphis when the guitar amp fell out of the car, tearing a hole in the speaker cone. When the group arrived at the studio, the resourceful Sam Phillips stuffed the amp with paper and actually featured the distorted sound in the mix. He later said, "It sounded like a saxophone." It stands today as one of the first examples of distorted guitar on record.

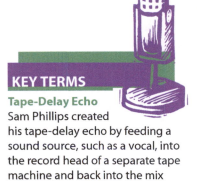

KEY TERMS

Tape-Delay Echo
Sam Phillips created his tape-delay echo by feeding a sound source, such as a vocal, into the record head of a separate tape machine and back into the mix after it passed the playback head a split second later.

man. He spent days and weeks on the road, driving thousands of miles with boxes of 45s in the trunk of his car to distribute to record shops and radio stations. Phillips's studio was a small room, so he experimented with an innovative **tape-delay echo** to enhance and fatten up the sound, a technique for which his Sun recordings would become famous. More importantly, he was on a mission to capture the passion and raw energy of the Memphis blues scene. He often spent hours in the studio with unknown performers to that end, while most other labels were trying to come up with a smooth, commercial sound. "My feeling was that there was more talent, innately natural, in the people that I wanted to work with—Southern black, Southern country white—than there was in the people who wrote the arrangements." Among the more unusual performers he took chances on in the early days were Joe Louis Hill, a one-man band, and the Prisonaires, a vocal group comprised of inmates from a local prison.

ROCKABILLY

Characteristics of Rockabilly

1. The earliest rock and roll style, influenced by R&B and honky-tonk
2. Fast tempos and jumping, nervous beat
3. Sparse instrumentation: electric and acoustic guitar, upright bass played in "slap" fashion to achieve percussive effect (in early Sun records); drums used in later Sun and other rockabilly records
4. Single vocalist using effects such as hiccuping and the use of heavy echo; backup vocals used in Bill Haley and Buddy Holly recordings

Key Rockabilly Recordings

- "Rock Around the Clock"—Bill Haley, 1954
- "That's All Right"/"Blue Moon of Kentucky"—Elvis, Scotty, and Bill, 1954
- "Blue Suede Shoes"—Carl Perkins, 1955
- "Be-Bop-A-Lula"—Gene Vincent, 1956
- "That'll Be the Day"—Buddy Holly, 1957

Phillips's first Sun hit came quickly: Rufus Thomas's "Bear Cat," the "answer" record to Big Mama Thornton's "Hound Dog," hit #3 on the R&B chart in 1953. Although he was hit with a copyright infringement lawsuit over the song (which he lost), it gave Phillips his first taste of success and put him on the map. He was still looking for something new and different, however, something that would reflect the honesty and personality of the common folk. Phillips's instincts told him that combining R&B and country music properly would have a huge crossover appeal. Even though the early recordings of Bill Haley had done this to a certain degree, it was Phillips's early Sun recordings that codified what would eventually be known as **rockabilly**, the first style of rock and roll.

Phillips also knew that he needed a distinctive vocal stylist to synthesize the "Southern black, Southern country white" sound he was looking for—someone "you'd know the moment you heard him." But he knew that as a culture steeped in the racial conventions of the 1950s, that vocalist would have to be white. He often said in those days, "If I could find me a white man who sang with the Negro feel, I could make a million dollars." As fate would have it, in August 1953 an 18-year-old truck driver walked in the front door of Sun Studios. Sam Phillips and Elvis Presley were about to change the world.

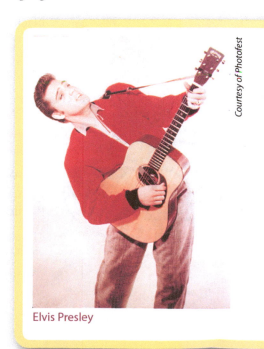

KEY TERMS

Rockabilly   The first style of rock and roll, characterized by merging elements of R&B and country, (the word is a combination of the words rock and hillbilly) slap bass, hiccupping vocals and a fast, nervous beat.

ELVIS PRESLEY

The Cat

Elvis Aron Presley (1935–1977) was born in Tupelo, Mississippi, to his parents Vernon and Gladys. The Presleys were dirt poor, moving frequently to stay a step ahead of missed rent payments; Vernon was even jailed for a brief time in 1938 for forgery. In 1948, the family moved to Memphis, where they lived in various public housing tenements before finally renting a house of their own. By this time Elvis was showing an interest in music, and his singing won a talent contest as a ten-year-old. For his eleventh birthday, his parents bought him his first guitar. He was also absorbing music from a variety of influences: country music from listening to the Grand Ole Opry, gospel music from singing at church, and from Memphis's black radio stations, R&B. One particular favorite R&B show was "Red, White, and Blue" on Memphis's WHBQ, hosted by "Daddy-O" Dewey Phillips (no relation to Sam). Of course, Elvis was also hanging out at the nightclubs along Beale Street in Memphis, where he heard artists like B. B. King and Wynonie Harris perform live.

Although he was painfully shy, by the time he had entered Humes High School Elvis was becoming the personification of the Southern "cat": greasing his long hair back, wearing brightly colored jackets, pants, and two-toned shoes that he bought at Lansky Brothers on Beale Street, a store with a primarily black clientele. He usually made an impression on those who met him, not only for his shyness and his clothes, but also for his sincere and burning desire to become somebody.

Elvis Presley

Courtesy of Photofest

The Discovery

When Presley first showed up at Sun Studios in August 1953, it was ostensibly to record two songs, which were supposedly a gift for his mother (whose birthday was actually in April). Although Sam Phillips was only mildly impressed ("We might give you a call sometime"), the next summer he teamed Elvis up with country musicians Scotty Moore (guitar) and Bill Black (bass) of the Starlite Wranglers to begin rehearsing. At the trio's first recording session on July 5, 1954, nothing was going particularly well. Finally they decided to take a break. Then, according to Scotty:

> All of a sudden Elvis just started singing this song, jumping around and acting the fool, and then Bill picked up the bass and he started acting the fool, too, and I started playing with them. Sam, I think, had the door to the control booth open . . . and he stuck his head out and said, "What are you doing?" And we said, "We don't know." "Well, back up," he said, "try to find a place to start, and do it again."

The song Phillips captured on tape was an R&B tune by Arthur "Big Boy" Crudup called "That's All Right," but Elvis had reinvented it as an electrifying cross between country western and R&B. For the B-side, they recorded a Bill Monroe bluegrass tune, "Blue Moon of Kentucky" using the same formula. The sound was different, yet puzzling—no one was quite sure how to categorize it. But the reaction was instantaneous: two nights later, when Dewey Phillips played it seven times in a row on his radio show, the phone lines lit up. In Memphis, Elvis was literally an overnight sensation. Over the next several months, Elvis, Scotty, and Bill performed around the region, including appearances at the Grand Ole Opry and Louisiana Hayride (they bombed at the conservative Opry, but were a hit at the Hayride). They also recorded a total of ten sides—five single releases—for Sun, which, over time, started to get the attention of *Billboard* magazine.

Promoting Presley presented Phillips with somewhat of a conundrum. Was he country or was he R&B? Because some listeners thought Elvis sounded "too black," in the beginning Phillips chose to market him as a country artist. Within

MUSIC CUT 7

"THAT'S ALL RIGHT" (ARTHUR CRUDUP)—ELVIS PRESLEY, SCOTTY AND BILL

Personnel: Elvis Presley: acoustic guitar, vocal; Scotty Moore: guitar; Bill Black: bass. Recorded July 5, 1954 at Sun Studio, Memphis, TN; produced by Sam Phillips. Released July 19, 1954 on Sun; did not chart.

The record that some say started it all, the first recording made by Elvis Presley with Scotty Moore on guitar and Bill Black on bass at Sun Studio in Memphis on July 5, 1954.

- "That's All Right"/"Blue Moon of Kentucky," 1954
- "Mystery Train," 1955
- "Don't Be Cruel"/"Hound Dog," 1956
- "Love Me Tender," 1956

KEY ELVIS PRESLEY RECORDINGS

a year, Presley had his first #1 hit on the country charts, "Mystery Train." Fueling his meteoric rise to fame were his electrifying live performances, in which he somehow combined surly bad boy fierceness and youthful charm that defied his off stage shyness. He wiggled his hips and kicked his legs like jackknives, eliciting an explosive effect on the crowd. Often he was forced to flee as young women rushed the stage, attempting to tear his clothes off. Jealous boyfriends were also chasing Elvis, but for different reasons.

RCA and Colonel Parker

Presley's sudden rise to fame caught the attention of **Col. Tom Parker**, a small time promoter and former carnival hawker, and in mid-1955 Parker, an illegal immigrant from the Netherlands (real name: Andreas Cornelius van Kujik), become Presley's manager. Parker immediately went to work, with a four-pronged strategy to monetize Elvis Presley. First, he began shopping Elvis to major labels, and in November 1955 engineered a deal in which RCA bought Presley's contract from Sun Records for $40,000. Parker also quickly began working to get the singer national TV exposure, Elvis-themed consumer products (Elvis perfume, Elvis sneakers, etc.), and starring roles in Hollywood movies. Over time, the Colonel took complete control of all business decisions while taking a 50-percent cut (as opposed to the usual 10 percent), all with Presley's blessing. Parker was also instrumental in shielding Elvis from the public, believing that whetting the public's appetite with only occasional appearances was a good marketing strategy. In reality this tactic contributed to isolating Elvis in his own private hell.

Presley's initial RCA recordings were done in Nashville and New York, and the change of locale coincided with some other subtle changes that began to take place. RCA was at first very nervous about their new investment, and to make the recordings more accessible to a wide audience brought in veteran studio musicians such as Chet Atkins on guitar, Floyd Cramer on piano, and the Jordanaires, a gospel backup chorus. At first the musical changes are minimal, but over time Presley's recordings became slicker and more polished, and lost most of the raw energy that Sam Phillips had honed at Sun. Eventually Parker fired Scotty and Bill, leaving the two longtime sidemen bitter and Presley even more isolated and alone. Nonetheless, RCA produced stunning results: by April of 1956, Presley had his first two #1 hits, "Heartbreak Hotel" and "I Want You, I Need You, I Love You." In August, the songs "Don't Be Cruel" and "Hound Dog" were released as flip sides on the same single, and became the first record in history to simultaneously hit #1 on the pop, country, and R&B charts.

TRIVIA NOTE

Elvis Presley's single release of "Don't Be Cruel" and "Hound Dog" became the first record in history to top the Billboard Pop, Country, and R&B charts. On the pop chart, "Hound Dog" was listed at #1 for five weeks, then "Don't Be Cruel" for six more weeks, for a total of 11 weeks at #1. The single also topped all the jukebox charts (pop, country, R&B) as well.

Elvis made his first national TV appearance on *The Dorsey Brothers Stage Show* on January 28, 1956, where he ultimately gave six appearances. He then moved up to the higher rated *Milton Berle Show* on June 5, which prompted a deluged of angry protest letters from older, conservative viewers. In response, Steve Allen had Presley appear on his show on July 1 as "the new" Elvis Presley, dressed in a tuxedo while singing to a real basset hound, also dressed in a tux. Elvis finally moved up to the top-rated variety program, *The Ed Sullivan Show,* on September 9. Sullivan initially refused to put Presley on his show, but changed his mind after seeing the huge audience the singer had garnered on Berle's show. Although Presley's first two appearances drew an astounding 60 million viewers, Sullivan's producers decided that for his third appearance on January 6, 1957 they would show only his upper body on screen—the famous "above the waist" show—because of the singer's suggestive hip movements. (They even shot his last song, the tame gospel ballad "Peace in the Valley" from the waist up!)

Sgt. Presley

Presley made his first movie, *Love Me Tender,* in 1956, and the title song produced yet another #1 hit. Eventually he made 31 films, and although many of them are of questionable value, the movies were commercially successful and Elvis did a creditable job with subpar scripts. Since Presley did not tour in the 1960s, it was mainly through his films that his fans were able to see him until the early 1970s. In March 1957 he bought Graceland, one of the most prestigious properties in Memphis, and moved in with his parents. In 1962, 17-year-old model/actress Priscilla Beaulieu moved in; the two were married in 1967 and had one child, Lisa Marie. Although Gladys Presley died in 1958, Vernon Presley lived at Graceland until his son's death in 1977.

On March 24, 1958, Presley entered the army, where he served in Germany with no special privileges until March 1960 when he was discharged after working his way up to the rank of sergeant. In the less than four years prior to being called up, Elvis remarkably had scored ten #1 hits and starred in four films. While in the service, Colonel Parker continued to release Presley recordings, with ten hitting the Top 25 and two going to #1 ("Hard Headed Woman" and "A Big Hunk O' Love"). Elvis continued to sell consistently well throughout the 1960s, but under Parker's guidance his material became increasingly pop oriented, and he fell out of touch with the younger rock audience. Although he staged a comeback on February 1, 1968, with the powerful live TV special *Elvis,* in the 1970s Presley was reduced to performing in Las Vegas in increasingly gaudy jumpsuits and flamboyant shows that cultivated a following of devoted mostly middle-aged female fans. Unbeknownst to the world, Elvis's life was becoming increasingly insular and depressing. His use of prescription drugs such as barbiturates and tranquilizers, which began in the army, increased. The breakup of his marriage to Priscilla in 1972 exacerbated the situation. His weight ballooned as his health declined, all of which contributed to his death of a heart attack in his second floor bathroom at Graceland in the early morning hours of August 16, 1977. Laboratory reports indicated that there were 14 drugs present in his system, ten in significant quantity.

The Presley Legacy

Elvis Presley gave his last performance in Indianapolis on June 25, 1977, but he left a legacy that will live forever. Even though his synthesis of R&B and country was not the first (Bill Haley, for one, was doing the same thing at least three years before Elvis made his first record), Presley did it with the attitude and conviction that would define rock and roll for many years. In essence, he was the first rock star. His records not only galvanized the teenage nation, but also influenced and inspired young rock wannabes all over the world. He had youthful good looks and charm, but at the same time brought an element of excitement, rebelliousness, and sexual energy to the stage that made his performances incendiary. Audiences weren't sure what he was going to do next, and it wasn't always clear how they would react to it. This explosive interaction between performer and audience, so common to rock performances ever since, was something new in American popular culture.

Elvis symbolized the American dream of growing up poor and becoming unimaginably rich. However, he also symbolized a much darker side of life, one that has tragically been repeated over and over by rock performers: drug abuse, selfishness, decadence, corruption, greed, and isolation. His performances in the last years of his career were sad, even pathetic, and unfortunately are the only memories that remain for many. But there is no doubt that he was a catalyst who changed our culture in ways that are perhaps incalculable. One thing is for sure: America in 1960 was a very different place than America in 1950. Elvis Presley was a major contributor to the changes that took place. He was, and will forever be, The King.

ELVIS LEGACY FACTS AND FIGURES

Elvis's sales figures dwarf everyone else in the history of rock music, including the Beatles.

- Over 500 million records sold worldwide, 134 million in the U.S.
- In America alone, 131 different albums and singles that have been certified gold, platinum, or multi-platinum by the Recording Industry Association of America.
- 149 songs on Billboard's Top 100 Pop Chart in America. Of these, 114 made the Top 40, 38 were in the Top 10, and 18 went to #1. His #1 singles spanned a total of 80 weeks at that position.
- Over 90 charted albums with nine reaching #1 (this figure is for the American pop charts only), and 16 reaching platinum or multi-platinum status. He was also a leading artist in the American country, R&B, and gospel fields, and his chart success in other countries was substantial.
- Eleven of his movie soundtrack albums went to the Top 10, and of those, four went to #1, and two, *Loving You* (1957) and *G.I. Blues* (1960), each stayed at the top for ten weeks. The album from *Blue Hawaii* was #1 for 20 weeks in 1961 and was on the chart for 79 weeks.

THE FIRST CROSSOVER ARTISTS

Rock and Roll Explodes

In the wake of Presley's success, record sales exploded and rock and roll became big business. The majors began to realize that they had misjudged the music entirely and were losing market share to the indies, who were busy scouring the South to find the next Elvis. Sam Phillips for one was well positioned, with a roster of explosive new talent that he was ready to unleash. Thousands of "cats" from all over the country (and in the United Kingdom where they were called "Teddy boys") were getting into the act as well, forming bands and recording demos. *Billboard* and *Cashbox* magazines sensed an epochal moment. A March 1956 *Cashbox* editorial entitled "Rock and Roll May Be The Great UNIFYING FORCE" stated that "The overwhelming sensation in the record business this week is the fact that two records which started essentially in the country field," (Presley's "Heartbreak Hotel" and Carl Perkins's "Blue Suede Shoes"), "have become hits also in the pop and rhythm and blues area." This demonstrated that the "possibilities exist . . . of bridging all three markets with one record" (which Elvis Presley did just five months later with "Don't Be Cruel" and "Hound Dog"). On February 16, 1957, *Billboard* announced a new format category— rock and roll. A revolution was underway.

Meanwhile, many in the industry were still uneasy with the growth of rock and roll. It was too sexual, vulgar, and obscene; its singers and songs carried a defiant attitude toward authority; and, especially in the South, it sounded "too black." Nonetheless, many black R&B artists had been enjoying significant commercial success throughout the 1950s. Some adopted a strategy of singing more sentimental or sing-along type songs that would appeal to whites, the downside of which was to cut them off from much of their black audience. Others sang in a more intuitive style with great **crossover** success to both black and white audiences.

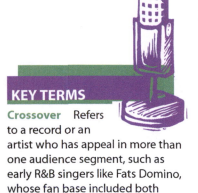

KEY TERMS

Crossover   Refers to a record or an artist who has appeal in more than one audience segment, such as early R&B singers like Fats Domino, whose fan base included both blacks and whites.

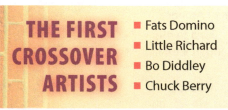

THE FIRST CROSSOVER ARTISTS

- Fats Domino
- Little Richard
- Bo Diddley
- Chuck Berry

In the early days of rock and roll, regional differences were an important part of the story. Just as Sun Records had defined the rockabilly sound of Memphis, studios in New Orleans and Chicago helped define the sound of those cities, where Fats Domino, Little Richard, Bo Diddley, and Chuck Berry—the first rock and roll crossover artists—made their most important records.

THE NEW ORLEANS SOUND

Antoine "Fats" Domino

As the birthplace of jazz, New Orleans has long been one of the most important music cities in America, with a rich mix of styles and influences from all over the world. The distinctive New Orleans R&B that emerged in the 1950s had loose shuffle rhythms (from jazz), tight bands (from gospel) and a preference toward walking bass lines (from boogie-woogie). The piano and tenor sax were the predominant instruments. Local bandleader **Dave Bartholomew** became a key figure as a songwriter and producer for many of the hits from this era that were recorded in the city, most notably those of Fats Domino. Engineer Cosimo Matassa also played a seminal role in defining the New Orleans sound at his **J&M Recording Studio** on the corner of Rampart and Dumaine Streets (later at 525 Governor Nicholls Street). Often using Red Tyler and Lee Allen on sax, Earl Palmer on drums, Huey Smith on piano, and Frank Fields on bass (all from Bartholomew's band), among the recordings made by Matassa were Roy Brown's original version of "Good Rocking Tonight" in 1947, Lloyd Price's "Lawdy Miss Clawdy" in 1952, Little Richard's "Tutti Frutti" in 1955 and many of Domino's hits.

- "Ain't That a Shame" (1955, #10)
- "I'm in Love Again" (1956, #3)
- "Blueberry Hill" (1956–1957, #2)
- "Blue Monday" (1957, #5)

FATS DOMINO'S GREATEST HITS

Except for Elvis Presley, Fats Domino (1929–) sold more records than any other rock pioneer from the 1950s. Born in New Orleans, he was playing the piano in juke joints and honky tonks in the city by the time he was ten years old. Domino's easygoing charm and demeanor made him likeable and non-threatening to white audiences, as was his distinctive Creole patois and his boogie-woogie piano playing. In the mid-1940s, Domino joined the band of trumpet player Dave Bartholomew, who helped him secure a contract with Lew Chudd and his newly formed Imperial Records in 1949. The first session produced the hit song "Fat Man" (#6) which ended up selling a million copies.

By the mid-1950s, Domino's records were already selling in the hundreds of thousands, but his greatest hits came between 1955 and 1960, including "Ain't That a Shame" (1955, #10), "I'm in Love Again" (1956, #3), "Blueberry Hill" (1956–1957, #2) and "Blue Monday" (1957, #5). Since 1955, Domino has garnered nine gold singles and 37 Top 40 hits. Fats Domino was still living in the New Orleans Lower 9th Ward when Hurricane Katrina hit in August 2005 and heavily flooded the neighborhood. He was thought to have died in the storm, but in fact a Coast Guard helicopter rescued him. His 2006 album *Alive and Kicking* was released as a benefit for the Tipitina's Foundation (www.tipitinasfoundation.org), which is dedicated to rebuilding the city's musical culture.

THE NEW ORLEANS SOUND

Characteristics of the New Orleans Sound

1. Shuffle "swing-like" rhythm influence from jazz
2. Walking bass lines borrowed from boogie-woogie
3. Extremely tight ensembles consisting of piano, bass, drums, and horn section

Key New Orleans Recordings

- "Good Rocking Tonight"—Roy Brown, 1947
- "Fat Man"—Fats Domino, 1949
- "Lawdy Miss Clawdy"—Lloyd Price, 1952
- "Tutti Frutti"—Little Richard, #17, 1955

Little Richard

Little Richard (1932–), born in Macon Georgia as Richard Wayne Penniman, was in many respects the opposite of Fats Domino—an aggressive, in-your-face wild man who shrieked and hollered and pounded the piano into submission. Growing up in a devout Seventh Day Adventist family, Richard learned to sing gospel music and play the piano at a local church. At age 13 he was kicked out of his family's house (reportedly because of his homosexuality); by 1951 he was performing on the radio with a jump band. In 1955 Richard sent a demo to Specialty Records in Los Angeles where it caught the attention of producer Bumps Blackwell. Blackwell brought him into New Orleans' J&M studio in September 1955 where Richard recorded his first hit, "Tutti Frutti." With its opening battle cry, "Awop bop a loo mop a lop bam boom! Tutti Frutti! Aw rooty," "Tutti Frutti" went to #17 in early 1956 and set the mold for many of Richard's hits to come, including "Long Tall Sally" (1956, #2), "Lucille" (1957, #1 R&B), and "Good Golly, Miss Molly" (1958, #10).

MUSIC CUT 8

"TUTTI FRUTTI" (RICHARD PENNIMAN, DOROTHY LABOSTRIE, JOE LUBIN)—LITTLE RICHARD

Personnel: Little Richard: piano, vocals; Alvin "Red" Tyler: baritone sax; Lee Allen: tenor sax; Earl Palmer: drums; Huey Smith: piano; Frank Fields: bass; guitarist unknown. Recorded September 14, 1955 at J&M Studio, New Orleans, LA; produced by Bumps Blackwell and Art Rupe; Dave Bartholomew, recording supervisor. Released December 1955 on Specialty; 12 weeks on the charts, peaking at #17.

The story of "Tutti Frutti" is one of the legends of early rock and roll. Signed by Art Rupe's Specialty Records, Richard's first day of recording at J&M Studio yielded nothing spectacular: four blues tunes. The next day, September 14, 1955, the results were pretty much the same. Finally the band took a break at a nearby club called the Drop. There, Richard sat down at the piano and belted out an obscene version of what was to become "Tutti Frutti." Up to this point, Huey "Piano" Smith had been playing piano on the session; after Richard took over on the keys, he was able to cut loose with his explosive vocal style. It took just three takes to come up with this jewel, after Dorothy LaBostrie was brought in to clean up Richard's lyrics. This recording shows off the tightly knit band of trumpeter Dave Bartholomew, who "supervised" this and many other sessions at J&M in the 1950s (the title "producer" had not been invented at this time, although that is essentially what Bartholomew was doing).

Little Richard's gospel influenced vocals and hard-driving piano playing was augmented by one of the tightest and most dynamic bands in early rock and roll. He often used **stop time** to punctuate vocal parts and honking saxophone solos. His lyrics were among the most sexually suggestive of the era. (The original lyrics to "Tutti Frutti," which included lines such as "Tutti Frutti, good booty/If it don't fit, don't force it/You can grease it, make it easy" had to be cleaned up by local songwriter Dorothy La Bostrie at the session.) On stage he was wild and aggressive, standing up while playing the piano. He took Presley's sexuality one step further, becoming rock's first androgynous performer by wearing mascara, lipstick, and a pompadour hairstyle combed high.

In 1957, at the height of his career, Richard left music to become an ordained minister. Among the reasons he gave were witnessing the Soviet satellite Sputnik fly overhead at an outdoor concert and a dream in which he claimed to have had a vision of the apocalypse. After throwing thousands of dollars worth of jewelry into the ocean, he entered a Seventh Day Adventist College in Alabama "to work for Jehovah and find that peace of mind." In 1962, Richard slowly began his return to music, but his greatest successes were behind him. His influence is undeniable, not only from his songs (which have been covered by the Beatles, Rolling Stones, and many others) but also from his outlandish, over-the-top stage persona.

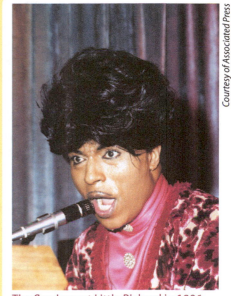

Courtesy of Associated Press

The flamboyant Little Richard in 1996.

CHICAGO R&B

Chess Records

Meanwhile, up north in Chicago, Chess Records was helping define that city's R&B sound. Phil Chess and Leonard Chess were Polish immigrants who came to Chicago as children in 1928. After dabbling in various business ventures, they eventually went into the nightclub business, owning and operating the Macomba Lounge on the South Side. In 1947 they sold the Macomba and invested in Aristocrat Records (which they later bought outright and renamed Chess in 1950) to record the artists they had seen performing in their club. Their earliest successes came with transplanted Delta musicians such as Muddy Waters and Howlin' Wolf, but by 1954 they were expanding into the growing crossover market, recording hits by doo-woppers such as the Moonglows and the Flamingos.

By 1957 business necessitated moving to a larger studio at 2120 South Michigan Avenue, where they remained until 1967 (the building remains today as a museum). Since South Michigan Avenue at the time contained the offices of several independent labels (such as Vee-Jay, Brunswick, and Constellation), distributors, rehearsal spaces, and other studios, it became known as Record Row. Many of the Chess sessions included veteran players **Willie Dixon** on bass, Fred Below on drums, Otis Spann on piano, and Little Walter on harmonica. (Dixon was also influential as a composer, penning such blues standards as "Hoochie Coochie Man" and "You Need Love." His songs have been covered by the Rolling Stones, Led Zeppelin and the Doors, to name a few.)

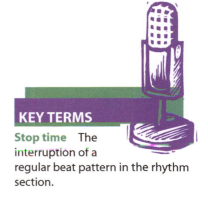

KEY TERMS

Stop time   The interruption of a regular beat pattern in the rhythm section.

Bo Diddley

One of Chess's first hit records came from a native Mississippian who was making a name for himself playing South Side clubs. Ellas McDaniel, going by the name Bo Diddley (1928–2008), turned his first recording, "Bo Diddley" (released on Checker Records, a Chess subsidiary) into a #1 R&B hit. The song consisted almost entirely of a one-chord vamp set to a repeating rhythm—*chunk-chunk-chunk-a-chunk, chunka-chunk-chunk*—which has since become known among musicians as the "**Bo Diddley rhythm**" (and has been co-opted by Buddy Holly ["Not Fade Away"], Johnny Otis ["Willie and the Hand Jive"], the Who ["Magic Bus"] and others). "Bo Diddley" was backed with "I'm a Man," a bump and grind blues number built on the five-note riff from Muddy Waters' "I'm Your Hoochie Coochie Man."

Bo Diddley had a distinctive physical appearance, often wearing cowboy hats and huge horn-rimmed glasses and playing unusual rectangular-shaped guitars. Although he never achieved the fame of other 1950s crossover R&B artists, he was an important guitar innovator who is the link between T-Bone Walker and Jimi Hendrix. His use of reverb and tremolo to enhance the sound of his guitar was as pioneering for the 1950s as the distortion and feedback that Hendrix used in the 1960s. He played his guitar as if it was a percussion instrument, giving his music a hypnotic, rhythmic feel. Diddley often propelled these rhythmic grooves with the use of maracas. His bands frequently included female musicians, which was unusual for the time.

THE CHESS R&B SOUND

Characteristics of the Chess R&B Sound

1. Raunchy, powerful, defining the Chicago blues sound
2. Instrumentation: distorted electric guitar, bass, drums, piano, sometimes harmonica

Key Chess Rock R&B Recordings

- "Bo Diddley"—Bo Diddley, #1 (R&B), 1955
- "Maybellene"—Chuck Berry, #5, 1955
- "Laura Lee"—Bobby Charles, 1956
- "Johnny B. Goode"—Chuck Berry, #8, 1958

Chuck Berry

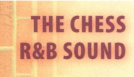

In 1955 Chess also signed the man who might easily qualify as the father of rock and roll. Chuck Berry (1926–) was born in St. Louis and grew up listening to gospel, country, blues, R&B, and popular crooners such as Nat "King" Cole and Frank Sinatra. After becoming somewhat successful in the local club circuit, Berry went to Chicago in May 1955 with hopes of making a record. There he met Muddy Waters, who referred him to Leonard Chess, who in turn set up a session to record Berry's tune "Ida Red." Although Chess liked the song, he knew of another with the same title, so he suggested renaming "Ida Red." Combining scorching guitar work, a country beat and a compelling story line, "Maybellene" shot up the charts, hitting #5 by the end of August. Over the next three years Berry had four more Top 10 hits—"School Day" and "Rock and

Roll Music" (#3 and #8, respectively, 1957), and "Johnny B. Goode" and "Sweet Little Sixteen" (#8 and #2, 1958).

Chuck Berry was the first great lyricist in rock and roll, with themes that often focused on three subjects that interested most teens: love, cars and school. His songs were interesting, humorous and often-ironic tales that transcended the usual boy-meets-girl story line. For instance, "School Day" told of racing down to the local juke joint as soon as the 3 o'clock bell rang. "Roll Over Beethoven" contained the warning "tell Tschaikowsky the news" to "dig these rhythm and blues," while "Sweet Little Sixteen" told a tale of a girl all dressed up ready to go out and rock, but who still needed mommy and daddy's permission. Berry also occasionally tackled deeper issues, as in the condemnation of racial injustice in "Brown Eyed Handsome Man." Many of these songs not only told great stories, but also contained unforgettable sing-along hooks, such as *"Go! Go! Johnny, Go! Go! Go!"* and *"Hail, Hail, Rock and Roll,"* which made them among the earliest rock and roll anthems. Berry combined elements of blues and country in his songs, and while this was a reflection of his early influences, it was also a calculated effort on his part to capture the widest crossover audience. He also sang very clearly, as did his crooner idols.

Berry was also the archetypal rock guitarist, creating double note lead lines that are among the most copied in rock. It is not inconceivable to believe that every rock guitar player since 1960 has learned to play the introductions to both "Roll Over Beethoven" and "Johnny B. Goode." Berry used imaginative call-and-response interplay between vocal and guitar on "School Day," recorded live in an era before overdubbing was common. His signature duck walk also inspired generations of guitarists to put on a better show.

Berry's initial success was due in part to Alan Freed, who recognized the hit potential of "Maybellene" early on and gave the song constant airplay. In return for his help, Leonard Chess credited Freed with one-third of the song's authorship, therefore assigning him a third of the royalty payments (the other one-third was assigned to Chess's landlord, Russ Fratto)—all without Berry's knowledge. This and other forms of outright payola were typical of how the industry operated in the mid-1950s. Within a few years, the practice of paying off DJs to get airplay would erupt into a major scandal (more on the payola scandal in Chapter 3).

MUSIC CUT 9

"MAYBELLENE" (BERRY/RUSS FRATTO/ALAN FREED)— CHUCK BERRY

Personnel: Chuck Berry: guitar, vocals; Johnny Johnson: piano; Willie Dixon: bass; Jasper Thomas: drums; Jerome Green: maracas. Recorded May 21, 1955 at Universal Studio, Chicago, IL; produced by Leonard and Phil Chess. Released July 30, 1955 on Chess; 11 weeks on the charts, peaking at #5 pop, #1 R&B.

Chuck Berry had originally titled his first hit—and his first recording for Chess Records—"Ida Red," but as pianist Johnny Johnson tells the story, Leonard Chess, who insisted on changing the name, came up with "Maybellene" after spotting a box of Maybellene mascara lying on the studio floor. All the essential Chuck Berry elements are here: proto-rock distorted guitar, a country two-beat, and a compelling story line, in this case about one of Berry's favorite subjects—cars ("As I was motorvatin' over the hill, I saw Maybellene in a Coupe de Ville . . ."). The record quickly worked its way up the R&B charts, and spent much of September and October at the #1 spot.

In 1959 Berry ran into trouble. While on tour in the southwest, he met Janice Escalante, a 14-year-old Mexican-Indian girl, and brought her back to St. Louis to work at his nightclub, Club Bandstand. After Escalante was picked up on prostitution charges, police launched an investigation into Berry on charges of violating the Mann Act, which prohibits transporting minors across state lines for immoral purposes. After two blatantly racist trials (the first was overturned), Berry was convicted in 1962 and spent two years in federal prison. When the embittered Berry returned to music, the British Invasion was underway, sweeping him and many other R&B artists out of the limelight. However, there is no doubt that the Beatles, Rolling Stones, and other British groups that came to prominence in the 1960s owed much of their success to the influence of Chuck Berry's musical genius.

OTHER IMPORTANT SUN ROCKABILLY ARTISTS

Meanwhile Back in Memphis . . .

Although it may have appeared that selling Elvis Presley's contract to RCA for only $40,000 was a bad business decision, it was one that Sam Phillips needed to make. Sun was nearing bankruptcy as it struggled to keep up with the up front costs of pressing thousands of records. In addition, by virtue of his connection with Presley, Phillips found a number of talented young Elvis wannabes were beginning to show up at his door to audition. Keep in mind also that no one knew at the time that Elvis was going to end up becoming as enormously popular as he did. Now flush with cash and without the time commitment Presley required, Phillips was able to move forward and seize what to him was a new business opportunity. Sensing that a major musical shift was at hand, he began turning away from the blues and R&B artists he had previously worked with and began turning his attention to country and rockabilly artists.

THE LATER YEARS OF SAM PHILLIPS AND SUN STUDIOS

In spite of the stunning success that Sam Phillips had during the 1950s, the glory years for Sun Studios were over by 1960. That was the year that he moved into a brand-new, state-of-the-art studio just a few blocks from his original location. Even though the new facility was much larger, the atmosphere was sterile and lacked the creative warmth of the cramped former studio. Phillips grew tired of the recording business and sold Sun in 1969. For a time he owned and operated WHER-AM, an all-female radio station in Memphis; he also was one of the original investors in Holiday Inn. The studio at 706 Union Avenue was eventually reopened as a tourist attraction, but still remains open today as a recording studio. Sam Phillips spent the last 30 some years of his life as a sort of living rock and roll legend. He died at age 80 on July 30, 2003.

Although he did have success in launching the career of a few country artists such as Johnny Cash and Charlie Rich, most of Phillips's success in the last half of the 1950s came from his rockabilly artists. The biggest of these, Carl Perkins and Jerry Lee Lewis quickly exploded to the top of the charts, but could not sustain any commercial success. In hindsight we are able to see that their greatest records, like those of Elvis Presley, were those that were made early in their careers under Phillips's supervision. One exception was **Roy Orbison**, who achieved his greatest success *after* leaving Sun. Orbison had nine Top 20 records between 1960 and 1964 for Monument Records, including the #1 hits "Running Scared" and "Pretty Woman." In trying to turn the balladeer Orbison into a rockabilly singer, Sam Phillips made one of the few artistic miscalculations in his career.

Carl Perkins and Jerry Lee Lewis

Carl Perkins (1932–1998) was born to poor sharecropping parents in northwest Tennessee. Despite his impoverished youth, he was able to start a band with his brothers Jay and Clayton, playing the honky-tonk circuit in the early 1950s. During these years Perkins was composing his own songs and developing his own rockabilly guitar and singing style. After hearing Presley's "Blue Moon of Kentucky" on the radio in 1954, the Perkins brothers auditioned for Phillips, and released two very country-sounding singles in 1955 with modest sales success. Their next release was a monster.

After a concert in Amory, Mississippi, in which they both appeared in the fall of 1955, singer Johnny Cash suggested that Perkins write a song based on a saying he had often heard while in the service, "Don't step on my blue suede shoes." Amazingly, a few nights later, Perkins heard a patron make the same comment on the dance floor in a Tennessee bar. At three o'clock the next morning, Perkins awoke with the song in his head, and wrote the lyrics down on an empty potato bag. Recorded and released in December 1955, "Blue Suede Shoes" shot up the charts, successfully fighting off numerous cover versions to end up at #2 (Presley's "Heartbreak Hotel" kept it from going to #1). By March 1956, the song was near the top of the country and R&B charts as well, becoming Sun's first million seller. Unfortunately, tragedy struck on March 21. Perkins and his brothers were on their way to make their network TV debut on *The Perry Como Show* in New York when their car slammed into a poultry truck in Delaware. Carl suffered a broken shoulder and cracked skull, was laid up for six months in the hospital, and never made it to New York.

Carl Perkins was unable to come up with another hit, and his career floundered. Although he continued his career after recovering from the auto accident, his sound (and even his look) was just a little too country for the emerging rock and roll audience. However, on a tour of England in 1964, he was received as a conquering hero, and met some of his most adoring fans, a certain moptop musical quartet. "I sat on the couch with the Beatles sitting around me on the floor," he later recalled. "At their request, I sang every song I had ever recorded. They knew each one. I was deeply flattered." The Beatles further showed their respect by covering both "Everybody's Tryin' to Be My Baby" and "Honey Don't" on their fourth album *Beatles for Sale*.

Jerry Lee Lewis (1935–) was the first bad boy of rock and roll. Born in Ferriday, Louisiana, Lewis's childhood, like Presley's and Perkins's, was spent in poverty. The cousin of tele-evangelist Jimmy Swaggart, Lewis was thrown out of Bible College his first night after tearing into a boogie-woogie version of "My

God Is Real." By the time he auditioned for Sam Phillips in 1956 at age 21, he had been married twice, in jail, and turned down by the Louisiana Hayride and every label he had auditioned for in Nashville. But Phillips took a chance on Lewis. In February 1957, after one lackluster release, Jerry Lee recorded "Whole Lotta Shakin' Going On," which quickly shot up the charts to #3, earning him a spot on *The Steve Allen Show* in July. He quickly followed up "Shakin'" with "Great Balls of Fire," which went to #2 in December, and "Breathless," which hit #7 in March 1958. After the Carl Perkins disappointment, Sam Phillips finally had a star that he could bank on.

But again, disaster struck. In May 1958, Lewis arrived in England for a promotional tour. With him was his newlywed third wife, Myra Gale Brown. She was 13 years old—and *his second cousin!* To make matters worse, Lewis married her before he was even divorced from his second wife. As the British press honed in on the scandal, Lewis was taken off the tour. Assuming that the Brits were just being their usual haughty selves, Lewis and his entourage retreated back to the safety of the States. Unfortunately, the American music industry reacted in much the same way as the British, and he was blacklisted from the Top 40 and cancelled from bookings on Dick Clark's *American Bandstand*. Even though Sam Phillips tried to make a quick buck off of the situation by releasing the novelty song "The Return of Jerry Lee," Lewis's career went into a tailspin less than a year after it started.

Despite his short stay at the top, Jerry Lee Lewis carved a niche for himself as one of rock and roll's originals. His story is of the very essence of rock and roll: a rebellious spirit, a natural-born performer, with an outrageous personality. Driven by one of the biggest egos in history, and an ongoing conflict with his lifestyle and his religious upbringing, he nicknamed himself "The Killer" (ironically, there is suspicion that he in fact killed his fifth wife, who was mysteriously murdered in their New Orleans home). He literally attacked his instrument, or as rock journalist Andy Wickham noted, "Elvis shook his hips; Lewis *raped* his piano." Jerry Lee Lewis drank too much, abused drugs, avoided paying taxes but did not avoid a number of scandals. And he is still alive to tell about it.

BUDDY HOLLY

Unlike many of the early rock and roll pioneers, Buddy Holly (1936–1959) grew up in a stable middle class home in Lubbock, Texas. His was a musical family, and the aspiring musician won $5 playing the violin in a talent contest when he was just five years old. Buddy soon gravitated to first the piano and ultimately the guitar. Most of his early musical influences came from listening to country music on the numerous barn dance radio programs; he in fact made his own radio debut in 1955 on local station KDAV playing songs like "Your Cheatin' Heart." Before long, his country-oriented group the Rhythm Playboys was gigging locally at nightclubs and public events. But like many other teenagers around the country in the mid-1950s, Holly was also fond of listening to R&B on black radio stations, and often times would venture into Lubbock's black neighborhood to listen to it performed live in cafés and juke joints. Then, in early 1955, Elvis Presley, Scotty and Bill came to town, and Buddy saw firsthand how Elvis intermingled R&B and country into rockabilly. "The day after Elvis left town, we turned into Elvis clones," his friend Sonny Curtis later remarked.

Over the next year, Buddy Holly experienced dramatic growth as a musician. He assembled three high school friends into a group that would eventually become the Crickets; he worked on his guitar playing and his stage appearance; he also began writing songs. Becoming supremely confident that he had what it takes to become famous, Holly was sure he had made it big when he signed a contract with Decca in early 1956. However, the sessions, held in Nashville, went badly, and even though Decca released a few of his singles, the contract was terminated early the next year. One of the recordings that the label refused to release was a Holly original entitled "That'll Be the Day."

Around the time Buddy and his band mates were giving up on Nashville, they began recording in Clovis, New Mexico at **Nor Va Jak Studio**, which was owned and operated by producer **Norman Petty**. Being that the young musicians were broke, Petty and Holly worked out a quid pro quo agreement to pay for the sessions: in exchange for giving Holly unlimited access to the studio and his technical expertise, Petty would be listed as co-composer and publish the songs with his Nor Va Jak Publishing Company. At the first session, held on February 25, 1957 the Crickets recorded two songs, including a revamped, faster version of "That'll Be the Day." While the group spent the next few weeks hard at work recording more of Buddy's originals, Petty worked out distribution deals to get the records released. The results were astonishing: "That'll Be the Day" entered the Top 40 in August and hit #1 in September. Two more singles, "Peggy Sue" and "Oh, Boy" followed in quick succession, peaking at #3 and #10. By the end of the year, the Crickets were booked into tours of the U.S., England and Australia (the U.S. tour included a stop at Harlem's Apollo Theatre, where the audience was surprised to find out the group was white). By 1958 Buddy Holly was a rock and roll star and living in New York's Greenwich Village.

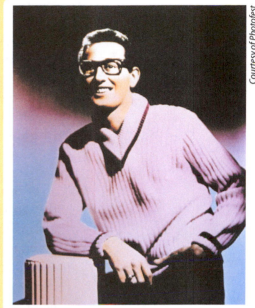

Buddy Holly

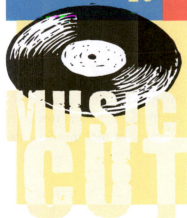

MUSIC CUT 10

"THAT'LL BE THE DAY" (BUDDY HOLLY/JERRY ALLISON/NORMAN PETTY) —BUDDY HOLLY AND THE CRICKETS

Personnel: Buddy Holly: guitar, vocals; Larry Welborn: bass; Jerry Allison: drums; Niki Sullivan, June Clark, Gary Tollett, Ramona Tollett: backup vocals. Recorded February 25, 1957 at Nor Va Jak Studio, Clovis, New Mexico; produced by Norman Petty. Released May 27, 1957 on Brunswick; 16 weeks on the charts, peaking at #1.

"That'll Be the Day" was Buddy Holly's first hit, and a monster at that. The song was originally recorded in Nashville in 1956 during Holly's short-lived tenure as a Decca artist. The newer, faster version was released in May 1957 but didn't hit the charts until August, where it quickly rose to #1 on September 23. The fact that the record took so long to start selling can be attributed to the popularity of Elvis Presley, who had eight #1 hits in 1957 and 1958, and the fact that the Crickets were at the time an unknown quantity. The record also sounded very unusual for its day, meaning that DJs were probably reluctant to play it initially. Nonetheless, it proved to be influential beyond its pop success: it was the first song ever recorded by the Quarrymen, who later became the Beatles, and clearly foreshadowed the sound of their early record releases.

By this time, important changes were beginning to take place in Holly's life. In August, he married Maria Elena Santiago after proposing to her on their first date. He recorded "True Love Ways," a song written for his new bride that was produced by Paul Anka and orchestrated with an 18-piece orchestra. The Crickets, tiring of being relegated to secondary roles and sensing a loss of camaraderie with the newlywed Holly, parted ways with him to form their own band, managed by Norman Petty. Holly's own relationship with the controlling Petty was becoming strained, and he took steps to sever their composing and publishing agreements. And suddenly without warning, the hits stopped coming. Struggling to get some momentum back in his career and the prospects of a lengthy and costly legal battle with Petty, Buddy Holly reluctantly agreed to join the Winter Dance Party tour in early 1959 that was to include several Midwestern stops.

On the tour, Holly was featured with Ritchie Valens (Richard Valenzuela) and Beaumont, Texas, DJ The Big Bopper (Jiles Perry Richardson), both up-and-comers with hits on the charts ("Oh, Donna" and "Chantilly Lace"). After the sixth show at the Surf Ballroom in Clear Lake, Iowa, the three stars chartered a plane to take them to the next show in Moorhead, Minnesota. They were supposed to take a bus, but wanted to arrive early to get their laundry done and get some extra rest. Flying into a quickly forming winter storm with a young pilot that was not certified to fly with navigational instruments, the plane crashed eight miles north of Clear Lake in the early morning hours of February 3, 1959, killing everyone on board.

Buddy Holly left an immense legacy, especially considering the brevity of his two-year career. He pioneered the four-piece combo of two guitars, bass, and drums that would be widely copied throughout the 1960s. Influences of his well-crafted, innocent love songs can be heard in the early works of the Beatles, the Hollies (who named themselves in his honor), and other groups. When the Beatles (who in fact renamed themselves from the Quarry Men to something that they thought would sound more like Holly's Crickets) made their first record in a small studio in Liverpool, the song they recorded was "That'll Be the Day." As an artist, Holly was the complete package: guitarist, singer, songwriter, and producer. He was the first of many rock guitarists to use the new Fender Stratocaster guitar. Holly was also one of the first rock musicians to push the limits of studio technology to enhance his recordings.

The End of an Era

Even though rock and roll created a musical and cultural revolution, the initial shock wave did not last long. A variety of forces came into play in the late 1950s and early 1960s that brought sweeping changes to the music—changes that were not all good. The transitional second phase of the history of rock music is the subject of the next chapter.

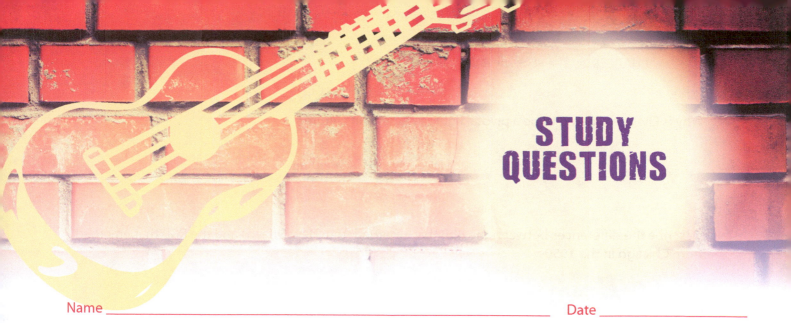

STUDY QUESTIONS

Name _____ Date _____

1. Describe some of the changes that were taking place in American society in the years leading up to the birth of rock and roll.

2. Why was Bill Haley important to the rock and roll explosion?

3. Why was Sam Phillips important to the rock and roll explosion, and in what ways was he a visionary?

4. Why are Elvis Presley's Sun recordings considered to be more important than his RCA recordings?

5. How did Sam Phillips and Col. Tom Parker differ in their nurturing of Elvis Presley's career?

6. Why is Elvis considered to be a pivotal figure in American culture?

7. Describe the differences between the R&B that emerged from New Orleans and the R&B that emerged from Chicago in the 1950s.

8. What are some of the important contributions that Chuck Berry made to rock and roll?

9. What are some of the important contributions that Buddy Holly made to rock and roll?

10. Name the most important non-musicians in this chapter and what roles they played to make them so.

HISTORICAL INTERLUDE: 1960s

A Decade of Change

The 1960s were defined by stark contrasts. A young, energetic president, John F. Kennedy, would take office in 1961, promising bigger and better things. The nation was feeling at the top of the world after winning World War II and spending the 1950s growing the economy. Many believed nothing could go wrong and a "golden age" was at hand. Unfortunately, numerous events in the late 1960s would create what many consider to be the least stable era the United States has ever experienced.

The first major event to create doubt in the United States was the assassination of President Kennedy on November 22, 1963. President Kennedy presented a model for the American youth and had given them a cultural identify. His death brought doubt and questions about who could be trusted. Numerous conspiracy theories were brought to the attention of the American public and many felt their questions were never answered. General attitudes of the youth culture magnified and instigated social movements that were more violent and critical than ever before.

Before his death, President Kennedy worked to reform laws to eliminate racial injustice in the United States. Although he would not live to see the law changes, President Lyndon B. Johnson would complete the charge, and the Civil Right Act, which outlawed discrimination based on race, was passed in 1964. Nonetheless, racial tensions would boil over throughout the 1960s, leading to numerous riots and protests. Martin Luther King Jr., a leader and face of the civil rights movement, was assassinated in 1968, bringing the racial riots to the highest and most extreme point of the decade.

The Vietnam War would be the final and most divisive issue facing the country during the 1960s. Although the United States had been involved in the Vietnam conflict since the late 1950s, the United States began sending combat troops to the region in 1965 and would officially enter the war in 1968 when involvement was at its peak. Over 500,000 combat troops were sent to Vietnam that year and the growing objection over American involvement produced massive protests and demonstrations, which often became violent. Many in the United States, who had thrown parades for its soldiers they returned from World War II, now picketed and protested any and all involvement in Vietnam.

The feminist movement began in earnest in 1963 after author Betty Freidan published the book, *The Feminist Mystique*. This best-selling book highlighted how the move to "normalcy" in the 1950s confined women to child raising and the traditional role of homemaker. Freidan became the first president of the National Organization of Women.

Many young Americans who were fed up with all of the conflict of the 1960s moved away from conflict altogether and were called "hippies." Some hippies went so far as to start communes and adopt other countercultural ideas. Echoes of these ideas would become part of the pop culture throughout the 1970s.

3

THE TRANSITION TO MAINSTREAM POP

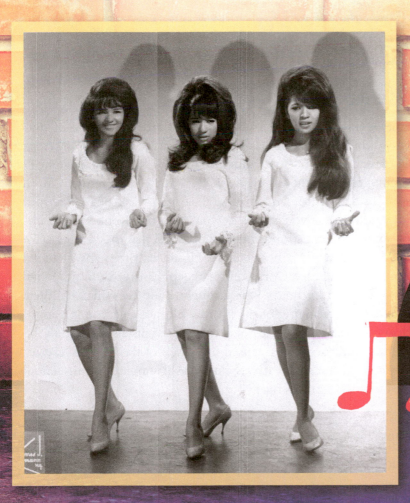

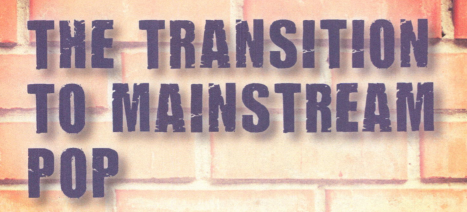

"We played a show for the American troops in Germany and the guys were having orgasms on the floor. I was like, 'What are they doin'? Ain't no dance I recognize.'"

— *Ronnie Spector (The Ronettes)*

KEY TERMS

Teen Idols
American Bandstand
The Ed Sullivan Show
Payola

Brill Building Pop
Aldon Music
Girl groups
Wall of Sound

Gold Star Studios
The Wrecking Crew
Bubblegum
Surf

KEY FIGURES

Dick Clark
Chubby Checker
Carole King/Gerry Goffin
Jerry Leiber/Mike Stoller
Phil Spector

Righteous Brothers
Burt Bacharach/Hal David
Dionne Warwick
Doc Pomus/Mort Shuman
The Monkees

Dick Dale and the
   Del-Tones
The Beach Boys
Brian Wilson

KEY ALBUMS

Pet Sounds—The Beach Boys

THE CHANGING LANDSCAPE

The Death of Rock and Roll

As the 1950s came to an end, America was poised to enter a decade of dramatic change that would become one of the most traumatic in its history. After eight years of the conservative and staid administration of President Dwight D. Eisenhower, the young charismatic John F. Kennedy was elected president. With his now famous call to action from his inaugural address, "Ask not what your country can do for you, ask what you can do for your country," Kennedy's youthful vigor and idealism made the nation's young people feel that they could make a difference in making the world a better place. His social programs included the Alliance for Progress, the Peace Corps, and new legislation to promote civil rights and fight poverty. With his pretty wife Jacqueline and two small children, the Kennedys represented a changing of the guard—old was out, young was in.

Rock was changing as well. A series of unrelated events that can only be chalked up to bad luck and bad timing caused the rebels of the first or "classic" rock era to disappear from the scene. It was almost as if someone from central casting had decided that the fun was over.

- Carl Perkins's career went unfulfilled after the car accident that almost killed him in 1956.

- Little Richard retired to the ministry in 1957.

- Elvis went into the army in early 1958, and would never regain the energy and excitement of his early career.

- Jerry Lee Lewis was shunned after news of his scandalous marriage broke in 1958.

- Chuck Berry was arrested in 1959 for violating the Mann Act.

- Tragic accidents claimed the lives of Buddy Holly in 1959 and Eddie Cochran in 1960.

These events were remarkably well timed for the major labels, which by 1960 were busy packaging a more refined and less vulgar product to a maturing audience. By this time, many of the teens that had originally embraced rock and roll were becoming adults and entering the world of mortgages, jobs, marriage, and children. They weren't so rebellious any more, and their music tastes were changing. Suddenly they were buying more LPs than singles (like their parents had done in the 1950s), and were "turning down the volume" so to speak, listening to music that wasn't quite as wild as five years ago. With a maturing audience, an increasingly watered-down product and the exiting of an entire generation of rock stars, many were inclined to believe that rock and roll was dead.

While this chapter focuses on how the pop music industry reclaimed its audience, two other important strains of pop were also emerging at the same time that will be covered in subsequent chapters. Chapter 4 will cover soul music, which emerged from the fusion of gospel and R&B in the 1950s to become a major force in pop music in the 1960s. Chapter 5 will cover folk music, which after breaking through to a mainstream audience after languishing for decades in the backwoods of rural America, would have a profound effect on the future of rock.

The Backlash

At the same time that the first generation of rock and rollers were fading from view, several conflicts associated with the music were beginning to emerge. The first of these was a backlash from alarmed religious, parental and white supremacist groups who began warning about the breakdown of morals and the poisoning of impressionable young minds that rock and roll was causing. To these groups, this was nothing less than an all-out culture war, and a many sided one at that. To some, rock and roll was a Communist plot; others placed the blame on the rock and roll DJs, while still others blamed the schools, government, or whatever other culprit was convenient. Pamphlets were distributed, meetings were held, "I Hate Elvis" clubs sprang up, and boycotts and record burnings were organized. The ugliest side of this backlash occurred where sex and race intersected, a particularly inflammatory hot button issue for many conservative-minded whites, especially in the segregated South. Many of these folks found it disturbing to see white girls shrieking and hyperventilating over black singers and white singers emulating black singers. Rock and roll is "sexualistic, unmoralistic, and brings people of both races together," warned the Alabama White Citizens Council, which took it upon themselves to publish a disciplinary guide for parents entitled *A Manual for Southerners.* "Help save the Youth of America. Don't buy Negro records," threatened a leaflet distributed throughout the South. Another moralized that "The entertainment world decides how our children will dress, speak, their moral conduct, and even their manners. At present, their theme is inter-racial friendship and tolerance. Now is the time to rise up in mighty protest."

Whether rock and roll was "unmoralistic" is a matter of opinion, but it was definitely bringing the races together. At many early rock and roll concerts black and white kids regularly mingled and even danced together despite the best efforts by security to keep them separate. This was a marked contrast from the traditional segregated audiences that Southerners were used to seeing. Chuck Berry described a concert where "Twice as many young whites as blacks rushed toward the stage . . . we knew the authorities were blazing angry, but they could only stand there and watch." In the end it was the kids who decided whether there should be any race mixing, and not surprisingly they broke stride with their parents. Even Pat Boone, a squeaky-clean pop singer that any white parent would love, cast his lot with the kids when he remarked that, "Racial segregation is sickening."

THE TEEN IDOLS

The Boy Next Door

A second battlefront was that of the major labels attempting to regain control of the youthful, record-buying market that the independent labels had so successfully taken away in the late 1950s. One strategy was to open their wallets and buy out the contracts of the artists signed to indie labels, as RCA had done with Elvis Presley. Or better yet, they could just buy the independent labels outright—if you can't beat 'em, *buy 'em*! It worked—by the end of the 1960s most of the important indies had been either bought out (including Atlantic, Sun and Chess) or run out of business entirely (Modern) by the major labels.

Another way to win back the youth audience was for the majors to develop their own artists that were—for the purpose of maximizing sales—as non-controversial and as socially acceptable as possible. (In other words, Little Richard wannabes need not apply.) This new crop of singers, who started to appear as early as the late 1950s, was a clean-cut and wholesome bunch—and conspicuously, they all were white. The **Teen Idols,** as they became known, were groomed for stardom not on the basis of their talent, but instead on their "boy-next-door" good looks. Many of them were of Italian ancestry who Anglicized their names to present a more All-American image—accordingly, Francis Avalone became Frankie Avalon, Walden Robert Cassotto became Bobby Darin, Concetta Franconero became Connie Francis. Unlike most of the classic rock and rollers, the Teen Idols did not write their own songs, but instead recorded songs written by professional songwriters who consciously smoothed out the rough edges of earlier rock and roll. The typical Teen Idols song contained little or no beat, lavish orchestration, and nonsexual, safe romantic themes of idealistic teen love. Among the most popular teen idols were Avalon, who had 13 Top 40 hits between 1958 and 1962; Paul Anka, with 22 during the same period; and Francis, with 28. Other popular Teen Idols included Fabian (Fabiano Forte), Bobby Rydell (Robert Ridarelli), and Freddy Cannon (Frederick Picariello).

One Teen Idol whose career extended beyond the early 1960s was Ricky Nelson. Nelson had grown up in front of the nation as a cast member of the popular family TV program *The Adventures of Ozzie and Harriet,* named for his

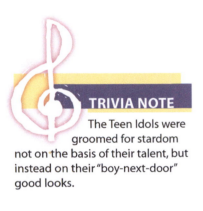

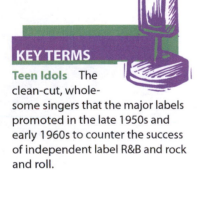

The Transition to Mainstream Pop

- "Who's Sorry Now?"—Connie Francis, #4, 1958
- "Venus"—Frankie Avalon, #1, 1959
- "Puppy Love"—Paul Anka, #2, 1960

KEY TEEN IDOL
RECORDINGS

parents, the stars of the show. Although Nelson's popularity was strongest before the British Invasion swept all the Teen Idols aside, he remained popular until his death in an airplane accident in 1985. Between 1957 and 1964 he had 33 Top 40 hits, two of which went to #1 ("Poor Little Fool" in 1958 and "Travelin' Man," 1961).

Philadelphia, Dick Clark, and *American Bandstand*

One reason for the huge success of the Teen Idols was their constant exposure on a television program that began broadcasting on Philadelphia's WFIL-TV in 1952. Originally called *Bandstand* and hosted by Bob Horn, the show was taken over by station staff announcer Dick Clark in 1956 after Horn was arrested for drunk driving (ironically right in the middle of a Don't Drink and Drive promotion). In 1957 the show was picked up by the national ABC-TV network and renamed *American Bandstand*. Within two years it was being broadcast on over 100 stations to an audience of 20 million. It aired until 1987.

The format of *American Bandstand* was simple: pack a TV studio with 150 clean-cut teenagers who danced to the latest hit singles, with weekly appearances by pop singers lip-syncing along with their records. Clark, who looked like a teenager himself, wielded enormous power by picking which songs were played and how often, and his choices frequently favored the pop-oriented Teen Idols and other non-threatening singers, including local Philadelphia boys Fabian, Avalon, and Rydell. Dick Clark also began building a music empire by investing in local record companies, publishing firms, a management company, and a pressing plant. Powered by the success of *American Bandstand*, Philadelphia played an important role in the pop music industry in the early 1960s.

Powered by the success of *American Bandstand*, Philadelphia played an important role in the pop music industry in the early 1960s.

Dance Crazes and Novelty Tunes

The most important record labels in Philadelphia at this time were Cameo/Parkway, Chancellor, and Swan (which

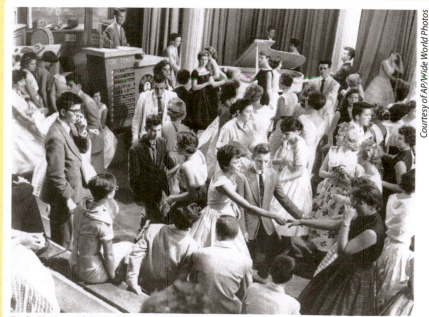

Courtesy of AP/Wide World Photos

Dick Clark on the set of *American Bandstand* in Philadelphia, June 30, 1958.

was half-owned by Clark). For a few years in the late 1950s and early 1960s, these companies were among the industry leaders in creating a pop music product, sometimes (in the case of the Teen Idols) literally creating stars out of less than stellar talents. Said Chancellor owner Bob Marcucci of meeting Fabian: "Somehow I sensed that here was a kid who could go. He looks a little bit like Presley. . . . I figured he was a natural. It's true that he couldn't sing. He knew it, and I knew it." Cameo/Parkway hit upon a tremendously successful strategy by producing a series of novelty dance tunes, starting with the 1960 #1 hit "The Twist" by **Chubby Checker**. Checker was a local unknown singer named Ernest Evans; his new name was conceived by Dick Clark's wife Bobbie as a play on the name Fats Domino. The label followed up "The Twist" with other dance tunes, including "The Hucklebuck," "Pony Time," "The Fly," and "Limbo Rock" by Checker, and "The Fish," "The Wah Watusi," "Mashed Potato Time," and several more by other artists. The dance craze scheme worked so well that "The Twist" returned to the #1 spot again in 1962, the only single since charting began in 1955 to top the charts twice. Usually instructions for the new dance were found somewhere in the lyrics of the song, and with exposure on *American Bandstand,* they quickly spread throughout the teenage nation.

DANCE CRAZES FROM THE EARLY SIXTIES

Twist	Pony	Fly
Dog	Madison	Popeye
Watusi	Loco-Motion	Hitch-Hike
Harlem Shuffle	Limbo	Swim
Wiggle Wobble	Bristol Stomp	Boston Monkee
Hully Gully	Cool Jerk	Duck
Mashed Potato	Monkee	Funky Chicken

Novelty tunes appeared from time to time as well, including Sheb Wolley's "The Purple People Eater" (#1, 1958), Brian Hyland's "Itsy Bitsy Teenie Weenie Yellow Polka Dot Bikini" (#1, 1960) and Bobby "Boris" Pickett's "Monster Mash" (#1, 1962). Dave Seville came up with one of the best pop gimmicks of all time when he created the Chipmunks by recording overdubs of his own voice at half speed and playing them back at full speed (making them sound an octave higher). He had two #1 hits in 1958 alone: "Witch Doctor" and "The Chipmunk Song."

Along with *American Bandstand,* other national TV programs began presenting rock and roll as well, albeit in small doses. At the time, variety shows were popular that presented comedians, acrobats, and jugglers as well as musical groups. Although they attracted some criticism from conservatives, the variety shows of Arthur Godfrey, Jackie Gleason, Steve Allen, Milton Berle, and Ed Sullivan all made a point of putting rock on their shows once they realized it increased ratings. The **Ed Sullivan Show**, on the air from 1948 to 1971 and one of the most-watched programs on TV, was particularly important for rock artists to gain national visibility. Appearances on the *Sullivan* show were milestones in the early careers of Elvis Presley, the Beatles, and the Rolling Stones.

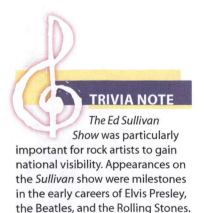

TRIVIA NOTE

The Ed Sullivan Show was particularly important for rock artists to gain national visibility. Appearances on the *Sullivan* show were milestones in the early careers of Elvis Presley, the Beatles, and the Rolling Stones.

PAYOLA

The Pay-for-Play Scandal

A third battle being waged at the time was a particularly ugly one. Although **payola**, the practice of DJs accepting cash (known euphemistically in the business as the "$50 handshake"), favors, and other gifts from record companies to play their songs was not specifically illegal at the time, it was at the very least a dubious enterprise. It was also so widely accepted as standard business practice that the entire industry shuddered when Congress decided to investigate the issue in 1959. The timing of the probe was convenient for politicians who wanted to score points among their constituents who hated rock and roll: 1960 was an election year. When the Special Subcommittee on Legislative Oversight, chaired by Arkansas Democratic Representative Oren Harris found that 335 DJs had been paid "consulting" fees totaling $263,245, a witch hunt commenced to find out who the guilty ones were. Although a few DJs were fired and some stations produced affidavits showing they were monitoring their jocks, the focus of the committee quickly turned to the two most highly visible rock entrepreneurs, Dick Clark and Alan Freed.

There were a number of issues suggesting that Clark had improper deals going on, including his ownership of publishing companies, 162 song copyrights (145 that had been given to him as gifts), and co-ownership of Swan Records. Since Clark often played songs on *American Bandstand* that benefited these business arrangements, it appeared that he was manipulating the system for his own profit. Clark was called to testify in April 1960, and although the questioning at times seemed to implicate that there was a case to be made against him, the committee could not prove that he actually accepted cash for playing songs. Clark defended himself as a businessman who was merely profiting from the performance royalties and taking advantage of legal business opportunities. He had also by this time divested himself from most of his various interests—except *Bandstand* of course. After two days the clean cut and youthful looking Clark was dismissed without further investigation. Committee chairman Harris even called him "an attractive and successful young man." Dick Clark stayed in the music business, amassing a vast entertainment portfolio that included one of the industry's largest independent production companies, and was worth hundreds of millions of dollars at the time of his death in 2012.

Alan Freed was not as fortunate. His problems began in 1958 when he was arrested for inciting a riot at a concert he promoted in Boston. He was promptly fired by his employer, WINS. By 1959, Freed was working at WABC radio in New York and facing new problems in light of the impending payola investigation. Although at the time he denied accepting payola, he refused to sign an ABC Network affidavit saying as much, and was fired by WABC in November. He was indicted by Congress on May 19, 1960 and charged with bribery, and although he eventually admitted to accepting a total of $2,500 in gratuities, he claimed that the money did not impact his decision to play any specific songs. But by this time, the shifty-eyed and controversial Freed had become the scapegoat of the entire scandal; *Cashbox Magazine* noted as much with an editorial stating he had "suffered the most and was perhaps singled out for alleged wrongs that had

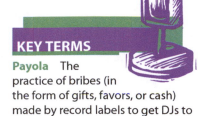

KEY TERMS

Payola   The practice of bribes (in the form of gifts, favors, or cash) made by record labels to get DJs to play their songs; *Variety Magazine* coined the term in 1938.

become a business way-of-life for many others." After pleading guilty to two counts of bribery in December 1962, Freed was fined $300 and dismissed. But unable to get a job in radio and cultivating a growing drinking problem, his career was essentially over; he died penniless and broken from the emotional and financial toll of the scandal in 1965 at age 43.

BRILL BUILDING POP

Aldon Music

In New York, where Tin Pan Alley composers had ruled pop music since the 1880s, a new breed of songwriters was beginning to emerge in the late 1950s. Rock and roll had presented a paradigm shift in the pop music business, and show tunes written in the Tin Pan Alley mold would not work anymore. New songs had to be written with a rock beat and story lines that related to teenagers but were not offensive to adults. Many of the older, established songwriters were simply not up to the task, leaving the door open for a new crop of younger writers. By the early 1960s this new pop songwriting scene was clustered in and around the Brill Building at 1619 Broadway, where over 150 music businesses were located. These songwriting shops became so influential to the industry that the pop music they produced in the late 1950s and early 1960s became known as Brill Building Pop. One of the most important, Aldon Music, at 1650 Broadway just across the street from the Brill Building, was founded in 1958 by songwriters Al Nevins and Don Kirshner. Nevins and Kirshner, who preferred their writers to work in pairs, assembled a stable of pop songwriting superstars that included the teams of Neil Sedaka and Howard Greenfield, Barry Mann and Cynthia Weil (who would marry soon after teaming up), and Carole King and Gerry Goffin, two 19-year-olds who were already married. (Interestingly, there was yet another highly successful Brill Building husband and wife team, Ellie Greenwich and Jeff Barry, although they didn't work for Aldon.)

Working at Aldon Music was typical of the Brill Building scene: each day writers worked out song ideas in cubicles with upright pianos, often soliciting

---

A SHORT LIST OF ALDON HITS THAT HELPED DEFINE BRILL BUILDING POP

Neil Sedaka/Howard Greenfield
- "Stupid Cupid"—recorded by Connie Francis, #14, 1958
- "Breaking Up Is Hard to Do"—Neil Sedaka, #1, 1960
- "Calendar Girl"—Neil Sedaka, #4, 1960

Barry Mann/Cynthia Weil
- "On Broadway" (with Jerry Leiber and Mike Stoller)—the Drifters, #9, 1963
- "You've Lost That Lovin' Feelin'" (with Phil Spector)—the Righteous Brothers, #1, 1964
- "We Gotta Get Out of This Place"—the Animals, #13, 1965

Carole King/Gerry Goffin
- "Will You Love Me Tomorrow"—the Shirelles, #1, 1961
- "The Loco-Motion"—Little Eva, #1, 1962
- "Go Away Little Girl"—Steve Lawrence, #1, 1963

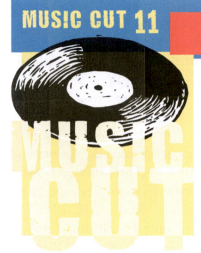

MUSIC CUT 11

"WILL YOU LOVE ME TOMORROW" (CAROLE KING/GERRY GOFFIN)—THE SHIRELLES

Personnel: Shirley Owens, Addie Harris, Beverly Lee, Doris Coley: vocals; other musicians unidentified. Recorded 1960 in NYC; produced by Luther Dixon. Released November 1960 on Scepter; 19 weeks on the charts, peaking at #1.

"Will You Love Me Tomorrow" was the first hit for newlyweds Gerry Goffin and 18-year-old Carole King. At the time he was working as a chemist; he and Carole (who were also new parents) would write songs at night in their cramped apartment in Brooklyn. Beverly Lee of the Shirelles at first rejected the song's demo as too white and too country, but once the group heard the final production with string arrangement by Carole, they were sold. "The song was completely different than the one on the demo. It was *beautiful*. All those *strings!* It blew our minds!" Lee later said. This record became a #1 hit for the Shirelles in December 1960, the first ever by a black female group. Soon after, Gerry quit his day job.

suggestions and criticisms from other company writers at the end of the day. The songs were then pitched to record companies, whose A&R men, arrangers, and producers cranked out product. It had all the glamour of an assembly line, but with impressive results. By 1962 Aldon had 18 writers on staff who had placed hundreds of hits on the radio, led by the top three writing teams of Sedaka/Greenfield, Mann/Weil, and King/Goffin. They were not only good, they were young—none were over the age of 26.

"Will You Love Me Tomorrow," while extremely popular, was also revolutionary for its time. While most songs of the era were stories of idealistic teenage love, this song was more direct. Being pressured by her boyfriend to "do it," the girl wants assurance that he will still love her in the morning—after all, her reputation was at stake. "The Loco-Motion" was inspired by King and Goffin's babysitter, 17-year-old Eva Narcissus Boyd, who was dancing while the two were working on some new material. Goffin asked what the name of the dance was—to him it looked like a locomotive train. After finishing the song, Goffin and King let Eva—who became "Little Eva"—sing it, and it became the first of her four Top 40 hits.

Leiber and Stoller

By this time another songwriting team was already making their own mark on the Brill Building scene. When Jerry Leiber and Mike Stoller met each other in Los Angeles in 1950, they discovered that they had remarkably similar backgrounds: both were from the East Coast, Jewish, 17 years old, and big fans of R&B and the blues. They hit it off right away, and began writing songs together. Their first taste of success came in 1953 with "Hound Dog," which Big Mama Thornton turned into #1 R&B hit. After forming their own Spark record label in 1954, Leiber and Stoller began to write songs for the R&B vocal quartet the Robins, including the classics "Smokey Joe's Café" and "Riot in Cell Block 9." Their first #1 pop hits came in 1956 when Elvis Presley recorded his own version of "Hound Dog" along with "Love Me Tender." Presley's version of "Hound Dog," (backed by the Otis Blackwell-penned song "Don't Be Cruel") became the first record in history to simultaneously hit #1 on the pop, country

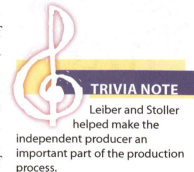

TRIVIA NOTE

Leiber and Stoller helped make the independent producer an important part of the production process.

and R&B charts. Presley had another #1 Leiber and Stoller hit in 1957 with "Jailhouse Rock"; in all, he recorded 24 of their songs.

In the mid-1950s Leiber and Stoller moved to New York and the Brill Building area and began an unusual (for the time) association with Atlantic Records as independent producers. By this time they had hit upon a formula of telling mini-stories with humorous lyrics, which they referred to as "playlets." They were also paying meticulous attention to every detail in the recording process, spending hours in the studio recording as many as 50 takes of a song if necessary. Claiming that "We don't write songs, we write records," Leiber and Stoller pushed the art of record production into new uncharted territory with the use of string orchestration, Spanish guitars, marimbas, and other exotic percussion instruments and Latin rhythms.

Their formula was well served in the string of nine Top 40 hits between 1957 and 1959 for the Coasters (the name given the newly reorganized Robins). These included the classics "Searchin'" and its flipside "Youngblood," "Yakety Yak" (#1, 1958), "Charlie Brown," "Along Came Jones," and "Poison Ivy." In addition to their success with another vocal group, the Drifters ("There Goes My Baby," "On Broadway," both Top 10 hits), they had two more Top 10s with Ben E. King—"Spanish Harlem" (written by Leiber with Phil Spector) and "Stand By Me." In 1964 they founded another label, Red Bird, which produced many of the hits of the so-called "girl groups." Although their songwriting productivity fell in the mid-1960s, many artists continued to record their songs, including the Beatles ("Kansas City"), Peggy Lee ("Is That All There Is?"), and Luther Vandros ("I [Who Have Nothing]").

Leiber and Stoller helped make the independent producer an important part of the production process. Their songs are still among the most enduring in rock history, using clean, witty lyrics teenagers could relate to, set to R&B chord progressions, rhythms, and melodies. They were also tremendously influential to the next generation of producers and songwriters such as Phil Spector, Barry Gordy of Motown, and Brian Wilson of the Beach Boys.

MUSIC CUT 12

"ON BROADWAY" (JERRY LEIBER/MIKE STOLLER/CYNTHIA WEIL/BARRY MANN)—THE DRIFTERS

Personnel: Rudy Lewis: lead vocal; Johnny Moore: tenor vocal; Charlie Thomas: tenor vocal; Gene Pearson: baritone vocal; Johnny Terry: bass vocal; Phil Spector: guitar solo; other musicians and singers unidentified. Recorded January 22, 1963 in NYC; produced by Jerry Leiber and Mike Stoller. Released April 1963; 8 weeks on the charts, peaking at #9.

"On Broadway" was the twelfth Top 40 hit for the Drifters in a four-year period. Notable in the Leiber/Stoller production of this record are the percussion instruments (including castanets and timpani), vibes, rhythm guitar playing a propulsive *chunk-chunk-chunk-chunk*, string section and female backup singers and brass section. And of course, Phil Spector's memorable twangy guitar solo.

PHIL SPECTOR

The Girl Groups

Of all the producer/songwriters in the early years of rock and roll, the most influential was Phil Spector. Spector (1940–) was born in the Bronx, but his mother moved the family to Los Angeles in 1953 after Phil's father committed suicide. In high school, he learned to play guitar, which helped the diminutive and socially awkward Spector gain respect from his classmates. After graduation, he formed a musical group with three friends called the Teddy Bears. At their very first recording session, Spector produced a song he had written called "To Know Him Is to Love Him," the title being a modification of "To Know Him Was to Love Him," the epitaph on his father's tombstone. Released on the tiny Dore label, the song (helped in part by airplay on *American Bandstand*) hit #1 in December 1958, just weeks before Spector turned 18. It eventually sold over one million copies. Around this time Spector came to realize that his future was in producing rather than performing, so in early 1960 he moved to New York to understudy with Jerry Leiber and Mike Stoller.

- Crystals
- Chiffons
- Dixie Cups
- Shangri-Las
- Ronettes

KEY "GIRL GROUPS"

The first song Leiber and Stoller gave him to produce, "Corrina, Corrina," became a #9 hit for Ray Peterson. His next project was co-writing "Spanish Harlem" with Jerry Leiber; it became a #10 hit for the Drifters. After working on a number of other records for the songwriting duo as both producer and session guitarist, Spector moved back to LA in late 1960, started his own label, Philles, and began looking around for new talent. He soon discovered a group made up of five schoolgirls called the Crystals, and sensing that an all-female group might succeed after years of male-dominated doo-wop groups, began producing records for them. Their first two releases, "There's No Other" and "Uptown" charted respectably at #20 and #13. The next two to chart were monsters: "He's a Rebel," went to #1 in 1962 and "Da Doo Ron Ron" (written by Spector with Ellie Greenwich and Jeff Barry) went to #3 in 1963.

Although the Crystals were not the first **girl group**, a genre characterized by young females singing songs of innocent love and devotion to their boyfriends, they were the first to achieve popular success, thereby creating the mold that others would copy. Other girl groups soon materialized, including the

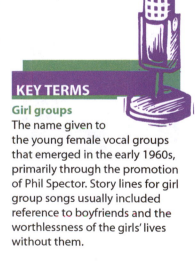

KEY TERMS

Girl groups
The name given to the young female vocal groups that emerged in the early 1960s, primarily through the promotion of Phil Spector. Story lines for girl group songs usually included reference to boyfriends and the worthlessness of the girls' lives without them.

PHIL SPECTOR— HE'S A REBEL

The story of "He's a Rebel" is an interesting commentary on Spector's role as visionary, and the record industry as well. Convinced the brand-new song (written by Gene Pitney) was going to be a #1 hit for the Crystals, he quickly booked time at L.A.'s Gold Star Studio, even though the Crystals themselves were unavailable. Spector brought in another group, the Blossoms (led by Darlene Love) to sing the song but released it as the Crystals anyway, since they already had name recognition. No one seemed to notice. In essence, the song and the production had become more important than the singers themselves.

Chiffons ("He's So Fine," #1, 1963, and "One Fine Day," #5, 1963), the Dixie Cups ("Chapel of Love," #1, 1964), and the Shangri-Las ("Leader of the Pack," #1, 1964). Spector himself soon focused his attention on a new group, a trio of inter-racially mixed girls from Spanish Harlem called the Ronettes. At only their second session in July 1963, the group recorded a song he had written with Ellie Greenwich and Jeff Barry entitled "Be My Baby." As it rose to its peak at #2, Phil and Ronettes lead vocalist Veronica (Ronnie) Bennett began a romance that eventually led to their marriage in 1968. They divorced in 1974.

KEY GIRL GROUP RECORDINGS

- "He's a Rebel"—the Crystals, #1, 1962
- "Da Doo Ron Ron"—the Crystals, #3, 1963
- "Be My Baby"—the Ronettes, #2, 1963
- "Leader of the Pack"—the Shangri-Las, #1, 1964

The Wall of Sound

By this time Spector was setting new standards in popular music with a production style that became known as the **Wall of Sound**. Spector wanted his records to sound like a symphony orchestra playing the *1812 Overture*, or as he once said, "Like God hit the world and the world hit back." The Wall of Sound began to evolve with "He's a Rebel" in 1962, and by the time he produced "Da Doo Ron Ron" in 1963, he had developed a system for creating it. Recording took place at **Gold Star Studios** in L.A.; although it was small by New York standards (25' × 35') and primitively equipped, it was where Spector had always recorded in L.A., going back to his Teddy Bear days. Spector also packed the studio with as many as 20 musicians at a time—usually using an informal collection of studio pros known as the **Wrecking Crew**. Rhythm sections usually contained three to five guitars (all playing the same part), three or four pianos (ditto), two bass guitars, a drummer and several percussionists. To this he added string and horn sections. Vocals were done at a second session; studio veteran Jack Nitzche did arrangements. Spector also doused his productions with liberal amounts of reverberation from the studio's echo chamber. After the recording was finished, he mixed everything down to monaural rather than stereo. "Back to mono" became his slogan.

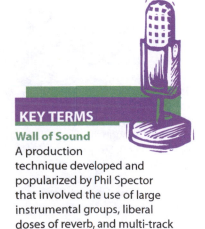

KEY TERMS

Wall of Sound
A production technique developed and popularized by Phil Spector that involved the use of large instrumental groups, liberal doses of reverb, and multi-track overdubbing.

Although Phil Spector used dozens of session musicians, his favorites were collectively known as the Wrecking Crew. Members of the Crew included Carol Kaye on bass, Hal Blaine on drums, guitarists Barney Kessel, Glen Campbell and Tommy Tedesco, pianists Don Randi, Larry Knechtel and Leon Russell, horn players Nino Tempo and Jay Migliori, and percussionists Victor Feldman and Sonny Bono. The Wrecking Crew musicians played on literally thousands of recordings during the 1960s and 1970s including pop, rock, TV themes songs and film scores. They were also a favorite of Brian Wilson of the Beach Boys, who used them on his monumental album *Pet Sounds*.

THE WRECKING CREW

Wall of Sound sessions generally took at least 3 to 4 hours as Spector meticulously tinkered with the parts, the mix, and microphone placement. But when he was done, the results were magical. "The musicians would come into the control room for the playback and just be blown away," recalled Gold Star engineer Larry Levine. "They simply couldn't believe that what they were hearing was what they'd been playing." Not that Spector was easy to deal with: although his track record as a producer between 1962 and 1965 was that of a musical Midas, he gained a reputation as an eccentric, a control freak, and an egomaniac. "Phil had quirks that nobody liked," recalled Don Kirshner. "He would work at being different and eccentric. Phil had to compensate for his size, his looks, by being different." Although he held great respect for the musicians, all of whom were pros, he treated the singers, most of whom were merely kids, as disposable parts. "He rode the singers hard," session player Don Randi later said. "He could be brutal to get that performance out of them." To Spector, the singers were not the stars. *He* was.

Like the teen idols, the British Invasion eventually killed off the girl groups, so Spector turned his attention to the blue-eyed soul group the **Righteous Brothers**. Working his magic once again, he produced "You've Lost That Lovin'

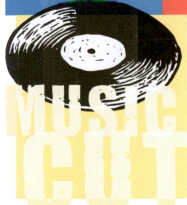

MUSIC CUT 13

"YOU'VE LOST THAT LOVIN' FEELING" (PHIL SPECTOR/BARRY MANN/ CYNTHIA WEIL)—THE RIGHTEOUS BROTHERS

Personnel: Bill Medley, Bobbie Hatfield: vocals; The Wrecking Crew: backing musicians. Recorded August-November 1964 at Gold Star Studios, Los Angeles, CA; produced by Phil Spector. Released December 1964 on Philles; 16 weeks on the charts, peaking at #1.

After signing the blue-eyed soul group the Righteous Brothers in 1964, Phil Spector's first job was to find new material for them. He turned to the Brill Building songwriting team of Barry Mann and Cynthia Weil, who after sketching out the basic song flew to Los Angeles to meet with the producer. Spector slowed it down to a dirge-like tempo and added the dramatic middle section ("Baby, baby, I get down on my knees . . ."), and ended up with a song that some thought was too long (at 3:45) and too slow for AM radio. (As lead vocalist Bill Medley later recalled, "When Phil played it for me over the phone I said, 'Phil, you have it on the wrong speed!'") Spector proved his doubters wrong as the song quickly climbed the charts, hitting #1 in February 1965; today it stands as arguably his greatest masterpiece. "Lovin' Feeling" was recorded, like all of Spector's Wall of Sound productions, at Gold Star Studio in Los Angeles.

Feeling" (#1, 1964), (co-written by Spector with Barry Mann and Cynthia Weil), and the King/Goffin "Just Once in My Life" (#9, 1965). However, his luck and career turned abruptly when his final and perhaps biggest wall of sound production, Ike and Tina Turner's "River Deep, Mountain High" flopped in 1965 without charting. Taken as a sign that the pop world had passed him by, Spector sank into reclusiveness, unsure of which direction to turn. He resurfaced in 1969 as producer of the Beatles *Let It Be* and the Ramones *End of the Century* in 1980. After years of staying out of the public eye, Spector made headlines in February 2003 after his arrest for the murder of 40-year-old starlet Lana Clarkson in the foyer of his Alhambra, California mansion. After a first trial failed to reach a verdict, a second trial convicted him of second-degree murder on April 13, 2009 and sentenced him to 19 years to life.

OTHER SIXTIES POP

Burt Bacharach and Hal David

Perhaps the most prolific pop composer of the last half of the 20th century has been Burt Bacharach (1928–). His first hit came in 1957 when "The Story of My Life," recorded by country artist Marty Robbins went to #15. It was also Bacharach's first collaboration with lyricist Hal David (1921–), with whom he would write most of his hits in the 1960s. After writing a few hits for Perry Como, the Drifters, and others, the two began to focus their attention on writing songs for **Dionne Warwick**, who was at the time a session singer aspiring to be a star. Between 1962 and 1972, Warwick recorded more than 60 of their songs, 23 of which hit the Top 40.

Other artists found success with Bacharach/David tunes as well, including:

■ Jackie DeShannon with "What the World Needs Now Is Love" (#7, 1965);
■ Tom Jones with "What's New Pussycat?" (#3, 1965);
■ Sergio Mendes & Brasil '66 with "The Look of Love" (#4, 1968);
■ Herb Alpert with "This Guy's in Love with You" (#1, 1968);
■ Aretha Franklin with "I Say a Little Prayer" (#10, 1968);
■ B. J. Thomas with "Raindrops Keep Fallin' on My Head" (#1, 1969);
■ The Carpenters with "(They Long to Be) Close to You" (#1, 1970).

The final tally for the duo was 66 Top 40 hits, 28 Top 10, with six going to #1.

A PARTIAL LIST OF BACHARACH/DAVID HITS RECORDED BY DIONNE WARWICK

■ "Don't Make Me Over"—#21, 1962
■ "Walk on By"— #6, 1964
■ "Alfie"— #15, 1967
■ "I Say a Little Prayer"— #4, 1967
■ "Do You Know the Way to San Jose"— #10, 1968
■ "This Girl's in Love with You"— #7, 1969
■ "I'll Never Fall in Love Again"— #6, 1969

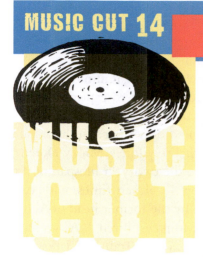

MUSIC CUT 14

"DON'T MAKE ME OVER" (BURT BACHARACH/HAL DAVID)— DIONNE WARWICK

Personnel: Recorded August 1962 at Bell Sound Studios, New York City; produced by Burt Bacharach and Hal David. Released 1962 on Scepter; 7 weeks on the charts, peaking at #21.

22-year-old Dionne Warwick was a newly signed artist to Scepter Records in 1962, and one of her first jobs was to record song demos written by Burt Bacharach and Hal David. Her first was "Make It Easy on Yourself," which she hoped the label would release as her recording debut. However, the song was given instead to Jerry Butler. Warwick found out this out while she was in the studio with the two songwriters, and in a fit of hurt and anger shouted out, "Don't make me over, man . . . you have to accept me for what I am" and walked out. Stunned, Bacharach and David looked at each other, with David telling Bacharach, "Burt, I think we just heard the title of a new song." The recording of the new song became Warwick's debut single, and one of more than 60 Bacharach/David songs that she recorded in her career. By the way, Butler's recording of "Make It Easy on Yourself" became a #20 hit, and Warwick herself had a #37 recording with it in 1970. Her amazing career has included 85 singles and 35 studio albums, with an estimated 100 million records sold.

While Bacharach and David never wrote about social or political change, their songs provided the soundtrack for much of the pop music world in the 1960s and 1970s. David's lyrics usually contained adult storylines that were straightforward and clever, while Bacharach's music often included interesting key changes and odd meters; his arrangements were usually pop savvy yet idiosyncratic. Although they split up in 1973, they reunited in 1993 for a project with Warwick. In the late 1990s Bacharach began collaborating with Elvis Costello.

Doc Pomus and Mort Shuman

Doc Pomus (1925–1991) began his career as a white blues singer in the 1940s before turning his attention to songwriting. In 1958, he teamed up with writer Mort Shuman (1936–1991), with whom he set up shop in the Brill Building. Over the next few years Pomus and Shuman wrote for:

- Dion and the Belmonts ("Teenager in Love," #5, 1959),

- The Drifters ("This Magic Moment," #16, and "Save the Last Dance for Me," #1, both 1960),

- Andy Williams ("Can't Get Used to Losing You," #2, 1963),

- Elvis Presley, who recorded more than 20 of their songs including "Surrender" (#1, 1961), "Little Sister" (#5, 1961), "(Marie's the Name) His Latest Flame" (#4, 1961), and "Viva Las Vegas" (#29, 1964).

Although Pomus was eleven years older than Shuman, the two died within months of each other in 1991, Pomus from cancer, Shuman from complications after liver surgery.

The Monkees

The ultimate manifestation of industry-manufactured pop came in 1965, when an ad was placed in *Daily Variety* magazine, announcing a casting call for "Folk and rock musicians-singers for acting roles in a new TV series; Running parts for four insane boys, age 17–24." The idea of the program was to capture the fun of the Beatles' *Hard Days Night* with four American mop tops. After narrowing down the 400 applicants (Stephen Stills was turned down because he wasn't good looking enough) to four—Michael Nesmith, Davy Jones, Micky Dolenz, and Peter Tork—the Monkees were born. During the two-year lifespan of the TV show (1966–1968), the Monkees hit the Top 40 eleven times, with two #3, one #2, and three #1 hits. Screen Gems (run by the former head of Aldon Music, Don Kirshner), who conceived of the Monkees, hired L.A. veterans Tommy Boyce and Bobby Hart to write songs such as "Last Train to Clarksville" in the mold of the Fab Four. The group also performed songs by Neil Diamond, Carole King, and others. They broke up after the TV show was cancelled and band members complained that they were not allowed to play their own instruments on recordings.

BUBBLEGUM The Monkees unleashed a short-lived strand of insipid pop that became known as bubblegum. Aimed at preteens, bubblegum was generally produced in the studio by session players working from carefully crafted sing-along songs. Among the "classics" of the genre are the unforgettable hits "Yummy, Yummy, Yummy" by the Ohio Express, "Simon Says" by the 1910 Fruitgum Co., and "Sugar, Sugar" by the Archies. Other bubblegum groups besides the Monkees who had their own TV shows were the Archies (an animated cartoon), the Partridge Family, and the Osmonds.

SURF

Surf Culture

Meanwhile, another pop music scene was developing on the West Coast. Surf music was not the brainchild of the record industry; rather, it was the offshoot of a lifestyle that was unique to its time and place. During the early 1960s, the sport of surfing spawned an entire subculture in Southern California that included carefree laid-back lives, hot rods, wood-paneled station wagons (called "woodies"), Hawaiian shirts and sandals, its own vernacular, and its own music. Surfing was brought to California from Hawaii around the turn of the 20th

CHARACTERISTICS OF SURF

1. Instrumental music (except the Beach Boys and other later groups), with a combo consisting of guitar, bass, and drums, with an occasional organ or horn player. Guitar usually plays the melody.
2. "Garage band" what-you-hear-is-what-you-get sound
3. High energy

- "Miserlou"—Dick Dale and the Del-Tones, 1962
- "Wipe Out"—The Surfaris, #2, 1962
- "Surfin' U.S.A."—the Beach Boys, #3, 1963

**KEY SURF/
INSTRUMENTAL
ROCK RECORDINGS**

century, where it was enjoyed by a relatively few hardy souls until Hollywood brought it to the rest of the country with a series of bikini beach party movies made between 1959 and 1963. The first, *Gidget,* was followed by others such as *Beach Blanket Bingo, Bikini Beach,* and *Beach Party,* starring Annette Funicello and Frankie Avalon. These movies tended to portray surfers and their girls as clean-cut, blonde, wholesome and good looking, leading affluent lives free of adult supervision. Unfortunately, the surf music in these movies was generally watered down, once again to offend as few viewers as possible.

The real music of the surf culture was driving, high energy, and primarily instrumental, dominated by the electric guitar. It had a raw, garage-band edge to it and was not overly produced. The first important surf band was **Dick Dale and the Del-Tones**, who had what is considered to be the first surf hit in 1961 with "Let's Go Trippin'." Of Lebanese descent, Dale often employed downward glissandos in his guitar playing to imitate the sound of waves, and tremolos that were reminiscent of the oud music of his native culture. These tricks are evident in the 1962 hit "Miserlou," which is based on a Middle Eastern folk song. Dale worked closely with Leo Fender, the creator of the first solid-body electric guitar, to develop the Dual Showman amplifier, which had two 15-inch speakers that made it possible to play loud with distortion. It also employed a metal spring to create a reverb effect. Because the Del-Tones were extremely popular in Southern California, they were reluctant to tour and therefore never achieved any substantial recognition in other parts of the country. It was up to other Southern California groups to take surf music to national prominence. Among the first to do so were the Marketts, whose "Surfer's Stomp" went to #31 in 1962, the Chantays with "Pipeline" (#4, 1963), and the Surfaris with "Wipe Out" (#2, 1963). Although Dick Dale was dubbed the "King of Surf Guitar," he became disillusioned with music after the surf boom died out and retired in 1965. He later returned to performing and developed a new fan base when "Miserlou" was included in the 1994 Quentin Tarantino film *Pulp Fiction.*

TRIVIA NOTE
The real music of the surf culture was driving, high energy, and primarily instrumental, dominated by the electric guitar.

The Beach Boys

Although surf first appeared as instrumental music, ironically the most famous of the surf groups was known for its beautiful vocal harmonies. Hailing from Huntington Beach, California, the Beach Boys consisted of three brothers—**Brian Wilson** (1942–), Dennis Wilson (1944–1983), and Carl Wilson (1946–1998)—their cousin Mike Love and family friend Al Jardine. The Wilson's father Murry was a frustrated part-time songwriter who was physically and emotionally abusive to his sons, often punishing them with beatings or humiliation. (Brian's deafness in one ear reportedly came from one such childhood beating. This may have been a factor in his preference for monaural mixes, although he was also a devotee of Phil Spector, who also preferred monaural over stereo.)

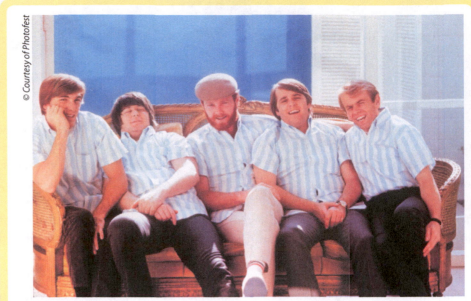

© Courtesy of Photofest

The Beach Boys. From left: Dennis Wilson, Brian Wilson, Mike Love, Carl Wilson, Al Jardine.

The one salve in the Wilson household was music. Murry built a music room in the garage, and with his encouragement the boys all learned to sing and play instruments at an early age. It soon became clear that the most talented son was Brian. For his sixteenth birthday, Murry gave Brian a Wollensak tape recorder, which he used to record himself singing vocal arrangements that were inspired by the popular 1950s vocal group the Four Freshmen. With their parents out of town for the Labor Day weekend in 1961, the Wilson Boys, Jardine, and Love (who were by now informally a band, calling themselves the Pendletones) wrote and recorded "Surfin'" to try to cash in on the burgeoning surf craze. The song became a regional hit and helped secure a contract with Capitol Records. They also changed their name around this time at the suggestion of a local record distributor. In the beginning, Murry served as their manager.

The Beach Boys' formula was simple: combine the driving rock and guitar licks of Chuck Berry with the lush vocal harmonies of the Four Freshmen. Over the next four years, they released seven albums with an impressive string of 17 Top 40 singles, including their first hit, "Surfin' Safari" (#14, 1962), and two #1s, "I Get Around" (1964) and "Help Me Rhonda" (1965). The subjects were girls, cars, hanging out with schoolmates, and of course, surfing. The primary songwriter was Brian, who also arranged the intricate vocal harmonies and produced the records. During these years Capitol put intense pressure on Brian to write as many songs as possible before the surf craze passed, and his output was astonishing. Eventually, however, the emotional stress of writing hit songs, producing, arranging, singing, and touring became overwhelming, and in December 1964 Brian made the decision to stop touring with the band. By this time he had started to use marijuana and other hallucinogens heavily, and in the next few years would become reclusive and increasingly unstable mentally. Despite his deteriorating state of mind, in late 1965 he began working on the monumental achievement of his career, the album *Pet Sounds.*

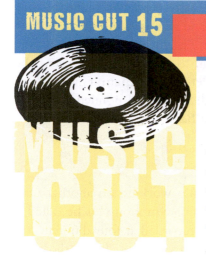

MUSIC CUT 15

"WOULDN'T IT BE NICE" (BRIAN WILSON/MIKE LOVE/TONY ASHER)— THE BEACH BOYS

Personnel: Brian Wilson: lead vocal; Mike Love: lead and backup vocals; Carl Wilson, Dennis Wilson, Al Jardine, Bruce Johnston: backup vocals; Larry Knetchel: piano; Al de Lory: piano; Bill Pitman: guitar; Jerry Cole: guitar; Barney Kessel: 12-string mandolin; Carl Fortina, Frank Marocco: accordion; Roy Caton: trumpet; Steve Douglas, Jay Migliori, Plas Johnson: saxophone; Ray Pohlman: 6-string bass guitar; Lyle Ritz: acoustic bass; Carol Kaye: bass guitar; Frank Capp: percussion; Hal Blaine: drums. Recorded January 22, 1966 (instrumental tracks) at Gold Star Studios, Los Angeles, March 10, 1966 and April 11 (vocal tracks) at Columbia Studios, Los Angeles; produced by Brian Wilson. Released July 18, 1966 on Capitol; 11 weeks on the charts, peaking at #8.

"Wouldn't It Be Nice" is the opening track on the Beach Boys highly praised *Pet Sounds,* and one of four singles released from the album. Brian Wilson composed the music to the song, with band mate Mike Love and lyricist Tony Asher writing the lyrics. The instrumental tracks—done in a very "Wall of Sound" fashion that included two pianos, two guitars, two accordions, mandolin, three basses, horns, drums and percussion—were recorded at Gold Star Studios, a favorite of both Wilson and his mentor, Phil Spector. The song was finished up at two later sessions at Columbia Studios, with backup vocals recorded at the first and lead vocals at the second. The lyrics address the sweet sentiment of youth from an era when young adults still 'saved themselves for marriage.' Wilson later said that the song, "Expresses the frustrations of youth, what you can't have, what you really want and you have to wait for." Lines that invoked waiting for marriage and happiness earned the song a #5 spot on the National Review's 2006 list of top 50 conservative rock songs.

Pet Sounds

Pet Sounds (released May 16, 1966) was inspired upon hearing the newest Beatles' release, *Rubber Soul*. Intrigued that they could record an album that contained only good songs and no "fillers," Brian set out to make "the greatest rock and roll album ever." The LP is a tour de force of his writing, arranging, and producing skills (although his friend Tony Asher wrote the lyrics, they were inspired by Brian). By this time, he had become a studio perfectionist, and spent many hours meticulously crafting the album primarily at three studios—Gold Star (where his idol Phil Spector often recorded), Western, and Sunset Sound—at an unheard of cost of $70,000. For the instrumental tracks Wilson used the famed Wrecking Crew, including Hal Blaine, Carol Kaye, and Barney Kessel, since the other Beach Boys were on tour. An array of unconventional (for rock) instruments and sounds were used, including tympani, Japanese percussion, harpsichord, glockenspiel, bass harmonica, and even barking dogs. The songs are generally all short in length with intricate and difficult vocal melodies and arrangements; most have a quiet, reflective, or otherworldly nature to them. The album's lyrics generally speak to a young man's difficult coming of age; Brian Wilson at the time was 23 years old.

Pet Sounds initially sold roughly a half million copies (it eventually went platinum in 2000), and two of its songs hit the charts, "Sloop John B" (#3), and "Wouldn't It Be Nice" (#8). Still, by Beach Boys' standards, those figures were a disappointment. Although critics hailed it as a masterpiece, the public by now expected a certain type of song from the group, and generally did not find them on the album. This was definitely *not* surf music. The innovations Brian Wilson brought to *Pet Sounds* were powerful motivation to the Beatles however, who realized Wilson had thrown the creative gauntlet back at them. Giving Brian Wilson credit for inspiring them, the next year the Beatles responded with their own masterpiece, *Sgt. Pepper's Lonely Hearts Club Band.*

A Teenage Symphony to God

While in production for *Pet Sounds,* Brian was also working on another masterpiece, the seminal "Good Vibrations." The "mini-symphony," as he called it, took six months to finish, used 90 hours of tape recorded at four different studios, and cost an astounding $50,000 (the cost of an expensive *album* at the time). It is as unlikely a pop tune as there ever was, utilizing exotic instruments such as the theremin, a complex form with constant key changes, and state-of-the-art studio effects. Nonetheless, "Good Vibrations" was as catchy as it was innovative, and went to the top of the charts in December 1966. Before "Good Vibrations" was even completed, however, Brian was already starting on what he determined was going to be his greatest achievement yet. Amid sky-high expectations, the next album, at first named *Dumb Angel* but eventually renamed *Smile,* was to be "a teenage symphony to God," and establish new standards of recording excellence. Ultimately the enormity of the task, coupled with his excessive drug abuse bogged the project down, and it was never completed (although the unfinished tracks were released in 1997). There would be more hits to come, but Brian Wilson's moment at the vanguard of the pop music world was more or less over.

The Beach Boys could never quite escape their clean-cut, wholesome image, and their popularity began to wane in the midst of the psychedelic era. They unwisely backed out of an appearance at the 1967 Monterey Pop Festival, which may have reinvigorated their image as that of a hipper band. In the 1970s and 1980s, the Wilson brothers eventually succumbed to the hedonistic Southern California lifestyle of too many drugs, too much partying, and too much self-indulgence. Drummer Dennis Wilson became friends with aspiring songwriter Charles Manson for several months in early 1968, but broke off the friendship just weeks before Manson and his family brutally murdered Sharon Tate and six others on August 9, 1969. Dennis drowned in a boating accident in 1983; Carl Wilson died of cancer in 1998. After years of mental and physical problems in the 1970s and 1980s, Brian Wilson has returned to recording and touring, while Al Jardine and Mike Love have established their own solo careers.

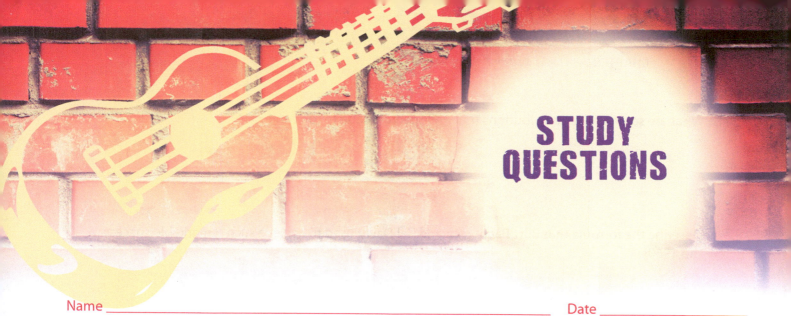

STUDY QUESTIONS

Name _____   Date _____

1. What were some of the factors that made some observers believe that rock and roll was dead by the early 1960s?

2. Describe the influence that Dick Clark and *American Bandstand* had on the music business.

3. What is payola and how did it affect the music and radio industries?

4. Describe the Brill Building scene and the major figures involved with it.

5. Why are Leiber and Stoller important?

6. What are some of the contributions that Phil Spector made to rock and roll?

7. Describe the formula that Burt Bacharach and Hal David used to achieve such remarkable success in the 1960s.

8. Describe the surf culture, surf music, and how it came into being.

9. Describe the formula used by Brian Wilson to achieve the Beach Boys' sound.

10. Why is *Pet Sounds* so important?

4

SOUL MUSIC

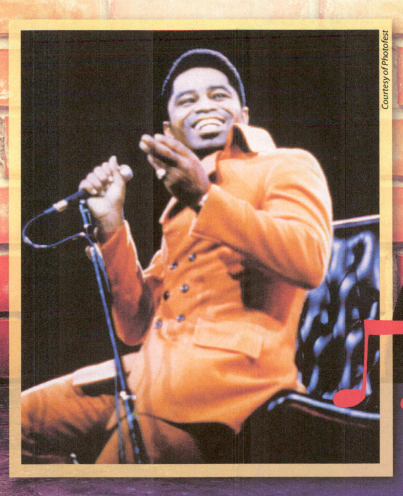

"Where I grew up there was no way out, no avenue of escape, so you had to make a way. Mine was to create JAMES BROWN."

—James Brown

KEY TERMS		
Soul music	Overdubbing	Stax Records
Minimalism	The Snakepit	Fame Studios
Motown Records	Falsetto	

KEY FIGURES		
Ray Charles	The Marvelettes	Booker T. and the MG's
Jerry Wexler	Stevie Wonder	Otis Redding
James Brown	Marvin Gaye	Wilson Pickett
Sam Cooke	The Four Tops	Sam and Dave
Berry Gordy	The Temptations	Rick Hall
Funk Brothers	The Supremes/Diana Ross	Muscle Shoals Rhythm
Holland/Dozier/Holland	Martha and the Vandellas	Section
Smokey Robinson and	Jim Stewart/Estelle Axton	Aretha Franklin
the Miracles	Isaac Hayes/David Porter	

KEY ALBUMS	
Live at the Apollo— James Brown	*What's Going On*— Marvin Gaye

THE ORIGINS OF SOUL

The First Soul Record

KEY TERMS

Soul music   A more pop oriented version of R&B containing heavy influences from gospel that is associated with the 1960s. Characteristics of soul include a powerful rhythmic drive from the bass and drums, melismatic singing, and in some cases, heavy orchestrations.

Soul music comes from the merging of rhythm and blues and gospel music. It seems entirely natural that these two styles would find common ground—they are the secular and the sacred counterparts of the black musical experience of the mid-20th century. However, the music of the church and the music of the nightclub traditionally served different purposes for different people, and until the mid-1950s the idea of marrying the two was strictly taboo. Although there were a few R&B recordings from the early 1950s that contained hints of gospel influence, the first real fusion of the two styles came in 1954 with Ray Charles's landmark record "I Got a Woman."

Charles's formula was simple—and for some, shocking. He transformed the traditional hymn "I Got a Savior, Way Over Jordan" into "I Got a Woman" by secularizing the lyrics ("Savior" became "woman," "Jordan" became "across town") and adding a rhythm-and-blues beat. "I Got a Woman" created the blueprint for soul music, and inspired other R&B singers, doo-wop groups and crossover artists to incorporate their own gospel roots into their records. Although black clergy vilified him at first, Ray Charles became a source of pride for the black community and ultimately a national treasure.

- "I Got a Woman"—Ray Charles, 1954
- *Live at the Apollo*—James Brown, 1962
- "A Change Is Gonna Come"—Sam Cooke, 1964
- "Cold Sweat"—James Brown, 1967
- "Respect"—Aretha Franklin, 1967

KEY SOUL RECORDINGS

Soul and the Civil Rights Movement

Also 1954 was the year when the U.S. Supreme Court handed down the *Brown v. Board of Education of Topeka, Kansas* ruling that effectively made legal segregation unconstitutional and jumpstarted the civil rights movement. Throughout the late 1950s and 1960s black political coalitions, often spearheaded by clergymen such as the Rev. Martin Luther King, Jr. became active throughout the South, demanding social changes and racial equality. King's strategy of using nonviolent demonstrations resulted in dramatic gains for the cause, even though there often were confrontations that did turn violent. During these years black Americans experienced a general sense of optimism and expectation that their dreams of freedom from racism and discrimination could finally be achieved. The zenith of the civil rights movement came between the years 1964 and 1968, when the two major Civil Rights Acts and the Voting Rights Act were passed. However, King's assassination on April 4, 1968 was a severe blow to the movement that made many blacks reexamine their expectations as the decade ended. Many became pessimistic and disillusioned, and the dream of integration and equality seemed to fade.

Not coincidentally, the ascent and decline of soul music mirrored that of the civil rights movement. While record sales rose impressively through the early 1960s, soul's popularity was greatest in the last half of the decade. Motown Records alone had 14 #1 singles on the pop charts and 20 #1 hits on the R&B charts between 1964 and 1967. Likewise, the best-selling soul artist at Stax Records was Otis Redding, whose greatest chart successes came in the two years before he died in a plane crash in 1967. Although Stax artist Isaac Hayes had impressive sales in the late 1960s and early 1970s with his albums *Hot Buttered Soul* and *Shaft* and the Jackson 5 began their run of four #1 hits in 1969, by this time the classic sound of 1960s soul was disappearing. Both Motown and Stax went into decline by the mid-1970s.

What Is Soul?

As soul became popular in the 1960s, the word came to have a number of cultural associations outside of its musical context. First and foremost, to have soul described a sense of pride in being black, of cultural solidarity, and aligning oneself with black consciousness and culture. It was hip to "have soul," or to be a "soul brother." The soul experience extended as well to hairstyles (the "Afro"), handshakes, "soul food" (ribs, chitlins, collard greens, etc.), clothing, and slang vernacular, all of which became ways of identifying with the movement. These

TRIVIA NOTE

The essence of all soul music is the emotional expression of the black experience in the 1960s—pride, struggle, love, ecstasy, hope, pain, and sorrow.

associations were often adopted by whites as well, especially Southern white musicians who played soul music.

The music itself took on great diversity, much of it on the account of regional origins. Much of rural Southern soul, where the music was born, had a raw, gritty, and powerful sound. In the Northern cities, such as Detroit, Chicago, and Philadelphia, soul took on a smoother, more pop-oriented sound. Regardless of these differences, the essence of all soul music is the emotional expression of the black experience in the 1960s—pride, struggle, love, ecstasy, hope, pain, and sorrow. Even though most of the soul music from the 1960s did not actually address the issues of the civil rights movement directly, soul songs were sometimes adopted by the black community and used as rallying cries to identify with the ongoing struggle.

Soul vocalists, using the melismatic delivery of gospel as well as a variety of moans, shrieks, and cries, sing in an uninhibited way that often gives the listener the impression that they are about to lose control at any moment. In doing so, they create a sense of anticipation and hope, as if they have just one more ounce of emotion left to give. As author Peter Guralnick has stated, soul is music that "keeps hinting at a conclusion, keeps straining at the boundaries of melody and convention that it has imposed upon itself." Add to this percolating, syncopated bass lines and the heavy drum backbeat of rhythm and blues, and you've got soul music.

The story of soul begins in the 1950s in the rural South. The main protagonists in the early years were Ray Charles, James Brown, and Sam Cooke.

THE FIRST IMPORTANT SOUL ARTISTS

Ray Charles

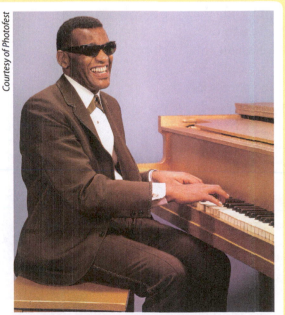

Courtesy of Photofest

Ray Charles created the blueprint for soul music with his 1954 recording of "I Got a Woman."

Ray Charles Robinson (1930–2004) was born in Albany, Georgia, and grew up in Greenville, Florida. After losing his sight at age six from glaucoma, his parents enrolled Ray at the St. Augustine School for the Deaf and the Blind where he learned how to play a variety of instruments while specializing in piano. During his youth he was exposed to jazz, R&B, gospel, and country music from listening to the radio and other sources. When he was 17, he moved to Seattle and began to work his way up through the city's nightclub scene, leading a Nat King Cole-style piano trio. He also mentored 15-year-old future producing legend Quincy Jones. In 1948 he made his first record, "Confession Blues" and changed his name to Ray Charles to avoid confusion with the middleweight boxing champ Sugar Ray Robinson.

THE ARCHETYPE

By 1954 Charles signed with Atlantic Records after Ahmet Ertegun and **Jerry Wexler** heard him perform "I Got a Woman" at a nightclub in New Orleans. To Ertegun and

MUSIC CUT 16

"I GOT A WOMAN" (RAY CHARLES/RENALD RICHARD)— RAY CHARLES

Personnel: Ray Charles: piano, vocals; Joe Bridgewater, Charles Whitley: trumpet; Don Wilkerson: tenor sax; David "Fathead" Newman: baritone sax; Wesley Jackson: guitar; Jimmy Bell: bass; Glenn Brooks: drums. Recorded November 18, 1954 at WGST Radio in Atlanta, GA; produced by Ahmet Ertegun and Jerry Wexler. Released January 1955 on Atlantic; predates *Billboard* pop charts, peaked at #1 on the R&B charts.

The song that is generally considered to have created the blueprint for soul came about almost by accident. Listening to a gospel radio station while on the road one night, Charles' music director Renald Richard recalled that, "We used to clown around a lot when we were traveling, and we started singing 'I Got a Woman' to the tune playing on the radio. Ray said, 'Can you do something with that?' I said, 'Sure!' And the next morning I had the lyrics written." The song wasn't recorded until several months later, the day after the band auditioned for Atlantic's Ahmet Ertegun and Jerry Wexler in Atlanta. The recording took place in the studios of the campus radio station at Georgia Tech University.

Wexler, the song was the "archetype" of a new music that as of yet had no name. For Charles, the song was nothing special. "I'd been singing spirituals since I was three, and I'd been hearing the blues for just as long. So what could be more natural than to combine them? It didn't take any thinking, it didn't take any calculating." Using the same hymn-to-pop formula, he also recorded "This Little Girl of Mine" (based on "This Little Light of Mine") and several other songs that became minor R&B hits before his first big breakthrough came in 1959 with "What'd I Say (Part 1)." The song captures the essence of Ray Charles's ability to galvanize different musical elements, including gospel, the blues, R&B, and jazz. It became his first Top 10 hit, peaking at #6.

Soon after the success of "What'd I Say (Part 1)," Charles left Atlantic and signed with ABC, and promptly scored two #1 hits, "Georgia on My Mind" (1960) and "Hit the Road Jack" (1961). In 1962 to the shock of many, Charles turned his attention to country music, but he was a convincing enough country stylist to earn another #1 hit, "I Can't Stop Loving You." From the early 1960s on, his career focused more on pop and easy listening, resulting in 22 more Top 40 hits. Although he was the target of some criticism over the years for his pop leanings, Charles always gave every song his own highly personal rendition with a singing style that was one of the most influential and widely copied in American music. The icon of soul music died on June 10, 2004, of liver disease. Before his death, Charles collaborated in the making of the film *Ray*, which was released in October 2004. Jamie Foxx won the 2005 Academy Award for Best Actor for his portrayal of Ray Charles.

James Brown

Alternately known as "Soul Brother #1," "The Godfather of Soul," and "The Hardest Working Man in Show Business," James Brown (1933–2006) unquestionably fits all three descriptions. He not only was one of the most consistent contributors to the soul catalogue of the 1960s, but played an important role in its evolution into 1970s funk, as well as being inspirational and influential to the birth of rap. His stage shows were legendary displays of athleticism and show-manship, and his many dance moves have been widely copied throughout the era of music videos.

James Brown was born in Barnwell, South Carolina and raised in Augusta, Georgia, by his father. Small of stature and dirt poor, Brown was picked on by other kids in his rough neighborhood and was often forced to defend himself. He came to school barefoot, and regularly resorted to searching through garbage cans for food and clothing. Early on, his self-determination and ambition became apparent: classmates recall that he had to be the best at everything he did, which included boxing, baseball, and singing the national anthem at school every morning. After an armed robbery conviction at age 16 sent him to prison however, he began to focus his attention solely on singing gospel music. Paroled in 1952 after serving three years of an 8–16 year sentence, Brown formed a gospel cum R&B vocal group he named the Flames, and began working the South's chitlin circuit. In 1956, the Flames caught the attention of Cincinnati's King Records, who signed the group to their subsidiary Federal label. Their first recording, "Please, Please, Please," was a showcase for Brown's sobbing, gospel-influenced vocals, and the Flames' doo-wop-styled background vocals. It became a regional hit in the South, eventually selling a million copies. Brown's first #1 R&B hit came in 1958 with "Try Me," and in 1960 he broke into the Top 40 for the first time with "Think."

MR. DYNAMITE

Throughout the late 1950s and early 1960s, Brown played an exhausting schedule of some 300 nights a year on the chitlin' circuit. His band, known as James Brown and The Famous Flames, now included an MC and a full horn section.

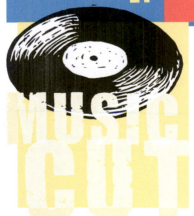

MUSIC CUT 17

"COLD SWEAT" (JAMES BROWN/ALFRED ELLIS)— JAMES BROWN

Personnel: James Brown: vocals; Joe Dupars, Waymond Reed: trumpet; Levi Rasbury: trombone; Alfred "Pee Wee" Ellis: alto sax; Maceo Parker, Eldee Williams: tenor sax; St. Clair Pinckney: baritone sax; Alphonso Kellum: guitar; Jimmy Nolen: guitar; Bernard Odum: bass; Clyde Stubblefield: drums. Recorded May 1967 at King Studios, Cincinnati, OH; produced by James Brown. Released July 1967 on King; 8 weeks on the charts, peaking at #7.

James Brown's "Cold Sweat" is a great example of minimalism, a technique that Brown often used in his music and which became common in later black pop music styles. Co-writer Pee Wee Ellis described the song's creation in a 2007 Down Beat magazine article. "After one of the shows, one night somewhere, James called me into the dressing room and grunted a bass line of a rhythmic thing, which turned out to be 'Cold Sweat.'" "The horn line is based on Miles Davis' 'So What.' I wrote that on the bus between New York and Cincinnati. The next day we pulled up in front of King Records studio, got off the bus, got in the studio, set up, and I went over the rhythm with the band. By the time we got the groove going, James showed up, added a few touches—changed the guitar part, which made it real funky—had the drummer do something different. He was a genius at it. Between the two of us, we put it together one afternoon. He put the lyrics on it. The band set up in a semicircle in the studio with one microphone. It was recorded live in the studio. One take. It was like a performance. We didn't do overdubbing."

Their music, now rougher-edged and grittier, was tightly honed, as was the precisely executed choreography. Brown's performances were becoming legendary, with innovative dance maneuvers, numerous costume changes, and a nightly feigned death sequence in which he was carried off by assistants only to miraculously come back to life by channeling the energy of the frenzied crowd. During this time the band was so well rehearsed and tight that recording new songs, which were usually done in after-hours sessions, rarely required more than one take. In late 1962 Brown decided to record an entire live performance and release it on an album. *Live at the Apollo*, recorded at Harlem's Apollo Theatre, is a tour de force of grit and sweat, power and raw energy that in one fell swoop made Ray Charles' style of soul seem old and stodgy. Self-financed at a cost of $7,500 (King president Syd Nathan refused to take the risk of releasing an entire album), it became a huge success, staying on the charts for 14 months and eventually selling over a million copies.

By the mid-1960s, James Brown had achieved reverential status in the black community as well as a wide crossover appeal with white audiences. In 1965 he had his two biggest chart successes with "Papa's Got a Brand New Bag Part 1" peaking at #8, and "I Got You (I Feel Good)" hitting #3. Brown was now taking pop music into uncharted territory by peeling away most of the melodic and harmonic elements and putting most of the emphasis on rhythm. The melodic instruments in the band—guitar, bass and horns—played one and two bar repeating phrases in short, staccato fashion, which, along with syncopated drum patterns produced created dense and hypnotic dance beats. This use of **minimalism** would later become a staple of the future styles of funk and rap. On occasion, Brown even went so far as to dispense with the traditional verse/chorus song form in favor of an open-ended, elastic form where each change was signaled by vocal cues such as, "To the bridge!" The most striking and revolutionary characteristic of Brown's music was his idiosyncratic vocal style, which incorporated shouts (including his patented "Good God!"), shrieks, screams, grunts, and wails, usually in perfect sync with the music.

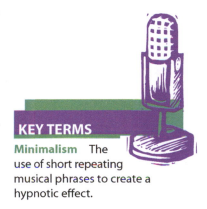

KEY TERMS

Minimalism   The use of short repeating musical phrases to create a hypnotic effect.

THE SPOKESMAN

Throughout the later 1960s and 1970s, James Brown further pursued this avant-garde, rhythm-oriented approach, and although at times it lost its crossover appeal with white audiences, his success made him a symbol of pride and cultural identity for many in the black community. He was a black man who triumphed over the white run record industry on the strength of his own convictions and self-determination. Brown did not take his role as spokesman lightly, and drew considerable praise for his key role in diffusing a tense situation when he performed at the Boston Garden on April 5, 1968, the night after Dr. Martin Luther King, Jr.'s assassination. After Dr. King's death, Brown's records, such as 1968's "Say It Loud, I'm Black and I'm Proud" and 1971's "Get Up, Get Into It, Get Involved," often became more politically involved with the civil rights movement. His bands became veritable schools of funk, showcasing players such as Maceo Parker on tenor sax, Clyde Stubblefield on drums, Fred Wesley on trombone, and Bootsy Collins on bass. As an inspiration to many current R&B and hip-hop artists, in many ways James Brown's music is even more influential today than it was during his peak years.

Sam Cooke

Unlike Ray Charles or James Brown, Sam Cooke (1931–1964) was an established star in the gospel world when he made his first pop recordings. His 1957 #1 hit "You Send Me" was easily the biggest crossover hit of the 1950s, selling nearly two million copies. His good looks, suave and debonair image, and sophisticated musical settings allowed him to quickly grab hold of a huge audience of both blacks and whites that could have served him well for a long and enduring career. Unfortunately, he was murdered at age 33 in a bizarre incident that is largely unexplained to this day.

PERFECTION

Cooke was born in Clarksdale, Mississippi (as Sam *Cook*), but grew up in Chicago, one of eight sons of a Baptist minister. As a teenager he became a member of the Highway QC's, a gospel vocal group whose inspiration was the Soul Stirrers, one of gospels most popular groups. Cooke's charisma and looks drew positive reviews from gospel insiders, and when the lead vocalist of the Soul Stirrers, Robert Harris, suddenly quit in 1950, Cooke was chosen to replace him. Almost immediately, Cooke's warm, velvety croon won over the older, established Soul Stirrers' audience and gained legions of new, younger gospel fans. But by 1956 Cooke was setting his sights on the pop world, and recorded his first pop tune "Lovable" under the name Dale Cook, hoping not to offend his loyal gospel fan base. The thinly veiled ploy did not work; shock and outrage followed in the conservative gospel community. Cooke was undeterred; his next record, "You Send Me," was released under his "real" name, and cemented him firmly in the pop world for the rest of his career.

Part of the appeal of "You Send Me" was the sweet, soulful, and restrained delivery that became Cooke's trademark. Jerry Wexler of Atlantic Records called him "the best singer who ever lived, no contest . . . everything about him was perfection." Cooke managed to appeal to young and old, black and white, transcending any and all barriers. In the wake of "You Send Me" came 28 more Top 40 hits—mostly crooning, romantic ballads—including "Wonderful World" (#12, 1960) and "Twistin' the Night Away" (#9, 1962). As his popularity grew, he moved from the chitlin' circuit to performing in Las Vegas and the upper tier of the nightclub circuit, including New York's Copacobana.

TRAGEDY

Cooke's ambitions did not limit him to singing: with his partner J. W. Alexander, he created Kags Music publishing company, the SAR record label and a production/management company that were beginning to establish him as a visionary black music entrepreneur. With such a bright future before him, the sordid events that led to his death on December 11, 1964, are puzzling. Picking up a young model at a restaurant in Los Angeles, Cooke drove her to the $3-a-night Hacienda Motel where he reportedly began to sexually assault her. After she escaped with his pants and disappeared, Cooke became enraged and went to the office of night manager Bertha Lee Franklin. A violent altercation ensued in which Franklin shot him once with a pistol in self-defense. He died at the scene. As grief and disbelief overtook the pop world, 200,000 fans viewed Cooke's body as it lay in state in both Chicago and Los Angeles. His most fitting epitaph was the posthumous release of "A Change Is Gonna Come," a spiritually fused comment on the state of race relations in America inspired by Bob Dylan's "Blowin' in the Wind."

MOTOWN

Hitsville, U.S.A.

At the pinnacle of black popular music in the 1960s was Detroit's: Motown Records, founded in 1959 by songwriter, producer, and erstwhile professional boxer **Berry Gordy**. Borrowing $800 from his family, Gordy bought an eight-room house at 2648 West Grand Boulevard, and put up a sign over the front door that read "Hitsville, USA." He then proceeded to create the largest black-owned business in the United States in the 1960s. Gordy's business strategy was simple: to bring young, black talent in off the streets of Detroit (where they seemed to be in unlimited supply), groom and cultivate them, back them up with highly polished production, and sell them to the largest possible crossover audience. He accomplished his version of the American dream with huge ambitions, auto-cratic control, hard work, and the production techniques he learned while working on the assembly line at the local Lincoln Mercury plant in 1955.

Motown's beginnings go back to 1957, when Gordy, then an independent producer, met William "Smokey" Robinson, aspiring songwriter and lead vocalist of the local group the Miracles. Gordy talked his way into producing the group's next single, "I Got a Job," the answer to the Silhouette's "Get a Job." The song went nowhere, but established an important working relationship between Gordy and Robinson, who would become Motown's first important songwriter and producer. Gordy at first used United Artists or Chess Records to distribute his records, but Robinson convinced him to start his own label and distribute them himself. In early 1959, Gordy formed Tamla Records and Jobete Music, a music publishing firm, both of which eventually fell under the Motown umbrella, and began signing local talent. Gordy formed another important business relationship in 1959 when he produced the #23 pop hit "Money" by singer Barrett Strong, who in time became another one of Motown's top songwriter/producers. ("Money" was later covered by the Beatles, who turned the song into a rock classic.) The upstart label's first blockbuster hits came in 1960 with the Miracles "Shop Around" (#2, 1960—Motown's first million seller) and the Marvelettes' "Please Mr. Postman" (1961—Motown's first #1 hit).

The Assembly Line

Motown was a tightly controlled business run by Berry Gordy, but his family played important roles as well. His father helped renovate the offices; two sisters worked as fiscal officers; brother-in-law Harvey Fuqua worked in production. Family outsiders were also drawn into the fold, some of whom eventually became stars: both Martha Reeves and Diana Ross started at the company as secretaries; Marvin Gaye originally was a session drummer who later married

Gordy's sister Anna. Another important aspect of Motown was the attention to quality control. Gordy and his producers held meetings each Friday morning at 9:05 to vote on whether to release each of that week's recordings. A no vote meant the song either died or had to be redone. Although there were producers and songwriters on staff that were in competition with each other (much like Aldon Music and the Brill Building scene), Gordy closely supervised every major decision that was made. This tight control of power later contributed to dissention within the company.

Because Motown was actively involved in the artistic development of each of its stars, careers were often patiently nurtured over a period of years. For instance, both the Temptations and the Supremes were signed in 1961, a good three years before either group had a hit single. The Motown process of transforming a street singer into a pop star was a model of assembly-line efficiency that gave their artists a consistent look and sound that was innovative in the music business at the time.

The results were stunning: during its peak years, from 1964 to 1967, Motown had 14 #1 pop singles, 20 #1 R&B singles, 46 additional Top 15 pop singles and 75 more Top 15 R&B singles. In 1966 alone, its best year, 75 percent of Motown's releases made one or more of the charts, far above the industry average of less than 15 percent.

THE MOTOWN PROCESS

- **Step 1:** Finishing School. Modeling expert Maxine Powell taught the proper way to walk, talk, and dress as successful young debutantes and debonair gentleman.
- **Step 2:** Dance Lessons. Choreographer Cholly Atkins, a well-known dancer from the heydays of the Swing Era in 1930s and 1940s Harlem, taught dance steps and graceful body moves coordinated to the music.
- **Step 3:** Stage Presence. Maurice King, executive musical director, taught stage patter, presence, and projecting a friendly, nonconfrontational persona.
- **Step 4:** Music Production. In-house songwriters, arrangers, producers, session musicians, and engineers produce the music to fit the individual sound of each artist.
- **Step 5:** Record Distribution. Records are pressed and distributed throughout the country by the various Motown labels.
- **Step 6:** Talent Agency. Artist contracts, management, and touring schedules are overseen by the in-house talent agency.

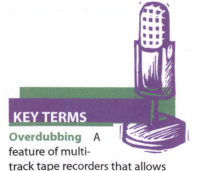

KEY TERMS

Overdubbing A feature of multi-track tape recorders that allows the recording of additional parts independently of each other while listening to previously recorded tracks with headphones.

The Sound of Young America

Above all else, Motown's greatest achievement was the music it produced. Gordy looked to the success of Phil Spector and the "wall of sound" to produce music that was thick in horns, strings, and background vocals, backed by a rhythm section with a hard-driving backbeat. Gordy called it "The Sound of Young America." Motown's recording studio, located in the basement of 2648 West Grand, was a tiny room affectionately called the **Snakepit**. Although at first all the musicians and singers were recorded together using two and three track recorders, in 1964 the Snakepit installed an eight-track recorder that allowed Motown producers to record more elaborate productions in stages, **overdubbing** strings, horns, and percussion on top of the rhythm section and vocals.

From the very beginning, the core of the Motown sound was the in-house rhythm section, known as the Funk Brothers. Although the personnel changed somewhat over the years, the core of the **Funk Brothers** was James Jamerson on electric bass, leader Earl Van Dyke on piano, drummer Benny Benjamin, and guitarist Robert White. Jamerson in particular was important in creating a syncopated bass style that helped define soul music and has been widely copied over the years by nearly all who have played the instrument. Gordy kept tight control over the Funk Brothers, not allowing them to go on tour or play sessions at other studios (although he did pay them well, reportedly $50,000 each per year).

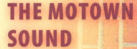

THE MOTOWN SOUND

Characteristics of the Motown Sound

1. Pop-oriented, smoothing over most of the rough edges of other soul music
2. Rock-solid groove, anchored by Benny Benjamin's drums and James Jamerson's innovative syncopated electric bass
3. Heavy use of string and horn orchestration and reverberation, ala Phil Spector's Wall of Sound
4. Use of added percussion to emphasize the backbeat
5. Vocal harmonies used extensively

Key Motown Recordings

- "My Girl"—the Temptations, 1965
- "You Keep Me Hangin' On"—the Supremes, 1966
- "Reach Out I'll Be There"—the Four Tops, 1966
- "I Heard It Through the Grapevine"—Marvin Gaye, 1968

Holland/Dozier/Holland

Although Gordy used a variety of writers and producers, including Smokey Robinson, Barrett Strong, Norman Whitfield, and Nicholas Ashford and Valerie Simpson (Ashford and Simpson), the most successful was the team of Lamont Dozier and brothers Brian and Eddie Holland, known as Holland/Dozier/Holland (or simply HDH). From their first hit, 1963's "Mickey's Monkey" (recorded by the Miracles) to the end of 1967 when they left the company, HDH racked up an astonishing 46 Top 40 hits, including twelve that went to #1. Although HDH's credits include hits for Martha and the Vandellas ("Heat Wave," #4, 1963) and Marvin Gaye ("How Sweet It Is [To Be Loved by You]," #6, 1964), their best material was written for the Four Tops and the Supremes. Their hits for the Four Tops included "I Can't Help Myself" (#1, 1965), "Reach Out I'll Be There" (#1, 1966), "Standing in the Shadows of Love" (#6, 1966), and "Bernadette" (#4, 1967). When Gordy assigned HDH to the Supremes in 1964, they pulled off an amazing string of ten #1 hits over the next three years. HDH not only wrote the songs (melodies primarily by Dozier, lyrics primarily by Eddie Holland) but produced the sessions as well, with Brian Holland engineering at the mixing console.

IMPORTANT MOTOWN ARTISTS

Smokey Robinson and the Miracles

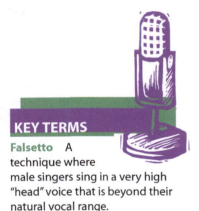

KEY TERMS

Falsetto A technique where male singers sing in a very high "head" voice that is beyond their natural vocal range.

William "Smokey" Robinson (1940–) has been called "America's greatest living poet" by no less than Bob Dylan. His work as lead singer and primary writer/ producer for the Miracles produced 27 Top 40 singles, six of which hit the Top 10. Robinson also made significant contributions to the Motown catalogue as a songwriter for other artists, including the Temptations ("My Girl," "The Way You Do the Things You Do," and "Get Ready"); Mary Wells ("My Guy"); and the Marvelettes ("Don't Mess with Bill"). Robinson was able to write love songs that spoke directly to such subjects as passion, loneliness, and forgiveness, as well as using clever rhyming schemes and metaphor. His **falsetto** singing was among the most soulful of all the Motown artists.

Robinson formed the Miracles (originally called the Matadors) in 1955 when all four singers were attending Detroit's Northern High School. It was when they auditioned for Jackie Wilson's manager Nat Tarnopol in 1957 that they met Berry Gordy, which led to their signing with Motown and eventually their first Top 10 hit, "Shop Around" in 1960. Among the other Miracles' Top 10 hits to follow were "You Really Got a Hold on Me" (#8, 1963), "I Second That Emotion" (#4, 1967), and "The Tears of a Clown" (#1, 1970). Robinson left the group in 1972 to pursue a solo career that produced nine more Top 40 hits. He was inducted into the Rock and Roll Hall of Fame in 1987.

IMPORTANT MOTOWN ARTISTS

- Smokey Robinson and the Miracles
- The Marvelettes
- Stevie Wonder
- Marvin Gaye
- The Four Tops
- The Temptations
- The Supremes
- Martha and the Vandellas

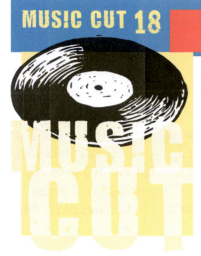

MUSIC CUT 18

"WHERE DID OUR LOVE GO" (BRIAN HOLLAND/LAMONT DOZIER/ EDDIE HOLLAND)—THE SUPREMES

Personnel: Diana Ross, Mary Wilson, Florence Ballard: vocals; the Funk Brothers: rhythm section; Mike Valvano: foot stomps. Recorded April 8, 1964 at Motown Studios, Detroit, MI; produced by Holland/Dozier/Holland. Released June 17 1964 on Motown; 13 weeks on the charts, peaking at #1 for two weeks.

"Where Did Our Love Go" was the first #1 hit for both the Supremes and the legendary production team of Holland/Dozier/Holland. It is an interesting song in that it consists of a simple, repeating three-chord, 8-bar progression, without a bridge or contrasting chorus. The arrangement, unlike later heavily orchestrated H/D/H productions, is simple and sparse, with the primary instrument being the foot stomping provided by teenager Mike Valvano. The song was originally pitched to the Marvelettes, who rejected it. It is also the title track to the Supremes second album, which was released in August 1964.

The Marvelettes

The Marvelettes were formed in 1960 by five schoolgirls attending Inkster High in suburban Detroit. After signing with Motown in 1961, they had their biggest hit with their first release, "Mr. Postman," which also became the company's first #1 pop hit. Over the next seven years, nine more Top 40 hits followed. The Marvelettes were in some ways a link to the past as the most purely "girl group" of any of the Motown vocal groups, and were ultimately swept aside by the more contemporary sound of such groups as the Temptations and the Supremes. Interestingly, the group refused to record Holland/Dozier/Holland's "Baby Love" when it was presented to them in 1964; the song was given to the Supremes, who turned it into a #1 hit.

Stevie Wonder

The blind and multitalented Steveland Morris (1950–) was rechristened "Little Stevie Wonder" by Berry Gordy soon after he signed with Motown at age ten in 1960. In less than three years Wonder had his first #1 hit with "Fingertips— Pt 2." The record is a live recording that features Wonder's harmonica playing and singing—which along with playing drums, piano, and organ were staples of his live performances. Presented initially in the Ray Charles mold (partly because both were blind), Wonder eventually forged his own unique and soulful singing style. He had 20 more Top 40 hits over the next eight years, including eleven Top 10s. Then, when turning 21 in 1971, he renegotiated his contract, giving him complete artistic control of his recordings, as well as more money (he had only earned $1 million up to that point, while Motown had kept over $30 million of his profits for themselves). By this time Wonder was playing nearly all of the instruments himself on his records, as well as producing, singing, arranging, and writing the songs.

With his new contract, Wonder's career after 1972 blossomed well into the 1980s as he explored the possibilities of synthesizer layering and fusing funk, jazz, reggae, R&B, soul, pop, and African rhythms. Beginning with the #1 singles

"Superstition" and "You Are the Sunshine of My Life," he had 24 more Top 40 hits, nine of which went to #1, and placed nine albums in the Top 10. He also won an amazing 15 Grammy Awards.

Marvin Gaye

The son of a Washington, DC, minister, Marvin Gaye (1939–1984) grew up singing and playing organ in his father's church. As a member of the Moonglows (led by Berry Gordy's brother-in-law Harvey Fuqua), Gaye was discovered and signed by Gordy in 1961; soon afterward, he married Gordy's sister Anna. Working at first as a session drummer on Miracles' recordings, Gaye began his solo career in 1962, which yielded a remarkable 40 Top 40 hits, including three that went to #1:

- "I Heard It Through the Grapevine" (1968),
- "Let's Get It On" (1973)
- "Got to Give It Up (Pt. I)" (1977).

From 1967 until 1970, he often teamed with Tammi Terrell, with whom he had seven Top 40 hits. Terrell died in 1970 from a brain tumor, three years after collapsing in Gaye's arms onstage during a concert in Virginia.

Like Stevie Wonder, Marvin Gaye was able to renegotiate his contract in 1971, bringing him more artistic control. That same year he released the album *What's Going On*, which contained three Top 10 singles that were politically charged statements on the Vietnam War ("What's Going On"), the environment ("Mercy Mercy Me [The Ecology]"), and civil rights ("Inner City Blues [Make Me Wanna Holler]"). His bitter divorce from Anna required him to give her the proceeds of his next album, resulting in 1978's dark and very personal *Here, My Dear*. The album so clearly detailed their marriage and subsequent breakup that Anna for a time considered suing him for invasion of privacy. Gaye's conflicts with his hedonistic, cocaine abusing lifestyle and his religious upbringing brought much self-inflicted anguish to his later life. In 1983, he moved in with his father, with whom he quarreled constantly. After one such heated argument on April 1, 1984, his father shot him to death from point-blank range.

The Four Tops

After meeting at a birthday party in 1954 while all four were high school students in Detroit, Levi Stubbs, Lawrence Payton, Renaldo Benson, and Abdul Fakir began singing together and soon secured a contract from Chess Records. After several years of record flops and countless appearances in Detroit-area supper clubs, the group signed with Motown in 1963. Berry Gordy originally had the group record a jazz-oriented album, which was never released; he then switched their style back to R&B and hooked them up with Holland/Dozier/Holland in 1964. The results were immediate: their first HDH release, "Baby I Need Your Loving" went to #11; the next year they hit the Top 40 four times, including the #1 "I Can't Help Myself." By the end of 1971, they had 13 more Top 40 hits, including another #1, "Reach Out I'll Be There" in 1966.

- Levi Stubbs
- Lawrence Payton
- Renaldo Benson
- Abdul Fakir

THE FOUR TOPS

With their distinct sound of the gritty lead vocal of Stubbs pleading and wailing over the creamy backup vocals, the Four Tops have remained together for nearly 50 years without a single change in personnel. Although they stagnated for a while when HDH left the label in 1967 (they resorted to recording cover tunes for a few years, such as "If I Were a Carpenter"), they continued on with a variety of other Motown producers before leaving the label in 1971.

The Temptations

Formed in 1960 by three Southerners, a Los Angeles transplant, and one Detroit native, the Temptations were the most commercially successful male vocal group of the 1960s. The group came together when two existing groups, the Primes and the Distants combined, initially calling themselves the Elgins. By 1961 they had changed their name to the Temptations and signed with Motown. After languishing with poor record sales for several years, the group's luck changed in late 1963 when lead vocalist David Ruffin was added and Berry Gordy assigned them to producer Smokey Robinson. Their next release, "The Way You Do the Things You Do" hit #11, the first of 38 Top 40 hits, 15 of which hit the Top 10, four hitting #1. The group's primary attractions were their precise choreography, the best of any of the Motown groups, and the alternating lead vocals of Eddie Kendricks's high falsetto and David Ruffin's low husk.

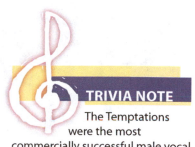

TRIVIA NOTE
The Temptations were the most commercially successful male vocal group of the 1960s.

In 1966 Norman Whitfield began producing the Temptations with an eye toward a rougher hewn soul style, evidenced by the #13 hit "Ain't Too Proud to Beg." In 1968, David Ruffin quit the group to pursue a solo career, and the group recorded the socially conscious song "Cloud Nine" (#6). Although "Cloud Nine" contained drug allusions, it became Motown's first Grammy Award winner. More socially aware songs followed, including "Message from a Black Man," "War," and "Papa Was a Rolling Stone," which went to #1 in 1972. Like many of the other original Motown groups, the Temptations left the label in the mid-1970s.

The Supremes

Unquestionably the most commercially successful of all the Motown groups, the Supremes hit the American radio waves in 1964 with unprecedented fury: ten of their first 14 releases, all produced by Holland/Dozier/Holland, went to #1, including a run of five in a row in 1964 and 1965. By the time Diana Ross left the group in 1970, their Top 40 total had reached 25, with two more #1 hits, "Love Child" in 1968 and Ross's 1969 farewell, "Someday We'll Be Together."

Originally known as the Primettes, the sister group to the Primes (later the Temptations), **Diana Ross** (1944–), Mary Wilson, and Florence Ballard grew up in Detroit's Brewster housing project. Rejected at their first audition with Berry

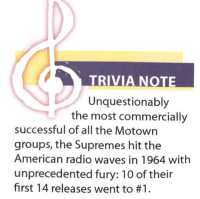

TRIVIA NOTE
Unquestionably the most commercially successful of all the Motown groups, the Supremes hit the American radio waves in 1964 with unprecedented fury: 10 of their first 14 releases went to #1.

THE SUPREMES

- Diana Ross
- Mary Wilson
- Florence Ballard (later replaced by Cindy Birdsong)

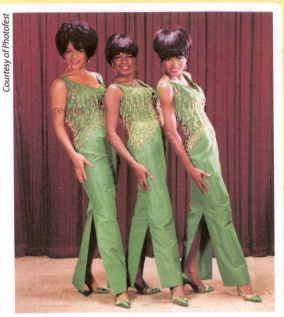

Courtesy of Photofest

The Supremes

Gordy because they were still in high school, the girls hung around Hitsville and sang in backup roles on recording sessions before Gordy finally signed them in 1961. After nine unsuccessful singles over the next three years, Gordy assigned the HDH team to produce the group in 1964. By focusing on Ross's sultry and dramatic vocal style, HDH hit on a winning formula for the group, which Gordy skillfully parlayed into weekly TV appearances and nightclub shows in Las Vegas and at the Copacabana in New York. As the attention increasingly centered on Ross (in 1967 they became known as "Diana Ross and the Supremes"), Ballard became disenchanted and left, replaced by Cindy Birdsong. Following her departure from the group, Ross went on to a successful film career (managed by Gordy), which included starring roles in 1972's *Lady Sings the Blues* (for which she received an Oscar nomination), *Mahogany,* and *The Wiz*.

Martha and the Vandellas

Martha Reeves (1941–) and her friends Annette Beard and Rosalind Ashford began singing together in high school in Detroit as the Del-Phis and had one single under their belt when in 1961 Reeves began working as a secretary at Motown. One day on short notice they were called in as background singers on a session for Marvin Gaye, which eventually led to their signing with the label as Martha and the Vandellas. With twelve Top 40 hits (including 1963's #4 "Heatwave" and 1964's #2 "Dancing in the Street"), the Vandellas were not one of the most commercially successful Motown groups, but were one of the earthiest and most soulful.

STAX RECORDS

Back to Memphis

At the same time that Motown was establishing itself in Detroit, a small record company was emerging in Memphis that would one day become its most formidable soul challenger. Unlike Motown, there was no advance business plan laid out for Stax Records—the company just sort of evolved with large doses of luck, being at the right place at the right time, and of course, hard work. Stax also benefited from the unique "transracial" (as historian Peter Guralnick has called it) environment in Memphis at the time. Although the city was as segregated as any Southern city in the early 1960s, there existed a harmonious relationship between blacks and whites that allowed them to mingle socially at many of the nightclubs around town. Especially among musicians, there were no prejudices based on the color of one's skin; the only thing that mattered was whether or not you could play.

The Stax story begins in 1957 when **Jim Stewart**, a country fiddler who worked at Memphis' First National Bank during the day, began a small record label out of a friend's garage at night. He named the company Satellite—"satellites were big at the time" he later recalled in reference to the Soviet Union's Sputnik. By 1958 he had piqued the interest of his sister **Estelle Axton**, ten years his senior, to the point where she invested in the company by buying a monaural Ampex 350 tape machine in order to make better recordings. The fledgling business quickly became a passion for the two, who spent all of their off-hours (she worked at Union Planters Bank) working with local talent producing records, none of which made any significant sales.

Stax Is Born

In the summer of 1960, the operation moved to the abandoned Capitol Theatre at 926 East McLemore Avenue, where a recording studio was set up in the theater and a recording booth on the stage. Because money was tight, the sloped floor of the theater was not leveled out. There was also no heating or air-conditioning, which meant that summer sessions were stifling hot while winter sessions were so chilly that musicians often wore their coats. A record store, the Satellite Record Shop, was set up in the popcorn concession area to bring in extra money. Around this time, local legend and DJ Rufus "Bear Cat" Thomas (see Chapter 2) recorded a duet with his daughter Carla called "Cause I Love You," which sold around 30 thousand records. The record caught the attention of Jerry Wexler of Atlantic Records, who for $1000 leased the master and took out a five-year option on all other duets by Rufus and Carla (or at least that's how Jim and Estelle interpreted it—more on that later). Wexler was impressed with the raw energy that came from the studio, something that was lacking from the professional arrangers and session musicians he was used to working with in New York. The association between the two companies that started with "Cause I Love You" would last until 1967, by which time the small mom-and-pop studio was firmly established as a major music production center.

Meanwhile, two recordings established the foundation for what would become the Stax sound. In the summer of 1961 a band of high school students calling themselves the Royal Spades (which included Estelle Axton's son Packy) released a single called "Last Night," which to everyone's surprise, went all the way to #3 on the national pop charts. With national exposure, the Royal Spades decided to change their name to the Mar-Keys; simultaneously, Jim and Estelle changed the name of the studio to Stax (derived from their last names: Stewart and Axton) to avoid a lawsuit with a label in California also named Satellite. The second important recording came in the summer of 1962 when two members of the Mar-Keys, guitarist Steve Cropper and bassist Donald "Duck" Dunn joined two other local musicians, Booker T. Jones on Hammond organ and Al Jackson on drums, and recorded a simple blues jam that they called "Green Onions." Again, surprisingly, "Green Onions" rose to #3 on the national charts.

The quartet began calling themselves Booker T. and the MG's (MG stood for "Memphis Group" or the English sports car, depending on who is telling the story), and became established as the house band for most of the recordings that came out of Stax over the next several years. Unusual for the times, but mirroring the unique workplace environment that emerged at Stax, the MG's was an integrated band: both Cropper and Dunn were white, Jones and Jackson black.

THE STAX SOUND

Characteristics of the Stax Sound

1. Raw, gritty, powerful, emotional
2. Bare bones instrumentation of bass, drums, guitar, piano or organ, horn section
3. Very tight yet uncluttered groove in rhythm section
4. Horns scored in punchy unison lines and chords
5. Generally no vocal harmonies or backup vocals; vocalists have more "elbow room" with bare bones arrangements

Key Stax Recordings

- "Green Onions"—Booker T. and the MG's, 1962
- "In the Midnight Hour"—Wilson Pickett, 1965
- "Soul Man"—Sam and Dave, 1967
- "(Sittin' on) The Dock of the Bay"—Otis Redding, 1967

Soulsville, U.S.A.

Stax grew quickly. Realizing that their destiny was in soul music, the company put up the words "Soulsville, U.S.A." on the theater marquee outside the studio. Over the next 15 years more than 800 singles and 300 albums were released that comprise one of the most enduring catalogues of American music. More than 160 singles made the Top 100 pop chart, while nearly 250 of them made the Top 100 R&B chart. By the start of the 1970s, the label (which included the subsidiary Volt Records) had over 100 artists signed and more than 200 employees. Like Motown, a variety of in-house songwriters were used to crank out songs, the most important of which were **Isaac Hayes** and **David Porter**. The Hayes/Porter team wrote more than 20 hits for Sam and Dave, including "Hold On, I'm Comin'" (#21, 1966), "Soul Man" (#2, 1967), "I Thank You" (#9, 1968), and "When Something Is Wrong with My Baby." Steve Cropper of Booker T. and the MG's was also an important contributor, cowriting such soul classics as "634-5789" (#13, 1966) and "Knock on Wood" (#28, 1966) with Eddie Floyd, "In the Midnight Hour" (#21, 1965) with Wilson Pickett and "(Sittin' on) The Dock of the Bay" (#1, 1968) with Otis Redding.

Sessions at Stax were conducted very differently than they were at Motown. Everything was done in a live and spontaneous environment, rather than the assembly-line production using composers, arrangers, and overdubbing. Songs were often composed on the spot, as was the case with "Green Onions," "In the Midnight Hour," and others. As Jerry Wexler said, "Memphis was a real departure, because Memphis was a return to head arrangements, to the set rhythm section, away from the arranger. It was a reversion to the symbiosis between the producer and the rhythm section, and it was really something new." Compared to Motown, the Stax sound is punchier, more direct and emotional, and not as overly produced, and in effect, more authentic.

- Booker T. and the MG's
- Otis Redding
- Wilson Pickett
- Sam and Dave

IMPORTANT STAX ARTISTS

IMPORTANT STAX ARTISTS

Booker T. and the MG's

The MG's were the Memphis version of Motown's Funk Brothers, serving as the in-house rhythm section for many of the Stax classic soul recordings. They also had their own chart successes, with six more singles besides "Green Onions" hitting the Top 40, including "Hang 'Em High" (#9, 1968) and "Time Is Tight" (#3, 1969). In 1967 the MG's performed in a backup role for many of the label's stars on the "Hit the Road, Stax!" European tour, and also appeared with Otis Redding at the Monterey International Pop Festival. The band paid tribute to the Beatles with one of their last albums, 1970's *McLemore Avenue,* which featured covers of 13 songs from *Abbey Road*. The cover photo shows them crossing the street in front of the Stax studios in a take-off on the famous *Abbey Road* cover.

- Steve Cropper
- Donald "Duck" Dunn
- Booker T. Jones
- Al Jackson

BOOKER T. AND THE MG'S

Otis Redding

Otis Redding (1941–1967) was born in Dawson, Georgia, 100 miles south of Macon. As a youth he sang gospel music at church and played the drums in a school band. As he grew older, he became a Little Richard-inspired lead singer with the group the Pinetoppers, and it was with them that Redding first recorded at Stax in October 1962. Although the song, "These Arms of Mine" only cracked the R&B chart at #20, Redding began to make a name for himself over the next several years as one of the hottest performers on the chitlin' circuit, performing with the Memphis-based backup band the Bar-Kays.

Redding's career was flourishing through the mid-1960s, especially after his electrifying performance at the July 1967 Monterey Pop Festival, which introduced him to a much larger white fan base. By this time he had chalked up seven Top 40 hits, including his classic "Respect" (#35, 1965). Just as his career was beginning to take off, on December 9, 1967, his private plane crashed on the way to a concert in Madison, Wisconsin, killing Redding and most of the members of the Bar-Kays. Three days before his death, Redding made his last recording, the melancholy "(Sittin' on) The Dock of the Bay." Released posthumously, the song became his only #1 hit.

Wilson Pickett

Although Wilson Pickett (1941–2006) signed with Atlantic in 1964, his records were not selling until Jerry Wexler brought him to Stax in May 1965. That session resulted in the soul classic "In the Midnight Hour," the first of 16 Top 40 hits over the next seven years. After his second hit, "634-5789" in late 1965, Pickett recorded at Fame Studio in Muscle Shoals, Alabama, as the Stax/Atlantic association began to dissolve. Pickett was known as the "Wicked Pickett" for his roughly hewn aggressive style and husky voice.

Sam and Dave

Sam Moore (1935–) and Dave Prater (1937–1988) were a hot Miami-based nightclub act when Wexler signed them to Atlantic and brought them to Stax in early 1965. There they were assigned to the Hayes/Porter writing team, who wrote more than 20 hits for the duo over the next two years, including the classic soul anthem "Soul Man." Despite the fact that their live shows were among the most exciting in the industry, the two became estranged after Prater shot his wife in a domestic dispute and did not talk to each other offstage for several years. They broke up in 1970. Both experienced drug problems over the next several years; Prater died in an automobile accident in 1988.

MUSIC CUT 19

"HOLD ON, I'M COMIN'" (ISAAC HAYES/DAVID PORTER)— SAM AND DAVE

Personnel: Sam Moore, Dave Prater: vocals; Booker T. Jones: keyboards; Isaac Hayes: piano; Steve Cropper: guitar; Donald "Duck" Dunn: bass; Al Jackson, Jr.: drums; Wayne Jackson: trumpet; Charles "Packy" Axton: tenor sax; Don Nix: tenor sax. Recorded 1966 at Stax Studios, Memphis, TN; produced by Jim Stewart. Released March 1966 on Stax; 7 weeks on the charts, peaking at #21.

Although "Hold On, I'm Comin'" was Sam and Dave's 13th single release, it was the first to break into the Top Forty pop chart. It also went to #1 on the R&B chart. The song is the epitome of the Stax sound, with a combination of emotionally charged call and response gospel vocals, powerful horn lines, and the clean, funky rhythm section of Booker T. and the MG's. The song grew out of a simple but humorous conversation in the studio; writer David Porter went to the bathroom, and when he didn't come back right away, his co-writer Isaac Hayes grew impatient. "Hold on, man, I'm coming," Porter yelled back. "I swear, right then I broke out of the rest room shouting, 'I got it!'" Porter later related. "When I told Hayes the title, he had the perfect thing for it on the piano. We had the whole song in five minutes."

MUSCLE SHOALS AND ARETHA FRANKLIN

Fame Studios

Nestled in the northwest corner of Alabama, 150 miles east of Memphis lies the sleepy metropolitan area known as Muscle Shoals. Actually made up of four small towns—Florence, Sheffield, Tuscumbia, and the township of Muscle Shoals (where Sam Phillips was born in 1923)—the area started on its way to becoming an unlikely music center in 1959 when local guitarist and entrepreneur **Rick Hall** opened a small recording studio and named it Fame Music (Fame being an acronym for Florence Alabama Music Enterprises). After a number of regional hits allowed him to move into a larger custom-built studio, Hall began to attract clients from Atlanta and Nashville, and eventually Jerry Wexler from Atlantic Records. Like Motown and Stax, one of the chief attractions to the recording environment at Fame was its house band, which through the 1960s became well known simply as the **Muscle Shoals Rhythm Section**. Important members of the MSRS were drummer Roger Hawkins, guitarist Jimmy Johnson, bassists Junior Lowe and David Hood, and pianists Spooner Oldham and Barry Beckett.

- Roger Hawkins
- Jimmy Johnson
- Junior Lowe
- David Hood
- Spooner Oldham
- Barry Beckett

IMPORTANT MEMBERS OF MUSCLE SHOALS RHYTHM SECTION

Muscle Shoals first came to the pop world's attention in the spring of 1966 with the release of "When a Man Loves a Woman" by local R&B singer Percy Sledge. With the help of local DJ Quinn Ivy, a copy of the song was sent to Jerry Wexler, who bought the distribution rights. "When a Man Loves a Woman" shot up to #1 and became Atlantic's first gold record. Once Wexler realized the benefits of recording at Fame (at a time when Stax was getting too busy with their own artists), he began bringing his Atlantic artists to Muscle Shoals. The most notable of these were Wilson Pickett, and in the spring of 1967, Aretha Franklin.

Aretha Franklin

Although Aretha Franklin (1942–) was born in Memphis and grew up in Detroit, her first recording contract came from neither Motown nor Stax, but Columbia Records. Her father, the Reverend C. L. Franklin, was the nationally known pastor of the 4,500-member New Bethel Baptist Church in Detroit, where Aretha began singing at age eight. By the age of 14, she released her first album, comprised entirely of gospel music recorded live at her father's church. At age 18 she was signed by the legendary John Hammond of Columbia, who tried to make her into

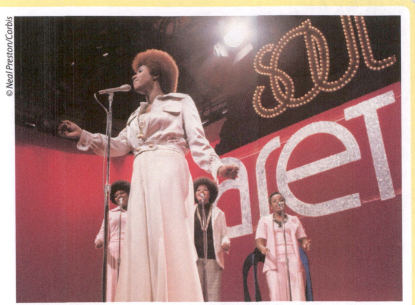

© Neal Preston/Corbis

Aretha Franklin, appearing on the *Soul Train* TV program.

the jazz/pop mold of his earlier discovery, jazz great Billie Holiday. After six years and ten albums that resulted in only one hit (the unremarkable "Rock-a-bye Your Baby with a Dixie Melody"), Aretha left Columbia and signed with Atlantic. Jerry Wexler immediately scheduled a session in Muscle Shoals in January 1967.

Although the session was the only one Aretha ever did in Muscle Shoals, it produced the landmark "I Never Loved a Man (the Way I Love You)," a #9 hit. Under Wexler's direction, for the first time Franklin was allowed the freedom to do what she did best, and her career took off. Following the Muscle Shoals session, Aretha moved to Atlantic's New York studios (taking the Muscle Shoals Rhythm Section with her) and recorded Otis Redding's "Respect," her first #1 hit. Over the next three years she sold millions of records, hitting the Top 10 constantly with hits like "Baby I Love You" (#4), "(You Make Me Feel Like) a Natural Woman" (#9), and "Chain of Fools" (#2), all from 1967 alone. Franklin has the ability to take a remarkably wide variety of songs and give them definitive soul renditions, as in Carole King's "Natural Woman," the Beatles' "Eleanor Rigby," or Simon and Garfunkel's "Bridge Over Troubled Water." She is also a fine pianist and composer in her own right, having penned "Think," "Since You've Been Gone," and many others. Like Ray Charles, her ecstatic, gospel-filled voice is an American institution, and one of the most recognizable and influential in the history of pop music. She also did a credible acting job in her role in the 1980 movie The Blues Brothers, singing both "Respect" and "Think."

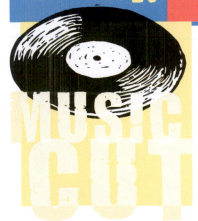

MUSIC CUT 20

"RESPECT" (OTIS REDDING)— ARETHA FRANKLIN

Personnel: Aretha Franklin: piano, vocals; Carolyn Franklin, Erma Franklin: backup vocals; Melvin Lastie: trumpet; King Curtis: tenor sax; Charles Chalmers: tenor sax; Willie Bridges: baritone sax; Jimmy Johnson: guitar; Spooner Oldham: keyboards; Tommy Cogbill: bass; Gene Chrisman: drums. Recorded on February 14, 1967 at Atlantic Studios, New York, NY; produced by Jerry Wexler. Released April 1967 on Atlantic; 12 weeks on the charts, peaking at #1.

Although "Respect" was written and originally recorded by Otis Redding for Stax/Volt in 1965, Aretha Franklin took possession of the song with her 1967 cover. Describing the differences in the two interpretations, producer Jerry Wexler said, "For Otis, respect had the traditional connotation, the more abstract meaning of esteem. The fervor in Aretha's voice demanded that respect; and more respect also involved sexual attention of the highest order. What else would 'sock it to me' mean?" Recorded in Atlantic's New York studio with the famed Muscle Shoals Rhythm Section just one month after her successful debut recording for the label, the song became her first #1 single.

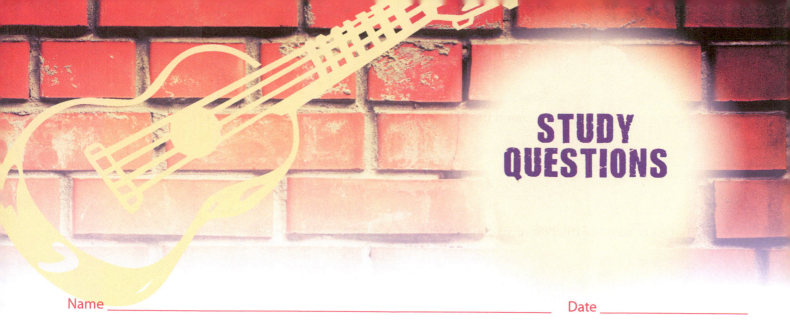

Name _____ Date _____

1. Describe how Ray Charles created the first soul recording.

2. Describe the close connection between the civil rights movement and soul music of the 1960s.

3. How did James Brown influence soul and later black music styles?

4. Describe the key elements to the way business was run at Motown.

5. What were some of the right and wrong things that Berry Gordy did in running Motown?

6. Describe the differences between the way sessions were run at Motown and Stax.

7. What were some of the differences in the Motown sound and Stax sound?

8. How did the "transracial" atmosphere in Memphis affect the operation of Stax?

9. What important role did Jerry Wexler of Atlantic Records play in the soul music of the 1960s?

10. Briefly describe why Atlantic was successful in making a star out of Aretha Franklin but Columbia wasn't.

5

THE FOLK INFLUENCE

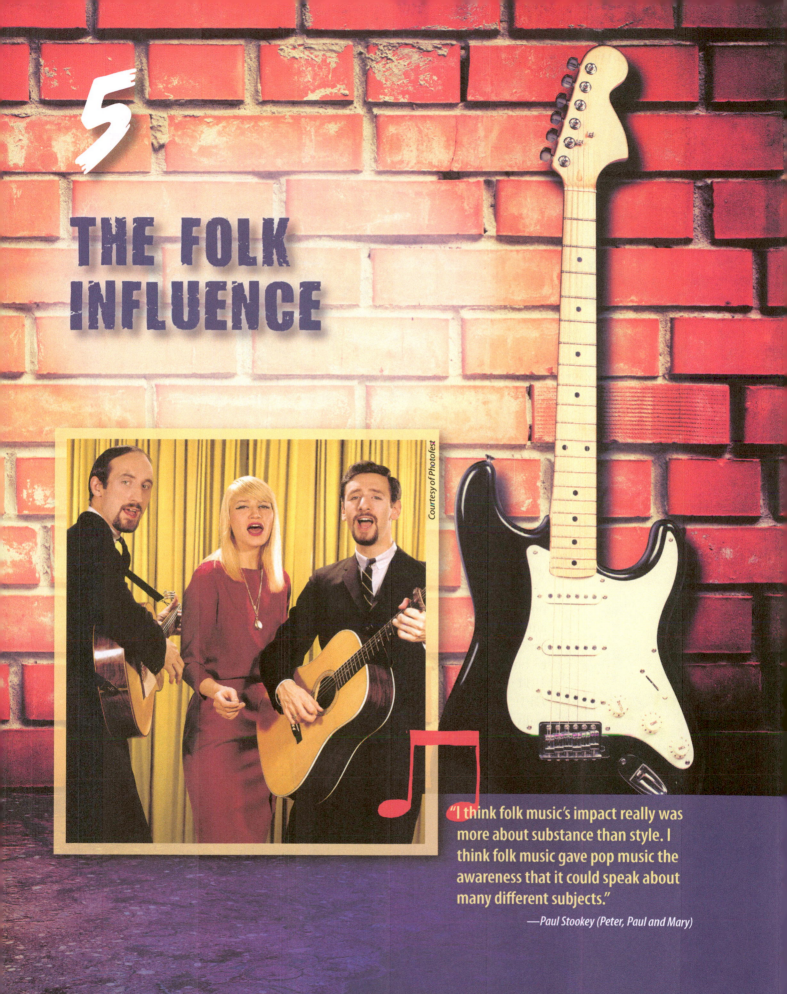

Courtesy of Photofest

"I think folk music's impact really was more about substance than style. I think folk music gave pop music the awareness that it could speak about many different subjects."

—*Paul Stookey (Peter, Paul and Mary)*

KEY TERMS	Left wing folk song conspiracy Wobblies Hootenanny	Fifties folk revival Calypso Newport Folk Festival	Beat writers Hammond's Folly Basement Tapes
KEY FIGURES	John and Alan Lomax Woody Guthrie Pete Seeger The Kingston Trio	Joan Baez Peter, Paul and Mary Bob Dylan Paul Butterfield Blues Band	The Hawks/The Band Rolling Thunder Revue Traveling Wilburys
KEY ALBUMS	*The Freewheelin' Bob Dylan*—Bob Dylan *Bringing It All Back Home*—Bob Dylan	*Blonde On Blonde*—Bob Dylan	*Blood on the Tracks*—Bob Dylan

THE FOLK TRADITION

The Left-Wing Folk Song Conspiracy

Just after the turn of the 20th century, there was a growing interest in traditional American folk music. Part of this interest came from preservationists who feared that the music would disappear due to the increasing urbanization of the country. However, folk music was also becoming popular as a tool for political organizations and labor unions to rally support and foster solidarity among their members. One union in particular, the International Workers of the World (IWW, or popularly known as the "**Wobblies**"), used folk songs to build morale, recruit new members, and stir up publicity for their cause. In 1911, the Wobblies published the first of 30 editions of their songbook entitled *IWW Songs: Songs of the Workers to Fan the Flames of Discontent,* which unofficially became known as *The Little Red Songbook.* Because many folk songs were protest songs against big business and government policies (such as America's involvement in World War I), and were often used by socialist groups and the fledgling Communist Party, by the 1920s conservatives began to speak of a "left-wing folk song conspiracy." This association between folk music, social activism, and liberal politics endured well into the 1960s.

By the 1930s folk radio shows began appearing, such as *The Wayfaring Stranger* hosted by folksinger Burl Ives on the CBS network. Folk songs also began to get published in newspapers. In 1933 **John and Alan Lomax**, a father and son team of musicologists from the Library of Congress, began taking trips through the backwoods of the South with a portable recording device to find and preserve folk songs. On their first trip they discovered an inmate at the Angola State Prison in Louisiana named Leadbelly (Huddie Ledbetter) who was a gifted singer, songwriter, and guitarist. Through the Lomax's persistence, Leadbelly was released in 1934 and went on to become an important influence to folk and blues performers until his death in 1949. Leadbelly also wrote countless numbers of folk songs, including his two most famous, "Goodnight Irene" and "Midnight Special."

Woody Guthrie and Pete Seeger

The 1930s also saw the emergence of the most important early folk singer, Woody Guthrie (1912–1967). Guthrie's impoverished childhood was spent in Oklahoma and Texas, where he witnessed first hand the tough life of the lower class during the Depression. He saw how easily banks were willing to evict farm families whose crops had been ruined by dust storms and other calamities. Guthrie himself was the victim of several tragedies in his youth, including his sister's death in an explosion and his mother's commitment to an insane asylum. He was on his own and living on the streets by age 13, singing and playing the harmonica to earn a living. At the age of 25, Guthrie began a lifelong crusade to help band the common folk together to fight for their rights through unions and other organizations. He traveled the country, often hobo-style on trains, talking to people and singing the songs he wrote. Guthrie's songs included dust bowl ballads, pro-union songs, anti-Hitler songs, and songs about the plight of migrant workers and common people. In all, it is estimated that he wrote well over 1,000 songs during his lifetime, including "The Great Dust Storm," "Pastures of Plenty," "Roll on Columbia," and his most famous, "This Land Is Your Land." Guthrie also developed a unique talking blues style of half singing and half speaking the lyrics to his songs while accompanying himself on guitar. With his songs, his idealism and his working-class blue jeans and uncombed hair, Guthrie became a hero and a legend in the folk community.

Hootenannies and Witch Hunts

In 1940, Guthrie met 21-year-old singer/guitarist Pete Seeger (1919–) at a benefit concert for migrant workers. Seeger's father Charles was a university professor who had registered as a conscientious objector during World War I, and had

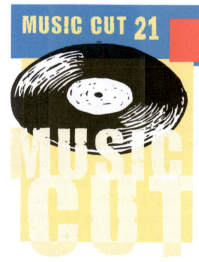

MUSIC CUT 21

"PRETTY BOY FLOYD" (WOODY GUTHRIE)— WOODY GUTHRIE

Personnel: Woody Guthrie: guitar, vocals. Recorded April 26, 1940 at RCA Victor Studio 1, Camden, NJ.

During his life, Woody Guthrie wrote a number of epic ballads about outlaws, often celebrating them as populist heroes that, like Robin Hood, stole from the rich and gave to the poor. "Pretty Boy Floyd" is just such a tale, about the real life bank robber Charles Floyd. After growing up in the dust bowl years on a small farm in Oklahoma, Floyd was inadvertently involved in a murder that forced him into a life of crime. Living in Kansas City during the corrupt years of the Pendergast administration, Floyd made connections with organized crime elements and learned to use a machine gun. As his reputation grew and federal agents began pursuing him, he hid out in the backwoods, often protected by the locals who viewed him as a folk hero. He was eventually killed by FBI agents in an open Ohio farm field.

Guthrie's song captures the essence of Floyd the folk hero. It was Guthrie's characteristic "talking blues" style that became so influential to Bob Dylan and other folk artists. It is also performed in the traditional folk style, with only acoustic guitar accompaniment.

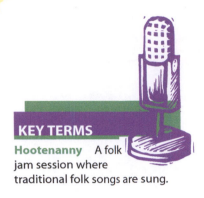

KEY TERMS

Hootenanny A folk jam session where traditional folk songs are sung.

exposed his son to folk music at an early age. Throughout the 1940s Guthrie and Seeger traveled the country as part of the Almanac Singers, singing original and traditional folk songs at **hootenannies** and rallies. In 1949 Seeger went on to form the Weavers, one of the first folk groups to break into mainstream visibility when their recording of Leadbelly's "Goodnight Irene" became a #1 hit in 1950. But both men fell on harder times in the 1950s, as did the folk community in general. Guthrie fell ill to Huntington's chorea, a central nervous system disorder that leads to distorted speech and progressive degeneration of the brain that kept him in and out of hospitals until it finally killed him in 1967. Seeger ran into problems of a political nature.

The conservative and Cold War climate of the early 1950s did not bode well for the folk community. With Senator Joseph McCarthy of Wisconsin on the prowl trying to "out" Communist infiltrators in the government, fingers began to point in all directions at those who were suspected of being Soviet spies or Communist sympathizers. Among those blacklisted were Hollywood writers, actors, and directors, as well as journalists and of course, folk singers. Pete Seeger's liberal politics eventually caught the attention of the FBI, and he was blacklisted in the 1950 publication *Red Channels: The Report of Communist Influence in Radio and Television*. Among other charges, the book exposed that he had joined the Young Communist League while a student at Harvard in the 1930s. In light of the revelations, Decca Records dropped the Weavers, as the group was suddenly too controversial. Seeger left the Weavers in 1953 to tour college campuses across the country as a soloist, singing political songs and inviting audience participation. But by 1955 Congress was on his trail: he was asked to testify before the House Un-American Activities Committee, which by now was on their own Communist witch hunt. Seeger appeared, but refused to cooperate. He was indicted, tried, and convicted on ten counts of contempt of Congress, although he was cleared in 1962 after a lengthy court battle. Seeger continued to be a political activist and went on to write some of the most important songs of the folk movement, including "If I Had a Hammer," "Where Have All the Flowers Gone," "Turn, Turn, Turn," and reworking an old spiritual into the civil rights anthem "We Shall Overcome."

THE FIFTIES FOLK REVIVAL

The Calypso Fad

The anti-Communist furor that engulfed the nation's attention for much of the early and mid-1950s forced many folk musicians to go underground. However, by the late 1950s, there was another popular folk revival. Many who were turned off by the vulgarities of R&B and rock and roll were drawn to the socially conscious nature of folk music. College students in particular saw folk as music that addressed the need for positive change in society, and much of its groundswell of support was fostered at coffeehouses and study halls on campus. One of the first signs that folk was about to have a revival came when actor and singer Harry Belafonte scored a series of calypso hits in 1956 and 1957. **Calypso**, a folk music of Trinidad, has a different rhythmic quality than

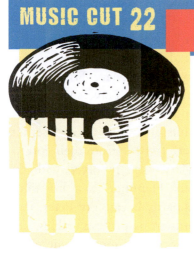

MUSIC CUT 22

"TOM DOOLEY" (TRADITIONAL)— THE KINGSTON TRIO

Personnel: Dave Guard: banjo, vocals; Bob Shane: guitar, vocals; Nick Reynolds: guitar, vocals. Recorded 1958 in Los Angeles, released on Capitol; 18 weeks on the charts, peaking at #1.

As discussed in Chapter 1, major components of the English folk tradition in America were ballads and lyric songs that often told tales of love and love lost. "Tom Dooley" is such a song, inspired by the 1866 murder of Laura Foster in North Carolina and subsequent hanging in 1868 of her lover and convicted murderer, Tom Dula (pronounced "Dooley"). Although details of the exact origins of the song are murky, the first recording of the song apparently was made by Gilliam Grayson and Henry Whitter in 1929. Several recordings of the song exist, but by far the most popular was the Kingston Trio's 1958 version, which hit #1 on the charts and eventually sold more than six million copies. The song was so popular that it helped renew interest in folk music, and helped kick-start what is today called the Fifties Folk Revival. It also earned the group a Grammy Award at the 1959 ceremonies.

traditional American folk, but the narrative verse structures and storylines are similar. Belafonte's commercial success included the 1957 #5 hit "Banana Boat (Day-O)," which started a short-lived calypso fad that was instrumental in renewing interest in folk. Belafonte's *Calypso* spent 31 weeks at #1 on the Billboard Top 100 Album chart.

The real start to the 1950s folk revival came in 1958 when the record "Tom Dooley" by the **Kingston Trio** became a #1 hit. The song was a traditional folk song about a convicted murderer named Tom Dula who was sentenced to death by hanging in 1866. The group was obviously influenced by the calypso fad (naming themselves after the Jamaican capital city), but played folk music that was pop oriented and without much trace of political protest. To help foster a squeaky clean image, they wore crew cuts and matching clothes. By 1963 the group had racked up ten Top 40 hits.

The Queen of Folk

In the summer of 1959 the first **Newport Folk Festival** was held in Newport, Rhode Island. One of the artists who performed was angel-voiced **Joan Baez** (1941–), who had been a favorite at Cambridge's Club 47 while a student at Boston University. Baez was beautiful, wore plain peasant clothes, sang traditional folk songs, and was committed to political and social issues. By embracing the values of the common person, Baez became the darling of the traditional folk crowd, who began calling her the "Queen of Folk." She also quickly developed a large mainstream audience as well—her second album *Joan Baez 2* went gold in 1961. Around this time she met Bob Dylan, with whom she fell in love and went on tour in the summer of 1963, introducing him to her loyal

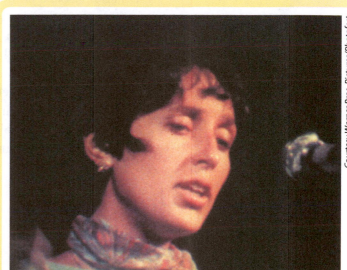

Joan Baez

Courtesy Warner Bros. Pictures/Photofest

fans. Because Baez stuck to traditional folk songs and resisted commercial pressures, she did not have any chart success until 1971 when her cover of the Band's "The Night They Drove Old Dixie Down" went to #3.

In 1961 **Peter, Paul and Mary** made their debut performance at New York's Bitter End. Peter Yarrow, Noel Paul Stookey, and Mary Travers came from different backgrounds—only Yarrow was a folksinger; Travers was an off-Broadway singer, Stookey a comedian. They ended up becoming the most popular folk group of the 1960s with 12 Top 40 hits, including two—"Lemon Tree" (#35) and Pete Seeger's "If I Had a Hammer" (#10)—from their eponymous first album. Like Baez, Peter, Paul and Mary were involved with the social issues of their songs. Although Seeger wrote "Hammer" as a pro-union song, it became a civil rights anthem in the 1960s partly because of Peter, Paul and Mary's recording. The group appeared at numerous protests, rallies, and marches, including the August 28, 1963, March on Washington where Dr. Martin Luther King gave his famous "I Have a Dream" speech. Also like Baez, Peter, Paul and Mary gave a boost to the early career of Bob Dylan, recording two of his songs in 1963 that outsold Dylan's own versions: "Blowin' in the Wind" (#2) and "Don't Think Twice, It's All Right" (#9).

The Greenwich Village Scene

In the wake of the commercial success of performers like the Kingston Trio, Joan Baez, and Peter, Paul and Mary came other popular folk groups such as the Highwaymen ("Michael Row the Boat Ashore," #1, 1961), the New Christy Minstrels ("Green Green," #14, 1963), and the Rooftop Singers ("Walk Right In," #1, 1963). Coffeehouses, cafés, and small clubs all over the country began to hire folk performers, and important folk scenes sprang up in New York; the Boston/Cambridge area; Ann Arbor, Michigan; Berkeley, California; and other cities. The most important of these was in New York's Greenwich Village.

The Village had long been a magnet for artists, musicians, writers, and bohemians, and by 1960 young aspiring folk musicians seemed to be everywhere. It was a compact and nourishing scene, where everyone knew and supported each other. Among the struggling folk performers in the Village at this time were Dave Van Ronk, Tom Paxton, Odetta, Ramblin' Jack Elliott, Tim Hardin, John Sebastian, and Phil Ochs. These and other folk singers often took part in impromptu hootenannies on Sunday afternoons in Washington Square Park. These gatherings routinely drew so many listeners that police had to stop traffic. Folk music was heard in the many clubs and coffeehouses in the area, most of which had open-mic policies on Tuesday nights where singers, both unknown and famous, could get up and perform. These venues were known as "basket

POPULAR FOLK GROUPS FROM THE EARLY SIXTIES

- Highwaymen
- The New Christy Minstrels
- Rooftop Singers

- Dave Van Ronk
- Tom Paxton
- Odetta
- Ramblin' Jack Elliott
- Tim Hardin
- John Sebastian

houses" because the musicians were paid in tips that were collected in baskets that were passed around. The most important were:

- The Gaslight, a basement coffeehouse on MacDougal Street

- Café Wha?, which often hired up-and-coming comedians like Bill Cosby and Richard Pryor, and where Bob Dylan made his first New York appearance

- Gerde's Folk City on West 4th Street and Mercer (an Italian restaurant during the day)

- Bitter End at 147 Bleecker Street. Folk music was so popular that for a while even the Village Vanguard, New York's premier jazz club was featuring it on off nights

One of the most important establishments in the Village was Izzy Young's Folklore Center on MacDougal Street. Young was a folk enthusiast who opened the center in 1957 as a sort of clearinghouse for folk musicians. It was a place where you could buy instruments, sheet music, books, and records, or just hang out and listen to records and talk. Young was one of Bob Dylan's most enthusiastic early supporters, and produced Dylan's first concert at Carnegie Chapter Hall in 1961.

TRIVIA NOTE

One of the most important establishments in the Village was Izzy Young's Folklore Center on MacDougal Street. It was a place where you could buy instruments, sheet music, books, and records, or just hang out and listen to records and talk.

Broadside

The Village had a long-standing tradition of publications that supported the folk scene. In 1946 *People's Songs,* a bulletin that promoted progressive causes through music, was first published by Pete Seeger and Oscar Brand. This gave way in May 1950 to *Sing Out!,* which was dedicated to keeping folksingers and songwriters in touch by publishing left-leaning political songs, a risky endeavor at the time. It is still published on a quarterly basis. In February 1962, Pete Seeger and three other folk musicians began publishing a mimeographed biweekly newsletter called *Broadside.* Designed to showcase new folk and protest songs and provide articles about protests, festivals, and recent record releases, *Broadside* provided a forum for the new generation of folk musicians to get their original songs noticed. Newsletters like *People's Songs, Sing Out!* and *Broadside* also provided outlets for the folk community to weigh in with criticisms and opinions of songs, events, and new artists. Broadside gave a struggling young songwriter like Bob Dylan the opportunity to write topical songs inspired by current events and get them published. One of Dylan's first songs, "Talkin' John Birch Paranoid Blues," a satirical piece about searching for Communists, was printed in the inaugural issue of the magazine. The next few years would be some of the most prolific in the long career of one of the most important figures in the history of American music.

BOB DYLAN

Boy from the North Country

Bob Dylan was born Robert Zimmerman in Duluth, Minnesota, on May 24, 1941, to Abe and Beatty Zimmerman. Bob received a good Jewish upbringing, although his father made sure he was well-versed in the New Testament as well. The family moved north to Hibbing in 1947, where Bob stayed until he finished high school. He became interested in music, playing the piano and guitar and forming a rock and roll combo called the Golden Chords. His musical idols included Hank Williams, Little Richard, and Elvis Presley. It was in high school that he began to experiment with various pseudonyms before eventually settling on Bob Dylan in honor of an idol, Welsh poet Dylan Thomas (he would also go by the names Blind Boy Grunt, Bob Landy, and Robert Milkwood Thomas at various times in his life). Dylan enrolled at the University of Minnesota in the fall of 1959 and quickly became a fixture of the hip bohemian section next to campus known as Dinkytown. Because the Dinkytown coffeehouse scene was heavily tilted toward folk, Bob's interest in it supplanted his rock and roll leanings. He learned the traditional folk songs and performed them in his own idiosyncratic and sometimes humorous style, unlike the solemn way in which most Dinkytown folkies presented themselves. During this time Dylan read and was inspired by the works of the **beat writers**, but his biggest influence was Woody Guthrie's memoir *Bound for Glory*. In the book Guthrie created fictional characters that used unusual speech patterns such as clipped words, double negatives, and non sequiturs. Dylan began to adopt these in his own speech, along with a fascination for Guthrie and his music. Deciding he had to meet the folk hero, Dylan left for New York in late 1960.

Dylan arrived in Greenwich Village in late January 1961 and performed an open-mic set at the Café Wha? his first night in town. Within a week he succeeded in meeting Guthrie, who by this time was bedridden and delusional from his battle with Huntington's chorea. After the meeting Dylan wrote his first important composition, "Song to Woody" and began to write other songs in Guthrie's talking blues style. Performing open-mic night sets and hanging out in the Village, Bob

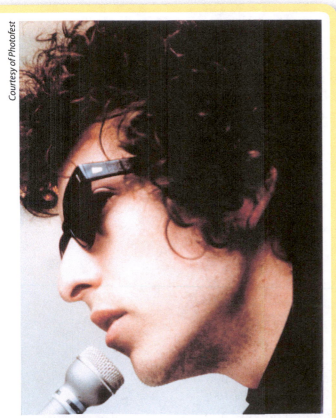

Courtesy of Photofest

Bob Dylan

started to establish himself and make friends with locals such as Dave Van Ronk, Ramblin' Jack Elliott, Paul Stookey, and Joan Baez. Even though he impressed the locals as intelligent and engaging, he was also mysterious, with far-fetched stories of his past. He soon worked his way into a Harry Belafonte recording session playing harmonica, which helped him get noticed by Columbia Records executive John Hammond. His big break came when *New York Times* writer Robert Shelton gave him a glowing review of a performance at Gerde's Folk City on September 29, 1961. Entitled "Bob Dylan: A Distinctive Song Stylist," the column convinced Hammond to sign Dylan to a five-year contract.

BEAT WRITERS

Writers such as Jack Kerouac, William S. Burroughs, and Allen Ginsberg who gained notoriety in the 1950s and espoused a philosophy of existentialism and a rejection of materialism. Kerouac himself coined the phrase Beat Generation, and defined it for the Random House Dictionary: "Members of the generation that came of age after World War II, who, supposedly as a result of disillusionment stemming from the Cold War, espouse mystical detachment and relaxation of social and sexual tensions."

Hammond's Folly

Dylan's first album was a vocal, guitar, and harmonica recording done in two days called simply **Bob Dylan** (released March 19, 1962). It contained two originals, including "Song to Woody" and an assortment of blues and traditional folk songs. The album sold poorly; around the Columbia offices it became known as "Hammond's Folly." In spite of the setback, Dylan began to compose new songs with a fervor. They came through him with ease, as if he was channeling them from some unknown source. As Tom Paxton said, "He felt he wasn't writing songs, he was [just] writing them down. They were there to be captured." He kept notebooks and wrote everywhere, all the time; songs of topical interest, social commentaries, protest songs, love songs. "The Death of Emmett Till" was about the gruesome unsolved murder of a 14-year-old black boy in Mississippi. "Let Me Die in My Footsteps" was a commentary on America's preoccupation with fallout shelters and air raid drills. Two were strong anti-war songs, "Masters of War" and "A Hard Rain's A-Gonna Fall." Two more were about failing relationships, "Don't Think Twice, It's All Right" and "Tomorrow Is a Long Time." Writers of good, original songs were unusual in the Village, and word spread quickly. "Everybody's talking about him," said none other than Pete Seeger.

- *The Freewheelin' Bob Dylan*, 1963
- *The Times They Are a Changin'*, 1964
- *Bringing It All Back Home*, 1965
- "Like a Rolling Stone," 1965
- *Blonde on Blonde*, 1966

KEY DYLAN RECORDINGS

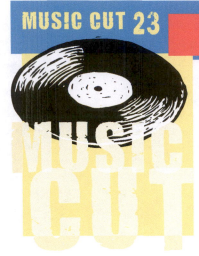

MUSIC CUT 23

"BLOWIN' IN THE WIND" (BOB DYLAN)— BOB DYLAN

Personnel: Bob Dylan: guitar, harmonica, vocals; Recorded July 9, 1962 at Columbia 7th Street Studio A, New York, NY; produced by John Hammond. Released May 27, 1963 on the Columbia LP *The Freewheelin' Bob Dylan*; released August 1963 as a single, did not reach Top Forty.

"Blowin' in the Wind," the opening track on Side A of Bob Dylan's second album *The Freewheelin' Bob Dylan,* is Dylan's first great anthem, and the song that is perhaps most associated with him to this day. It is an adaptation of the Negro spiritual "No More Auction Block," and is one of many examples of Dylan's appropriation of traditional songs for his own purposes (another song from the album, "A Hard Rain's A-Gonna Fall" was based on the folk ballad "Lord Randall"). Dylan himself admitted as much in 1978, saying, "'Blowin' in the Wind' has always been a spiritual. I took it off a song called 'No More Auction Block'—and 'Blowin' in the Wind' follows the same feeling." He first performed the song at Gerde's Folk City in Greenwich Village on April 16, 1962, where several audience members recorded it. In May it was published for the first time in Pete Seeger's *Broadside* magazine, and in June it was published in *Sing Out!* In that magazine, Dylan said of the song, "There ain't too much I can say about this song except that the answer is blowing in the wind . . . Too many of these hip people are telling me where the answer is but oh I won't believe that. I still say it's in the wind and just like a restless piece of paper it's got to come down some." The song has an interesting verse structure, in that each verse contains a series of rhetorical questions that are usually interpreted as addressing human dignity, peace, and freedom. Each verse concludes with the ambiguous, "The answer my friend, is blowin' in the wind/The answer is blowin' in the wind." It has been widely regarded as an anthem to the civil rights era, and inspired Sam Cooke to write "A Change is Gonna Come" in 1964. "Blowin' in the Wind" has been covered many times, most famously by Peter, Paul and Mary, whose version went to #2 and sold over one million copies.

Dylan's second album, ***The Freewheelin' Bob Dylan*** (released May 27, 1963) consisted almost entirely of his new original material, including his first great anthem "Blowin' in the Wind." "Blowin' in the Wind" was composed in a café across the street from the Gaslight Club in just a few minutes, and within weeks it was being played throughout the Village by other folk singers. The song struck a chord with many in the community who pondered the meaning of its lyrics, set in the form of a series of rhetorical questions. Peter, Paul and Mary's 1963 cover of "Blowin' in the Wind" went to #2 on the charts, putting Bob Dylan on the national map for the first time. When they performed the song at the Newport Folk Festival in July, Peter, Paul and Mary brought Dylan onstage, introducing him as "the most important folk artist in America today" to a thunderous ovation. Bob had also endeared himself to the folk community when he refused to appear on *The Ed Sullivan Show* on May 12 when the CBS censors, fearing a lawsuit, requested that he not perform his intended selection "Talkin' John Birch Paranoid Blues." Later in the summer, he sang at the March on Washington with Joan Baez and Peter, Paul and Mary. Around this time his on-and-off love affair with Baez began as she took him on tour with her; he was an appropriate folk "King" for the "Queen."

The Times They Are a Changin'

More topical protest songs filled Dylan's third album, *The Times They Are a Changin'* (released January 13, 1964), which helped solidify his leadership of the folk community. The title track was a rallying call to action that cleverly addresses different segments of society with each verse. Also on the album were protest songs such as the antiwar "With God on Our Side," "Only a Pawn in Their Game" about the death of civil rights worker Medgar Evers, and "The Lonesome Death of Hattie Carroll," about a privileged white man who kills his black servant and escapes serious punishment. However, just as his audience was warming up to their new prophet, Dylan suddenly changed directions with his next LP, *Another Side of Bob Dylan* (released August 8, 1964), which turned away from political activism toward a more introspective stance. The album was recorded in one 6-hour session on June 9 and contained no protest songs—the dominant themes were relationships—a fact that was noted with consternation by critics. Even the album's title seemed to signal that Dylan was abandoning his role as leader of the folk movement. When he appeared at the 1964 Newport Festival in July, Dylan's crowd response was lukewarm—a noticeable change from the resounding reception from the previous year.

Still, Bob was now a major celebrity, and when in the summer of 1964 the Beatles came to New York, an introduction was set up at the Hotel Delmonico. It was at this famous meeting that Dylan reportedly turned the Fab Four on to marijuana, although there is evidence to suggest that they were already experimenting with it and other hallucinogens on their own. As Dylan, McCartney, and Lennon spent more time together over the next few days, a bond of friendship grew between them. Dylan's influence on the Beatles is well documented, as their lyrics became more socially relevant and political starting with their August 1965 album *Help!* But it's also clear that the Beatles and other rock groups such as the Animals (see Chapter 6) were also influencing Dylan, as his next album would prove.

In January 1965 Dylan recorded his fifth and possibly most important album, ***Bringing It All Back Home*** (released March 22, 1965). It was clear by now that he was not interested in staying within the narrow parameters of acoustic folk music, and wanted to incorporate the energy of electric rock. In the process, the songs on side one, recorded with a rock rhythm section, did nothing less than redefine popular music. By combining original, thought-provoking and poetic lyrics with an electric rhythm and blues sensibility, Dylan changed rock forever. From this moment on, rock artists such as the Beatles began to write lyrics that went beyond girls and cars and tackle issues of social significance. In doing so Dylan paved the way for the creation of folk rock, a style that would be further defined by the Byrds, Simon and Garfunkel, Crosby, Stills, Nash and Young, and others (in June 1965, the Byrds took their pop-oriented version of "Mr. Tambourine Man" to #1). Although side two of *Bringing It All Back Home* was made up of all acoustic material (including the original version of "Mr. Tambourine Man"), the dye had been cast. Predictably, folk purists reacted angrily, but the album peaked at #6, higher than any of Dylan's previous LPs.

Newport 1965

Dylan's most controversial moment came at the Newport Folk Festival on July 25, 1965. Appearing before an audience of primarily traditional purists, he performed his new electric material with the **Paul Butterfield Blues Band**. The audience was stunned and angry. To many, like folk singer Oscar Brand, "The electric guitar represented capitalism . . . the people who were selling out." In attendance was Pete Seeger, who was so angered by the music that he tried to cut the power to the band. After performing three songs, the band left the stage to lusty boos from the crowd. Dylan did return in a few minutes to play "Mr. Tambourine Man" and "It's All Over Now, Baby Blue" by himself, with acoustic guitar and harmonica. This time he was cheered.

On August 30, 1965, *Highway 61 Revisited* was released, an album that continued to explore the sound of *Bringing It All Back Home* and contained one of Dylan's most powerful rock songs, "Like a Rolling Stone." Rising to #2, "Rolling Stone" was to become the highest charting single of his career. On the surface, the song is about a privileged girl who falls on hard times, but it has also been interpreted to be a commentary on America's own state of turmoil, and also as a response to those who were critical of Dylan's endeavors into rock music. In any analysis, the song's refrain of "How does it feel/How does it feel/To be without a home/Like a complete unknown/Like a rolling stone?" makes it one of rock's most vengeful compositions.

In September Dylan toured with the **Hawks**, a band from Canada who would later be known simply as the **Band**. Each concert consisted of Bob doing a solo acoustic set, followed by an electric set with the Hawks. As expected, each night the acoustic set was warmly applauded, the electric set was booed. During breaks in the tour, Dylan went to Nashville and recorded ***Blonde on Blonde*** (released May 16, 1966) using mostly Nashville session players. The double album (considered

MUSIC CUT 24

"LIKE A ROLLING STONE" (BOB DYLAN)—BOB DYLAN

Personnel: Bob Dylan: guitar, vocals; Mike Bloomfield: guitar; Al Kooper: organ; Paul Griffin: piano; Russ Savakus: bass; Bobby Gregg: drums. Recorded June 15, 1965 at Columbia 7th Street Studio A, New York, NY; produced by Tom Wilson. Released July 20, 1965 on Columbia; 12 weeks on the charts, peaking at #2.

1965 was *the* pivotal year for the merging of folk music with rock; it began with the Byrds recording of Bob Dylan's "Mr. Tambourine Man" hitting the #1 spot on the charts and ended with Simon and Garfunkel's "The Sound of Silence" doing the same. It was also the year that many folkies such as Marty Balin of Jefferson Airplane and Jerry Garcia of the Grateful Dead began to plug in electric guitars for the first time. But the year's defining moments came courtesy of Dylan, who within one month's time recorded what some call his greatest song and then shocked the folk community with his electric performance at Newport. "Like a Rolling Stone" evolved during May and early June from a 20-page rant, which was, as Dylan later said, "Just a rhythm thing on paper all about my steady hatred, directed at some point that was honest." Eventually it was edited down to four verses and a chorus, but the completed song still ended up being a convention-defying six minutes in length. In spite of its length, "Rolling Stone" still managed to peak at #2 and help propel its LP *Highway 61 Revisited* to a #3 spot and sell a million and a half copies. Dylan himself later said that, "'Rolling Stone' 's the best song I wrote." Amen.

to be the first double album in rock history) contains a variety of songs, some of which can be considered the hardest rocking of his career. *Blonde on Blonde* also includes the absurd and jovial "Rainy Day Women #12 & 35" and the poignant "Sad Eyed Lady of the Lowlands," written for his wife Sara Lownds, whom he married in November 1965. In 1967 filmmaker D. A. Pennebaker released **Don't Look Back**, a documentary covering Dylan's 1965 tour of the United Kingdom that features among others, Joan Baez, John Mayall, Ginger Baker, and Allen Ginsberg. The opening of the film contains the famous take of Dylan holding lyric placards in an alley while his song "Subterranean Homesick Blues" from *Bringing It All Back Home* plays.

The Basement Tapes

In the summer of 1966, Dylan was involved in a motorcycle accident that to this day is shrouded in mystery. Bob, Sara, and their children had purchased a mansion outside of the artistic community of Woodstock, New York, in July 1965, which they named Hi Lo Ha. On the morning of July 29, Bob apparently fell off his bike somewhere along the winding, wooded roads surrounding their home. The extent of his injuries has been the subject of considerable debate ever since—some say he was only bruised, some say his neck was broken, rumors even flew for a while that he had died. Dylan was in fact injured to some extent, but the accident may have actually been a blessing, allowing him to get away from the intense pressure of his celebrity. While recuperating, Dylan centered his attention on his family life in the peaceful settings of upstate New York, out of the public eye for the first time in nearly three years. He also started to record new songs with the Band, who had moved into a nearby house they called Big Pink (so named because of its exterior paint color). These recordings were originally distributed by Dylan's publishing company to artists looking to record his songs, but over time they fell into the hands of bootleggers who sold them illegally. They became known as the **Basement Tapes**. Because of the mystery surrounding Dylan's accident and his reclusiveness during this time, the Basement Tapes were widely copied; they were officially released in 1975.

John Wesley Harding, released in January 1968 and Dylan's first album in almost two years, was recorded in Nashville and signaled yet another paradigm shift in his career. Released at a time when big productions like *Sgt. Pepper's* and *Pet Sounds* were in vogue, the album is quiet and reflective with simple instrumentation. Its influences lie in the music of Hank Williams and the Bible—Dylan called *JWH* "the first biblical rock album." It includes one of his classics, "All Along the Watchtower," a modern morality parable, as well as other songs that flirt with country influences. His next album, *Nashville Skyline,* continued the country trend to an even greater degree. Dylan's voice seemed to have changed into a smoother sort of croon, most noticeable on the album's only hit, "Lay Lady Lay." Once again, the critics complained, this time because country music was not currently "in" with the rock establishment (Nashville and country music were equated with right-wing, pro-war politics). However, the album proved to be immensely influential in creating the country rock genre. Dylan continued to confuse fans with the release of *Self Portrait,* an album comprised entirely of cover tunes. Once again, the critics were less than enthusiastic.

Dylan's Later Career

Throughout the 1970s, Bob Dylan's career continued to evolve. In 1971 a book of his poetry and prose entitled *Tarantula* was published. In 1972 he acted in and scored Sam Peckinpah's movie *Pat Garrett and Billy the Kid,* which included his song "Knockin' on Heaven's Door." In 1974 he resumed touring for the first time since 1966, once again backed by the Band. Late 1974 saw him work on his 15th studio album ***Blood on the Tracks***, which is often called one of, if not the very best of his career. Although the album was recorded in New York in September, at the last minute Dylan re-recorded several of the songs at Sound80 Studio in Minneapolis with local musicians. Many of the album's songs reflect the impending breakup of his marriage to Sara, including the tender "If You See Her, Say Hello." In 1975 Dylan toured with the **Rolling Thunder Revue**, a loose collection of friends that included Joan Baez, Ramblin' Jack Elliot, Alan Ginsberg and other assorted musicians. In 1976, he released *Desire,* which like *Blood on the Tracks* before it, went to #1. It contained the haunting "Hurricane," which protested the murder conviction of former middleweight boxer Rubin "Hurricane" Carter.

Sometime in early 1979, Dylan converted to Christianity. Throughout his career his songs had contained references to religion, and although he was raised a Jew, he had always had a strong connection to Christian teachings. Three albums followed that reflected his new faith: *Slow Train Coming, Saved,* and *Shot of Love.* The albums, together with Dylan's new habit of opening concerts with sermons, had a negative effect on his career, and record sales and concert audiences dwindled. In 1988, at a particularly low point in his career, Dylan recorded an album with his friends George Harrison, Tom Petty, Jeff Lynne, and Roy Orbison who called themselves the **Traveling Wilburys**. It was a major commercial success. He has continued to record and tour into the 21st century, recently winning a Grammy in the Contemporary Folk Album category in 2001 for *Love and Theft,* which ranks among the best albums of his career.

TRAVELING WILBURYS

- George Harrison
- Tom Petty
- Jeff Lynne
- Roy Orbison

The Dylan Legacy

Bob Dylan is one of the most important and innovative musicians in American history. He brought to rock the idea that lyrics can be poetry, a call to action, a political commentary, or a personal statement. He was a major influence on the music of the most popular group of the 1960s, the Beatles. Emerging at a time when pop music was increasingly a manufactured product, Dylan was raw, a warts-and-all performer who was not a particularly good singer or guitar player, inspiring an "anybody can be a rock star" ethic that continues to be an important part of what rock is all about. He brought the worlds of folk, country, R&B, and rock together as no one else had previously done. He was influential to the late 1960s singer/songwriters (of which he was the first), and in the creation of folk rock and country rock, two genres that continue to flourish to this day. As a songwriter, he is one of the most prolific in music history, and has released more than 60 albums, 10 of which are listed in *Rolling Stone's* list of 500 Greatest Albums of All Time. Two, *Highway 61 Revisited* (#4) and *Blonde on Blonde* (#9) are listed in the top ten.

TRIVIA NOTE

Bob Dylan is one of the most important and innovative musicians in American history. He was a major influence on the music of the most popular group of the 1960s, the Beatles.

STUDY QUESTIONS

1. Why did folk get a reputation as the music of left wing radicals?

2. Why were Woody Guthrie and Pete Seeger so important, and what were some of their contributions to folk music?

3. Who were some of the important players in the 1950s folk revival and what roles did they play?

4. How did Jamaican music influence the folk scene in the 1950s?

5. Why was the Greenwich Village scene so important?

6. In what ways did Woody Guthrie influence Bob Dylan?

7. Describe some of the difficulties Bob Dylan encountered with critics' and his audience's expectations of him in the mid-1960s.

8. What are some of the later rock styles that Bob Dylan was influential to?

9. What were the Basement Tapes?

10. How did his motorcycle accident affect Dylan's career?

6

THE BRITISH INVASION

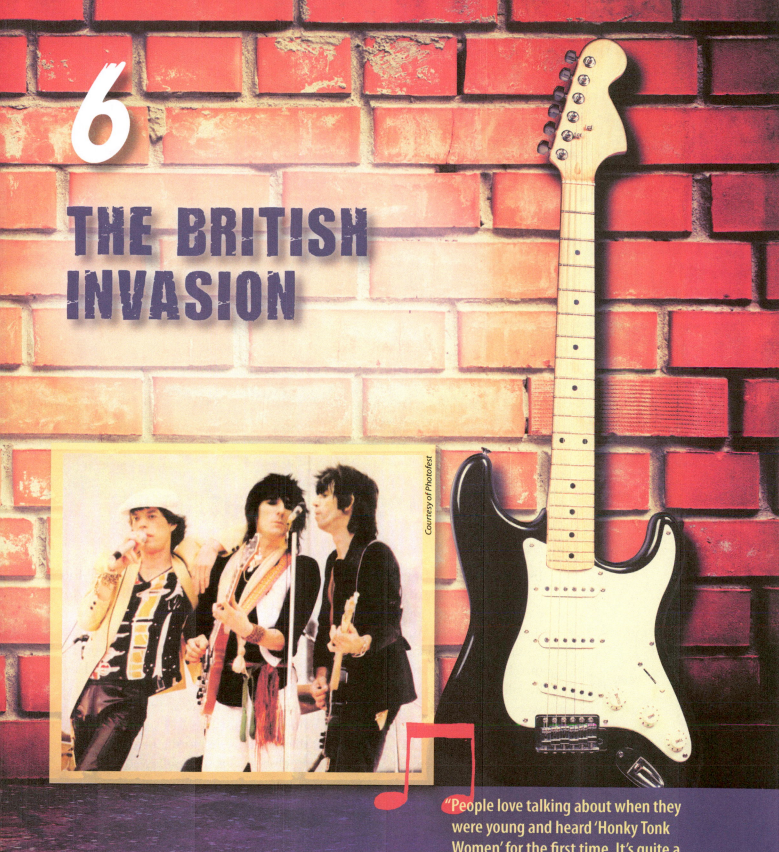

"People love talking about when they were young and heard 'Honky Tonk Women' for the first time. It's quite a heavy load to carry on your shoulders the memories of so many people. I like it but I must be careful not to get trapped in the past."

—Mick Jagger (The Rolling Stones)

KEY TERMS

Trad jazz
Skiffle
Pirate radio stations
Teddy boy
Reeperbahn

Cavern club
Abbey Road Studios
Beatlemania
Our World

Altamont Speedway Free
   Festival
Mods
Mersey Beat

KEY FIGURES

The Beatles
Brian Epstein
George Martin
The Rolling Stones
Andrew Loog Oldham

Jimmy Miller
The Who
Meher Baba
Herman's Hermits
The Hollies

The Dave Clark Five
The Kinks
The Yardbirds
The Animals

KEY ALBUMS

Revolver—the Beatles
*Sgt. Pepper's Lonely Hearts
   Club Band*—the Beatles
The Beatles—the Beatles
Abbey Road—the Beatles

Aftermath—the Rolling
   Stones
Beggar's Banquet—the
   Rolling Stones
Sticky Fingers—the
   Rolling Stones

Tommy—the Who
Who's Next—the Who

THE BRITISH POP SCENE IN THE FIFTIES

Post-War England

In early 1964, the Beatles came to America for the first time. Their arrival had been highly anticipated for weeks: bumper stickers reading "The Beatles Are Coming" were popping up; grown men suddenly started wearing mop top wigs; the press was reporting the group's every move. When they finally touched down at New York's Kennedy Airport on February 7, there were approximately 10,000 screaming fans waiting (mostly teenage girls) who would have literally torn the group apart if not for the police officers on duty. By the last week in March, they held the *top five* positions on the *Billboard* pop chart, with seven more records in the Hot 100, while their first two LPs were positioned at #1 and #2 on the album chart. But the Beatles were just the beginning. Like a dam bursting open, a flood of other English groups soon followed, sweeping American rock stars aside as they took control of radio playlists and record sales. The British Invasion of America had begun in earnest. And the music the Brits were playing? Their own unique brand of good old American rock and roll.

Throughout the years following WWII, English youth had absorbed whatever American music they could get their hands on. One of the first manifestations of this was a fascination with **trad jazz**—traditional New Orleans jazz. Trad jazz bands became popular throughout the country for a while, and a few recordings even became hits in the United States. Somewhere in the mid-1950s, tastes changed to **skiffle**, an English adaptation of traditional American jug band music. The most popular English skiffle musician was Lonnie Donegan, whose

KEY TERMS

Trad jazz   Traditional New Orleans jazz, sometimes called Dixieland.

Skiffle   A do-it-yourself music played by small groups, using guitars, washboards, empty jugs, etc.

"Rock Island Line" also became an American hit in 1956. Skiffle was easy to play, and the fad encouraged many British youth to start playing music, including Liverpudlians John Lennon and George Harrison. Once the skiffle fad wore out, British music fans turned to other indigenous American music styles, most notably the blues and R&B. By the late 1950s there was an entire generation of young people who were turning on to Muddy Waters, Chuck Berry, Little Richard, Bill Haley, and Elvis Presley. Many were learning to play the songs they heard on the American records—and some were forming their own bands.

English Pop Culture

The English popular music culture in the 1950s and early 1960s was very different than in America. There were only three radio stations to choose from, all of which were run by the government-sponsored British Broadcasting Corporation (BBC). The closest any of these came to programming pop was the BBC Light, which played light opera, musical comedy, and light orchestral music for dancing—but it was hardly the kind of station where one might hear American R&B. There were only four major record labels, the largest of which were EMI and Decca. There were few independent labels willing to take risks on wannabe pop stars like there were in America, and American records heavily dominated the English pop charts. With few opportunities to break into the national music scene, up until the early 1960s most rock and roll bands in the UK were pale imitations of their American counterparts. However, the Beatles proved that Brits *could* rock, and after their 1964 landing on American soil, they and other bands from across the pond began to have a dramatic impact on the American music industry. The chart below is indicative:

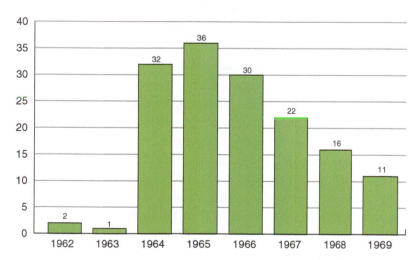

Top Ten Hits in America by British Artists, 1962–69

Of course, the British Invasion started with the Beatles, and our story begins with them.

PIRATE RADIO STATIONS

Early 1960s British rock and roll fans could still get a fix of their music even though the BBC wouldn't program it. Many turned to Radio Luxembourg, the "Fabulous 208" (named for its frequency at 208 on the British dial), which had been catering to a youth audience since the late 1950s. The 208 featured American style DJs and even had Alan Freed—on tape. In the early 1960s, illegal stations began broadcasting from ships offshore the British coast—the so-called pirate radio stations—that were largely funded by American record companies. These stations—which included Radio Caroline (named for John F. Kennedy's daughter), Radio London, Radio Veronica, and Radio Nord—enjoyed tremendous ratings until 1967, when the British government shut them down. The BBC finally relented to the demands of the youth market when their own pop station, Radio One went on the air on September 30, 1967.

THE BEATLES

It has now been more than 50 years since much of the world was introduced to the Beatles, and they are still very much with us. Yes, they had a dramatic effect on the way music was composed, performed, and consumed, but they also impacted us on a much broader social level. Although they wrote music that became very popular, it was also meaningful. It spoke of making the world a better place; it challenged us to become better people; it made social commentary but provided hope; it was about the essence of what it is to be human. Of course, part of the Beatles early success can be attributed to incredibly good timing. When they first set foot in New York on February 7, 1964, the nation had been mourning the murder of President John F. Kennedy for exactly 11 weeks. It seemed that at the very moment Americans were ready to begin mending their collective hearts, the Beatles arrived with their funny haircuts, their carefree attitude and their uplifting music. Let the healing begin!

The Beatles—John Lennon (1940–1980), Paul McCartney (1942–), George Harrison (1943–2001), and Ringo Starr (1940–)—were THE cultural phenomenon of the 1960s. They were smart, funny, irreverent, idealistic, and eclectic, and the baby boom generation ate them up. In many ways, everything about the 1960s can be looked at from a Beatles perspective. At the start of the decade as they emerged with their infectious pop tunes, there was optimism, a feeling of hope of how we were going to make the world a better place. In the middle 1960s, life became more complicated: there were drugs and a sexual revolution, there was a counterculture and an older, conservative generation locked in ideological warfare. The Beatles music in turn became more complicated, asking questions that made us search for answers. When the 1960s came to a crashing halt, the Beatles broke up. With the country in turmoil in the wake of political assassinations, a controversial war and troubling civil rights issues, we had to face the future without them.

THE BEATLES
- John Lennon
- Paul McCartney
- George Harrison
- Ringo Starr

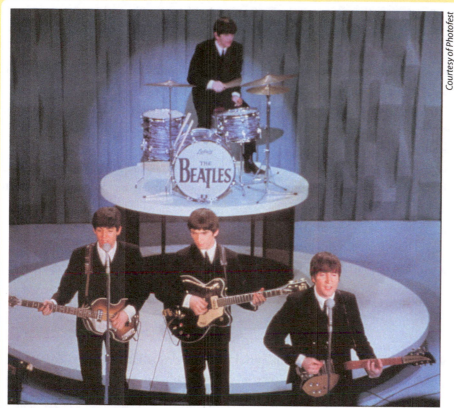

Courtesy of Photofest

The Beatles on *The Ed Sullivan Show,* February 9, 1964. Front row, from left: Paul McCartney, George Harrison, John Lennon. Back row: Ringo Starr.

But today, it is the music that matters most. One of the most astounding things about the Beatles was their constant appetite for growth and change. Their music literally matured in front of our eyes. By the time they broke up, they were writing innovative art that still sounds fresh today. Looking at record sales alone, the numbers are impressive, with fourteen #1 albums and twenty #1 singles. But these numbers are just a starting point in measuring the impact of the greatest rock band in history.

- *Revolver,* 1966
- "Strawberry Fields Forever"/"Penny Lane," 1967
- *Sgt. Pepper's Lonely Hearts Club Band,* 1967
- *The Beatles* (aka *The White Album*), 1968
- *Abbey Road,* 1969

KEY BEATLES RECORDINGS

THE BEATLES IMPACT ON ROCK

1. The Beatles are the most popular rock group in history, with worldwide sales of all albums, singles, music videos, and downloads estimated at 600 million.

2. More than anyone or any group, the Beatles made rock the dominant pop music format that transcended age and demographic. It was no longer music just for teens.

3. The Beatles changed the way music was recorded and presented; they constantly pushed the envelope with their use of studio technology; they pioneered the basic format for contemporary music videos; and they were innovative in their music packaging.

4. The Beatles transcend generation and era; although they are a symbol of the 1960s, their music does not sound out of date today. It is still fresh and meaningful, and still appeals to all ages.

5. They combined exceptional songwriting and performing both live and in the studio as no other artist(s) in the twentieth century.

6. They forced the recognition of pop music as art, and were the forerunners of art rock.

TRIVIA NOTE

At the heart of the Beatles' magic is the coming together of two powerful yet very different musical forces that in friendly competition brought out the best in each other. John Lennon and Paul McCartney could never have achieved the greatness they did on their own. They clicked immediately.

While the Beatles were influential to music and culture of the 1960s, it's clear that from the beginning they absorbed influences from everything and everywhere, including the blues, American R&B, doo-wop, Tin Pan Alley, country, European classical music, and Indian music. It's easy to hear Little Richard in the "oooooo" of "She Loves You," Bob Dylan in the raspy vocals of "You've Got to Hide Your Love Away," Carl Perkins in the jangly guitar of "Run for Your Life" and Brian Wilson in the intricate melody of "Here, There and Everywhere." They absorbed the psychedelic zeitgeist of the San Francisco scene and the larger than life production ethic of Phil Spector. But perhaps the greatest influence on the group came from producer George Martin. It was he who guided the band in their formative early years, offering gentle suggestions without being overbearing or heavy handed. Martin turned them on to the possibilities of new instruments and orchestration, studio effects, and technology. He was smart enough to never say, "You can't do that!" to the curiosity, creativity, and imagination that emerged from the band. The Beatles without the steadying hand of George Martin simply would not have been the Beatles as we know them today.

At the heart of the Beatles' magic is the coming together of two powerful yet very different musical forces that in friendly competition brought out the best in each other. John Lennon and Paul McCartney could never have achieved the greatness they did on their own. They clicked immediately—they were inseparable in the early days, writing songs together, harmonizing together, or letting the other finish a song when they got stuck. But the competitive nature of their friendship was also hard work, and in the end, when it finally burned itself out, the group broke up.

The Early Years

The story of the Beatles begins in Liverpool in the early 1940s as Britain was engaged in World War II. As an important seaport on Britain's northwest shore, the city was a target for German bombers and had suffered mightily during the Battle of Britain in the fall of 1940. The very night John Lennon was born, October 9, 1940, bombs were falling outside the maternity home where he lay with his mother Julia. Sunken ships littered the Mersey River. But the city survived.

Liverpool in the 1950s was an interesting town: despite its working-class ethic and depressed economy, it was a sponge for pop culture from America, especially the rock and roll records brought over by sailors. As the rock and roll culture of American youth flourished, the English counterpart of the cat was born: the Teddy boy. Teddy boys greased their hair up and wore leather jackets, boots and sneers. Although young John Lennon was not yet a Teddy boy in 1956, he was so completely taken with Elvis Presley that he put together his own group called the Quarry Men—named after the Quarry Bank Grammar School he attended. Sometime after Paul McCartney first heard the group play on July 6, 1957, he ended up auditioning for them—and got the job. Lennon and McCartney had one thing in common besides their love for music: both of their mothers had recently died, and their pain clearly had a bonding effect on them. Each would later write love songs to their mums—Lennon's "Julia," and McCartney's "Let It Be." McCartney soon brought along his schoolmate George Harrison to play lead guitar. Even though he was only fourteen years old at the time, George could play solos, while John and Paul could only strum chords. The drummer was Lennon's friend Pete Best, who stayed with the group until 1962.

KEY TERMS

Teddy boys A term describing disaffected English youth in the 1950s and 1960s who greased up their hair and wore leather clothing; comparable to the Southern U.S. "cat."

The Audition

By 1960, the group had changed its name to the Beatles and added Stu Sutcliff on bass (Sutcliff quit the next year to pursue a career in art). Beginning in August, they played the first of a string of engagements over a two-year period in the raunchy clubs in the **Reeperbahn** section of Hamburg, Germany. It was here that the Beatles honed their group sound, as they were often required to play for up to eight hours a night. In early 1961 they first appeared at Liverpool's **Cavern Club**, a dank, underground pub where they performed nearly 300 times over the next two and a half years. By the time they played their last Cavern Club show, they were drawing long lines to see their polished, high-energy shows. The Beatles were becoming a phenomenon, both locally and regionally.

In late 1961, **Brian Epstein**, the manager of the nearby NEMS record store became the Beatles manager and quickly went to work. Over the next few months, the group's Teddy boy image changed to more upscale matching mohair suits with white shirts, thin ties, and mop top haircuts. Although Epstein searched for a record contract for the group, his initial efforts were in vain: the only label that expressed any interest at all was industry giant Decca, who quickly turned them down. Finally, as Epstein was exhausting his options, he

THE CONTRIBUTIONS OF JOHN, PAUL, GEORGE, AND RINGO

1. All four were great musicians; even Ringo, albeit not the greatest drummer of the era, made impressive contributions to the band.

2. The variety of instruments they played was staggering: Paul, the bassist, also played piano, acoustic and electric guitar, and drums; John played guitar, piano, harmonica, and banjo; George played guitar, sitar, tamboura, bass, violin, synthesizer, and organ; and Ringo played drums and all sorts of percussion instruments.

3. They were great singers—John and Paul were simply two of rock's best. The combination of John, Paul, and George singing harmony was powerful and exciting on rockers, gorgeous on ballads.

4. Their compositions cover a diversity of styles that was unprecedented: from hard rockers ("Helter Skelter"); to tender ballads ("She's Leaving Home"); world music ("Within You, Without You"); the avant-garde ("Revolution 9"); children's songs ("Yellow Submarine"); folk ("Blackbird"); and Tin Pan Alley ("When I'm Sixty-Four"). Although Lennon and McCartney often wrote together to one degree or another, each had unique styles. John tended to write songs that were more complicated rhythmically, simpler melodically, and often more avant-garde. Paul was a superior pop craftsman in the Brill Building mold, writing some of the most endearing pop tunes of the last 50 years ("Yesterday" has been covered by more artists than any song in history), while also bringing a classical music influence.

5. The lyrics, among the most meaningful of their generation (along with those of Bob Dylan), reflect the different styles of the two main writers. (One way to identify the authorship of a Beatles song is by identifying the lead singer.) John tended to write songs about himself, asking questions and seeking answers that were both personal, yet could be viewed in the larger communal sense as well. Paul tended to write songs about other people, pointing out the peculiarities of their lives or situations they were in. Of course, there were exceptions to this rule—John's "Good Morning, Good Morning" is written in the fashion of Paul; Paul's very direct and personal "Let It Be" is more typical of John.

6. Often the important contributions of George and Ringo are overlooked. George Harrison was without exaggeration one of the best guitarists in the 1960s, creating some of the most melodic and lyrical solos of the era. He was a master of studio technology, utilizing a huge variety of sounds and effects. By the time the group broke up, he had also turned into a great songwriter—his "Something" is the second most covered Beatles tune. In addition, he turned in several other masterpieces, such as "Here Comes the Sun," "Taxman," and "Within You, Without You." His interest in Indian music and culture inspired the conception of the world music movement. Ringo was the perfect compliment for the other three, never competing for attention, often playing understated but perfect parts. And, he contributed some of the most memorable lead vocals as well ("Yellow Submarine").

managed to get his foot in the door at EMI's small Parlophone subsidiary. His contact was **George Martin**, a classically trained composer and staff producer at EMI who was willing to give the group an audition. On June 6, 1962, the Beatles went into the London office building on Abbey Road where the EMI studio (later referred to as **Abbey Road Studios**) was located and recorded four songs. Martin decided to sign them, although he was admittedly not so much impressed with their music as he was with their personal charm. "It was love at first sight . . . we hit it off straight away . . . the most impressive thing was their engaging personalities."

Beatlemania!

After the Beatles signed with Parlophone, things began to happen very quickly. The band went to work on their first album amid a hectic touring schedule. After the audition, Martin told them they had to replace Best, which they did with their friend Richard Starkey, who went by the name Ringo Starr. Four songs were recorded on various off days, and the other ten were recorded in one ten-hour marathon on February 11, 1963. The resulting album was called *Please, Please Me*. Eight of the songs on the LP were originals, highly unusual at the time for a debut album. At this point, many of the songs were written by John and Paul "eyeball to eyeball"; however, even in the early days, the two were also writing apart from each other, often only getting help from the other for a hook or extra phrase. The Beatles' first single, "Love Me Do" (written by Paul), and their first #1 (UK), "Please, Please Me" (written by John), came from these sessions. Ringo did not play on two of the songs—producer Martin felt that his playing wasn't up to par, so session drummer Andy White was used instead.

The band continued their hectic touring schedule as their popularity soared throughout England. By July 1963, they went back into the studio to start on the second album, *With the Beatles*. It was released on November 22, 1963, (the day that John F. Kennedy was assassinated) and immediately went to #1 (UK) where it stayed for 21 weeks. The album is a mix of originals (including "All My Loving" and "I Wanna Be Your Man") and covers (such as "Roll Over Beethoven" and "You Really Got a Hold on Me"). By this time fans all over England were constantly mobbing the group whenever they appeared in public. After a performance at London's Palladium in October, the *Daily Mirror* coined the term "Beatlemania!" in a headline, and it stuck.

Coming to America

Initially, Beatlemania went largely unnoticed in America (due in large part to the preoccupation with the Kennedy assassination), but it hit with sudden and tremendous impact. The group's first appearances on *The Ed Sullivan Show* on February 9th, 16th, and 23rd were viewed by approximately 73 million people each, the largest audiences in the 23 year history of the program. EMI's American subsidiary, Capitol Records had been slow to release any Beatles singles, but when "I Want to Hold Your Hand" was finally released in January 1964, it shot straight to #1 where it stayed for seven weeks. By the end of March, the Beatles held the top five records in America: #1: "Can't Buy Me Love," #2: "Twist and Shout," #3: "She Loves You," #4: "I Want to Hold Your Hand," and #5: "Please, Please Me."

July 10, 1964 saw the release of the third album, *A Hard Day's Night*, which stayed at #1 for 21 weeks (only to be knocked off by the group's next album). *A Hard Day's Night* is significant on several accounts. It is the first Beatles album that utilized a four-track tape machine, allowing the group to overdub parts and begin using the studio in more innovative ways. It is also their only album consisting entirely of Lennon and McCartney songs. *A Hard Day's Night* was a tie-in to the pioneering feature film of the same name, whose jocular plot evolves around whether the Fab Four would make it through another madcap day being chased by fans. Directed by Richard Lester, the film is a blueprint for many of the first music videos made in the 1980s. The album itself is a tour de force for Lennon, who wrote most of the songs, including the title track (inspired by one of Ringo's favorite catch phrases), the lovely "If I Fell," and "I Should Have Known Better." McCartney's contributions, while fewer in number, were still noteworthy, including "Can't Buy Me Love" (a beautifully disguised 12-bar blues) and the tender "And I Love Her."

The fourth album, *Beatles for Sale,* released on December 4, 1964, was the first Beatles LP to receive luke-warm critical acclaim. In many ways it is a reflection of the rigors of Beatlemania—constant touring, constant screaming mobs, no privacy—which made writing difficult. As George Martin put it, the band was "war weary." However, there were still some gems: "Eight Days a Week," a collaborative effort from John and Paul actually fades *in,* one of the first examples of the group trying out new ideas in the studio. John's "I'm a Loser" philosophically questions the high price of fame. The album was filled out with several covers, including Chuck Berry's "Rock and Roll Music," Leiber and Stoller's "Kansas City" and two Carl Perkins's tunes, "Everybody's Tryin' to Be My Baby" and "Honey Don't."

Meeting Dylan

The first album to signal the experimental future of the Beatles recordings was *Help!,* released on August 6, 1965. Part of the evolution was the result of the famous meeting with Bob Dylan in the summer of 1964 at New York's Hotel Delmonico. Dylan and the Beatles reportedly spent several hours hanging out and smoking marijuana. The meeting was an epochal moment in rock, as Dylan's influence was immense and immediate, revitalizing the group at the very moment that they were ready to evolve both musically and lyrically (as mentioned in Chapter 5, the Beatles also had a profound influence on Dylan). From this point on, the lyrics of McCartney and particularly Lennon and Harrison began to take on increasing social, political, and cultural significance. The group also began to expand into more musically diverse styles, evidenced on *Help!* by the use of outside session musicians for the first time (a flautist at the end of "You've Got to Hide Your Love Away" and strings on "Yesterday"). Lyrically and musically from this moment on the Beatles would begin to change rock into an art form.

Help! was the first album in history to have an advance order of over one million copies. It was also a tie in to the group's second movie, once again directed by Richard Lester. The title song, composed by John, was written as an expression of his self-loathing "Fat Elvis" period: tiring of the trappings of wealth and fame, he was drinking and eating too much, bored with his marriage and with living in the suburbs. Dylan's influence is overpowering on Lennon's

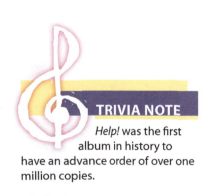

TRIVIA NOTE

Help! was the first album in history to have an advance order of over one million copies.

"You've Got to Hide Your Love Away." Tucked away near the end of Side B is McCartney's masterpiece "Yesterday," uniquely set to only acoustic guitar and string quartet accompaniment (arranged by Martin). It became the most performed pop song in the world for the next several years.

Coming of Age

Rubber Soul is often considered the Beatles' "coming of age" album. Released on December 3, 1965, it is comprised of fourteen original songs written over a four-week period. With a number of songs tackling social issues, *Rubber Soul* shows more lyrical depth and intelligence than any previous release. Musically and instrumentally the album is a harbinger of things to come, as the Beatles introduce a variety of new instruments, including sitar on Lennon's "Norwegian Wood" and fuzz bass on Harrison's "Think for Yourself." There is also a baroque piano solo played by George Martin on John's autobiographical "In My Life" recorded at half speed to make it sound like a harpsichord when played back at normal speed.

On August 5, 1966, the Beatles released ***Revolver***, an album that many call their finest work. It is also considered to be the first album of the psychedelic era because of its use of exotic instruments, studio effects, and several drug allusions. Where *Rubber Soul* headed, *Revolver* continued on to the next level. There are no "fillers" on the album, as every song has merit, most are brilliant. George Harrison contributed three strong tracks: "Taxman," a social commentary about the high taxes in Britain for the wealthy; "Love You To," written specifically for sitar and tablas (recorded using only himself and Indian musicians), possibly the first piece of the coming "world music" movement; and "I Want to Tell You." Lennon contributed six, including three with drug references ("She

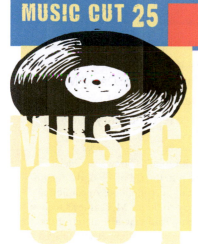

MUSIC CUT 25

"TOMORROW NEVER KNOWS" (JOHN LENNON/PAUL MCCARTNEY)— THE BEATLES *(NOTE: THIS CUT IS NOT ON RHAPSODY)*

Personnel: John Lennon: organ, tambourine, tape loops, lead vocals; Paul McCartney: bass, drums, tape loops, guitar; George Harrison: guitar, sitar, tape loops; Ringo Starr: drums, tape loops; George Martin: piano, tape loops. Recorded April 6, 1966 at Abbey Road Studios, London; produced by George Martin. Released August 5, 1966 on the Parlophone LP Revolver; not released as a single.

As the first song recorded for *Revolver*, "Tomorrow Never Knows" set the tone for the album and for the psychedelic era. The foundation for the song, a one-chord drone, was made by creating a tape loop of John and Ringo playing a simple riff that engineer Geoff Emerick configured to play continuously. On to this was added such otherworldly effects as a sitar drone, cut up tape loops of Paul laughing (which sound like science fiction seagulls) and a backwards guitar solo. One of the more interesting effects came as a result of John's request to, "Make me sound like the Dalai Lama chanting from the mountaintop." Emerick, in his first of many sessions as engineer for the group, responded by running John's voice (in the verse after the guitar solo) through the rotating speakers of a Leslie tone cabinet, which is normally used for a Hammond organ.

Said She Said," "Dr. Robert," and "Tomorrow Never Knows"). "Tomorrow Never Knows" was inspired by Timothy Leary's *The Psychedelic Experience,* a guide to spiritual enlightenment through the use of LSD based on *The Tibetan Book of the Dead.* McCartney's contributions were more of his usual well-crafted pop gems, including the haunting "Eleanor Rigby," the tender "Here, There, and Everywhere" inspired by Brian Wilson's "God Only Knows," and the sing-along children's song "Yellow Submarine."

Sgt. Pepper's

After the release of *Revolver,* the Beatles announced their decision to discontinue touring. Although they had toured worldwide since 1963 with spectacular success, live concerts were plagued by poor sound reinforcement and screaming mobs; now their music was getting too dependent on studio technology to be reproduced adequately in a live setting. Their last concert was at Candlestick Park in San Francisco on August 30, 1966. The announcement fueled rumors that the Beatles were about to break up, which the lack of their expected year-end album release only intensified. To silence critics, on February 17, 1967, the band released "Penny Lane" and "Strawberry Fields Forever" as two A sides on one single. Both songs are remembrances of real places in Liverpool from McCartney and Lennon's childhoods.

"Penny Lane" and "Strawberry Fields Forever" were originally supposed to be included on the group's next album, the highly anticipated *Sgt. Pepper's Lonely Hearts Club Band,* released on June 1, 1967. Restless fans and critics were overjoyed, and for several months in the summer of 1967, it captivated

MUSIC CUT 26

"PENNY LANE" (JOHN LENNON/PAUL MCCARTNEY)— THE BEATLES *(NOTE: THIS CUT IS NOT ON RHAPSODY)*

Personnel: John Lennon: guitar, piano, congas, backup vocals; Paul McCartney: bass, piano, lead vocal, recorder; George Harrison: lead guitar, fire bell, backup vocals; Ringo Starr: drums, percussion; George Martin: piano; David Mason: piccolo trumpet. Recorded December 1966–January 1967 at Abbey Road Studios, London; produced by George Martin. Released February 1967 on Capitol; 10 weeks on the charts, peaking at #1.

Released as one of the two A sides on the same single (along with John's "Strawberry Fields Forever"), "Penny Lane" is pure McCartney pop magic. Written in the fall of 1966, the song is about a bus roundabout in Liverpool that Paul used to frequent in his childhood. According to engineer Geoff Emerick, each instrument was recorded separately to honor McCartney's request to produce a "really clean American sound," in hopes of matching Paul's favorite album at the time, the Beach Boys *Pet Sounds.* The highlight of the song is the piccolo trumpet solo, played by David Mason, principal trumpet player in the Royal Philharmonic Orchestra. Paul fell in love with the instrument after seeing Mason—a friend of producer George Martin's—play it on a television broadcast of Bach's *Brandenburg Concerto* that aired during the songs production. The single with "Penny Lane" and "Strawberry Fields Forever" set a record for Capitol with advance sales orders of over a million copies, an indication of the pent-up demand for new Beatles records in the months leading up to the release of *Sgt. Pepper's Lonely Hearts Club Band.*

the world of popular culture. The album took five months and 700 hours to record and cost an unheard of $100,000. Stemming from Paul's idea to fabricate an alter ego band where each Beatle could assume the role of another musician, the album was originally intended to give the experience of having attended a royal performance, with each song segueing into the next. In the end, only the first two songs were done this way, but with an overture to open Side A, a reprise of the overture and an encore to close out Side B, the effect is nearly the same. *Sgt. Pepper's* also contains what is arguably the most famous music album cover in history, showing celebrities and famous people gathered around the Beatles in costume. It is the first album to print song lyrics on the inside cover. *Sgt. Pepper's* is also noteworthy for the stunning use of studio technology, used with great skill and effect throughout. The album's encore, the Lennon/McCartney collaboration "A Day in the Life" is a chilling commentary on bureaucracy, materialism, the specter of nuclear annihilation, and is perhaps their finest work.

All You Need Is Love

After the release of *Sgt. Pepper's,* the Beatles took part in the first worldwide satellite TV broadcast on the program *Our World*, performing Lennon's "All You Need Is Love" live to 350 million viewers. Then, in August, the band suffered a major setback when manager Brian Epstein died from an accidental drug overdose. From this point on the Beatles would try to manage themselves, one of the first of many bad business decisions that ultimately contributed to the group's downfall. In February 1968, the band, along with actress Mia Farrow and her sister Prudence, the singer Donovan, Mick Jagger, the Beach Boys' Mike Love, and assorted girlfriends all went to the ashram of guru Maharishi Yogi in Rishikesh, India, to learn about Transcendental Meditation. Within just a few weeks the group ascertained that the Maharishi was a charlatan, and one by one returned home to England. Lennon later wrote the vindictive "Sexy Sadie" about the experience, which appeared on the upcoming *The White Album*.

Magical Mystery Tour, a six-song double EP (an "extended play" 45-rpm) was released on December 8, 1967, accompanying the film of the same name. The movie and artwork of the EP was inspired by the cross-country journey of Ken Kesey and his Merry Pranksters in their psychedelic bus, *Further* (see Chapter 7). Although the EP was panned by the critics as too self-indulgent, sloppy, and not very good, it did contain John's brilliantly bizarre and surrealistic "I Am the Walrus," whose two-note melody was inspired by the sound of an English police siren. In the months following the release of *Magical Mystery Tour,* the Beatles released two singles written by Paul, "Lady Madonna" and "Hey Jude," the latter ultimately becoming their best-selling single with sales of nearly ten million copies.

Impending Doom

By the time *The Beatles* (aka *The White Album*) was released on November 22, 1968, the inner tensions that would eventually break the band apart were surfacing. Lennon and McCartney were losing control of their song publishing rights, and Apple, their new but poorly managed production company was losing money. John's new lover Yoko Ono was a constant presence, and an often-unwelcome one at that (she would often submit criticisms at recording sessions, and at one point when she was ill, John even rolled a bed into the studio for her). Other signs of impending dissolution were becoming apparent: George began recording a solo album, Ringo quit for a few days when he discovered that Paul was re-recording the drum parts himself after Ringo left the studio. Nonetheless, *The White Album* is a remarkable double album with thirty songs that cover a wide range of styles. Many of the songs were recorded without the full group in attendance, giving the effect of John, Paul, and George essentially taking turns doing solo pieces with backing musicians. Some of the group's best material can be found on *The White Album,* including John's "Happiness is a Warm Gun," "Julia," and the avant-garde "Revolution 9"; Paul's "Blackbird," "I Will," and "Ob-la-di, Ob-la-da"; and George's "While My Guitar Gently Weeps" (featuring his friend Eric Clapton on guitar) and "Piggies."

The year 1969 saw the release of *Yellow Submarine,* which is often called the worst Beatles album, a manifestation of the ever-worsening band morale. Only six songs are on the album, two of which had already been released. Side B of the album contains orchestral scorings by George Martin from the accompanying movie.

The End

The next album recorded was not immediately released. *Let It Be* was originally planned as a no overdubs, back-to-live concept to be called *Get Back.* To get a truly live recording, the Beatles staged a surprise noontime concert on the rooftop of Apple's Savile Row offices on January 30, 1969, and performed five songs (including Paul's "Get Back") before the police shut them off because of neighbors' complaints. The concert was filmed, as were most of the sessions, and were included in the accompanying documentary of the same name. However, with tempers flaring over Paul's overbearing control and the worsening management situation, the task of finishing the project was just too much for the band. George Martin quit; George Harrison walked out for a few days. By the time the recording was done, no one wanted to stick around to mix it, so the job was left to a session engineer. The resulting mixes were sloppy with too many mistakes, so Phil Spector was brought in to re-produce the entire album. Spector added lush string orchestration to some of the songs, including Paul's "The Long and Winding Road," which angered McCartney. In the end *Let It Be* was unsatisfying to everyone involved and not released until May 8, 1970, after the Beatles had broken up.

The last album recorded by the Beatles was *Abbey Road* (released September 26, 1969) and it is perhaps their finest work. George Martin was persuaded to return as producer, and by this time the studio had installed a new eight-track recorder for the band to use for the first time. Synthesizers were also used for the first time on several of the songs. Once again, George Harrison contributed two very fine songs, "Something" and "Here Comes the Sun." Lennon's contributions include "Come Together," based loosely on Chuck Berry's "You Can't Catch Me" and "Because," inspired by hearing Yoko play Beethoven's

TRIVIA NOTE

The last album recorded by the Beatles was *Abbey Road* (released September 26, 1969) and it is perhaps their finest work.

"Moonlight Sonata" backwards. The centerpiece and masterstroke of *Abbey Road* is the 16-minute, eight-song medley that closes Side B. The songs, written mostly by Paul, seamlessly segue together and cover a variety of styles, from the serenely beautiful "Sun King," the polka-like "Mean Mr. Mustard," the tongue-in-cheek "Polythene Pam" and ending up with the rocking "The End." The last song features a jam session where Lennon, McCartney, and Harrison trade two-bar guitar solos before closing with the words, "And in the end, the love you take/Is equal to the love you make." A fitting finale to leave their millions of fans.

The Beatles breakup was messy. Although Paul had lobbied the others on the idea of a return to performing live at small clubs without public announcement, John had had enough. In September he announced to the rest of the band that he "wanted a divorce," but was persuaded by McCartney to remain silent to keep from jeopardizing pending business dealings. In the ensuing months, McCartney went to work on his solo album debut, and ultimately came to the conclusion that he too wanted out. When *McCartney* was released on April 10, 1970, its liner notes included a faux self-interview in which Paul implied that the Beatles were done. Lennon, who had kept his desire to quit a secret out of respect for Paul, felt betrayed. Business entanglements, lawsuits, and Lennon's anger would continue on for years, but one thing was clear: the Beatles would never record or perform together again.

The Aftermath

After the breakup of the band, solo albums were forthcoming from Lennon and McCartney. Now that they were no longer chained together, each was free to pursue his natural musical instincts. McCartney continued to write well-crafted pop tunes, but without Lennon's gravity they became lightweight and sugary sweet. In 1972 he formed Wings with wife Linda Eastman, whom he married in 1969. Nine #1 hits followed, including duets with Stevie Wonder and Michael Jackson. In 1971, George Harrison organized the first ever all-star concert to raise money for a cause, the Concert for Bangladesh, which raised over $10 million for the people of that country. In 1988 he formed the Traveling Wilburys with friends Bob Dylan, Tom Petty, Jeff Lynne, and Roy Orbison. Harrison died of cancer on November 29, 2001. Ringo, after having two #1 hits in 1973 went on to a career in TV and movie acting.

John Lennon had a turbulent and brief post-Beatles life. In the early 1970s, his festering anger over what he perceived was McCartney's double-crossing sent him into primal scream therapy, which was reflected in his dark and disturbing 1970 album *Plastic Ono Band*. In 1971 he released *Imagine,* which contained the poignant title track as well as "How Do You Sleep," a scathing attack on McCartney. By the late 1970s, as he and Yoko settled down at their Dakota apartment in New York to raise their family, Lennon was gradually becoming more at peace with the world. Just as hopes of a long awaited Beatles reunion were rising, Lennon was murdered outside the Dakota by crazed fan Mark David Chapman on December 8, 1980.

THE ROLLING STONES

Image

In the 1960s, the Rolling Stones began calling themselves "The World's Greatest Rock and Roll Band," and by many standards they were. But because their rise to fame so closely followed that of the Beatles, to many they were the world's *second* greatest band. The Stones were forced early on to portray themselves as dangerous and surly, creating a sort of "anti-Beatles" image as a way to find a niche for themselves in the midst of Beatlemania. The ploy worked. There are two ironies to the public images of the Stones and the Beatles: the first is that despite a general perception of the Beatles as middle class and lovable versus the low-class and dangerous Stones, the Stones came from a generally higher class upbringing than the Beatles. The second is that the Stones have been much more influential and widely imitated in this regard than the Beatles. The marketing of rock musicians as rebellious hoodlums has become an accepted part of the rock canon.

The Rolling Stones were the quintessential kick ass rock band throughout much of the 1960s and 1970s. Unlike most British bands of the era that cut their teeth playing American-influenced blues and R&B and then moved on to their own brand of pop, the Stones only occasionally strayed far from their roots, and always returned (their worst digression was a brief flirtation with disco in the late 1970s). Their on-stage image, in the persona of Mick Jagger, was the most boldly sexual and threatening of their time. Off stage, the scandals and bad behavior of their personal lives only served to intensify their reputations as scoundrels. During their most creative period from 1965 to 1972, the Rolling Stones created some of rocks most memorable anthems and produced five albums that are among the most memorable of the era.

The Early Years

Mick Jagger (1943–) and Keith Richards (1943–) both grew up in London and briefly went to the Dartford Wentworth Primary School together. Around 1950, Richards moved to a housing project on the other side of town and the two did not see each other again until a chance meeting on a commuter train in 1961. The two fledgling guitarists began jamming together after discovering their common love for American rhythm and blues. Brian Jones (1942–1969), also an aspiring blues guitarist, had grown up in the exclusive resort city of Cheltenham before joining Alex Korner's influential Blues Incorporated. Jones became acquainted with Jagger and Richards through London's blues bar scene,

KEY ROLLING STONES RECORDINGS

- "(I Can't Get No) Satisfaction," 1965
- *Aftermath*, 1966
- *Beggars Banquet*, 1968
- "Sympathy for the Devil," 1969
- *Sticky Fingers*, 1971

and by mid-1962 the three musicians, along with Dick Taylor on bass and Mick Avory on drums played their first gig as the Rolling Stones at the Marquee Club (taking their name from the Muddy Waters tune). By January 1963 Taylor and Avory had been replaced by Bill Wyman (1936–) on bass and Charlie Watts (1941–) on drums, and the Stones personnel for the next six years was set.

Sometime in the spring of 1963 public relations man **Andrew Loog Oldham** (a former employee of Brian Epstein) heard the Stones at the Crawdaddy Club, where they had established a residency. After taking on the group as clients, Oldham realized that "In just a few months the country would need an opposite of what the Beatles were doing," and went about packaging the group as such. On the advice of George Harrison (by this time the two bands had become acquainted), Decca Records signed the group, and in May 1963 they released their first single, a cover of Chuck Berry's "Come On," which went to #21 in the UK. Their second single, the Lennon and McCartney tune "I Wanna Be Your Man" was released in October and hit the British Top 15. Other early recordings included covers from their American role models: Willie Dixon's "I Just Want to Make Love to You," "Little Red Rooster," and "I Want to Be Loved," Holland/Dozier/Holland's "Can I Get a Witness" and Buddy Holly's "Not Fade Away," which went to #3.

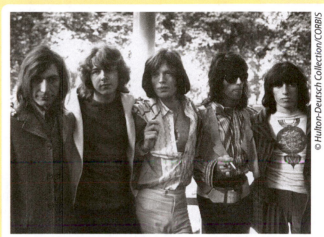

The Rolling Stones, 1964. From left: Mick Jagger, Bill Wyman, Brian Jones, Keith Richards, Charlie Watts.

© Hulton-Deutsch Collection/CORBIS

Breaking Through

Starting in late 1963, the Stones embarked on an arduous three-year touring schedule. On their first tour, they warmed up for the Everly Brothers, Bo Diddley, and Little Richard; in early 1964 they headlined their own tour of the UK. Crowds at their concerts were decidedly more aggressive than Beatles audiences, and often times the band could only perform four or five songs before violence erupted. At a concert in Dublin, fans rushed on stage and tackled Jagger while Wyman was crushed against a piano. One report said "three boys were throwing punches at Brian while two others were trying to kiss him." When the Stones went on their first American tour in June 1964, they had moderate success in the larger cities while being virtually ignored in the Midwest. The tour ended on a high note when Oldham booked a recording

- Mick Jagger
- Keith Richards
- Brian Jones
- Bill Wyman
- Charlie Watts

THE ROLLING STONES

session at Chicago's Chess Studio that was attended by idols Muddy Waters, Willie Dixon, and Chuck Berry. From that session came their first #1 hit in the UK, a cover of Bobby Womack's "It's All Over Now." Of their Chicago concert, *Vogue Magazine* wrote: "The Stones have a perverse, unsettling sex appeal with Jagger out front of his team-mates. . . . To women, he's fascinating, to men a scare."

By the end of 1964, the Stones were finally beginning to break through in the United States. They released their first LP, *England's Newest Hit Makers/ The Rolling Stones,* and by the end of 1965 they had four hits break into the Top 10. Jagger and Richards by this time were composing their own material (initially under the pseudonym Nanker Phelge), with Richards typically writing the music and Jagger the lyrics. After two Top 10 hits in late 1964 and early 1965 ("Time Is On My Side" and "The Last Time"), in June the Stones finally hit #1 in the States with "(I Can't Get No) Satisfaction," which stayed at the top for four weeks. Richards reportedly conceived the song's memorable guitar riff in the middle of the night in a motel room in Florida. Four months later "Get Off My Cloud" knocked the Beatles "Yesterday" off the #1 spot. Five more Top 10s in 1966 signaled that the Stones had finally conquered America.

Rock and Roll's Bad Boys

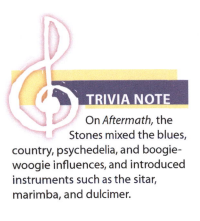

TRIVIA NOTE

On *Aftermath,* the Stones mixed the blues, country, psychedelia, and boogie-woogie influences, and introduced instruments such as the sitar, marimba, and dulcimer.

In mid-1966 the Stones released the pivotal *Aftermath*, their first album consisting entirely of Jagger/Richards's compositions. Influenced by the Beatles' musical experimentations, the Stones mixed the blues, country, psychedelia, and boogie-woogie influences, and introduced instruments such as the sitar, marimba, and dulcimer. The overall tone, set by the Indian raga-esque opening track "Paint It Black" (#1) is dark and sneering, helping to cement the Stones' reputation as rock and roll's bad boys. Two songs, "Stupid Girl" and "Under My Thumb," contain misogynistic lyrics, with the latter being particularly nasty. The final song, the 11-minute "Going Home" includes a hypnotic, extended vocal improvisation by Jagger.

Meanwhile, the Stones were living up to their rowdy image on and off stage. In January 1967 they appeared on *The Ed Sullivan Show* with the intention of performing their risqué (for the time) "Let's Spend the Night Together." While CBS censors protested, the group played the song anyway, but Jagger mumbled the words "some time" instead of "the night" as he rolled his eyes for the camera. Then, on February 12 both Richards and Jagger were arrested after police raided a party at Richards's home—Richards for allowing drugs on his property, Jagger for possession of amphetamines. On the same day that the two appeared at the court hearing, Brian Jones was arrested at his London flat for possession of cocaine, Methedrine, and marijuana. Although Jagger and Richards were convicted and sentenced to serve jail time, their convictions were overturned. Jones, however, continued to be harassed by police, and was later arrested again. Because of his eventual conviction, touring abroad became impossible, and as a result, the Stones would not perform in the US again until late 1969.

From their earliest years, Brian Jones had been the most flamboyant member and the de facto leader of the group. However, Jagger's athletic and sexually suggestive onstage antics and Richards's high-energy guitar playing had shifted

MUSIC CUT 27

"SYMPATHY FOR THE DEVIL" (MICK JAGGER/KEITH RICHARDS)— THE ROLLING STONES

Personnel: Mick Jagger: vocals; Keith Richards: guitar, vocals; Bill Wyman: bass, maracas, vocals; Brian Jones: guitar; Nicky Hopkins: piano; Rocky Dijon: congas; Charlie Watts: drums. Recorded June 1968 at Olympic Studios, London; produced by Jimmy Miller. Released December 6, 1968 on the ABKCO LP *Beggar's Banquet;* not released as a single.

Recorded in the heady days of 1968 when the Rolling Stones were just beginning to reach their creative peak, "Sympathy for the Devil" is one of the most enduring rock anthems of the decade. Mick Jagger's lyrics were inspired by Russian author Mikhail Bulgakov's novel *The Master and Margarita,* in which the Devil appears disguised as a mysterious gentleman in 1930s Moscow. Jagger poignantly updates the premise of the Devil lurking inside humankind with his line, "I shouted out 'Who killed the Kennedys?' when after all it was you and me." Keith Richards' music, quite unusual for both the Stones and for the era, is set to a samba beat with the most prominent instruments throughout much of the song being maracas, congas and piano. Richards' guitar does not make an appearance until the song is nearly half over. The song is one of the first recorded with new producer Jimmy Miller.

the public focus of the group away from him. Jagger and Richards were also taking artistic control of the Stones with their songwriting, further relegating Jones to the sidelines. As Brian Jones sensed he was being reduced to the role of a second-class citizen within the band (to add insult to injury, his girlfriend Anita Pallenberg left him for Richards), his paranoia increased, as did his drug use. He finally left the group in June 1969, ostensibly to clean himself up, but less than one month later, he was found dead in his swimming pool. The official coroner report cited the cause as "death by misadventure." Two days later, on July 5 the Stones performed at Hyde Park in London before 250,000 fans who heard Jagger open the show by reading from Percy Shelley's *Adonais:* "Peace, peace! He is not dead, he doth not sleep." Brian Jones was replaced by guitarist Mick Taylor.

Creative Triumph, Tragedy

Despite the inner turmoil, the Rolling Stones in 1968 were entering their most creative period. Following the critically panned release of the psychedelic *Their Satanic Majesties Request* (which the group seemingly patterned after *Sgt. Pepper's,* even down to the cover), the Stones hired producer **Jimmy Miller**. Miller gave the Stones a tighter, more focused sound, and ironed out the rough spots that had sometimes plagued earlier recordings. By making Richards's guitar more prominent and highlighting percussion instruments, the Stones sounded tougher and meaner than ever before. The first Miller production was the classic "Jumpin' Jack Flash" (#3), released in May 1968. Next up was *Beggars Banquet,* released in December, which contained two of the Stones' most memorable anthems, "Sympathy for the Devil" and "Street Fighting Man." Both songs made powerful musical and lyrical statements: "Sympathy" was a commentary on the dark side of society's soul, while "Street" became an anthem for student protests. In May 1969, the Stones released yet another rock classic, "Honky

Tonk Women," which became their fifth #1 single. Critics and fans warmly greeted the November 1969 release of *Let It Bleed,* which contained two more masterpieces, "Gimme Shelter" and "You Can't Always Get What You Want." Some viewed *Let It Bleed* as a satirical take on the Beatles' soon-to-be-released *Let It Be,* and "You Can't Always Get What You Want" as a response to "Hey Jude." Whether they were or not is arguable, but it was more proof that at least for some the Stones seemed destined to live in the shadow of the Beatles.

As the Stones wound up their first American tour in five years at the end of 1969, plans were made to stage a free "thank you America" concert in the San Francisco Bay Area. After several possible locations were turned down, the site was set at the last minute for the Altamont Speedway just south of San Francisco. Hastily prepared, the **Altamont Speedway Free Festival** held on December 6, 1969 was mismanaged from the start. Hell's Angels were hired to provide security (and paid in *beer*); the stage was inadequate, as were the rest room facilities. Throughout the early performances by Santana, Jefferson Airplane, Crosby Stills Nash and Young, and others, the Angels applied brute force to keep things under control. By the time the Stones took the stage, the overflow crowd was getting unruly and the situation was rapidly becoming dangerous. Then, with cameras rolling (for the documentary film *Gimme Shelter*) and the band playing "Under My Thumb," the Hell's Angels violently stabbed to death audience member Meredith Hunter directly in front of the stage. With order breaking down and fearful for their lives, the Stones fled the scene in a helicopter. Coming as it did at the very end of the decade, Altamont became a metaphor of sorts for the end of the peace and love 1960s.

Although Altamont dealt the Stones another serious public relations setback, it had surprisingly little effect on the intensely creative streak they were undergoing. In April 1971, they released **Sticky Fingers**, recorded in part in Muscle Shoals, Alabama. Critics hailed it as one of their best albums. The album contained the #1 hit "Brown Sugar," which became the latest of the Stones' songs to draw criticism as being demeaning toward women. However, what drew perhaps the most attention to the album was the cover, designed by Andy Warhol, which contained a real zipper within a photo of a man's jeans. The album also introduced for the first time the famous tongue and lips logo on the inner sleeve. In May 1972, the fourth Jimmy Miller produced album *Exile on Main Street* was released to mixed reviews. A double album, *Exile* is swampy, bluesy, and captures the essence of the Mississippi Delta, mixing elements of rock and roll, soul, and country. Over time, many have come to view *Exile on Main Street* as the Stones' best ever.

The Later Years

Since the early 1970s, the Stones have continued to tour and record. Since *Exile on Main Street,* their albums have hit the Top 40 18 more times, eight of which went to the Top 10. Six of their post-*Exile* albums have hit #1, although none since 1981. Their personnel has stayed remarkably consistent over the years, with the exceptions of Mick Taylor leaving in 1975, replaced by Ron Wood (formerly of the Faces), and mainstay Bill Wyman leaving in 1994 after more than 30 years, replaced by bassist Darryl Jones. In the last few years they have stayed naughty, although no longer dangerous, and have become more venerable institution than creative force. But the Stones have persevered. Their 2005/2006 tour included performances at Boston's Fenway Park, Super Bowl XXX, and a free concert on February 18, 2006, at Copacabana Beach in Rio de Janeiro, Brazil, before an estimated crowd of 1,200,000.

THE WHO

The Early Years

Although never as commercially successful as the Beatles or the Rolling Stones, the Who were unquestionably one of rock's most innovative and influential bands. Not only were they the prototype of the "power trio" format, they were inspirational to several later rock genres, including punk, heavy metal, and art rock. The Who were the first rock band to incorporate synthesizers into the compositional process rather than just as an added-on effect. They brought stage violence and drama to rock like no other band before them. They also produced a catalogue of highly unique and powerful original music that had social relevance and relied heavily on the exceptional musicianship of the four group members. And, in 1969 they produced the first rock opera *Tommy*, which was universally hailed as a masterpiece and was later made into not only a feature film but also a Broadway musical. The Who did all this despite (or perhaps because of) the friction caused by the constantly clashing personalities within the band.

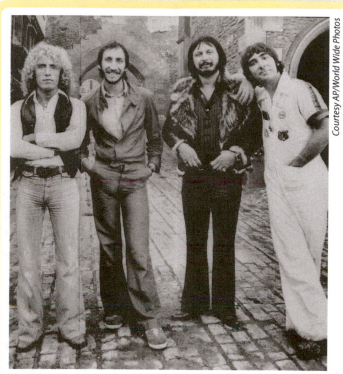

The Who, from left: Roger Daltry, Pete Townshend, John Entwistle, Keith Moon.

Courtesy AP/World Wide Photos

Roger Daltrey (1944–), Pete Townshend (1945–), and John Entwistle (1944–2002) grew up in the west London suburb of Shepherd's Bush and went to school together. All three were drawn to music: Townshend and Entwistle played in a trad jazz band for a while before Entwistle left in 1962 to join the Detours, a rock band that included Daltrey on lead guitar. In 1963, Daltrey switched to lead vocals and Townshend joined as lead guitarist. When Detours' drummer Doug Sandom quit that same year Keith Moon (1947–1978), who had been in the surf band the Beachcombers, replaced him. With a repertoire that consisted primarily of American R&B covers, the Detours developed a popular fan base playing wedding receptions, bar mitzvahs, and birthday parties and even once on the same bill with the Rolling Stones. In early 1964, after discovering that another band already was named the Detours, they changed their name to the Who.

From Mods to Maximum R&B

Around this time public relations man Pete Meaden took over management of the Who and repackaged them with the look of London's **mods**. The mods, a youth cult that burst onto the London scene in early 1964, wore snappy clothes,

THE WHO
- Roger Daltrey
- Pete Townshend
- John Entwistle
- Keith Moon

short hair, rode scooters, and consumed massive amounts of amphetamines that allowed them to dance continuously at all-night raves. Meaden, himself a mod, changed the name of the band to the High Numbers—an obscure mod reference—to identify the band with the scene. However, after the unsuccessful release of "I'm the Face" ("face" being another mod reference), the band split with Meaden and teamed up with Kit Lambert and Chris Stamp, who went about the task of reversing the bands fortunes. The first thing Lambert and Stamp did was to change the name back to the Who. They also introduced a new motto—Maximum R&B—with the now-famous poster that included an arrow emerging from the "o" on Who, forming the medical symbol for the male. It was a perfect assessment of the band's masculine attitude—this was very much a "guys" band—in a pop world that idolized females.

One night in late 1964 while playing at London's Railway tavern, Townshend broke the neck of his guitar when it accidentally hit the club's low ceiling. When he saw some of the audience laughing at him, he picked up his other guitar and resumed playing as if the incident were part of the show. As word of mouth spread about Townshend's act of destruction, the crowds at the Railway grew; before long Moon was joining in, kicking over his drums at the conclusion of each show. The notoriety from these acts of stage violence helped secure a contract with Decca Records and the January release of "I Can't Explain," which featured session guitarist Jimmy Page on rhythm guitar. Then, on January 29, 1965, the Who appeared live on the British TV show *Ready, Steady, Go* (sort of the British equivalent of *American Bandstand*) and once again Townshend and Moon destroyed their equipment. With a national TV audience witnessing the incident, "I Can't Explain" entered the charts three weeks later, eventually reaching #8 and selling over 100,000 copies. The group appeared on *Ready, Steady, Go* a total of ten times in 1965.

In late 1965 the group's first album (*The Who Sings*) *My Generation* was released, featuring nine Townshend originals, one Bo Diddley and two James Brown covers (maximum R&B indeed!). "My Generation," an attack on the establishment and older generation, was an immediate hit, rising to #2 in the UK. With lines like "People try to put us down," "Hope I die before I get old,"

KEY RECORDINGS BY THE WHO
- "My Generation," 1965
- *Tommy,* 1969
- *Live at Leeds,* 1970
- *Who's Next,* 1971
- "Baba O'Riley," "Won't Get Fooled Again," 1971

and the unforgettable "Why don't you all f-f-f-fade away," Townshend connected with the disaffected teenage nation, and became their spokesman. The song also set the template for the group's basic structure: bass and drums exploding in a flurry of notes, vocals dripping with attitude, and persistent guitar power chords holding it all together. The song ends in a flurry of feedback and drum cacophony, a prototype of the violence and anger of punk.

Monterey

In December 1966 the second album *A Quick One* was released (titled *Happy Jack* in the United States), which featured a ten-minute mini-opera and the single "Happy Jack." With little success in the U.S. market up to that point, the Who embarked on a tour of America in the summer of 1967 that included a stunning performance at the Monterey Pop Festival. Their show concluded with Townshend and Moon again destroying their equipment while playing "My Generation." The band capitalized on the media stir that followed with the hit "I Can See for Miles," which at #9 became their best-ever U.S. chart appearance. With Townshend's deafening power chords and Moon's bombastic drumming, "I Can See for Miles" is a predecessor to heavy metal. The song was part of the December 15, 1967, album *The Who Sell Out,* a concept album built on the premise of being a broadcast from the offshore pirate station Radio London that included faux radio jingles and ad parodies on the cover.

By this time the Who's stage act was a flurry of perpetual motion: Townshend attacked his guitar with a windmill right hand as he leapt across the stage; Moon was a wild man on his huge drum set, which included two bass drums; when not screaming into the microphone, Daltrey would swing it by the cord as if he was roping cattle. In the midst of all this, bassist Entwistle stood statue-like,

MUSIC CUT 28

"WON'T GET FOOLED AGAIN" (PETE TOWNSHEND)— THE WHO

Personnel: Pete Townshend: guitars, synthesizer programming (Arp 2500, EMS VCS 3), organ; Roger Daltry: vocals; John Entwistle: bass guitar; Keith Moon: drums. Recorded April-May 1971 at Rolling Stones Mobile Studio, Stargroves, Berkshire, England, and Olympic Studios, London; produced by the Who and Glyn Johns. Released June 25, 1971 MCA; 10 weeks on the charts, peaking at #15.

"Won't Get Fooled Again" is one of two innovative songs (the other being "Baba O'Riley") built around synthesizer foundations from the 1971 LP *Who's Next.* The signature sound of the song is the repeating organ sequence that continues through most of its 8½ minutes. Townshend created the sound by playing chords on a Lowrey organ and feeding its output into a sample and hold filter on an Arp 2500 synthesizer and then a low frequency oscillator (LFO) on an EMS synthesizer. For its single release the song was edited down to 3½ minutes. Of the song's meaning, Townshend has said, "It is not precisely a song that decries revolution—it suggests that we will indeed fight in the streets—but that revolution, like all action can have results we cannot predict. Don't expect to see what you expect to see. Expect nothing and you might gain everything." However, he also acknowledged the impact that Daltrey's inspired performance had on the song: "When Roger Daltrey screamed as though his heart was being torn out in the closing moments of the song, it became something more to so many people. And I must live with that."

seemingly oblivious to everything. Much of the fury on stage was fueled by the constant amphetamine and alcohol usage by the band members, which also intensified the frequent personality clashes between Daltrey and Townshend, who battled over control of the band. (At one point, Daltrey was even kicked out of the band for a while and was not let back in until he promised to become less combative.)

Tommy

In 1968, Pete Townshend became a follower of the Indian guru **Meher Baba**, stopped taking drugs, and began to reflect upon ways in which to define his new spirituality through music. He came up with the idea of telling a story of spiritual enlightenment through song lyrics rather than the conventional spoken narrative accompaniment. It would be, in effect, a rock opera, the first of its kind. Released in 1969 and named after its main character, *Tommy* is the story of a boy who traumatically loses all sensory skills—becoming deaf, dumb, and blind—and becomes famous for his superior skills at playing pinball. After he is miraculously cured, he is manipulated into selling his secrets and exposed as a fraud. The story line was one that could be interpreted on several levels by a wide range of people; but most of all, the music in the 90-minute *Tommy* is exceptional, from "Overture," "Pinball Wizard," "I'm Free," "We're Not Gonna Take It," and others. *Tommy* became a critically acclaimed hit and put the Who at the front of the creative vanguard in rock. It was turned into a controversial film in 1975 and a Broadway musical in 1993.

In August 1969 the band appeared at Woodstock, and their set is one of the highlights of the documentary film. In 1970 *Live at Leeds* was released, capturing the Who live in concert and cementing their reputation as one of the most dynamic live acts in history. Not taking time to bask in the glory of *Tommy,* Townshend began work on his next project, which was to be an album and science fiction film entitled *Lifehouse*. Because the enormous scope of the project proved to be too much for Townshend, *Lifehouse* was never fully realized. However, four of the songs were included in the 1971 LP **Who's Next**, which like *Tommy* and *Live at Leeds* went to #4 on the album charts. Included on Who's Next are two stunning and innovative pieces, "Baba O'Riley" (named for Meher Baba and minimalist composer Terry Riley) and "Won't Get Fooled Again," in which Townshend programmed an ARP 2600 synthesizer to provide a sequenced foundation for the songs to be built upon. Both songs became staples of FM radio playlists.

Final Triumph, Tragedy

In 1973 Townshend completed his second rock opera, the double album *Quadrophenia,* which charted at #2. The hero, Jimmy, is a member of the mid-1960s London mod scene with a four-way split personality, which reflected the personalities of each of the Who's band members. The story is a "study in spiritual desperation," which leads Jimmy to the realization that "the only important thing is to open [his] heart." Like *Tommy, Quadrophenia* was critically hailed and turned into a film in 1979. In 1978, the aptly named *Who Are You* was released as Townshend began to experience somewhat of an identity crisis as he agonized over becoming an elder statesman in the wake of the punk movement. Almost simultaneously, on September 7, 1978, Keith Moon died of an overdose of a sedative he had been taking to treat alcoholic seizures. Although the group continued on for another three years with Kenney Jones on drums (formerly of the Small Faces), the group was never the same again.

Although Townshend at first downplayed it, Keith Moon's death affected him deeply, and he returned to heavy drug and alcohol abuse in the early 1980s (although he eventually cleaned up and became active in drug rehab projects). In the post-Moon years, the remaining members of the Who involved themselves in solo album projects and regrouped periodically to tour. In October 2001 they played the Concert for NYC, a benefit concert for families of the victims of the September 11 attack on the World Trade Center. Pete Townshend still performs as a solo act, although he is afflicted with tinnitus, a constant ringing in his ears. However, since the June 2002 death of John Entwistle, Townshend and Daltrey have officially drawn the final curtain on the Who.

OTHER BRITISH INVASION BANDS

The Mersey Beat Groups

In the wake of the Beatles' success, many of the first wave of British Invasion bands sounded predictably very much like the Fab Four. Because there were reportedly more than 300 bands in Liverpool alone in the early 1960s, it was inevitable that a few would make it to the charts. The style of these bands—upbeat and joyous, with a relentless drive—became known as Mersey Beat (from the Mersey River), or simply beat. One of the first Liverpool groups was Gerry and the Pacemakers, who like the Beatles, were signed by Brian Epstein, played Hamburg and the Cavern Club, and were produced by George Martin. Formed in 1959 as a skiffle band, the Pacemakers had three UK #1 hits in 1963 and hit in the United States with "Don't Let the Sun Catch You Crying" (#4) in 1964 and "Ferry Across the Mersey" (#6) in 1965. Also from Liverpool were the Searchers, whose sound could best be described as a precursor to the Byrds—tight, four-part harmony, and chiming guitars. Their biggest hit came in 1964 with "Love Potion Number Nine" (#3 U.S.). Billy J. Kramer and the Dakotas were another Epstein/Martin group from Liverpool, although Kramer was more of a 1950s-type pub crooner than a rock singer.

MERSEY BEAT GROUPS

- Gerry and the Pacemakers
- The Searchers
- Billy J. Kramer and the Dakotas
- Herman's Hermits
- The Hollies
- Freddie and the Dreamers
- Dave Clark Five

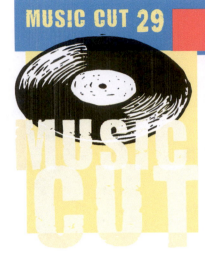

MUSIC CUT 29

"BUS STOP" (GRAHAM GOULDMAN)— THE HOLLIES

Personnel: Allan Clarke: vocals; Graham Nash: guitar, vocals; Tony Hicks: guitar, vocals; Bernie Calvert: bass; Bobby Elliot: drums. Recorded May 18, 1966; produced by Ron Richards. Released June 17, 1966 on Parlophone; 9 weeks on the charts, peaking at #5.

The Hollies were formed in Manchester England in late 1962 by Allan Clark and Graham Nash. Their name was in tribute to Buddy Holly. By 1963 they were performing at the Cavern Club in Liverpool, where Parlophone Records producer Ron Richards heard them and offered the group an audition. A song from that audition resulted in their first single release. The Hollies went on to release an astounding 28 singles in the 1960s, with 15 hitting the Top Ten in the UK. "Bus Stop" was their highest charting record in the US in the decade, and was the opening and title track to their 1966 album release. The song was written by Graham Gouldman, who also wrote hit songs for the Yardbirds ("For Your Love"), and Herman's Hermits ("No Milk Today") and several other British Invasion bands. Gouldman was inspired to write the song while riding home from work on the bus one day. Amazingly, the Hollies are still together, although co-founder Nash left the group in late 1968 and eventually help form Crosby, Stills, Nash & Young.

By 1964, groups from other English cities had emerged. Manchester was home base to **Herman's Hermits**, the **Hollies**, and Freddie and the Dreamers. Freddie Garrity, with Buddy Holly-nerdish looks, started out playing skiffle; with the Dreamers his biggest hit was "I'm Telling You Now" (#1 U.S., 1965). The Hermits, led by Peter Noone, were as cute and cuddly as the Beatles, with whom they actually went toe to toe with in record sales for a while. Between 1964 and 1967, they had eleven Top 10 hits, six of which were in 1965, when they practically dominated the charts. They hit with two #1s that year: "Mrs. Brown You've Got a Lovely Daughter" and "I'm Henry the Eighth, I Am." When the Hermits were unable to musically evolve out of lightweight pop, they quickly fell from grace. The Hollies, led by Graham Nash, formed in 1962 and became best known for their Everly Brothers-influenced harmonies and jangly guitars. They began making inroads into the American market in 1966 with Top 10 hits "Bus Stop," "Stop Stop Stop," and "On a Carousel," but by 1968 Nash had become unhappy with the group's direction and left for the United States (and helped start Crosby, Stills and Nash). From Tottenham came the **Dave Clark Five**, whose peak years also were from 1964 to 1967. Their first hit, 1964's "Glad All Over" (#6 U.S.) was the first of 17; they also were the second British group (after the Beatles) to appear on *The Ed Sullivan Show,* and ultimately did so a total of 18 times.

The Blues-Oriented Groups

Also starting around 1964, groups with a rougher, blues orientation started emerging from Britain. These groups tended to be sinister and menacing looking, with rude and defiant attitudes—definitely more Rolling Stones than Beatles. The most prominent and influential were the Kinks, the Yardbirds, and the Animals.

- Kinks
- Yardbirds
- Animals

BLUES-ORIENTED GROUPS

Brothers Ray Davies and Dave Davies (vocals and guitars), Mick Avory (the original Rolling Stones drummer), and Peter Quaife (bass) formed the **Kinks** in London in 1963. Their first hit single came the following year, "You Really Got Me" (#1 UK, #7 U.S.), which was followed in 1965 with "All Day and All of the Night" (#7 U.S.) and "Tired of Waiting for You" (#6 U.S.). The Kinks sound was heavily based on blues-based distorted power chords—making them an important predecessor to hard rock and heavy metal. Even though the group continued to record and perform after their early hits, for the next ten years or so they went largely unnoticed until punk and metal bands rediscovered their power chord-filled catalogue of songs (Van Halen recorded "You Really Got Me" in 1978). That catalogue also includes one of rock's all-time sing-along anthems, 1970's "Lola."

The **Yardbirds** have achieved immortal status by virtue of the three legendary lead guitarists that passed through the band. Soon after forming in 1962, they became the house band at London's Crawdaddy Club with a repertoire of Chicago blues standards such as Howlin' Wolf's "Smokestack Lightning" and Bo Diddley's "I'm a Man." In October 1963 18-year-old Eric Clapton joined, and the band released the first important live British rock album, *Five Live Yardbirds*. When the group decided to become more pop-oriented, Clapton quit in 1965; his replacement was Jeff Beck, a virtuoso guitarist with a volatile personality. Propelled by their hit "For Your Love" and the eventual addition of Jimmy Page on bass, the band gradually moved from pop to psychedelic, as exemplified by their 1966 LP *Roger the Engineer*. In October 1966 Beck was forced out, and Page became the group's lead guitarist and leader. A disagreement over the band's direction ultimately led to its demise: singer Keith Relf and drummer Jim McCarty wanted to go folk; Page wanted to get heavier. After the final Yardbirds gig in mid-1968, Page reformed the group as the New Yardbirds with the lineup that ultimately became known as Led Zeppelin.

Led by singer Eric Burdon, the **Animals** were formed in Newcastle in 1962. In addition to Burdon the group included Alan Price (keyboards), Bryan "Chas" Chandler (bass), Hilton Valentine (guitar), and John Steel (drums). Most of the group's first album, *The Animals*, was recorded in one day in 1964 at EMI's Abbey Road studio and included their only #1 hit (UK and U.S.), "House of the Rising Sun." The song is one of two traditional folksongs from

- Eric Clapton
- Jeff Beck
- Jimmy Page

LEGENDARY YARDBIRDS GUITARISTS

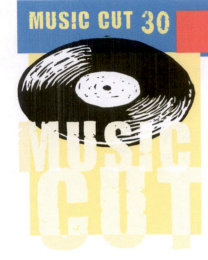

MUSIC CUT 30

"HOUSE OF THE RISING SUN" (TRADITIONAL)— THE ANIMALS

Personnel: Eric Burdon: vocals; Alan Price: keyboards, arranger; Hilton Valentine: guitar; Chas Chandler: bass; John Steel: drums. Recorded May 18, 1964 in London; produced by Mickie Most. Released July 1964 on MGM; 11 weeks on the charts, peaking at #1.

As much credit as Bob Dylan is given for infusing folk traditions into rock music, the Animals did it first with their version of the venerable folk standard "House of the Rising Sun." Dylan had actually recorded the song on his debut album in 1962, but it was done in the traditional fashion using only acoustic guitar as accompaniment. The Animals decided to add it to their repertoire while on tour with Chuck Berry in 1964. "We were looking for a song that would grab people's attention," said singer Eric Burdon. However, to make their rendition work, Burdon had to adapt the song lyrics to a male perspective from the traditional confessional of a "poor girl" trapped in a whorehouse in New Orleans. Burdon sang the new lyrics with a blues drenched howl, which, combined with the menacing guitar and jazzy organ riffs make this one of the most ominous records in early rock.

the album that were also on Bob Dylan's first album—an indication of one of the group's main influences. However, it was the reciprocal influence that ultimately had the biggest impact on rock history: upon hearing the Animals play "House of the Rising Sun" while touring England in 1964, Dylan is reported to have said, "My God, ya oughta hear what's going down over there. Eric Burdon, the Animals, ya know? Well, he's doing 'House of the Rising Sun' in rock. Rock! It's fucking wild! Blew my mind." The group disbanded in 1966; Burdon reformed it as Eric Burdon and the Animals later that same year. Chandler went on to a management career, and played an important role in the discovery of Jimi Hendrix.

STUDY QUESTIONS

Name _____ Date _____

1. What were some of the differences between the British and American pop scenes in the 1950s and early 1960s?

2. Describe how John Lennon and Paul McCartney wrote songs in the early years.

3. In what ways did songs written by Lennon differ from those written by McCartney?

4. Name three significant things about the album *Revolver*.

5. What were some of the factors that led to the breakup of the Beatles?

6. What were some of the ways in which the early years of the Rolling Stones were different than those of the Beatles, including their public relations, records, and audience reaction?

7. What were the most important Rolling Stones albums?

8. What later music styles did the Who influence, and how?

9. What were some of the difficulties encountered by the Beatles, Rolling Stones, and the Who in live performances?

10. Describe the differences between the Mersey Beat groups and the blues-oriented groups that emerged from the British pop scene in the 1960s.

7

SIXTIES BLUES AND PSYCHEDELIA

Courtesy of Photofest

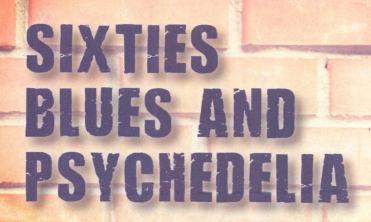

"So all of a sudden you're at the acid test and . . . we weren't required to play anything even acceptable. We could play whatever we wanted. So it was a chance to be completely free form on every level. It was just what we needed, because we were looking to break out."

—*Jerry Garcia (Grateful Dead)*

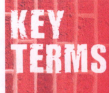

KEY TERMS

1968 Democratic Convention
Merry Pranksters
Acid tests
Hippie
Summer of Love
Haight-Ashbury
Electric ballrooms
Trips Festival

Human Be-In
Rolling Stone magazine
Progressive rock radio
Acid rock
Deadheads
Wall of Sound
Sunset Strip/Whisky a Go Go
Riot on Sunset Strip

Lizard King
Monterey International Pop Festival
Woodstock Music and Arts Fair
Hard rock
Power chord
Electric Lady Studio

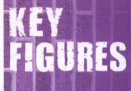

KEY FIGURES

Dr. Timothy Leary
Ken Kesey
Owsley
Jefferson Airplane
Grace Slick
The Grateful Dead
Jerry Garcia
Big Brother and the Holding Company
Janis Joplin

The Charlatans
Quicksilver Messenger Service
Country Joe and the Fish
Santana
The Doors
Jim Morrison
The Mothers of Invention
Frank Zappa
Flo and Eddie

Blues Incorporated
John Mayall and the Bluesbreakers
Cream
Eric Clapton
Derek and the Dominoes
Duane Allman
The Jimi Hendrix Experience
Jimi Hendrix

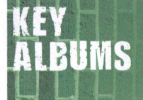

KEY ALBUMS

Surrealistic Pillow—Jefferson Airplane
Workingman's Dead—the Grateful Dead
American Beauty—the Grateful Dead

Cheap Thrills—Big Brother and the Holding Company
The Doors—the Doors
Freak Out!—The Mothers of Invention

Bluesbreakers with Eric Clapton
Disraeli Gears—Cream
Are You Experienced?—the Jimi Hendrix Experience

THE SIXTIES COUNTERCULTURE

Seeds of Discontent

When historians look back at the 20th century in America, no doubt they will cast the 1960s as one of its most traumatic and turbulent decades. Political assassinations, an unpopular war, social revolution, and new liberal lifestyle choices based upon personal freedom marked the era, and with them came extraordinary changes in our culture. In some ways we are still trying to absorb the full impact that the 1960s brought; some pundits even credit the demise of the New Left and the rise in religious fundamentalism in the 1990s and early 2000s as a reaction to the "harmful effects" of the 1960s. Even now, with the passing of more than 40 years, it is clear that the decade was a touchstone moment in our history.

The single most important factor driving this upheaval was the emerging youth culture, as the huge influx of children from the postwar baby boom began coming of age. This new generation was not one that was content with the social status quo. As author John Markoff has written, this generation was "certain it was going to change the world. Even those who weren't standing in the barricades were deeply caught up in a set of events that was to thoroughly

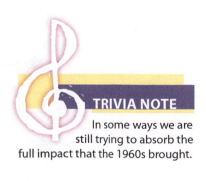

TRIVIA NOTE

In some ways we are still trying to absorb the full impact that the 1960s brought.

change America." More than the teenagers of the 1950s, the youth of the 1960s questioned the middle-class values of their parents. These traditional values—being achievement oriented, adhering to social conformity, acquiring material goods, "keeping up with the Jones's," and so on—were to many young people as outdated as the America portrayed on the 1950s *I Love Lucy* show. Although discontent was nothing new to the realities of being a teenager, the world was a much different place in the mid-1960s than it was in the mid-1950s. New social aggravators—including the civil rights movement, the increased usage of hallucinogenic drugs, and the Vietnam War—were now emerging that had a profound impact on youth, giving them even more reason to reject the values of the older generation—the "establishment."

The new youth culture was the beneficiary of some of the most remarkable music to emerge from the rock canon. By addressing the social issues of the day rather than just the issues important to teens, rock now gave young people a more direct and meaningful voice and identity than ever before; in other words, "Peggy Sue" gave way to "The Times They Are a Changin'." The most vital and important music of the era called for change, tolerance, and freedom. It rallied for opposition to the war and an end to racial discrimination. It became a mouthpiece for the sexual revolution, which followed the introduction of the first oral contraceptive in 1960. Rock in the 1960s truly became a soundtrack to the cultural revolution that was going on around it, and as a result the new, idealistic and motivated generation of young people became intensely passionate about their music.

However, no issue polarized young Americans against the establishment more than the Vietnam War. America began sending military advisors to the area in 1955, and our involvement slowly escalated until the first troops were deployed in 1965. By this time the first small antiwar protests had begun on college campuses as young men were drafted into military service. The first large-scale rally was staged by the radical Students for a Democratic Society (SDS) in Washington, D.C., in April 1965. By the time the Tet Offensive began in January 1968, popular opinion was turning against the war to such an extent that President Lyndon Johnson announced in March that he was not running for reelection (despite being elected in a landslide in 1964). From this point on, antiwar protests and rallies became more commonplace—and violent. One of the bloodiest confrontations occurred during the August **1968 Democratic Convention** in Chicago as protesters clashed with police in the streets. When the draft lottery was installed in late 1969 (the first such lottery since WWII), many of draft age defiantly burned their draft cards or became draft-dodgers and

ANTI-VIETNAM WAR SONGS

- "Feel Like I'm Fixin' to Die Rag" by Country Joe and the Fish
- "Chicago" by Graham Nash
- "The Unknown Soldier" by the Doors
- "Machine Gun" by Jimi Hendrix
- "Fortunate Son" by Creedence Clearwater Revival
- "Masters of War" by Bob Dylan
- "Ohio" by Crosby, Stills, Nash and Young

fled to Canada. On May 4, 1970, four students were killed by National Guard troops during a demonstration on the campus of Kent State University, resulting in an outbreak of angry, violent nationwide protests and the closing of hundreds of college campuses for several days. The war finally ended in 1975 at a cost of more than 58,000 American soldiers killed.

As one might guess, most of the songs about the Vietnam War were protest songs, but there were a few exceptions. The most famous pro-military song was SSgt. Barry Sadler's "Ballad of the Green Berets," a #1 hit in 1966. Among the many songs that expressed antiwar sentiments were "Feel Like I'm Fixin' to Die Rag" by Country Joe and the Fish, "Chicago" by Graham Nash, "The Unknown Soldier" by the Doors, "Machine Gun" by Jimi Hendrix, "Fortunate Son" by Creedence Clearwater Revival, "Masters of War" by Bob Dylan (one of his many), and "Ohio" by Crosby, Stills, Nash and Young. Interestingly, the Vietnam War also continued to inspire rock musicians into the 1980s and beyond; later war-related songs included "Goodnight Saigon" by Billy Joel (1982), "Born in the U.S.A." by Bruce Springsteen (1984), "Long Walk Home" by Neil Young (1987), and "Beach Party Vietnam" by the Dead Milkmen (1997).

Drugs

Another issue that became a barometer of the changing times was the increasing recreational use of psychoactive drugs such as LSD, marijuana, hashish, and mescaline. Many young people preferred these drugs to alcohol and "uppers" such as amphetamines (speed) because they tended to induce a general state of increased creativity and enlightenment—a "oneness of life"—rather than aggressive behavior. During the mid-1960s rock musicians such as Bob Dylan, the Beatles, Jimi Hendrix, the Grateful Dead, and others began to experiment with these drugs and explore their mind-expanding possibilities. In June 1967, Paul McCartney announced that he had taken LSD four times in the past year, and that it made him "a better, more honest, more tolerant member of society, brought closer to God." The Beatles album *Revolver*, released in August 1966 and often called the first album of the psychedelic era, contains several allusions to drugs, most notably in the song "Tomorrow Never Knows." Other 1960s rock songs of the era that reportedly had drug connotations include Jimi Hendrix's "Purple Haze" (named after a type of LSD), the Byrds' "Eight Miles High," Bob Dylan's "Mr. Tambourine Man," Donovan's "Mellow Yellow," Jefferson Airplane's "White Rabbit," and the Amboy Dukes' "Journey to the Center of the Mind."

SIXTIES ROCK SONGS THAT REPORTEDLY HAD DRUG CONNOTATIONS

- Jimi Hendrix's "Purple Haze"
- The Byrds' "Eight Miles High"
- Bob Dylan's "Mr. Tambourine Man"
- Donovan's "Mellow Yellow"
- Jefferson Airplane's "White Rabbit"
- Amboy Dukes' "Journey to the Center of the Mind"

Unlike marijuana, which had been used illegally for years by jazz musicians and beat writers, LSD-25 (lysergic acid diethylamide, or simply acid) was relatively new, and in fact was legal in the United States until October 1966. Discovered in 1943 by Swiss chemist Albert Hofmann, acid first became widely known in part through highly publicized experiments by Harvard psychologist **Dr. Timothy Leary** (author of *The Psychedelic Experience* and the catch phrase "Turn on, tune in, drop out") and author **Ken Kesey** (*One Flew Over the Cuckoo's Nest,* 1962). Kesey first encountered the drug at the Stanford Research Institute at Menlo Park (just south of San Francisco), and began sharing it with his friends the **Merry Pranksters** at parties called "acid tests." Acid tests featured live music by the Grateful Dead, psychedelic light shows, and LSD spiked Kool-Aid. Prior to the acid tests, Kesey and the Merry Pranksters had journeyed to New York in the summer of 1964 in their day-glow-painted school bus named Further, dropping acid and playing crude homemade music to astonished onlookers along the way. Author Tom Wolfe chronicled the Merry Pranksters trip in his book *The Electric Kool-Aid Acid Test.*

SAN FRANCISCO AND ACID ROCK

The Hippie Culture

The focal point of the new underground culture was San Francisco, a well-established haven for creative intellectuals, bohemians, radical political activists, and eccentrics. The San Francisco Bay Area had been the West Coast base for beat writers in the 1950s, and in the 1960s it became the birthplace of the Free Speech Movement (at the Berkley campus of the University of California), the personal computing industry and the Internet. With cheap rent and relatively safe neighborhoods, the city became a magnet for thousands of free-spirited youth who nurtured an air of spontaneity and an anything goes, "let's try something and see what happens" attitude. With the liberal use of psychoactive drugs thrown into the mix, the result was an explosion of long hair, headbands, VW buses, incense, beads, peace signs, tie-dyed shirts, and bell-bottom pants. On September 5, 1965, in a *San Francisco Examiner* piece entitled "A New Paradise for Beatniks," reporter Michael Fellon first used the word **hippie** to describe the young bohemians (who were only slightly hip), and the name stuck, describing the movement that ultimately spread far beyond the Bay Area.

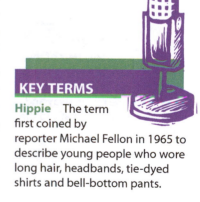

KEY TERMS

Hippie   The term first coined by reporter Michael Fellon in 1965 to describe young people who wore long hair, headbands, tie-dyed shirts and bell-bottom pants.

Hippies eschewed the trappings of the rat race and dropped out of society, often living communally in large houses or on farms where they shared chores, listened to music, consumed drugs, and pursued peaceful and artistic activities. In 1965, the first hippie community was established in San Francisco's **Haight-Ashbury** district, which was full of Victorian mansions that had been built after the 1906 earthquake and in recent years converted into apartment houses as the neighborhood went into decline. After the new immigrants moved in, stores and boutiques such as the Psychedelic Shop, the Blushing Peony, the Drogstore Café, and the I/Thou coffee shop opened to serve the various spiritual and daily needs of the burgeoning scene. For the next two years (before the area became infested with heroin pushers and the crime that came with them) the Haight was ground zero to the 1960s cultural revolution.

The counterculture milieu also included radical theater groups such as the San Francisco Mime Troupe, and the Diggers, who also ran free-food pantries and a free medical clinic. There were local rags such as *The Berkeley Barb* and *The Oracle*. The famous City Lights Bookstore owned by beat writer Lawrence Ferlinghetti was the first all-paperback bookstore in the country and the first to publish Allen Ginsberg's controversial poem *Howl*. A loose collective that called itself the Family Dog formed in 1965 with the sole purpose of promoting dances where there was no booze but where hallucinogens were available. Their first event, called A Tribute to Dr. Strange, was held at Longshoreman's Hall on October 16, 1965, and featured bands such as the Charlatans, Jefferson Airplane, and the Great Society (which included singer Grace Slick). The event was so successful that others like it soon followed, and were often staged at one of the **"electric" ballrooms** in the city such as the Avalon and the Fillmore.

The Summer of Love

By January 1966, the San Francisco scene was in full bloom. Nearly 10,000 people showed up at Longshoreman's Hall for the three-day **Trips Festival** (January 21–23) organized by Kesey and his Merry Pranksters that featured music by the Grateful Dead and Big Brother and the Holding Company, among others. The event also included Native American tepees, strobe lights, slide shows, poetry readings, and free acid samples dispensed by local chemist/acid activist Augustus Owsley Stanley III, better known as **Owsley**, or simply "Bear." (Between 1965 and 1967, Owsley was the prime caterer of the Bay Area drug culture, producing more than one million hits of acid in his lab.) It was publicized with colorful and stylized psychedelic posters that became in themselves part of the local flair. Another creation that emerged from the San Francisco scene was the psychedelic light show, which used the crude technology of the time: colored liquids that pulsated over classroom overhead projectors onto bare walls and dancers. By early 1966 the Fillmore and Avalon Ballrooms were having concerts nearly every weekend. Legendary promoter Bill Graham used the Fillmore to stage his shows, while Family Dog leader Chet Helms, worked the Avalon. Free concerts in city parks were not unusual either—as Mickey Hart of the Grateful Dead recalled: "I loved playing for free. It felt good to give the music away and let people who couldn't afford the music hear it."

On January 14, 1967, the **Human Be-In**, described as "A Gathering of the Tribes" drew 20,000 to the Polo Grounds in Golden Gate Park to hear Allen Ginsberg, Lawrence Ferlinghetti, Dr. Timothy Leary, and radical activist Jerry Rubin speak and listen to Jefferson Airplane, the Grateful Dead, Quicksilver Messenger Service, Big Brother and the Holding Company, and others. Newspaper writer Ralph J. Gleason described the audience as "a wild polyglot mixture of Mod, Paladin, Ringling Brothers, Cochise, and Hell's Angels' formal." The event was the first in the year that culminated in the so-called "Summer of Love." By the summer, the Haight was a tourist attraction (complete with Gray Line Bus "Hippie Hop" tours), the focus of national media attention and an overflow of hippie wannabes from all over the country. There was even a song, "San Francisco (Be Sure to Wear Flowers in Your Hair)," written by John Phillips of the Mamas and the Papas and sung by Scott

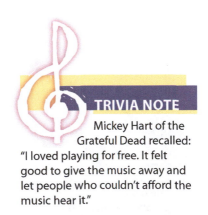

TRIVIA NOTE

Mickey Hart of the Grateful Dead recalled: "I loved playing for free. It felt good to give the music away and let people who couldn't afford the music hear it."

McKenzie that celebrated the moment (although many locals were angered that Los Angeles-based Phillips would capitalize on a grassroots, noncapitalist movement). The highpoint of the year occurred on the weekend of June 16–18, when the Monterey International Pop Festival was held at the Monterey County Fairgrounds south of San Francisco. This landmark event was the first major outdoor rock festival, and was a blueprint for the many that followed in the next few years, including Woodstock. Monterey was instrumental in launching the careers of Jimi Hendrix, Janis Joplin, and other Bay Area bands that were discovered by record executives in attendance.

Counterculture Media

The Bay Area counter culture spawned what has become the standard-bearer of rock journalism, *Rolling Stone* Magazine. The first issue appeared on November 9, 1967, with a photo of John Lennon wearing a WWI doughboy helmet on the set of the film *How I Won the War* on the cover. The brainchild of local journalists Jann Wenner and Ralph J. Gleason, *Rolling Stone* has over the years effectively integrated political, cultural, and music reporting, using such writers as Hunter S. Thompson, Greil Marcus, Cameron Crowe (now a Hollywood film producer), and Ben Fong-Torres. To be on its cover is considered such an achievement that it inspired a song, "The Cover of Rolling Stone," by Dr. Hook and the Medicine Show (which earned the group a cover photo on the March 29, 1973, issue).

San Francisco was also the birthplace of underground or **progressive rock radio**. In spite of the burgeoning psychedelic music culture, in early 1967 the city's AM radio stations were still programming Top 40, which effectively excluded any local bands from getting airplay. Although the FM band broadcast in stereo and was of superior quality to AM, in the mid-1960s it was still routinely programmed with classical music and jazz. Then, on April 7, 1967, music entrepreneur and former DJ Tom Donahue took over the evening shift at ratings cellar-dweller KMPX-FM and began playing an eclectic mix of blues, R&B, Beatles and comedy, interspersed with his low pitched and slow paced conversation that he backed with Indian ragas. The program proved to be such a hit that the idea quickly spread across the country; Donahue became known throughout the industry as the "Father of Free Form." The new format allowed rock artists to get airplay for songs that were too long, too noncommercial, or too experimental for Top 40. Although radio programmers began to replace it with tighter formatting in the early 1970s, the progressive rock format turned FM radio into the most popular band for listening to music.

Acid Rock

The lively music scene that developed in San Francisco in the 1960s was a mirror image of the "anything goes" ethos of the city. Because of the association with the drug culture (especially LSD), the music became known as **acid rock**. Unlike earlier rock styles, the term really describes the music that emerged from San Francisco more than it denotes a specific style. Acid rock bands played a wide variety of music styles, although that is not to say there weren't common elements. The influence of the blues is ubiquitous. Many of the musicians that

TRIVIA NOTE

Monterey International Pop Festival was held at the Monterey County Fairgrounds June 16–18, 1967. This landmark event was the first major outdoor rock festival, and was a blueprint for the many that followed in the next few years, including Woodstock. Monterey was instrumental in launching the careers of Jimi Hendrix, Janis Joplin, and other Bay Area bands that were "discovered" by several record executives who were in attendance.

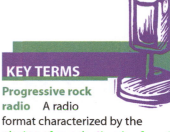

KEY TERMS

Progressive rock radio   A radio format characterized by the playing of an eclectic mix of music, particularly long, non-commercial album cuts, usually accompanied by low key, spaced-out DJ conversation.

Acid rock   An umbrella term, usually associated with the music of the San Francisco Bay Area in the 1960s, that encompasses a wide variety of stylistic approaches, often with free form improvisations and heavy influences from the blues and folk music.

played acid rock were former folkies who went electric, so there is also an undeniable folk influence in the music and the lyrics. Acid rock lyrics covered the gamut from the existential to the mundane, but were often socially relevant, critical of the establishment, and extolling the virtues of altered states of consciousness and free love. From its roots in jam sessions came an almost jazz-like approach to spontaneous improvisation, most often in the form of extended free-form guitar solos. There was a decided noncommercial bent to the whole musical culture: bands tended to promote an egalitarian image of themselves while downplaying the notion of a leader or a star within the group. Acid rock also did not easily mesh with AM radio formatting, and as a result there was a noticeable absence of hit singles from the genre (Jefferson Airplane being the most obvious exception, with two Top 10 hits in 1967).

IMPORTANT SAN FRANCISCO ACID ROCK PERFORMERS

Jefferson Airplane

On August 13, 1965, the Matrix, a tiny new folk club co-owned by folksinger Marty Balin opened in San Francisco's Marina District. The night also marked the first appearance of Balin's new band, Jefferson Airplane, which included fellow folkie Paul Kantner, blues guitarist Jorma Kaukonen, and jazz vocalist Signe Anderson. In the audience that night was the respected jazz critic from the *San Francisco Chronicle,* Ralph J. Gleason, whose glowing review "Jefferson Airplane—Sound and Style" is regarded as the first public announcement of the city's new music scene (coming just a few weeks before the *Examiner's* "hippie" column). Performing at the Matrix often over the next several months, the Airplane developed a strong fan base, solidified their personnel (adding drummer Skip Spence and bassist Jack Casady) and gradually evolved their sound from folk rock to electric psychedelic. By the end of the year they signed a contract with RCA, becoming the first area acid rock band to secure a major label deal. But just as their first album, *Jefferson Airplane Takes Off* was about to be released in August 1966, Anderson quit to care for her newborn baby and Spence departed to form the group Moby Grape. Jazz drummer Spencer Dryden replaced Spence; Anderson's replacement was **Grace Slick** (1939–), who had previously sung with another local group, the Great Society. By this time Jefferson Airplane was a much-improved band.

JEFFERSON AIRPLANE

- Paul Kantner
- Jorma Kaukonen
- Grace Slick
- Spencer Dryden
- Jack Casady

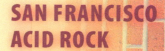

SAN FRANCISCO ACID ROCK

Characteristics of San Francisco Acid Rock

1. Umbrella term encompassing a wide variety of stylistic approaches, including heavy influences from the blues and folk music

2. Typical instrumentation: distorted electric guitar, acoustic guitar, bass, drums, piano, or organ; backup singers frequently used

3. Long, free-form guitar improvisations common (hard rock influence)

4. Lyrics could be about nearly anything, but were often socially relevant (a folk influence) rather than pop-oriented songs of romance; references to drugs and their usage common

5. Noncommercial—bands promoted an egalitarian image and generally had little if any commercial success (although FM airplay was common)

Key San Francisco Acid Rock Recordings

- "Feel Like I'm Fixin' To Die Rag"—Country Joe and the Fish, 1966
- *Surrealistic Pillow*—Jefferson Airplane, 1967
- *Anthem of the Sun*—the Grateful Dead, 1968
  - *Cheap Thrills*—Big Brother and the Holding Company, 1968

Slick brought with her a more powerful voice than Anderson, and two songs from the Great Society's repertoire, "White Rabbit" (written by Slick) and "Somebody to Love" (written by Slick's brother-in-law Darby Slick). Both songs were included on the Airplane's second album *Surrealistic Pillow* (released in February 1967), and buoyed by their successful appearance at the Monterey Pop festival, both hit the Top 10 (#8 and #5 respectively). In many ways these two songs capture the essence of San Francisco psychedelia: "Somebody to Love" extols the virtues of free love, while "White Rabbit," inspired by Lewis Carroll's *Alice's Adventures in Wonderland,* criticizes the misguided older generation and

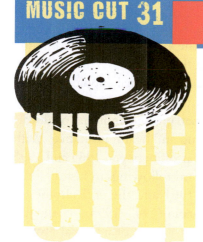

MUSIC CUT 31

"WHITE RABBIT" (GRACE SLICK)—JEFFERSON AIRPLANE

Personnel: Grace Slick: vocals; Marty Balin: guitar; Paul Kantner: guitar; Jorma Kaukonen: lead guitar; Jack Casady: bass; Spencer Dryden: drums. Recorded November 3, 1966 at RCA Victor's Music Center of the World, Hollywood, CA; produced by Rick Jarrard. Released June 24, 1967 on RCA; 10 weeks on the charts, peaking at #8.

When Grace Slick joined Jefferson Airplane in 1966, she brought two songs with her: "Somebody to Love" and her own "White Rabbit." Both songs were included in the seminal LP *Surrealistic Pillow,* and both hit the Top 10 as singles. Slick's lyrics were inspired by *Alice's Adventures in Wonderland,* and include references to several of the novel's characters, including the White Knight, the Dormouse, the Red Queen, and the hookah-smoking caterpillar. Her message? "Our parents read us stories like *Peter Pan, Alice in Wonderland* and *The Wizard of Oz,*" Slick said. "They all have a place where children get drugs, and are able to fly or see an Emerald City or experience extraordinary animals and people. . . . And our parents are suddenly saying, 'Why are you taking drugs?' Well, *hello!*" Adding drama to the trippiness of the lyrics was the bolero rhythm that builds to a climax with Slick's final exhortation to "Feed your head!"

suggests that the listener "feed your head," commonly interpreted as an invitation to take drugs. The album got its name from Jerry Garcia (assisting in the production), who described the songs as "surrealistic as a pillow." Completed in just 13 days, *Surrealistic Pillow* is a classic.

SAN FRANCISCO ACID ROCK PERFORMERS

- Jefferson Airplane
- Grateful Dead
- Big Brother and the Holding Company/Janis Joplin
- Charlatans
- Quicksilver Messenger Service
- Country Joe and the Fish
- Santana

After two less successful album releases, the Airplane in 1969 released the anti-establishment manifesto *Volunteers,* which included the call to action song "We Should Be Together." By this time, the group was at its creative peak, and performed at the Woodstock and Altamont festivals. The 1970s brought shifting personnel and several name changes. In 1970, drummer Spencer Dryden left to form New Riders of the Purple Sage, Kaukonen and Casady left to form Hot Tuna, while Slick and Kantner had a baby together. Founder Marty Balin left in 1971. After taking some time off, in 1974 the group reformed as Jefferson Starship, and released *Red Octopus* in 1975, which became the group's (Airplane or Starship) only #1 album. When Kantner departed in 1984, he took the legal rights to the word "Jefferson," so the group continued on as simply "Starship" until 1989 when Jefferson Airplane regrouped once more with nearly all the original members. In all, the various renditions of the band placed 21 albums in the Top 40 charts.

The Grateful Dead

By more or less defining the sound of acid rock, the Grateful Dead became the heart and soul of the San Francisco music scene in the late 1960s. Although they will forever be remembered as the quintessential communal-hippie-tripping-acid rock band, they outlived that era and continued to perform well into the 1990s, becoming a privately held corporation that grossed millions of dollars annually while providing an employee pension fund and health insurance. With a relentless touring schedule that took only one year off between 1965 and 1995 (1975), they also cultivated one of the most die-hard followings in history—the **Deadheads**. The roots of the band go back to 1961 and the coffeehouses of Palo Alto, where bluegrass banjo player **Jerry Garcia** (1942–1995), having just been discharged from the army, began playing in a variety of informal groups. Garcia had the sort of personality that brought people together, a gentle soul with an insatiable curiosity, an interest in existentialism as well as intense musical ambitions. After several years on the scene, his musical circle had grown to include Robert Hunter, an aspiring guitarist/lyricist; Ron "Pigpen" McKernan, a blues-loving, Harley Davidson-riding piano/harmonica player; and the athletic and dyslexic washtub bass/jug player Bob Weir. In January 1964, Garcia, McKernan, Weir, and two other friends (minus Hunter, who had temporarily left the band) began gigging as Mother McCree's Uptown Jug Champions.

THE GRATEFUL DEAD

- Jerry Garcia
- Mickey Hart
- Ron "Pigpen" McKernan
- Bob Weir
- Phil Lesh
- Bill Kreutzman

By early 1965, Garcia and Co. decided to go electric. Heavily influencing their decision were the Rolling Stones (who were just starting to break into the United States market), Bob Dylan (especially his *Bringing It All Back Home* album), and LSD, with which they had begun experimenting. Filling out the new band, now called the Warlocks, was Phil Lesh on bass, a classically trained trumpeter and violinist who had studied composition and jazz in college (and had never played bass before), and Palo Alto's hottest jazz drummer Bill Kreutzman. In November, learning of another band with the same name (who later became ZZ Top), they again changed their name to the Grateful Dead, a phrase that Garcia had stumbled upon in a dictionary. Among the first gigs that the Dead played were the now-famous acid tests staged by Ken Kesey's Merry Pranksters. Playing in the trippy, anything goes environment of the acid tests where they were not the main focus of the evening's entertainment (the hallucinations were) allowed the band to experiment musically in long free-form jam sessions. This, along with their eclectic musical backgrounds and common interest in jazz saxophonist John Coltrane's recent experimental recordings, produced some truly idiosyncratic results. As their music began to gel, in September 1966 the band members moved into a large Victorian mansion at 710 Ashbury Street in the Haight, where they famously resided until the following May.

> **TRIVIA NOTE**
>
> By defining the sound of acid rock, the Grateful Dead became the heart and soul of the San Francisco music scene in the late 1960s.

In 1967 the Dead added second drummer Mickey Hart, who brought an interest in Native American and world music, and signed with Warner Brothers. After recording an unsatisfactory first album (*The Grateful Dead*), the group released the innovative *Anthem of the Sun* (1968), in which they attempted to capture the essence of their jam sessions by interweaving studio recordings with those of live performances. The third album, *Aoxomoxoa* (1969), was a continuation of the experimental phase of the band, which now included second keyboardist Tom Constanten and the return of Garcia's old friend Robert Hunter as lyricist. Also from 1969 came *Live/Dead,* comprised of live recordings made at the Fillmore and Avalon Ballrooms. Among the songs on the double album was Hunter's 23-minute anthem "Dark Star." Although by the summer of 1969 the Dead had become nationally known through appearances at Monterey and Woodstock, their albums were not selling and they were nearly $200,000 in debt to Warners.

In 1970 the group responded to their dire financial situation by releasing two of their finest albums, *Workingman's Dead* and *American Beauty*. Both albums signaled a dramatic change of direction by focusing on their musical roots with songs that were surprisingly tightly structured, including "Uncle John's Band" and "Casey Jones" from *WMD* and "Friend of the Devil" and "Truckin'" from *AB*. Over the next several years the band experienced limited personnel changes, including the departures of Constanten and Hart (the drummer returned in 1975), the addition of Keith and Donna Godchaux on keyboards and vocals respectively, and the departure of McKernan, who died in 1973 due to complications from alcohol abuse. In 1973 the Dead revealed the **Wall of Sound**, an innovative sound reinforcement system that consisted of 604 speakers and 26,400 watts of power. Designed and built by Owsley Stanley and Dan Healy, the 75-ton Wall was the largest portable sound system ever built (requiring four semi trucks and 21 crew members to haul and assemble), and could be heard distortion-free for distances up to a quarter mile.

The Grateful Dead continued to tour and record prolifically throughout the 1970s, 1980s, and 1990s. However, Jerry Garcia, the founder and spiritual leader of the band, began to suffer health problems in 1985 from his prolonged drug usage. He died of a heart attack at a drug treatment center on August 9, 1995. Although the final Grateful Dead concert was at Soldier Field in Chicago on July 9, 1995, their legacy continues to this day in the form of jam bands such as Phish and the String Cheese Incident, and the continued popularity of their music. As band biographer Dennis McNally put it, "As long as there are Dead Heads, they will be guided by the principles of freedom, spontaneity, caring for each other and their planet, fellowship, and fun."

Big Brother and the Holding Company/Janis Joplin

Big Brother and the Holding Company emerged out of the 1965 Wednesday night jam sessions that Family Dog member Chet Helms was running out of the basement of a condemned mansion on Page Street in Haight-Ashbury. The band (Sam Andrews and Jim Gurley on guitars, Peter Albin on bass and Dave Getz on drums) quickly became a fixture on the local scene, performing at the Trips Festival and as the house band at many of the Helms produced Avalon Ballroom shows. By early 1966 however, they felt the need for a strong lead vocalist, and Helms recommended Texas blues singer Janis Joplin (1943–1970), whom he had met when they hitchhiked together from Austin, Texas, to San Francisco in early 1963.

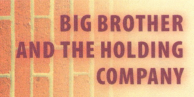

BIG BROTHER AND THE HOLDING COMPANY

- Sam Andrews
- Jim Gurley
- Peter Albin
- Dave Getz
- Janis Joplin

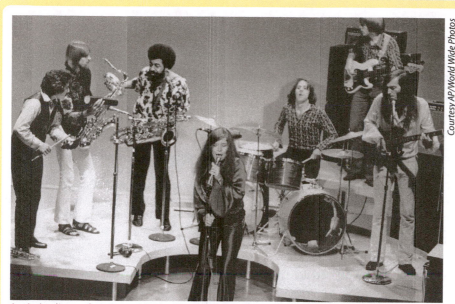

Janis Joplin performing with the Kozmic Blues Band in December 1969.

Janis Joplin was born in Port Arthur, Texas. Although she tried to fit in with the conservative mores of her hometown for much of her childhood, in high school she began to exhibit streaks of wild and independent behavior that increasingly labeled her as a nonconformist. She found solace painting and reading the writings of the beats, and also began to love the music of black blues singers. Eventually she developed enough courage to begin singing in local coffeehouses. Music emboldened her, allowing her to develop a tough-as-nails nonconformist persona to hide her vulnerabilities. She developed a singing style inspired by blues singers Bessie Smith and Big Mama Thornton that was rough edged, gritty, and raw. In late 1962 she moved to Austin where she became a student at the University of Texas and began assimilating into the local folk scene. After one semester she left school, and traveled around the country before moving to the Bay Area in June 1966 to sing with Big Brother.

Joplin revitalized the band. With her dynamic ability to move from a barely audible whisper one moment to full tilt screaming the next, she transfixed audiences. When Big Brother performed at the Monterey Pop Festival in June 1967, Joplin stole the show with her amazing performance, and the band was rewarded with a contract from Columbia Records. After a six-month delay getting out of an earlier contract with a small label, the album *Cheap Thrills* (with a cover designed by cartoonist R. Crumb) was released in July 1968 and promptly went gold, staying at #1 on the charts for eight weeks. The album's strongest track "Piece of My Heart" was released as a single and also charted at #12. But at the height of their success, the world was changing quickly for Janis. After months of being told that she was better than the rest of the band, she left Big Brother at the end of 1968 to pursue a solo career. By this time she had also begun drinking heavily and using heroin.

MUSIC CUT 32

"PIECE OF MY HEART" (BERT BERNS/JERRY RAGOVOY)— BIG BROTHER AND THE HOLDING COMPANY

Personnel: Janis Joplin: vocals; Sam Andrew: guitar, vocals; James Gurley: guitar, vocals; Peter Albin: bass; Dave Getz: drums. Recorded at Columbia Studio B in New York, April 1968; produced by John Simon. Released September 28, 1968 on Columbia; 12 weeks on the charts, peaking at #12.

"Piece of My Heart" was the only hit from Big Brother and the Holding Company's debut album *Cheap Thrills*. One of the most anxiously awaited albums of its day, *Cheap Thrills* (whose working title was *Sex, Dope, and Cheap Thrills*) quickly went gold and stayed at #1 for eight weeks. To capture the raw energy of Janis Joplin and BB&HC's live shows, producer John Simon recorded the band live rather than with the more conventional (and laborious) overdubbing method. Co-written by Bert Berns (who also wrote "Twist and Shout" and "Hang on Sloopy" under the name Bert Russell), "Piece of My Heart" was originally recorded by Aretha Franklin's sister Erma, who had a #10 R&B hit with the song in 1967. Big Brother's version was recorded in Studio B of Columbia's complex at 799 7th Avenue (next door to where Bob Dylan recorded "Like a Rolling Stone" in the larger Studio A).

TRIVIA NOTE

Janis Joplin embodied the spirit of the 1960s "liberated" woman who took control of her life and her career.

Joplin's new band, the Kozmic Blues Band, a classic soul revue, was much tighter and more professional than Big Brother. Although they appeared with her at Woodstock, they disbanded in January 1970 after one album release. In April Joplin assembled a new band, the Full Tilt Boogie Band, and began work on what would be her last album, *Pearl* (her nickname). However, before the album was completed, Joplin's body was found in her room at the Landmark Hotel in Los Angeles on October 4, 1970. Like Brian Jones and Jimi Hendrix who died before her, and Jim Morrison who would die the following July, Janis Joplin died of a drug overdose at age 27. *Pearl* was released posthumously and went to #1 in early 1971. The single "Me and Bobby McGee" (written by Kris Kristofferson) also hit #1. Two other songs from *Pearl* left chilling legacies: "Buried Alive in the Blues" is missing the vocal overdub that Joplin did not live to record, and the a cappella "Mercedes Benz," a demo recorded three days before her death is simultaneously full of pain and whimsy—and is perhaps her greatest recording.

Janis Joplin embodied the spirit of the 1960s "liberated" woman who took control of her life and her career, becoming a star and role model for future women rockers in a male-dominated field. Her extroverted stage image (which included a constant companion bottle of Southern Comfort and wildly colorful clothes) and her soulful, passionate voice will live on forever as icons of a unique time and place in rock.

Other Bay Area Acid Rock Bands

Even though the **Charlatans** were more or less an amateur group, they set the tone both musically and stylistically for the Bay Area music scene. On June 29, 1965, they began playing in Virginia City, Nevada, at the Red Dog Inn, a bar they had remodeled to resemble an Old West-style saloon. Throughout the summer, the Charlatans played the Red Dog while donning cowboy outfits, dropping acid, and using a crude sound sensitive light box. They also attracted hippies from San Francisco with eye-catching psychedelic posters. **Quicksilver Messenger Service**, formed in 1965, was on par with the Grateful Dead as a quintessential acid rock jam band. Led in its early years by guitarist John Cipollina, one of the finest guitarists to emerge from the Bay Area, QMS was a fixture in the electric ballroom scene throughout the late 1960s. In 1970, Dino Valenti joined as vocalist and became the group's main songwriter. QMS is perhaps best known for the song "Fresh Air" (1970), which became an FM radio staple. **Country Joe and the Fish**, also formed in 1965 by Joe McDonald and Barry Melton, was the most political of the Bay Area bands. Originally a loose knit skiffle-type band, in 1966 the band electrified and released what was to become their most famous recording, the Vietnam protest song "Feel Like I'm Fixin' to Die Rag." The Fish appeared at Monterey and Woodstock, and their performance of "Fixin' to Die" preceded by the famous "Fish Cheer" ("Give me an *F,* give me a *U,* give me a *C,*" . . . and so on) is one of the highlights of the Woodstock documentary film.

One group from the San Francisco Bay Area that lent a slightly different slant to the local music scene was **Santana**, led by Mexican guitar virtuoso Carlos Santana (1947–). Santana put together his band in 1967 from musicians that he jammed with regularly in San Francisco's Latin district. Their public debut at the Fillmore in 1968 electrified the audience and won them a spot at Woodstock, where their performance of "Soul Sacrifice" had a similar effect. In the ensuing years the group had ten Top 40 hits, including 1970's "Evil Ways" and "Black Magic Woman" (#9 and #4, respectively). The Santana sound is steeped in Afro-Latin instruments and rhythms, the Hammond B-3 organ, and Carlos Santana's unique guitar styling. It is one of the few bands to reach pop superstar status without a clearly defined lead vocal identity—their popularity stems from their infectious dance rhythms and the guitar wizardry of their leader. Santana has remained one of rock's most venerable bands, and scored a dramatic comeback in 1999 with their multi-Grammy Award-winning album *Supernatural.*

Other Bay Area bands from the 1960s include the Sons of Champlin, Sopwith Camel, the Vejtables, the Beau Brummels, the Great Society, and Moby Grape.

THE 1960s LOS ANGELES PSYCHEDELIC SCENE

The Strip

Meanwhile, Los Angeles was developing its own music scene in the mid-1960s. For many young people in the city, there was the same independent spirit of infinite possibilities that characterized the era. "The universe was changing," observed Ray Manzarek of the Doors. The heart of L.A.'s live music scene was the **Sunset Strip**, a stretch of Sunset Boulevard running through West Hollywood that had been a hangout for movie stars, bohemians, and the incurably hip since Prohibition. Among the many clubs on the Strip that featured live music in the 1960s were the Galaxy, the London Fog, Gazzari's, the Action, the Trip, Pandora's Box, the Roxy, and Ciro's. There were also recording studios and record label offices, as well as popular all-night

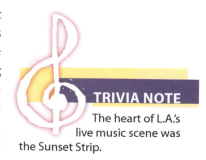

TRIVIA NOTE

The heart of L.A.'s live music scene was the Sunset Strip.

dining hangouts like Ben Frank's and Cantor's Deli. The most important and most famous nightclub was the **Whisky a Go Go**, which after its opening in January 1964 was an immediate hit featuring singer Johnny Rivers and a female DJ in a fringed mini-dress with big hair and no bra—the first "Go-Go girl"—dancing in a glass cage suspended above the floor. (*Johnny Rivers at the Whisky au Go Go* spent 45 weeks on the charts in the summer of 1964, with the single "Memphis" peaking at #2 nationally.)

The Strip was a 24/7 party atmosphere for young people. The L.A. hipster scene had its own dress code: boots and bellbottoms for girls and tunics for boys. ("The girls all looked like Cher, and the boys like Brian Jones," according to author Barney Hoskins.) But like the scene in San Francisco, the good times ethos of the Strip would not last. By November 1966 traffic congestion and the constant influx of teenagers grew so bad that area businesses began requesting police intervention, and confrontations between the two sides quickly escalated. A protest held on the night of November 12 attracted several thousand demonstrators; the so-called **"Riot on Sunset Strip"** that ensued resulted in nothing more than a few fistfights and broken windows. Nonetheless, it inspired both the film *Riot on Sunset Strip* and Buffalo Springfield's "For What It's Worth" ("There's something happening here/What it is ain't exactly clear . . ."). By the end of the decade, things turned ugly when the zeitgeist of the Strip became more about drugs than music and having a good time.

L.A. PSYCHEDELIA

The L.A. Psychedelic Music Scene

1. More theatrically oriented than San Francisco scene
2. Instrumentation included electric guitar, keyboards, drums, bass
3. Darker lyrics, eschewing the peace and love ethos of San Francisco
4. Wide variety of styles and influences, including folk, the blues, and hard rock

Key L.A. Psychedelic Recordings

- *Freak Out!*—Frank Zappa and the Mothers of Invention, 1966
- *The Doors*—the Doors, 1967

L.A.'s music scene was more musically diverse than San Francisco's—and definitely more commercial oriented. As an important center of the record industry, L.A. was home to a well-established pop scene in the early 1960s consisting of recording studios, music publishers, production companies, and record labels. Whereas the San Francisco scene eschewed commercialism as part of its ethic, Los Angeles drew many musicians, arrangers, and producers who specifically wanted to be part of the mainstream pop scene. Starting in 1965, Los Angeles-produced singles began to take control of the pop charts away from New York and London. That same year, the folk rock movement (discussed in Chapter 8) was finding its legs with the emergence of groups like the Byrds ("Mr. Tambourine Man," #1) and the Mamas and the Papas ("California Dreamin'," #4).

Of course, Los Angeles is home to Hollywood and the television industry, and an entire ecosystem of thespian activity, and this also had an impact on the psychedelic music scene. Two groups in particular, the Doors and the Mothers of Invention (and later, Alice Cooper) made great use of theatre in making their performances among the most provocative of the 1960s. Both the Doors and the Mothers rejected the peace and love ethos of the San Francisco scene and explored darker messages in their lyrics, and both explored a wide variety of musical approaches and influences as well.

The Doors

The Doors were one of the most unique groups of the era, with no bass player and a sound that owed more to the haunting sound of the Vox Continental combo organ than the electric guitar. However, the most identifying attribute of the Doors sound came from their enigmatic lead vocalist, **Jim Morrison** (1943–1971). Even though he had never sang before joining the Doors at age 21, Morrison's hypnotic rich baritone voice is instantly identifiable even today, more than 30 years after his death. Morrison was the most charismatic and controversial rock performer of his era. His performances were mesmerizing and hypnotic, at other times menacing and dangerously out of control. Offstage he was an impossible drunk, an insatiable bisexual, a loner and a drifter. In spite of all this, Jim Morrison was one of the most important and gifted rock poets, and published two books of his writings during his lifetime.

Morrison's childhood was rocky: his father, Captain Steve Morrison, was a naval commander whose job kept the family moving constantly. Young Jim was smart—with an IQ of 149—but rebellious, and did not take well to the authoritarian discipline of his parents. Detached and alienated as a teen, he was drawn to the writings of the beats, Friedrich Nietzsche, and eventually French Symbolist poet Arthur Rimbaud. After moving from school to school, he graduated from UCLA in June 1965 with a degree in cinematography. One month later, Morrison ran across former classmate Ray Manzarek on the beach at Ocean Park and read to him several poems he had written, including "Moonlight Drive." Manzarek, a classically trained pianist, immediately saw that Morrison's talent along with his Greek god looks would be a natural for his rock band, Rick and the Ravens. Once the moody and temperamental Morrison joined the band, one by one the other original members quit; replacing them were guitarist Robby Krieger and jazz drummer John Densmore. They could not find a bass player to their liking, so Manzarek played bass with his left hand on a small bass keyboard. With a new lineup came a new name, inspired by the book *The Doors*

■ Jim Morrison
■ Ray Manzarek
■ Robby Krieger
■ John Densmore

THE DOORS

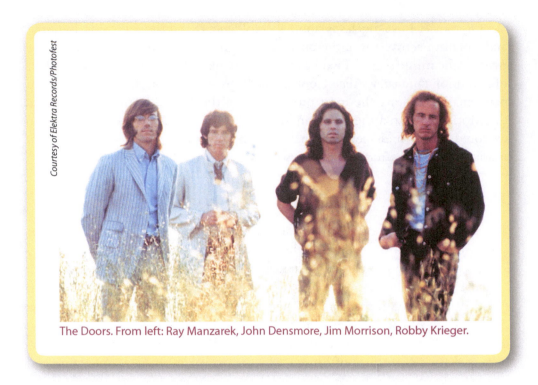

Courtesy of Elektra Records/Photofest

The Doors. From left: Ray Manzarek, John Densmore, Jim Morrison, Robby Krieger.

of Perception, Aldous Huxley's account of his hallucinogenic drug experiences. The group also began to write their own songs.

In March 1966 the Doors secured a steady gig at the low-rent London Fog; by May they had improved enough to get hired by the Whisky a Go Go as the house band. Despite being inconsistent—with dynamite shows often followed by incredibly bad ones—the band drew the attention of Elektra Records, who signed them on August 18. Just three nights later Morrison went into a spontaneous chant during the hypnotic 15-minute song "The End" that included a spellbinding poetic retake on the Oedipus myth. It was an incendiary moment was for the band and the audience; the Whisky exploded into what Manzarek later called "a Dionysian frenzy" that resulted in the band's firing from the Whisky at the end of the set. "The End," as it appears as the last song of the Doors' eponymous first album, contains a riveting recreation of Morrison's oration. *The Doors* is one of the 1960s most dynamic debut albums; in the summer of 1967 it peaked at #2, fueled by the #1 smash hit single "Light My Fire."

Over the next four years the group released seven more albums, including the psychedelic masterpiece *Strange Days* (1967) and *The Soft Parade* (1969), the latter having an innovative multi-movement suite title as its track. During this time, Morrison's behavior became increasingly unpredictable due to his excessive drinking, and as a result the band was not invited to perform at either Monterey or Woodstock. However, they did appear on *The Ed Sullivan Show* on September 17, 1967, and despite warnings not to sing the word "higher" during their live performance of "Light My Fire," Morrison did just that— twice. Morrison was a quick study on how to use his charisma on stage, and invented the **Lizard King**, a shaman-like alter ego he used to incite audiences and drive the band to explosive heights. From late 1967 through much of 1968, the Doors were the top band in America, and played to sellout crowds in huge indoor and outdoor venues, essentially pioneering arena rock in the process.

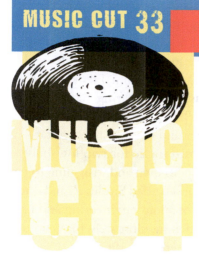

MUSIC CUT 33

"BREAK ON THROUGH" (MORRISON/MANZAREK/KREIGER/DENSMORE)—THE DOORS

Personnel: Jim Morrison: vocals; Ray Mansarek: organ; Robby Kreiger: guitar; John Densmore: drums. Recorded August 1966 at Sunset Sound Studios, Los Angeles, CA; produced by Paul Rothchild. Released January 1, 1967; did not chart.

The opening cut from their 1967 debut album *The Doors,* "Break on Through" seems to summarize the Doors' innovative musical strategy: to "break on through to the other side." Even though the LP eventually sold more than three million copies and its hit "Light My Fire" went to #1, "Break on Through" did not manage to chart. The song contains all the characteristics of the Doors sound: driving ostinato bass line, jazz-influenced drums, ominous combo organ, and most of all, Jim Morrison's spellbinding vocals. The group was also one of the decade's most explosive and dynamic, as they prove here by going from a soft bossa nova intro to the highly charged middle section where Morrison screams "She gets high" four times (although the word "high" was edited out in the single release).

However, Morrison's public drunkenness and confrontational stage behavior eventually caught up to him and the band. On March 1, 1969, the Doors played a concert in Miami in which the singer reportedly exposed himself and simulated masturbation. Although authorities could produce no photographs or actual witnesses of him doing any such thing, Morrison was arrested, tried in August 1970, and convicted of misdemeanor counts of indecent exposure and open profanity. During the year and a half between the Miami concert and the trial, the Doors were blacklisted by many concert promoters and found touring increasingly difficult. Their last gig, on December 12, 1970, in New Orleans, ended early after Morrison had a mental breakdown on stage. Soon after completing *L.A. Woman,* his last album with the Doors, Morrison moved to Paris with his long-time girlfriend Pamela Courson, ostensibly to take a break from his turbulent life. It was there that he died in the bathtub of his apartment in the early morning hours of July 3, 1971. His body was quickly sealed in a coffin and buried at Pere-Lachaise cemetery. Because there was no autopsy and the police and doctor who arrived at the scene could not be traced, rumors have persisted that he is still alive. The mysterious circumstances surrounding his death have only served to enhance the legendary status of one of rock's most charismatic and mysterious figures.

Frank Zappa/The Mothers of Invention

Frank Zappa (1940–1993) was a musical anarchist who tore down convention and accepted norms in creating some of rock's most sophisticated and intellectual music. Zappa's lyrical themes were often dark, but he effectively used humor, biting satire, and vulgarity; in some cases his lyrics were downright gross. He was an admirer of 20th century avant-garde composers, surrealist artists such as Salvador Dali, "sick" comics like Lenny Bruce and Mort Sahl, and the musical comedian Spike Jones. He also had great love and respect for R&B, doo-wop and jazz. His great accomplishment is that he somehow managed to bring all these influences into his highly original and idiosyncratic music. Because Zappa received much

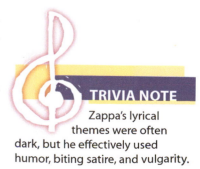

TRIVIA NOTE

Zappa's lyrical themes were often dark, but he effectively used humor, biting satire, and vulgarity.

critical acclaim in his life as a composer, arranger, and studio innovator, the fact that he was also a brilliant and inventive guitarist is often overlooked.

Zappa's father was a guitar-playing government research scientist who worked a variety of jobs that forced the family to move frequently during Frank's childhood. In 1954 the Zappas settled in Lancaster, California, and Frank began to develop an interest in 20th century classical music after hearing recordings of Edgard Varese's *Ionisation* and Igor Stravinsky's *The Rite of Spring*. As he grew older he started listening to doo-wop, R&B, and the blues, and began playing guitar in a series of garage bands. After high school he composed music for two low-budget films and briefly flirted with college. In late 1963, on his own and struggling to get by, he lived for a while in a small studio he bought and named Studio Z, and often spent twelve hours a day or more learning the art of audio engineering and tape editing. In 1964, Zappa joined the Soul Giants, which he ultimately took control of and renamed the Mothers (appropriately on Mother's Day, 1965).

After moving to L.A., the Mothers began working their way up the club circuit playing Zappa's original music. Once they made it to the Whisky, they caught the attention of MGM-Verve producer Tom Wilson, who signed the band in March 1966. As a precondition to releasing any recordings, MGM insisted that the words "of Invention" be added to "Mothers"—apparently to make the name less offensive. Their debut, *Freak Out!* (July 1966), one of the first ever double albums, is a manifesto on individual freedom, nonconformity, and the hypocrisy of American society. The music ranges from electronic sci-fi to doo-wop parody to an eight-minute collage of sound called "Help, I'm a Rock." The album was unlike anything that came before it, and a harbinger of things to come from Zappa. It received critical acclaim but attracted little attention from buyers.

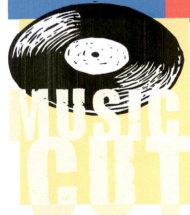

MUSIC CUT 34

"WHO ARE THE BRAIN POLICE?" (FRANK ZAPPA)— THE MOTHERS OF INVENTION

Personnel: Frank Zappa: guitar, vocals; Jimmy Carl Black: drums, vocals; Ray Collins: vocals, harmonica, "bobby pin and tweezers," sound effects, percussion; Elliot Ingber: alternate lead and rhythm guitar with "clear white light"; Roy Estrada: bass, vocals; additional session musicians also used. Recorded March 8–12, 1966 at Sunset-Highland/TTG Studios, Los Angeles, CA; produced by Tom Wilson. Released June 27, 1966 on the Verve album *Freak Out!;* later released as a single in 1966, did not chart.

Freak Out!, the first album by the Mothers of Invention, is one of the most inspired debut albums in history. It is one of rock's first double albums, and is arguably the first rock concept album. The variety of music on the record is astonishing, from the sci-fi psychedelia of "Who Are the Brain Police?" to the social commentary of "Trouble Every Day" to the collage-like minimalism of "Help, I'm a Rock" to the indescribable madness of "It Can't Happen Here." It is also the album that unleashed Frank Zappa's satiric brilliance on the world. Zappa, who wrote all 14 of the albums songs, declared in the liner notes that the album is a celebration of freakdom. "WHAT IS 'FREAKING OUT'," he asked. "On a personal level, *Freaking Out* is a process whereby an individual casts off outmoded and restricting standards of thinking, dress, and social etiquette in order to express CREATIVELY his relationship to his immediate environment and the social structure as a whole" . . . "We would like to encourage everyone who HEARS this music to join us . . . become a member of *The United Mutations . . . FREAK OUT!*" Of "Who Are the Brain Police?" Zappa writes, "At five o'clock in the morning someone kept singing this in my mind and made me write it down. I will admit to being frightened when I finally played it out loud and sang the words."

A prolific composer, Zappa began recording his music at an exhausting rate, eventually releasing more than 60 albums during his lifetime. 1968's *We're Only in It for the Money* (a *Sgt. Pepper's* parody) satirized hippies and eerily foretold the Kent State massacre of 1970. In 1968 Zappa also released two other albums— *Lumpy Gravy,* in which he experimented with mixing spoken word, taped noise, and sound effects (a Varese influence) into the music of a 50-piece orchestra, and the doo-wop parody *Cruising with Ruben & The Jets.* In 1969 the Mothers released the mostly instrumental double album *Uncle Meat,* a compositional tour de force with 28 tracks, some of which include spoken dialogue. After its release, Zappa abruptly disbanded the Mothers, who were by this time receiving attention for their live shows that combined incredible musicianship with zany, anarchic humor. In October 1969, with a new jazz-influenced band, Zappa released *Hot Rats,* one of the first albums recorded using a 16-track recorder and which some consider to be the first jazz/rock fusion album. Soon after, Zappa reformed the Mothers and hired vocalists Mark Volman and Howard Kaylan from the pop group the Turtles, who for contractual reasons had to go by the pseudonyms **Flo and Eddie**. The first album release with his new singers, 1970s's *Chunga's Revenge,* was the first of many to show a penchant for gross, sophomoric lyrics dealing with everything from cheap sex to excrement.

Zappa worked on several film projects during his life, most notably 1971's 200 Motels, a self-parody about a band playing a series of one-nighters that starred Ringo Starr and Keith Moon. The year 1971 also marked two tragic events for Zappa. On December 4, a fire broke out during a concert at Montreux, Switzerland, that destroyed the band's equipment and became the inspiration for Deep Purple's "Smoke on the Water." One week later in London, an enraged fan climbed on stage and pushed Zappa off the stage and into the orchestra pit, damaging his spine, fracturing his skull, and crushing his larynx, lowering his singing voice by a third of an octave. His new baritone voice was featured in 1973's *Overnight Sensation,* which included the cult hit "Don't Eat the Yellow Snow." In 1975 Zappa once again disbanded the Mothers—this time for good—and released all future recordings under his own name. In the 1980s he began working with the Synclavier, a state-of-the-art digital synthesizer that allowed him to compose, edit, and orchestrate music by himself in his home studio. Albums such as *The Perfect Stranger* (1984) and *Jazz from Hell* (1985) are innovative ventures into computer-based music.

Zappa used innovative editing and studio techniques in the creation of his recordings, often splicing together snippets from many different live recordings and adding studio overdubs to create a finished song. A good example of this technique is in the title track of 1982's *Ship Arriving Too Late to Save a Drowning Witch,* which used 15 edits, some of which lasted only two bars. He also was known for his unusual and sometimes silly album covers. His orchestral works, including "Pedro's Dowry" from *Orchestral Favorites* brought critical acclaim from heavyweights in the classical music world. In the years preceding his death, Zappa became a politically active voice against the censorship of rock lyrics. In 1985 he appeared as a dissenting voice before a Senate subcommittee inspired by the Parents Music Resource Center (PMRC), a group led by Tipper Gore (wife of future Vice President Al Gore) that advocated warning labels on CDs whose lyrics were determined to be offensive (see Chapter 12).

For a short while he also became a trade representative for the Czech Republic, named to the post by Czech President Vaclav Havel, a longtime fan. In 1991, Frank Zappa was diagnosed with the inoperable prostate cancer from which he died in 1993.

WOODSTOCK AND THE ERA OF THE ROCK MUSIC FESTIVAL

The psychedelic era also marked the beginning of an era when large out-door music festivals became popular. The first of these was the **Monterey International Pop Festival** in June 1967, which drew an audience of approx-imately 30,000 and was both an artistic and a financial success (with a profit of nearly $250,000). In addition, the resulting documentary film *Monterey Pop* showed the rest of the rock world just how much fun a three-day marathon of music, psychedelia, peace, and love could be. In Monterey's wake, other festi-vals in Palm Springs, Toronto, Los Angeles, Atlanta, and other cities were held, some of which drew upwards of 150,000 fans. Although there were occasional problems—bad drug trips, not enough restroom facilities or first aid, trouble with local authorities over the influx of longhaired youth—in large part most went off without major disruptions.

The landmark event of the era was the **Woodstock Music and Arts Fair**, held from August 15–18, 1969. Originally scheduled for the small art-ists' community in upstate New York, problems with local townsfolk forced a last-minute move to Max Yasgur's farm in nearby Bethel, 50 miles away from Woodstock. Despite assurances by festival organizers Michael Lang and Artie Kornfeld that no more than 50,000 would attend, an estimated 450,000 showed up, creating a mini-nation of counterculture youth who for the most part enjoyed the music and behaved themselves (and closed down the New

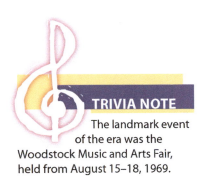

TRIVIA NOTE

The landmark event of the era was the Woodstock Music and Arts Fair, held from August 15–18, 1969.

WOODSTOCK PERFORMERS

Joan Baez	The Incredible String Band
Blood, Sweat and Tears	Janis Joplin
The Paul Butterfield Blues Band	Jefferson Airplane
The Band	Melanie
Creedence Clearwater Revival	Mountain
Canned Heat	Quill
Country Joe McDonald and the Fish	John Sebastian
Crosby, Stills, Nash & Young	Ravi Shankar
Joe Cocker	Sly and the Family Stone
Arlo Guthrie	Bert Sommer
Grateful Dead	Santana
Tim Hardin	Sweetwater
Jimi Hendrix	Ten Years After
Richie Havens	Johnny Winter
Keef Hartley Band	The Who

York State Thruway with one of the worst traffic jams in history). More than 30 artists were signed, including many of the top names in the business: Jimi Hendrix, the Who, the new supergroup Crosby, Stills, Nash & Young, the Grateful Dead, Janis Joplin, and Jefferson Airplane. New groups that made stunning debuts included Sly and the Family Stone, Santana, and English blue-eyed soul singer Joe Cocker. The festival in time became an indelible icon of the 1960s peace-love generation, and a cultural bookmark of the times. The documentary film and accompanying soundtrack double album were also released to great fanfare, capturing many of the remarkable musical moments of the festival.

Although Woodstock left many with a renewed hope in the goodwill of the human spirit, much of the innocence of the entire 1960s era was shattered with the disaster of the Altamont Festival outside San Francisco just four months later (discussed in Chapter 6). Even if Altamont wasn't the only event that sent counterculture spirits crashing, it was much closer to home for many in the rock audience.

BRITISH BLUES AND THE EMERGENCE OF HARD ROCK

Meanwhile, Across the Pond . . .

The British rock scene in the mid-1960s was gearing up for a second assault on American shores with a sound that was harder, louder, and more blues-oriented than the first invasion. Leading the pack were two guitar players that would become rock legends by the end of the decade, Eric Clapton and Jimi Hendrix. Clapton, a native son who had inspired London graffiti proclaiming, "Clapton is God" while still barely twenty years old, grabbed the world's attention when he formed the power trio Cream in 1966. Hendrix, a transplanted American who would do nothing less than redefine guitar playing before his untimely death in 1970, was a well-kept secret in the United States until his appearance at the 1967 Monterey Pop Festival. Before we examine the lives of these two guitar heroes, a little background on the thriving London blues scene in the mid-1960s is in order.

As mentioned in Chapter 6, the British had a long-standing fascination with American music, such as trad jazz, and R&B dating back to the 1940s. By the early 1960s, a burgeoning blues scene was developing in London, led by guitarist Alex Korner and guitar/harmonica player Cyril Davies, who in 1962 formed the band **Blues Incorporated**. Their 1962 LP *R&B at the Marquee*, recorded live at the famed London club, was the first ever full-length British blues album. Over the next few years, Blues Incorporated's changing lineup would include bassist Jack Bruce (later of Cream) and most of the members that would become the Rolling Stones. The band also inspired a young **John Mayall** to start his own blues group, the **Bluesbreakers** in January 1963. Like Blues Incorporated, the Bluesbreakers' lineup was constantly changing, and at one time or another included John McVie and Mick Fleetwood (later of Fleetwood Mac), Mick Taylor (later of the Stones), Jack Bruce, and Eric

HARD ROCK

Characteristics of Hard Rock

1. Instrumentation: electric guitar, bass, drums; occasionally Hammond organ
2. Songs often based on blues riffs, often using power chords
3. More intense, louder, bombastic than previous rock styles
4. Guitar player emerges as the focal point of the group
5. Lyrics do not include connections to Satan and the occult, which are more typical of heavy metal

Key Hard Rock Recordings

- *Are You Experienced?*—the Jimi Hendrix Experience, 1967
- *Disraeli Gears*—Cream, 1968
- *Steppenwolf*—Steppenwolf, 1968
- *In-A-Gadda-Da-Vida*—Iron Butterfly, 1968

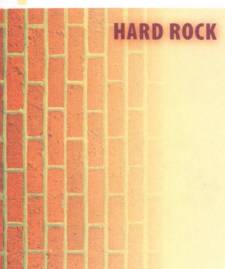

KEY TERMS

Hard rock   A style emerging in the 1960s that incorporated blues riffs, power chords and distorted guitar, typically played by a power trio (guitar, bass and drums).

Power chord   A two-note chord (using the root and the 5th of a chord) using distortion; a common characteristic of hard rock and heavy metal.

Clapton. During Clapton's brief tenure with the band (1965–1966), Mayall released the landmark album ***Bluesbreakers with Eric Clapton*** that put the guitarist on the map and hit the Top 10 in Britain.

Hard Rock—The Forerunner to Heavy Metal

Blues Incorporated and the Bluesbreakers, along with British Invasion bands the Who, the Animals, the Yardbirds, and the Kinks were influential to the emerging style that became known as **hard rock**. English bands such as Cream, Deep Purple, and the Jimi Hendrix Experience, as well as American bands such as Steppenwolf, Iron Butterfly, Grand Funk Railroad, and Vanilla Fudge were among the earliest to play in this style. Hard rock songs were often based on blues riffs and **power chords**; the guitar is usually distorted, and all the instruments (bass, drums, guitar, and sometimes Hammond organ) are played with more intensity—louder, in other words—than previous styles. These bands also tended to include blues-based guitar solos, which were often of extended length. Because of these characteristics, hard rock is considered to be the forerunner to heavy metal (which is covered in Chapter 9).

EARLY HARD ROCK BANDS

- Cream
- Deep Purple
- The Jimi Hendrix Experience
- Steppenwolf
- Iron Butterfly
- Grand Funk Railroad
- Vanilla Fudge

Eric Clapton/Cream

Throughout a career that has lasted more than 50 years, Eric Clapton (1945–) has established himself as one of rock's premier guitarists while performing in a variety of different groups and musical settings. Although he has become a pop icon as the leader of several commercially successful bands and has written a number of pop hits, he has never strayed far from his true calling—playing the blues. Clapton had a rocky childhood, having been raised by his grandparents after his mother abandoned him in his infancy. As a teen, he attended art school for a brief time, but turned his attention to music and the guitar after being expelled for poor grades. From the beginning Clapton was drawn to American blues and R&B while immersing himself in the records of Robert Johnson, B. B. King, Muddy Waters, and Chuck Berry. In October 1963 he joined the Yardbirds, at the time an up-and-coming R&B cover band, but left when the band began to pursue a more pop-oriented direction. Just as the Yardbirds were breaking through to the pop charts with "For Your Love" (#6 UK), Eric Clapton was laboring as a construction worker.

However, his construction career did not last long; in late spring 1965 John Mayall asked Clapton to join the Bluesbreakers. Although he only stayed with the band for slightly over a year, during his tenure Clapton established himself as Britain's premier blues guitarist and developed a devoted cult following. In July 1966 he left Mayall and formed the seminal hard rock power trio Cream with bassist Jack Bruce and drummer Ginger Baker. Clapton had played with Bruce and Baker at informal jam sessions, and although the two did not personally get along all that well, they agreed to put their differences aside for the sake of the group. After their debut at the 1966 Windsor Jazz and Blues Festival, Cream concerts became renowned for their high-volume extended blues jams. Audiences in the United States seemed to especially like this aspect of their shows: "When we saw that in America they actually wanted us to play a number for a whole hour—one number—we just stretched it," Clapton later said.

Cream became immensely popular in both the UK and America, eventually selling 15 million records internationally. After their first album *Fresh Cream* failed to chart, their second, **Disraeli Gears** sold a million copies and went to #4, propelled by the hit single "Sunshine of Your Love" (#5, 1968). The song is a 24-bar blues based on one of the most memorable blues riffs in all of rock, and Clapton's solo is a masterpiece of lyricism and understatement. The groups next LP, *Wheels of Fire,* was a live/studio double album partially recorded at the Fillmore Ballroom, which contained the hit "White Room" (#6, 1968) and an inspired electric cover of Robert Johnson's "Cross Road Blues" entitled "Crossroads." However, by mid-1968 the fragile Bruce/Baker truce was beginning to unravel, and Clapton was becoming increasingly tormented by

- Eric Clapton
- Jack Bruce
- Ginger Baker

CREAM

the pressures of being a guitar idol. At the height of their popularity, Cream disbanded after giving a farewell concert at the Royal Albert Hall on November 26, 1968. The final album *Goodbye Cream*, which included the Clapton/George Harrison effort "Badge" was released early the next year and peaked at #2 in the U.S.

Clapton's life and career was on a roller coaster of change over the next several years. His first musical endeavor was the so-called "supergroup," Blind Faith, which included Baker again on drums, Rick Gretch on bass and violin, and blue-eyed soul singer/keyboard player Stevie Winwood. Despite a successful concert tour and a self-titled #1 album, Clapton quit after six months. In 1970, he released two solo albums, *Eric Clapton* and *Layla and Other Assorted Love Songs*. *Layla* was released under the pseudonym **Derek and the Dominoes**, a short-lived group made up of studio musicians Jim Gordon, Carl Radle, Bobby Whitlock, and guitarist **Duane Allman** of the Allman Brothers Band. The title song, written about Clapton's unrequited love for George Harrison's wife Patti (who would later leave Harrison and marry Clapton), is one of rock's greatest anthems, with soaring guitar work by Clapton and Allman and a beautiful extended coda written by drummer Gordon. Despite an amazing string of popular successes and a standing in the rock world that was approaching legend-in-his-own-time status, Clapton in the early 1970s sunk into what he calls his "Lost Years" of heroin addiction and alcohol abuse. In 1974 he released *461 Ocean Boulevard,* which hit #1 on the album charts and included his cover of Bob Marley's "I Shot the Sheriff," which also peaked at #1. In the late 1970s Clapton began to overcome his addictions, and although his recent years have had rocky moments (most notably the tragic death of his son Conor in 1991), he has emerged remarkably healthy. Since the 1990s he has achieved 13 Top 40 singles and two #1 albums. In 1994 he established a drug and alcohol rehabilitation clinic in the Caribbean called the Crossroads Centre.

Jimi Hendrix

Although Jimi Hendrix (1942–1970) was only an international superstar for less than four years, in that time he expanded the sonic possibilities of the electric guitar as well as redefined the relationship between music and noise with his startling use of feedback and other guitar effects. In addition to establishing himself as perhaps the most innovative guitarist in history, he became the premier showman and studio technician of his generation. Although his musical universe included electric psychedelia, jazz, hard rock, R&B, and folk, he was always deeply rooted in the blues. When he died in 1970 at age twenty-seven, Jimi Hendrix left a profound legacy that is still highly influential to musicians of all stripes.

He was born in Seattle as John Allen Hendrix. His childhood was difficult: John's father was away in the military much of the time, and his mother abandoned the family when he was ten. He taught himself to play the guitar from listening to his father's jazz and blues records, and by 15 he was playing in mediocre cover bands in area clubs. Down on his luck, in 1959 Hendrix joined the army and served in the 101st Airborne as a paratrooper, but in 1962 got a discharge after feigning homosexual tendencies. (In later years he often claimed

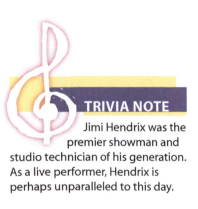

TRIVIA NOTE

Jimi Hendrix was the premier showman and studio technician of his generation. As a live performer, Hendrix is perhaps unparalleled to this day.

that he was discharged for breaking an ankle on a jump.) He then moved to Nashville where he played in a variety of R&B and soul bands on the chitlin' circuit, but was often fired for ad libbing "wild stuff that wasn't part of the song," as one-time employer Solomon Burke put it. In early 1964 he moved to Harlem, and by this time was good enough to get employment with the Isley Brothers, Little Richard, King Curtis, and at occasional recording sessions. Eventually he began to write songs, using influences from Delta blues, R&B, and his idol Bob Dylan, especially Dylan's newly released *Blonde on Blonde*. Around this same time (early 1966) Hendrix also began experimenting with LSD, and his experiences with the drug had a profound effect on his look, his music, and his poetry. When he began playing Greenwich Village clubs in mid-1966 under the name Jimi James (with a pickup band he called the Blue Flames), he was an immediate smash, although with his outlandish psychedelic clothes, Dylan-esque hair and whacked out feedback-laced solos, no one knew quite what to do with him. Playing at the Café Wha? in August, Hendrix was heard by Chas Chandler of the Animals, who advised him that he would become a star if he moved to England and let Chandler be his manager. In September, Hendrix left New York for London.

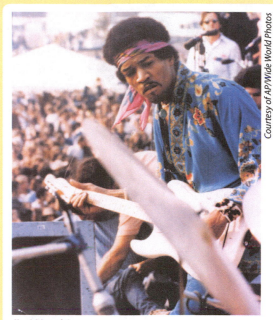

Jimi Hendrix

Courtesy of AP/Wide World Photos

The Experience

In England, Hendrix quickly made the rounds and was introduced to the Beatles, Eric Clapton, Pete Townshend, and other members of the London rock elite. Seeking a power trio format as a working band, he and Chandler put together the **Jimi Hendrix Experience** with Mitch Mitchell on drums and Noel Redding on bass. After playing their debut gig in October 1966, the trio recorded three singles, "Hey Joe" (#6 UK), "Purple Haze" (#3), and "The Wind Cries Mary" (#6). The success of these records—along with several BBC-TV appearances—made Hendrix a national sensation. In May 1967 the Experience released their debut LP *Are You Experienced?*, a stunning showcase for Hendrix's talents as a composer (with ten original songs), guitarist, and studio experimentalist. The musical styles on the LP cover jazz jams ("Third Stone from the Sun," "Manic Depression"), Dylan influenced electric folk ("The Wind Cries Mary"), hard rock ("Purple Haze," "Fire"), the blues ("Red House"), and Beatles-influenced psychedelia ("Are You Experienced"). Hendrix also makes innovative use of spoken poetry, backward tapes, occasional Dylanesque "talking blues" style vocals, and an array of guitar-produced sound effects, along with his distinctive use of feedback and noise. Redding and particularly Mitchell also make substantial contributions with powerful supporting roles.

- Jimi Hendrix
- Mitch Mitchell
- Noel Redding

THE JIMI HENDRIX EXPERIENCE

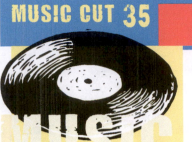

"THIRD STONE FROM THE SUN" (JIMI HENDRIX)— THE JIMI HENDRIX EXPERIENCE

Personnel: Jimi Hendrix: guitar, vocals; Noel Redding: bass; Mitch Mitchell: drums; Chas Chandler: voice of "Scout Ship." Recorded October 1966–April 1967 at De Lane Lea Studios and Olympic Studios, London; produced by Chas Chandler. Released August 23, 1967 on the MCA LP *Are You Experienced?;* not released as a single.

"Third Stone from the Sun" is an innovative mash up of styles and studio techniques, all designed to create the illusion that Jimi Hendrix is some sort of alien space captain contemplating the destruction of Earth (the third planet from the sun) as he approaches. The song is one of the first fusions of jazz and rock, as it alternates back and forth between the two styles. What is perhaps most interesting about the song is that there is no singing—only spoken word. After an slowed-down opening dialogue between Hendrix and producer Chas Chandler and vocal sound effects, Hendrix reads a poem later on during the free jazz jam in the song's middle section, Hendrix reads another poem. Then you'll never hear surf music again." The song is one of the reasons why Hendrix's debut LP *Are You Experienced?* is such a masterpiece.

As a live performer, Hendrix is perhaps unparalleled to this day. Left-handed, he played the Fender Stratocaster upside down, strung in reverse order, although he was equally at ease playing a normally strung guitar in the same fashion. He played the guitar behind his back, over his head, while doing somersaults, and with his teeth, all with ease and proficiency. Being self-taught, Hendrix developed an unusual technique of using his thumb to hold down strings on the neck of the guitar instead of the more conventional use of the thumb on the back of the neck to support the hand. His startling feedback effects were created with an array of processing pedals, including a Vox wah-wah, a Fuzz Face (for distortion), and a Univox Univibe (for a phasing effect). He also played with incredible volume produced by stacking English-made Marshall amplifiers on top of each other, in what became known as the Marshall stack. Hendrix was also adept at getting an astounding range of sounds and effects in the studio, and often spent endless hours doing multiple takes to achieve perfection.

Coming to America

Even though he was becoming a star in England in 1967, Hendrix was still pretty much unknown in his native America until his June performance at the Monterey Pop Festival. Performing on the last night of the festival before final act the Mamas and the Papas, the Experience played an electrifying show of six songs that concluded with a slow, psychedelic version of the Troggs' "Wild Thing." Watching "Wild Thing" (it is included in the documentary film of the festival), one gets to see the complete Hendrix package: coaxing feedback out of his guitar, playing it behind his back and while doing somersaults, using it as a phallic symbol, and ultimately setting it on fire and smashing it. Even though the performance got mixed reviews from critics, it put Jimi Hendrix on the map in America. *Are You Experienced?* hit #5 on the U.S. charts, and the Experience began their first tour of the United States as the unlikely warm-up band for the Monkees (they were quickly dropped however, as the band was too psychedelic for Monkees' audiences).

The year 1968 saw Hendrix busy releasing two new albums, touring extensively, and beginning construction on his dream studio, **Electric Lady** in Greenwich Village. The albums *Axis: Bold as Love,* released in January, and *Electric Ladyland,* released in November, were commercial successes, hitting #3 and #1, respectively. The critics, who were divided on the merits of *Are You Experienced?* were coming around as well: *Rolling Stone* reviewer Jon Landau called for Hendrix to win the magazine's Performer of the Year Award for *Electric Ladyland. Ladyland* is the apotheosis of Hendrix's short career, and a continuation of the variety of musical styles, guitar artistry, and studio wizardry that first appeared on *Are You Experienced?* It also contains a cover of Bob Dylan's "All Along the Watchtower" that has become the definitive version of the song (Dylan himself has adopted this version for his own live shows).

In 1969, Redding and Mitchell left the Experience and returned to England. Hendrix, in a portent of things to come, was arrested in Toronto in May for possession of heroin, a charge that was later dismissed. The highlight of the year came at Woodstock where with a loosely organized band he called "Gypsy, Sun, and Rainbow," Hendrix performed his now legendary version of "The Star Spangled Banner" as the festival's headline act. (Because the Sunday night program, which Hendrix was supposed to close, ran long, his performance took place on Monday morning in front of just 40,000 fans.) On New Year's Eve, he played New York's Fillmore East Ballroom with a new trio, Band of Gypsys, consisting of Billy Cox, an old army buddy on bass, and Buddy Miles on drums, a band mate from his days playing as a sideman for Wilson Pickett. In the audience that night was jazz legend Miles Davis, with whom Hendrix was making plans to record. Unfortunately the recording never materialized when Miles demanded $50,000 in advance of the first session.

Electric Lady Studios were finally completed in August 1970, but Hendrix only spent a few weeks actually recording there. On August 27 he headed to England to perform in front of 600,000 fans at the Isle of Wight Festival. By this time his health was rapidly deteriorating due to his increasing use of alcohol and a reckless intake of drugs. His last performance was at the Love and Peace Festival on the German island of Fehman on September 6. Exhausted and sick, he returned to London where he was found dead on the morning of September 18 at the Samarkand Hotel. Although the circumstances surrounding his death are still mysterious, it is believed that he took nine tablets of the sleeping aid Vesperax (recommended dosage: ½ tab) after a night of heavy drinking and drug taking. His body was returned to Seattle where he is buried at Greenwood Memorial Park in suburban Renton.

STUDY QUESTIONS

Name _____ Date _____

1. What were some of the social issues that led to the formation of a youth counter culture in the 1960s?

2. How and why did San Francisco give birth to the hippie movement?

3. What were some of the events and cultural trappings that resulted from the San Francisco scene and the Summer of Love?

4. What were some of the musical and non-musical influences on acid rock?

5. Name some similarities and differences between the early careers of the Jefferson Airplane and the Grateful Dead.

6. What were some of the differences between the psychedelic scenes in San Francisco and Los Angeles?

7. Describe some of the reasons that the Doors' sound was unique.

8. Describe some of the different music styles that Frank Zappa experimented with and the albums that they are found on.

9. What were some of the hallmarks of Cream's sound, and why did they break up after such a short existence?

10. Describe how Jimi Hendrix got such a unique sound, both in terms of his equipment and his playing technique.

8
CHANGING DIRECTIONS

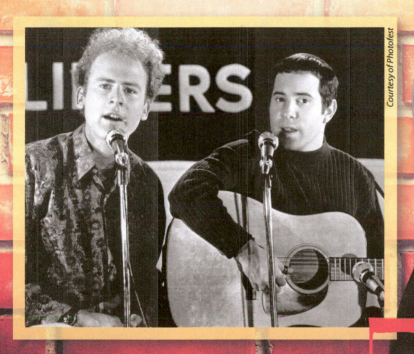

Courtesy of Photofest

"[Rock 'n roll] really is not given to thinking—and resents thinking. It's always aspired to be the music of the working class. And it's never been looked upon as a vocabulary for art and artistic thinking. . . . We have to be able to expand the vocabulary to express more complex thoughts."

—*Paul Simon (Simon and Garfunkel)*

KEY TERMS	Folk rock Laurel Canyon The Troubadour	Singer/songwriter Country rock The Basement Tapes	*The Last Waltz* Southern Rock

KEY FIGURES	Charles Manson
	The Byrds
	The Mamas and the Papas
	Buffalo Springfield
	Crosby, Stills, Nash &
	  Young
	Simon and Garfunkel
		Carole King
		Joni Mitchell
		Carly Simon
		James Taylor
		Van Morrison
		Gram Parsons
		The Band
			Creedence Clearwater
			  Revival
			Lynyrd Skynyrd
			Duane Allman
			The Allman Brothers Band
			The Eagles
			Fleetwood Mac

KEY ALBUMS	*Sweetheart of the Rodeo*—
	  the Byrds
	Déjà vu—Crosby, Stills,
	  Nash & Young
	*Bridge Over Troubled
	  Water*—Simon and
	  Garfunkel
	Tapestry—Carole King
	Blue—Joni Mitchell
		Sweet Baby James—James
		  Taylor
		Astral Weeks—Van
		  Morrison
		*The Gilded Palace of
		  Sin*—the Flying Burrito
		  Brothers
		Music from Big Pink—the
		  Band
			At Fillmore East—the
			  Allman Brothers Band
			*Eagles/Their Greatest Hits
			  1971–1975*—the Eagles
			Rumours—Fleetwood
			  Mac

THE 1970s

The Changing Landscape

As we have seen, the 1960s were a time when dramatic changes were taking place in American society—changes which often did not come easily. Entering the 1970s, it seemed as if the turmoil from the past decade had spoiled the chances for any hope or optimism from the upcoming decade. The assassinations of Dr. Martin Luther King and Senator Robert Kennedy in 1968 had certainly thrown their share of cold water on any momentum that had been gained by the anti-war and civil rights movements. In November 1968, Republican candidate Richard M. Nixon, who campaigned on a promise of bringing an end to the Vietnam War, was elected President. However, many young people viewed Nixon with suspicion, and their fears seemed to be justified when he ordered the invasion of Cambodia by U.S. troops in 1970—an obvious expansion of the war. In response, protests intensified on college campuses all over the country, and the mainstream media increasingly began to question the motives for continuing the war. With his shifty eyes and perennial 5 o'clock shadow, Nixon was a polarizing agent who stoked the fears and angers of many young people, and as the nation would soon find out, for good reason. Although the 1960s were over, America still had many troubling questions to answer as it entered the 1970s.

Rock was going through a similar rite of passage, and there seemed to be a convergence of tragic events in 1969 and 1970 indicating that its Aquarian age was over. The first came on the night of August 8, 1969, when the "family" members of **Charles Manson**, a wannabe songwriter who had befriended the Beach Boys' Dennis Wilson and had become a regular presence among Southern California rock circles, brutally murdered seven wealthy Los Angelos. Five of the victims were stabbed to death in the former home of producer Terry Melcher, who had repeatedly rejected Manson's songs. Was Manson sending a message to Melcher and others in the L.A. music industry? It would take four months for police to crack the case, during which time the city's music scene became decidedly less friendly and more guarded and suspicious. Up north in the Bay Area on December 6, the Altamont Festival was marred by violence and murder, and seemed to kill the good vibes created by the Woodstock Nation just four months earlier. While all this was going on—although no one knew it at the time—the Beatles, the group that had essentially started and led the pop-cultural side of the 1960s, were breaking up. And just as the rock community was adjusting to life without them, Janis Joplin, Jimi Hendrix and Jim Morrison all died from drug overdoses within nine months of each other, all at the age of 27. For many, the cumulative effect of all these events was a loss of innocence, a darker outlook on life, retreat, and a re-evaluation of what had been and what might lie ahead.

Fragmentation

For a variety of reasons, rock was also beginning to fragment into a number of different styles and musical paths by the 1970s. It had matured significantly during the 1960s, and the pursuit of different paths of expression is a natural part of the growing process of any art form, which rock by now had indeed become. Through the leadership of the Beatles and others at the creative vanguard, musicians had witnessed the expansion of rock's musical boundaries, and many were ready to begin pursuing their own musical paths. The breakup of the Beatles actually encouraged the fragmentation of rock, as there was no longer a clear-cut leader for musicians to line up behind and follow. The rock audience had also expanded tremendously during the 1960s, and by 1970 rock was no longer the music of the counterculture, but the music of the mainstream culture. This larger audience, which now cut across two generations, was itself much more diverse and fragmented, and also willing to accept a number of different forms of expression within the rock context.

The radio and record industries also contributed to the fragmentation. Late 1960s progressive rock radio, with its free form, anything goes programming was by 1970 deemed too haphazard and inefficient; radio executives began to tightly format their stations to target specific segments of the audience. These new formats included soft rock (target group: women), urban contemporary (blacks), oldies (mature adults), and AOR, or album-oriented rock (young white males). The expanded rock audience was also buying more records: in the early 1970s the record industry was growing at an astounding 25 percent a year. A gold record (sales of 500,000) was no longer a benchmark—the biggest selling records were now expected to go platinum (sales of one million). Like the radio industry, record companies also bought into the strategy of marketing rock as a product, and assigned user-friendly labels to the newly emerging music styles: folk rock, singer/songwriters, country rock, soft rock, art rock, and so on.

This chapter will examine the new mainstream pop styles and artists that began emerging in the late 1960s and early 1970s that changed the face of the rock world. Other styles that emerged in the 1970s will be covered in later chapters: heavy metal and art rock in Chapter 9; black pop in Chapter 10; and punk in Chapter 11.

FOLK ROCK

The Dylan Influence

Folk rock actually had its beginnings well before the onset of the 1970s; as discussed in Chapter 5, Bob Dylan's first experiments into combining the folk philosophy with rock occurred in early 1965 with *Bringing It All Back Home.* In April the Byrds released their cover of "Mr. Tambourine Man," the record that is generally considered to have started the folk rock movement. It peaked at #1 in June, just one month before Dylan's infamous appearance at the Newport Folk Festival with the Paul Butterfield Blues Band. Later that year Dylan released *Highway 61 Revisited,* which included the #2 single "Like a Rolling Stone," and in December Simon and Garfunkel's "The Sounds of Silence," a folk song with an overdubbed rhythm section went to #1. Although folk purists vilified Dylan for abandoning traditional folk and "selling out," folk rock became a popular style in the late 1960s and early 1970s with that segment of the audience looking for music containing a meaningful message. That most essential element of folk rock—socially relevant lyrics—combined with strumming acoustic guitars and beautiful vocal harmonies to define the new genre.

Ground zero for folk rock was Los Angeles, which by the mid 1960s was wresting control of the pop music industry from New York and London. Around this time the rock royalty, especially the folk rockers and singer/song-writers, were beginning to nestle into what became an artistic sanctuary of sorts in the mountainous wooded area north of West Hollywood known as **Laurel Canyon.** The Canyon was "the holy hills of the hip," a place where "bungalows perched precariously on Lookout Mountain, Wonderland Avenue, Ridpath Drive, and a handful of other dusty Canyon roads became a de facto rock and roll colony," writes author Fred Goodman. During its heyday, the Canyon was home to Roger McGuinn and Chris Hillman of the Byrds, David Crosby, Graham Nash and Neil Young, all four members of the Mamas and the Papas, Carole King, Joni Mitchell (who shared a cottage with Nash), Frank Zappa, Brian Wilson and many others. Doors it seemed were always

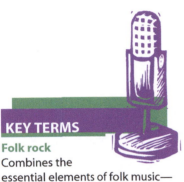

KEY TERMS

Folk rock
Combines the essential elements of folk music—socially relevant lyrics, strumming guitars and a softer manner—with the electric instruments of rock.

Laurel Canyon   The mountainous wooded area north of West Hollywood where many rock artists lived in the mid to late 1960s.

FOLK ROCK GROUPS
- The Byrds
- Buffalo Springfield
- The Nitty Gritty Dirt Band
- The Mamas and the Papas
- The Lovin' Spoonful
- Crosby, Stills, Nash & Young

he cohosted a network TV special with Elvis Presley on which the two sang each other's signature songs, "Love Me Tender" and "Witchcraft."

Characteristics of Folk Rock

1. Commercial pop oriented, combining elements of rock and folk
2. Instrumentation built around strumming acoustic guitar with rock rhythm section
3. Generally softer dynamics
4. Emphasis on rich choral vocal harmonies, often three and four part
5. Emphasis on lyric story lines, which could include romantic love, social or political themes, traditional folk songs, etc.

FOLK ROCK

Key Folk Rock Recordings

- *Bringing It All Back Home*—Bob Dylan, 1964
- "Mr. Tambourine Man"— the Byrds, 1965
- "The Sound of Silence"—Simon and Garfunkel, 1965
- "For What It's Worth"—Buffalo Springfield, 1967
- *Déjà Vu*—Crosby, Stills, Nash & Young, 1970

open; parties always commencing; and live, informal music making was a way of life. One of the Canyon's legends has it that David Crosby, Stephen Stills and Graham Nash first sang together at Mama Cass' Canyon bungalow. Another has it that Stills wrote his protest anthem "For What It's Worth" at a party there. "Stephen picked up his guitar and started playing this little riff—and he started singing," recalled singer Robin Lane. "He just wrote the song right there in front of everybody."

The Los Angeles club circuit was as varied as the city was sprawling. As we saw in Chapter 7, the clubs on and around Sunset Strip such as the Whisky a Go Go and Pandora's Box supported the psychedelic scene. Folk rock also had its venues, some of which had traditions dating back to the 1950s of hiring folk performers and hosting open mic nights that generally nurtured a growing folk scene. These included the Ice House, the Unicorn, and the Ash Grove, but the most important was **The Troubadour**, located just a few blocks away from the Whisky, on Santa Monica Boulevard. Starting in 1961 the Troub started hosting Monday night hootenannies, where big names like Judy Collins and Phil Ochs might intermingle performances with unknown up-and-comers. The club was also where networking was done, acquaintances made, and bands formed. It was at the Troubadour in 1964 that folksinger Jim McGuinn met David Crosby and Gene Clark, who together started the Byrds.

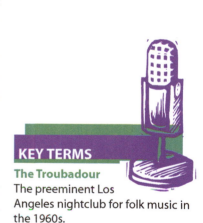

KEY TERMS

The Troubadour
The preeminent Los Angeles nightclub for folk music in the 1960s.

The Byrds

The Byrds were led by Jim McGuinn (who in 1967 began going by the first name Roger), a singer/guitarist from Chicago who had worked with folk groups the Limelighters and the Chad Mitchell Trio before moving to Los Angeles in early 1964. While hanging out and playing at the Troubadour he met former New Christy Minstrel singer/guitarist Gene Clark and folk-singer David Crosby. Inspired by seeing *A Hard Day's Night* in the summer of 1964, the three decided to form an electric band and enlisted bass player

Chris Hillman and drummer Michael Clarke to fill things out. After rehearsing for a few months as the Jet Set and then as the Beefeaters, in November they signed with Columbia Records and changed their name to the Byrds (the name being misspelled purposely in homage to the Beatles). In January 1965, after receiving a demo tape of Dylan singing his unreleased song "Mr. Tambourine Man," the group recorded their innovative cover of the song. By smoothing out the rough edges of Dylan's original version with Beatle-esque vocal harmonies and adding a rock rhythm section (mostly L.A. studio musicians), the group defined the folk rock style. Their sound was new, but familiar: rock columnist Lillian Roxon asked rhetorically whether the Byrds were a "Dylanized Beatles" or a "Beatlized Dylan." "Mr. Tambourine Man" hit #1 in June. Interestingly, it was McGuinn's prominently featured Rickenbacker electric 12-string guitar and not the group's vocals that was their most distinctive feature.

THE BYRDS

- Jim (Roger) McGuinn
- Gene Clark
- David Crosby
- Chris Hillman
- Michael Clarke

In November 1965 the Byrds scored a second #1 hit, "Turn! Turn! Turn! (To Everything There Is a Season)," a song whose lyrics were adapted from Ecclesiastics with a melody written by Pete Seeger. In early 1966 the Byrds retooled slightly with a more psychedelic sound, and released the LP *Fifth Dimension,* which included the #14 hit "Eight Miles High." The song, which included a trippy John Coltrane-influenced 12-string guitar solo, would have charted even higher if not for being blacklisted by many radio stations for using the word "high" in the title and supposedly having drug references in the lyrics (even though the group denied it). Unfortunately, *Fifth Dimension* and the follow up *The Notorious Byrd Brothers* (1968) were not well received by the general public. Meanwhile, internal squabbling began to tear the group apart, and by 1967 both Gene Clark and the quarrelsome David Crosby were gone. In early 1968 the Byrds began working with country singer/songwriter Gram Parsons, who managed to take control of the band and revamp them into a country/rock hybrid. In mid-year the group moved to Nashville and spent three months recording their next LP, ***Sweetheart of the Rodeo***. They also became the first rock group to play at the Grand Ole Opry, although their set was controversial. Sweetheart is a pioneering album, one of the first in the country/rock vein, but in a sense it was the last gasp of the Byrds. Soon after its release, Parsons quit after refusing to accompany the group on tour in apartheid South Africa, and the group sputtered along without much success until finally disbanding in 1973.

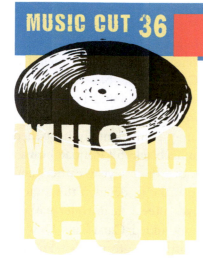

MUSIC CUT 36

"MR. TAMBOURINE MAN" (DYLAN)— THE BYRDS

Personnel: Jim McGuinn: vocals, Rickenbacker electric 12-string guitar; Gene Clark: vocals; David Crosby: vocals; Leon Russell: electric keyboards; Jerry Cole: rhythm guitar; Larry Knechtel: bass; Hal Blaine: drums. Recorded January 20, 1965 at Columbia Studios, Hollywood, CA; produced by Terry Melcher. Released April 12, 1965 on Columbia; 13 weeks on the charts, peaking at #1.

Widely credited with starting the folk rock movement, the Byrds recording of Bob Dylan's anthem was actually recorded before Dylan's own version was released in March on his seminal LP *Bringing It All Back Home.* For this recording, producer Terry Melcher (son of actress Doris Day) augmented Byrds McGuinn, Clark and Crosby with musicians of the famed Wrecking Crew (Blaine, Cole, Knechtel and Russell). With this rhythm section, the now famous sound of the Rickenbacker electric 12-string guitar and Everly Brothers inspired vocals, the Byrds completely transformed Dylan's own diamond-in-the-ruff version and created the template for their early sound. Just as this record was climbing to the #1 spot, the Byrds released their first LP, *Mr. Tambourine Man,* which contained three other Dylan songs and eventually reached the #6 spot on the charts during its 38-week stay.

The Mamas and the Papas

The Mamas and the Papas were made up of Denny Doherty, "Mama" Cass Elliot and husband and wife John Phillips and Michelle Phillips, all of whom were regulars in the early 1960s Greenwich Village folk scene. Originally known as the New Journeymen, the group moved to the Virgin Islands to rehearse new material before relocating in Southern California. After serving as backup vocalists in recording sessions, in 1965 the group changed their name to the Mamas and the Papas and signed with Dunhill. Their first release, "California Dreamin'" peaked at #4 later that year; the group eventually went on to release five albums and have ten Top 20 singles, including 1966's #1 "Monday, Monday" and 1967's #2 "Dedicated to the One I Love." The M&P's were known for their strong four part multi-tracked vocals and their good time hippie look; however, by 1968 the good times were coming to an end as the Phillips' began having marital problems that ultimately broke up the group. Mama Cass went on to have a successful solo career before dying of a heart attack in 1974. John Phillips wrote a number of hit songs (including most of the M&P's) before his death in 2001, including Scott McKenzie's 1967 #4 hit "San Francisco (Be Sure to Wear Flowers in Your Hair)" and the Beach Boys 1988 #1 hit "Kokomo." The Phillips' had three daughters, including actress McKenzie (who starred in TV's *One Day at a Time*) and singer Chynna of the popular 1990s group Wilson Phillips.

- Denny Doherty
- "Mama" Cass Elliot
- John Phillips
- Michelle Phillips

THE MAMAS AND THE PAPAS

Buffalo Springfield

One of the most promising but shortest-lived folk rock groups was Buffalo Springfield, who despite having a lineup that at one time or another included future stars Stephen Stills and Neil Young (later of Crosby, Stills, Nash & Young), Richie Furay (later of Poco), and Jim Messina (later of Poco and Loggins and Messina), only managed to last two years before internal bickering broke them up. The group formed in 1966 after Stills and Furay coincidentally happened to see Young stuck in traffic on the Sunset Strip in his black '59 Pontiac hearse. The three had met in Young's native Canada more than a year earlier, and now finding themselves all living in L.A. trying to make it, decided the logical thing to do was to start a band. Naming themselves after a steamroller parked outside their producers house, Stills, Young, Furay added Canadians Dewey Martin on drums and Bruce Palmer on bass to form the groups first lineup. Their debut gig was at the Troubadour in April, and by mid-year they were gigging at the Whisky a Go Go and touring with the Byrds. By the end of 1966 the band had signed with Atlantic and released their eponymous debut album. In the meantime, Stills had written what would prove to be the band's only lasting artifact "For What It's Worth" about the November 1966 Sunset Strip riots; unfortunately it was recorded too late to be included on the LP. After the song rose to #7, *Buffalo Springfield* was repressed, this time with "For What It's Worth" included. They further solidified their reputations as up and comers with a successful appearance at the Monterey Pop Festival. But infighting (ironically mostly between Stills and Young) and bad management ultimately took their toll, and the group folded in May 1968 after releasing three commercially unsuccessful albums.

Crosby, Stills, Nash & Young

Supergroup Crosby, Stills, Nash & Young, perhaps the most influential folk rock band, was formed by four of the genre's most talented and decorated singers and songwriters. Their intricately crafted high four-part harmonies are among the most distinctive of the genre. In May 1968, former Byrd David Crosby began jamming with Stephen Stills of the recently disbanded Buffalo Springfield; they were soon joined by Graham Nash, a former member of the group the Hollies. Their first LP, *Crosby, Stills & Nash,* recorded in early 1969, went to #6 and contained two minor hits, "Marrakesh Express" and "Suite: Judy Blue Eyes" (which Stills wrote for singer Judy Collins). Canadian singer/songwriter and ex-Springfielder Neil Young, joined the band as a sort of part-time member (as he was already leading his own group, Crazy Horse) in time for their summer tour, which included a performance at Woodstock. In early 1970 CSN&Y released what is perhaps their finest recording, **Déjà Vu**, which went to #1 on advance orders of two million copies. The album also contained two hit singles, "Woodstock" (written by Joni Mitchell, #11) and "Teach Your Children" (#16). *Déjà Vu* features songs written by each of the members that encompass a wide assortment of musical influences, including acoustic folk, rock, country, and pop.

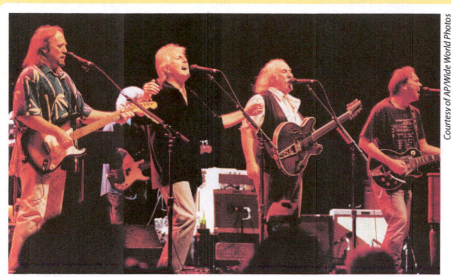

Stephen Stills, Graham Nash, David Crosby, and Neil Young perform in Los Angeles on February 12, 2000.

Courtesy of AP/Wide World Photos

Soon after the release of *Déjà Vu,* the Kent State massacre inspired Young to write "Ohio" ("Tin soldiers and Nixon's comin'/We're finally on our own/Last summer I heard the drumming/Four dead in Ohio"), a #14 single release. Young later reflected on the song: "It's still hard to believe I had to write this song. It's ironic that I capitalized on the death of these American students. Probably the biggest lesson ever learned at an American place of learning. My best CSN&Y effort. Recorded totally live in Los Angeles. David Crosby cried after this take." The group toured again in the summer of 1970, but afterward broke up due to internal conflicts (Stills and Young had a history of feuding going back to their days in Buffalo Springfield). A live album from the tour, *Four Way Street* was released in 1971 and like *Déjà Vu* went to #1. A brief reunion tour in 1974 resulted in their third straight #1 LP, a greatest hits compilation entitled *So Far*. Since 1977 the group has reunited from time to time without Young and has released three Top 20 albums as well as three Top 20 singles.

Simon and Garfunkel

Paul Simon (1941–) and Art Garfunkel (1941–) first got to know each other as classmates in the sixth grade in Forest Hills, New York. Singing together as the folk duo Tom and Jerry throughout their schooldays, they recorded a single called "Hey, Schoolgirl" in 1957 that went to #49 and earned them an appearance on American Bandstand. After their next records flopped, both went off to college, Garfunkel to study architecture and Simon to study English literature. In 1962 they reunited and began working the Greenwich Village folk club scene. Around this time Simon took one of his originals to Columbia Records producer Tom Wilson (Bob Dylan's producer at the time), who bought the song and signed the duo. The resulting album, *Wednesday Morning, Three A.M.,* a combination of traditional folk songs, Simon originals, and Dylan covers, went nowhere. Once again, the two went their separate ways, with Simon moving to England to try to get his career back on track.

Meanwhile, sensing a trend was afoot with the successes of "Mr. Tambourine Man" and "Like a Rolling Stone," Columbia's Wilson took one of the songs from *Wednesday Morning, Three A.M.,* "The Sound of Silence," and added a rock rhythm section and electric guitar without Simon or Garfunkel's knowledge. Within six months "The Sound of Silence" was the #1 song in the country. Simon immediately returned from England and reunited with Garfunkel to tour and record a new album in the folk rock vein. In 1966 the duo placed five singles and three albums in the Top 30, including the Top 5 hits "Homeward Bound" (#5) and "I Am a Rock" (#3). Although their two voices blended perfectly, the real magic in the group came from Simon's songwriting, which mixed pop-oriented melodies with intelligent, relevant lyrics that appealed to a wide audience base. However, after their initial success Simon's output slowed and the duo did not have another major hit until 1968 when the soundtrack album from the film *The Graduate* and its single release "Mrs. Robinson" both went to #1. *The Graduate* was followed by *Bookends,* which also went to #1 (the two albums occupied the top spot on the charts for a combined 16 weeks). In 1970, after another two-year drought, Simon and Garfunkel released ***Bridge over Troubled Water,*** which also went to #1 for ten weeks and contained the hit singles "The Boxer" (#7) and "Bridge over Troubled Water" (#1) and won the 1970 Grammy for Album of the Year. Unfortunately, *Bridge over Troubled Water* would be Simon and Garfunkel's last album as they separated to pursue other interests.

Other Folk Rock Artists

Other important folk rock groups include the Lovin' Spoonful, led by John Sebastian; Ian and Sylvia, led by Ian and Sylvia Tyson; the Turtles, and the Beau Brummels.

SINGER/SONGWRITERS

The Dylan Influence (Again!)

By the end of the 1960s, a new label was being given to solo performers who wrote and sang original songs that tackled personal issues and emotional struggles. **Singer/songwriters** were nothing new to rock: Buddy Holly, John Lennon, Paul McCartney, and Paul Simon had all fit that description, but they first became established stars as members of the bands they belonged to. The new breed of songpoets eschewed the traditional route of joining a band, and instead found fame on their own singing and composing merits. Up to this point, the only artist who had really established himself in this fashion was Bob Dylan, who, because of his emergence in the early 1960s was labeled a folk singer. In fact, many of the new singer/songwriters might have been called folk singers if they had come along ten years earlier, but in the new era of selling rock as

KEY TERMS

Singer/ songwriters An umbrella term to describe the solo singer/composers that emerged in the late 1960s and early 1970s; characterized by personal, confessional lyrics and soft, soothing music.

Characteristics of the Singer/Songwriters

1. Solo artists who recorded and performed with backup bands

2. Personal, confessional, reflective, narcissistic lyrics

3. Soft, soothing music, with acoustic pianos and acoustic guitars prominent

4. Willingness to experiment with influences from a variety of styles, including jazz, R&B, folk, etc.

5. Important outlet for women performers and their viewpoints

Key Singer/Songwriter Recordings

■ *Astral Weeks*—Van Morrison, 1968

■ *Sweet Baby James*—James Taylor, 1970

■ *Blue*—Joni Mitchell, 1971

■ *Tapestry*—Carole King, 1971

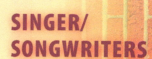

SINGER/ SONGWRITERS

a retail product, labels were an essential part of a record company's marketing strategy. Whatever they were called, the singer/songwriters owed a mountain of indebtedness to Dylan's influence.

Having said that, there were important differences between the new singer/ songwriters and the folkies that were due specifically to their timing. Although the 1960s were a time of communal thought, sharing, and a spirit of working together to change society, by the 1970s many people were ready for a moment of introspection and reflection, and to focus on making their own lives better and more meaningful. This attitude was widespread enough that many observers began calling the 1970s the "me first" decade. The singer/songwriters reflected this mood, and tended to write about themselves rather than socially conscious issues, as the earlier folkies would have done. The personal and confessional themes of these songs—along with a soft, slow and soothing musical context— connected with the maturing rock audience. Pianos and acoustic guitars rather than drums and distorted electric guitars became the prominent instruments. Other instruments such as orchestral strings and light percussion were also used to soften the sound.

But one of the most important developments that the singer/songwriters brought to rock was as a voice for female performers to reflect on the dramatic cultural changes that were taking place for women regarding their sexuality, independence, and their roles in the workplace. True, there had been previous instances of women who sang feminist manifestos of sort—Aretha Franklin's "Respect" and Grace Slick of Jefferson Airplane with "Somebody to Love" come to mind—but the songs were usually written by male songwriters (as in the examples given) and given a female perspective only by virtue of who was

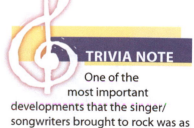

TRIVIA NOTE

One of the most important developments that the singer/ songwriters brought to rock was as a voice for female performers.

■ Buddy Holly

■ John Lennon

■ Paul McCartney

■ Paul Simon

■ Bob Dylan

SINGER/ SONGWRITERS

doing the singing. Even "Will You Love Me Tomorrow," a song about a girl asking for assurance that her boyfriend will still love her the day after "doing it" had lyrics written by a man (Gerry Goffin). The women singer/songwriters—Carole King, Joni Mitchell, Carly Simon, et al—wrote their own songs, and their lyrics reflected the new era of enlightenment and opportunities that characterized the emerging women's liberation movement. Songs like Simon's "That's the Way I've Always Heard It Should Be" and King's "It's Too Late," both of which hit the Top 10 with messages of criticizing marriages and ending relationships connected with young women of the day in powerful ways. Of course, lyrical topics were not limited by any means: there was always love (Mitchell's "Help Me"), companionship (King's "You've Got a Friend"), the meaning of life (Laura Nyro's "And When I Die"), and regret (Mitchell's "Big Yellow Taxi").

Carole King

By the mid 1960s Carole King (1942–) was already a legend in the music business, with a solid resume as a respected Brill Building songwriter with her husband Jerry Goffin. But when her marriage to Goffin broke up in 1967, she moved to Laurel Canyon to reinvent herself. Once in Los Angeles she released one album with a recording only group, the City, and a commercially unsuccessful solo album, *Writer*. In January 1971 King went back into the studio to record *Tapestry*, one of the decade's defining albums. With heartfelt songs and sparse production, King emotionally was at the right place at the right time with songs like "It's Too Late," "You've Got a Friend," and soulful reworkings of her earlier hits "Will You Love Me Tomorrow" and "(You Make Me Feel Like) A Natural Woman." *Tapestry* peaked at #1 for 15 weeks and stayed on the charts for six years; it also won four Grammies, including Album of the

MUSIC CUT 37

"IT'S TOO LATE" (CAROLE KING/TONI STERN)—CAROLE KING

Personnel: Carole King: vocals, keyboards; Danny "Kootch" Kortchmar: guitar; Ralph Schuckett: electric piano; Curtis Amy: soprano sax; Charles Larkey: bass; Joel O'Brien: drums. Recorded January 1971 at A&M Studio B, Los Angeles, CA; produced by Lou Adler. Released April 1971 on Ode; 17 weeks on the charts, peaking at #1.

"It's Too Late" was one of three songs recorded (along with "You've Got a Friend" and "I Feel the Earth Move") on the first day of sessions for Carole King's blockbuster album *Tapestry*. It was the first single released from the album, and the only to reach #1, where it stayed for five weeks. The single was named Record of the Year at the 1972 Grammy Awards, one of four Grammies King won for *Tapestry*, including Album of the Year. Part of *Tapestry's* appeal is its straightforward production, which was completed in less than three weeks. With its heartfelt lyrics and soothing music, "It's Too Late" is a perfect representation of the album as a whole, which struck a chord with the pop audience and spent 15 weeks at #1. "Carole spoke from the heart, and she happened to be in tune with the mass psyche," wrote songwriter Cynthia Weil. "People were looking for a message, and she came to them with a message that was exactly what they were looking for."

Year and Best Female Pop Vocal Performance. "It's Too Late," b/w "I Feel the Earth Move" peaked at #1; the former song also won a Grammy for Record of the Year. King remained popular throughout the 1970s: two more albums, *Music* and *Fantasy* both hit #1, while another, *Rhymes and Reasons* peaked at #2. She also had 13 Top 40 singles in the decade. King's songs have also been popular for other artists to cover; "You've Got a Friend" alone has been covered by everyone from jazz singer Ella Fitzgerald to Michael Jackson to James Taylor, whose version went to #1. The Beatles also covered her song "Chains" on their first album.

Joni Mitchell

With stunning Nordic looks and beautiful soprano voice, Joni Mitchell (1943–) made an indelible first impression on people—especially men—when she moved to Los Angeles in 1967, but it was her songs that first won her rave reviews. Born Roberta Joan Anderson, she was raised in the wide-open prairies of Alberta and Saskatchewan, Canada where she survived a bout with polio at age nine and learned to play the guitar while recuperating. After moving to Saskatoon to enter college, Joni began to sing and write songs, and became a fixture in the local coffeehouse scene. It was there that she met and married fellow folksinger Chuck Mitchell, with whom she moved to Detroit in 1965 and began performing with as Chuck & Joni. The next two years were intensely creative for Joni as she went on a prolific songwriting tear, and because the Mitchell's apartment was a way station for traveling folksingers, her songs began to get heard by the likes of Buffy Sainte-Marie, Tom Rush and others. By early 1967 the Mitchells had divorced, and Joni moved to New York to pursue a career as a solo artist. By this time her songs were being enthusiastically received and recorded by other artists, including Sainte-Marie, Rush, and Judy Collins, who had a #8 hit with "Both Sides, Now."

Late in 1967 Mitchell moved to L.A., where new boyfriend David Crosby used his clout to secure a contract with Reprise Records. Her eponymous debut LP (later known as *Song to a Seagull*) was released to positive reviews but modest sales in 1968; 1969's *Clouds,* containing Mitchell's own version of "Both Sides, Now," sold even better, peaking at #31 and winning a Grammy for Best Folk Performance. Around this time she bought a cottage in Laurel Canyon in which she lived with new boyfriend Graham Nash. Traveling with Nash to New York in August 1969 while CSN&Y appeared at Woodstock, Mitchell wrote her classic anthem "Woodstock" after watching the festival on TV from a hotel room in New York City; the group's cover of the song became a #11 hit. Mitchell's own version of the song was included on her next album, 1970's *Ladies of the Canyon*. Her 1971 album ***Blue***, written in the heartache that followed the breakup of her relationship with James Taylor, is often considered to be her best. Mitchell writes sometimes painfully confessional, sometimes subtly humorous lyrics, which she sings with an idiosyncratic, playful vocal style. Along with "Both Sides, Now" and "Woodstock," her most popular songs include "The Circle Game," "Big Yellow Taxi," and "Help Me," a #7 hit in 1974.

Carly Simon

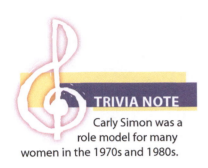

As the daughter of Richard Simon, co-founder of Simon and Shuster, Carly Simon (1945–) grew up in a world of wealth and privilege in the West Village of New York City. The Simon's were a musical family, and Carly and her two sisters recorded three albums as the Simon Sisters in the 1960s. After briefly attending the exclusive Sarah Lawrence College, Carly returned to New York and in 1968 sang in the jazz-flavored pop group Elephant's Memory, for which she also wrote songs. By 1969, after intensifying her songwriting efforts, she signed with Elektra Records, and in 1970 began working on her eponymous debut album. Her first single release, "That's the Way I've Always Heard It Should Be" struck a nerve with many women who were becoming disillusioned with the institution of marriage, and became a #10 hit. To promote the single, she made her L.A. debut at the Troubadour on April 6, 1971 and was warmly received. Her second album, *Anticipation,* was released in 1971, and propelled by the #3 charting title track (written while waiting for singer Cat Stevens to pick her up for a date), peaked at #30. 1972's *No Secrets,* was Simon's pop breakthrough; both the album and its signature song, "You're So Vain" hit #1. "Vain" has ignited a controversy of sorts as to who the song is about. Many have suggested Mick Jagger, with whom Simon reportedly had a brief fling, and who sang backup vocals on the song. Simon has never revealed the identity of the mystery person, however.

Carly Simon was a role model for many women in the 1970s and 1980s who were rethinking their status at home, work, and society as a whole. "Women adored her," said her manager Arlyne Rothberg. "Women looked at her and said: 'Oh, you can be gorgeous and smart and educated . . . *and* be a rock star?'" In 1972 Simon married James Taylor, and the two immediately became rock's *über* couple. *Rolling Stone* depicted them as embodying the "intelligent, self-conscious style and sex appeal that characterized soft-rock stardom in the Seventies." The couple divorced in 1983 after having two children.

James Taylor

Boston born James Taylor's (1948–) life has certainly seen its ups and downs, but he has managed to persevere and become a successful and often imitated star. He first garnered fame as the quintessential sensitive soft rock performer, but he has worked in a variety of musical settings over the course of his career. Taylor began writing songs after being admitted to a mental institution as a teen. Upon his discharge in 1966, he moved to New York and put together the Flying Machine with guitarist Danny Kortchmar. The group split up the next year due to Taylor's heroin addiction, which would plague him until 1969. In 1968 he moved to London and was signed to the Beatles' Apple Records, which produced his little noticed debut LP. After another stay at an institution to clean up his drug habit, he appeared at the 1969 Newport Folk Festival and signed with Warner Brothers. His next album, 1970's **Sweet Baby James** was his breakthrough, peaking at #3 with the help of the autobiographical single "Fire and Rain," which also hit the #3 spot on the charts. Taylor has since gone on to record thirteen more Top 40 albums and thirteen more Top 40 singles, including Carole King's "You've Got a Friend," a #1 hit in 1971, and 1974's "Mockingbird," a duet with his then wife Carly Simon, which peaked at #5.

Van Morrison

The career of George Ivan Morrison (1945–) has been chameleon-like, ranging from writing enigmatic song stories to poignant love songs to enduring Top 10 classics. His soulful, quirky vocal style and intelligent lyricism have been widely copied, while he in turn has been influenced by a wide range of styles including folk, jazz, soul, and the blues. Morrison was born and raised in a working-class family in Belfast, Northern Ireland. At 16 he quit school to tour Europe for a year with an R&B band; when he returned, he formed the group Them which secured a steady gig as the house band at Belfast's Maritime Hotel. Cut in the mold of the Rolling Stones and the Animals, Them became extremely popular in Ireland playing tough R&B-influenced rock. In 1964 the group moved to London where they released two albums, the #2 UK single "Here Comes the Night" and Morrison's classic "Gloria" before breaking up in 1966. In 1967 Morrison returned to Belfast before moving to New York, where he signed with Bang Records, who against his wishes released his first solo LP, *Blowin' Your Mind*. Despite the fact that the album contained the #10 hit single "Brown Eyed Girl," it sold poorly and Morrison retreated back to Belfast.

He rebounded quickly. In 1968 Morrison returned to New York and signed with the newly formed Warner Brothers label and in November released one of the most innovative and influential albums of the singer/songwriter genre, **Astral Weeks**. The album is not your typical rock and roll record, as Morrison used a jazz rhythm section (noted session men Richard Davis on bass, Connie Kaye on drums, and Jay Berliner on guitar), a vibraphonist, woodwinds, and string quartet to create a jazz/folk/blues/classical hybrid. Recorded in only two days, *Astral Weeks* is an enduring masterpiece that the critics loved; unfortunately, once again sales were poor. Morrison's commercial fortunes began to turn in the early 1970s with the release of five albums in four years that cracked the Top 40 (*Moondance, His Band and the Street Choir, Tupelo Honey, Saint Dominic's Preview,* and *Hard Nose the Highway*), and his highest charting single in late 1970 with "Domino" (#9). Morrison continues to record and tour despite suffering from severe stage fright. Many of his songs have also been covered by other artists, including "Have I Told You Lately That I Love You," a #5 hit for Rod Stewart in 1993 and "Wild Night," a #3 hit for John Mellencamp in 1994.

Other Singer/Songwriters

Other singer/songwriters that emerged in the late 1960s and early 1970s include Laura Nyro, Judy Collins, Jackson Browne, Randy Newman, Cat Stevens, Jim Croce, and Gordon Lightfoot.

COUNTRY ROCK

Dylan Strikes Yet Again

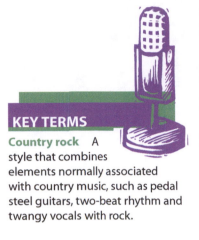

As we have discussed in Chapter 1, country music was one of the primary influences on the birth of rock and roll, and was an important component of the first rock and roll style, rockabilly. After rockabilly faded in the late 1950s, there was minimal country influence on rock for the next several years. However, when Bob Dylan recorded the country-influenced *John Wesley Harding* and *Nashville Skyline* in Nashville in 1968 and 1969, respectively, interest in country-tinged rock began to resurface. The use of Nashville studio musicians and a guest vocal by Johnny Cash on *Nashville Skyline* made that album a particularly important landmark. However, there were predecessors even to Dylan in the merging of country's ethos with rock. As early as 1963 the Hawks (which later became the Band) were playing music that could be loosely categorized as **country rock**; their association with Dylan in 1965 and 1966 on tours and on the Basement Tapes was no doubt mutually influential. Former teen idol Rick Nelson was also on the front end of the movement, recording the country-influenced *Bright Lights and Country Fever* as early as 1966. Often cited as the first country rock album is *Safe at Home,* recorded in late 1967 by the Gram Parsons led International Submarine Band.

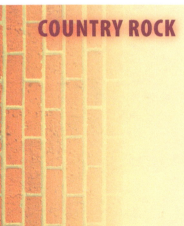

COUNTRY ROCK

Characteristics of Country Rock

1. Use of pedal steel guitar and other instruments normally associated with country/western
2. Two-beat country rhythm
3. Occasional use of twangy vocal delivery and vocal harmonies reminiscent of country/western
4. Rock rhythm section

Key Country Rock Recordings

- *Safe at Home*—the International Submarine Band, 1967
- *Music from Big Pink*—the Band, 1968
- *Sweetheart of the Rodeo*—the Byrds, 1968
- *Bayou Country*—Creedence Clearwater Revival, 1969

Gram Parsons

Gram Parsons (1946–73) grew up in a wealthy but dysfunctional Southern family. As a teen he played in several rock and roll bands and folk groups before moving to Boston to attend Harvard for a semester. While there, he became interested in country music, and formed the International Submarine Band to explore his new interest. In 1967 the ISB moved to Los Angeles and recorded the pioneering country rock LP *Safe at Home,* but before it was released Parsons left the group and began working with the Byrds. In his short time with the Byrds (there is some question whether or not he was an official member), Parsons wrote songs and sang on the album *Sweetheart of the Rodeo,* but due to legal entanglements from his ISB days most of his vocals were omitted from the final release. Parsons left the group in the summer of 1968 after refusing to tour in South Africa in protest of their apartheid policies.

In 1969, Parsons formed the Flying Burrito Brothers with ex-Byrd Chris Hillman. Their first album release, ***The Gilded Palace of Sin***, is yet another example verifying Parsons' influence on early country rock. Around this time he began hanging out with the Stones' Keith Richards and using heroin and cocaine, habits that grew worse and led to his untimely death from an overdose in 1973. Before his death, Parsons recorded one more album with the Flying Burrito Brothers and two solo albums. He is remembered today not only for his work with the ISB, the Byrds and the Burritos, but for the classic country rock songs that he wrote including "One Hundred Years from Now," "Do You Know How It Feels," and "$1000 Wedding."

The Band

Never fully appreciated by the public but loved by rock critics, the Band none-theless made a unique musical statement in the late 1960s and early 1970s that while influential, has never quite been replicated. Their music was an eclectic mix of folk, blues, country, classical, and rock and roll that managed to bring out the unique talents of each individual member. The Band evolved between 1958 and 1963 as the Hawks, the backup band for Arkansas-born rockabilly singer Ronnie Hawkins. One by one, Hawkins assembled the core of the group, adding

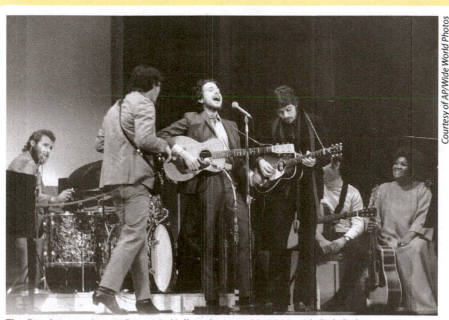

The Band appearing at Carnegie Hall on January 20, 1968 with Bob Dylan.
From left: Levon Helm, Rick Danko, Dylan, Robbie Robertson.

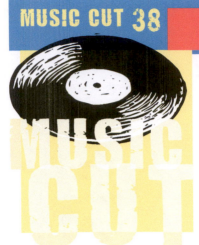

MUSIC CUT 38

"THE WEIGHT" (ROBBIE ROBERTSON)— THE BAND

Personnel: Levon Helm: drums, lead and backup vocals; Rick Danko: bass, vocals; Garth Hudson: piano; Richard Manuel: organ, vocals; Robbie Robertson: acoustic guitar. Recorded January 1968 at A&R Recorders Studio A, New York, NY; produced by John Simon. Released July 1, 1968 on the Capitol LP *Music from Big Pink;* single release peaked at #63.

"The Weight" is the last song on Side A of the Band's seminal 1968 album *Music from Big Pink,* and is one of the few single releases from the group to ever enter the Hot 100 chart. The lyrics reveal a song full of what appears to be biblical imagery, starting with the opening line and references to the Devil, Miss Moses, and Luke. But in a later interview, songwriter Robbie Robertson revealed his real inspiration came at least partly from filmmaker Luis Bunuel. "People like Bunuel would make films that had these religious connotations to them but it wasn't necessarily a religious meaning. In 'The Weight', it was this very simple thing. Someone says, 'Listen, will you do me this favor? When you get there will you say "hello" to somebody or will you pick up one of these for me? Oh, you're going to Nazareth, that's where the Martin guitar factory is. Do me a favor when you're there.' This is what it's all about." The song is an example of what made the Band so unique, in that it simultaneously sounds like the blues, country, folk, and pop. Or, as Robertson said, "It was North American folklore in the making."

fellow Arkansan Levon Helm in 1958, guitarist Robbie Robertson in 1959, and bassist Rick Danko, pianist Richard Manuel, and organist Garth Hudson in 1961. Robertson, Danko, Manuel, and Hudson were all Canadians, picked up as the group played its way through the rough and tumble bars in the mining towns in the middle of the country. The band members' various musical influences meshed well, and the Hawks developed a reputation as one of the hardest rocking bands around. By 1963, the egotistical Hawkins was forced out of his own group, and the group became at various times Levon and the Hawks or the Canadian Squires, with Helm as the de facto leader. In 1964, John Hammond Jr. heard them perform at a Canadian club and arranged a series of recording sessions in New York. It was there that they were introduced to Bob Dylan.

The Hawks toured with Dylan in late 1965, and after his motorcycle accident in the summer of 1966, they moved to Woodstock, New York, to collaborate with him on the informal recording sessions that would in time be known as the **Basement Tapes**. Those recordings, many of which were done in the basement of their sprawling pink house, provided the inspiration for the group to begin working on their own material and the eventual release of their first album, *Music from Big Pink* in 1968. The album was a revolutionary surprise; coming at a time when the rest of the rock world was immersed in psychedelia, *Big Pink* is unadorned and earthy, and lacking the flash of albums such as *Sgt. Pepper's* or *Are You Experienced?* Following its release, the group moved to Hollywood where in 1969 they released *The Band,* the album that proved to be their commercial breakthrough, peaking at #9, and containing their only Top 40 single, "Up on Cripple Creek" (#25). As the Band's popularity increased, the focus increasingly turned to the charismatic Robertson, the group's primary songwriter, and the egalitarian inner dynamics of the group began to change. Although they released six more LPs, including *Stage Fright* from 1970 and *Rock* *of Ages* in 1972, their days were numbered. The Band toured for the last time in 1976, concluding with a gala concert on Thanksgiving Day at San Francisco's Winterland Ballroom that included guest appearances by Dylan, Van Morrison, Eric Clapton, Muddy Waters, the Staple Singers, and many others. The documentary film of that concert, *The Last Waltz*, directed by Martin Scorsese, is one of rock's best.

Creedence Clearwater Revival

Formed in 1959 by four junior high school classmates from El Cerrito, California, Clearwater Revival was one of America's most popular bands from 1969 to 1971. Led by brothers John Fogerty (guitars/vocals/chief songwriter/producer) and Tom Fogerty (guitars/vocals), with Stu Cook (bass) and Doug Clifford (drums), CCR signed with Fantasy Records in 1964 when they were known as the Blue Velvets. After briefly calling themselves the Golliwogs, the band adopted their permanent name in 1967. CCR scored 13 Top 40 hits beginning in 1969 with the release of their LP *Bayou Country,* including 11 in the Top 10 and five that went to #2: 1969's "Proud Mary" (from *Bayou Country*), "Bad Moon Rising" and "Green River," and 1970's "Travelin' Band" and "Lookin' Out My Back Door." The band's sound was easily identifiable with strumming, country-influenced rockabilly guitars and John Fogerty's raspy blues enriched voice. Although most of their songs have rather down-to-earth and nonpolitical storylines, 1969's "Fortunate Son" was an attack on the privileged class who could afford to stay out of Vietnam through college draft deferments.

- John Fogerty
- Tom Fogerty
- Stu Cook
- Doug Clifford

CREEDENCE CLEARWATER REVIVAL

Other Country Rock Bands

Other bands and artists that played music in the country rock style include Linda Ronstadt, Poco, the Nitty Gritty Dirt Band, the Stone Canyon Band, Pure Prairie League, and Loggins and Messina.

SOUTHERN ROCK

The Rural Cousin

Southern rock is the rural cousin to the citified country rock. Whereas many country rock groups had a close musical connection to folk with strumming guitars and harmonious vocals, Southern rock bands were deeply rooted in country

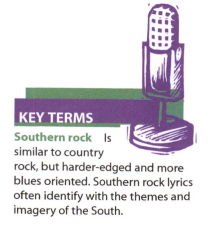

KEY TERMS

Southern rock Is similar to country rock, but harder-edged and more blues oriented. Southern rock lyrics often identify with the themes and imagery of the South.

SOUTHERN ROCK

Characteristics of Southern Rock

1. Heavier instrumentation, often including two drummers, two or three lead guitar players
2. Harder edge than country rock, similar to hard rock
3. Deep roots in the blues
4. Lyric themes identifying with Southern "good old boy" image: male swagger, drinking, cheating, fighting, etc.

Key Southern Rock Recordings

- *At Fillmore East*—the Allman Brothers, 1971
- "Free Bird"—Lynyrd Skynyrd, 1973
- *Second Helping*—Lynyrd Skynyrd, 1974
- *My Home's in Alabama*—Alabama, 1980

music and the blues. They were grittier, and played louder and harder than their country rock cousins. Their lyrics reflected less emphasis on intellectual subjects and more on identifying with the legacy of the South and the "good old boy" Southern stereotypes of male posturing and swagger. The bands were often bigger as well, sometimes including two lead guitarists (Lynyrd Skynyrd had three), and in the case of the Allman Brothers, two drummers. With its harder edge and blues base, Southern rock is conceptually somewhere between country rock and hard rock, and like hard rock, its audience was predominantly young, white and male. The power and drive of Southern rock also made the music popular in concert settings.

Lynyrd Skynyrd

Formed in 1965 in Jacksonville, Florida, Lynyrd Skynyrd was the prototypical Southern rock band, combining the rebellious attitude of rock and roll with the blues and a country twang. In 1965 while still in high school, classmates Ronnie Van Zant (vocals), Allen Collins (guitar), Gary Rossington (guitar), Leon Wilkeson (bass), and Billy Powell (keyboards) formed a band they named in mock honor of their gym teacher, Leonard Skinner, who was known to punish students with long hair. After adding drummer Bob Burns, the band spent the next several years playing bars throughout the South before they were discovered and signed to MCA Records by producer Al Kooper. After adding third guitarist Ed King, the band recorded their debut album *Pronounced Leh-Nerd Skin-Nerd* in 1973, which included the anthemic tribute to Duane Allman, "Free Bird." They also became the warm-up act on the Who's Quadrophenia Tour. By the time their second album *Second Helping* was released in 1974,

LYNYRD SKYNYRD

- Ronnie Van Zant
- Allen Collins
- Gary Rossington
- Leon Wilkeson
- Leon Wilkeson
- Bob Burns

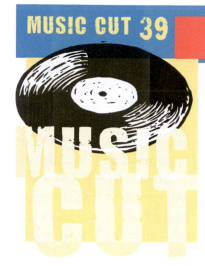

MUSIC CUT 39

"SWEET HOME ALABAMA" (ED KING/GARY ROSSINGTON/ RONNIE VAN ZANT)—LYNYRD SKYNYRD

Personnel: Ed King: lead guitar, backup vocals; Gary Rossington: rhythm guitar; Allen Collins: rhythm guitar, acoustic guitar; Leon Wilkeson: bass, backup vocals; Billy Powell: piano; Bob Burns: drums; Ronnie Van Zant: lead vocals; Al Kooper, Clydie King, Merry Clayton, Sherlie Matthews: backup vocals. Recorded June 1973 at Studio One, Doraville, GA; produced by Al Kooper. Released April 1974 on MCA; 17 weeks on the charts, peaking at #8.

"Sweet Home Alabama" was inspired by Neil Young's disparaging lyrics about racism and slavery in the South found in the songs "Southern Man" (from *After the Gold Rush*, 1970) and "Alabama" (*Harvest*, 1972). Although Lynyrd Skynyrd, in mentioning him by name in the lyrics, appear to be provoking Young into a war of words, there was in fact a mutual respect between the two adversaries. Young later said, "I'd rather play 'Sweet Home Alabama' than 'Southern Man' anytime"; Skynyrd lead singer Ronnie Van Zant responded by wearing a Neil Young T-shirt on the cover of the band's final album *Street Survivors*. "Sweet Home Alabama" was the highest charting record for Skynyrd, peaking at #8, and was included on their second LP *Second Helping*.

Lynyrd Skynyrd was acquiring a devoted fan base. The album went multi-platinum, and also contained what was to be their highest charting hit, "Sweet Home Alabama" (#8), a reply to Neil Young's song's "Southern Man" and "Alabama." Three more albums were forthcoming by late 1976, topped by the triple-platinum double live *One More from the Road*. Then, tragedy struck.

On October 20, 1977, three days after the release of their sixth album *Street Survivors,* the plane carrying the band to a gig in Baton Rouge, Louisiana, crashed outside of Gillsburg, Mississippi, killing Van Zant, new guitarist Steve Gaines, and Gaines's sister Cassie, a backup singer. The other members were injured but lived to continue on with the band. Ironically, the *Street Survivors* cover showed the band surrounded by flames; after the crash, the flames were removed on a redesigned cover. *Street Survivors* ultimately peaked at #5, becoming their biggest seller.

The Allman Brothers Band

Although they weren't as commercially successful or as typically a Southern rock band as Lynyrd Skynyrd, the Allman Brothers Band became one of the 1970s greatest bands by forging a unique combination of blues, boogie, R&B, country and jazz. Their legendary onstage jamming outdid even the Grateful Dead, with songs that often lasted 30 minutes or more and featured the tasteful playing of their three main soloists, the brothers themselves and guitarist Dickey Betts. The band was formed in 1969 in Macon, Georgia, the hometown of guitarist **Duane Allman** (1946–1971) and his organist brother Greg Allman (1947–). At the time, Duane was a session guitarist at Fame Studios in Muscle Shoals, Alabama, where he had earned a solid reputation by playing on records by Wilson Pickett, Aretha Franklin, and others. At the suggestion of Phil Walden, head of the newly formed Capricorn Records, Allman put together the band by recruiting friends Dickey Betts on guitar, Jai Johanny Johanson and Butch Trucks on drums, Berry Oakley on bass, and Greg. After some touring to jell their sound, they released their eponymous debut album, which garnered respect from critics and sold modestly, mainly in the South. Two more releases followed in the next two years, 1970's *Idlewild South,* which sold moderately well and peaked at #38, and the double live **At Fillmore East** from 1971, recorded at the Fillmore East Ballroom. By this time the Allmans were being praised as "America's best rock and roll group," while Duane was further cementing his reputation as a guitar hero by appearing on Eric Clapton's *Derek and the Dominos* album.

On October 29, 1971, as the band was working on its third album, Duane was killed in a motorcycle accident in Macon. Determined to continue, the rest of the members completed *Eat a Peach,* which climbed to #4, and added pianist Chuck Leavell as a quasi replacement for Allman. But tragedy struck again—before they could finish their next album, bassist Oakley was also killed in a motorcycle accident on November 11, 1972, only three blocks from where Duane had died. Forging ahead once again in the face of misfortune, Dickey Betts assumed the leadership of the band and wrote most of the band's new material while steering them away from their deep blues roots to a more pop friendly sound. 1973's *Brothers and Sisters* became their only #1 album and contained the Allman's highest charting single, "Ramblin' Man" (#2). The band began to break apart in the mid-1970s after Greg married actress Cher (who had a disruptive influence) and later was forced to testify against a band employee in a federal drug trial, alienating him from the other band members.

Other Southern Rock Bands

With the success of the Allman Brothers Band and Lynyrd Skynyrd, other Southern rock bands emerged in the 1970s that achieved commercial staying power. They include the power trio ZZ Top from Texas, with ten Top 40 albums beginning in 1973; South Carolina's the Marshall Tucker Band, with eight Top 40 albums starting in 1973; Florida-based .38 Special, led by Donnie Van Zant (younger brother of the late Ronnie from Lynyrd Skynyrd), five Top 40 LPs; the Charlie Daniels Band, led by the former Nashville session guitarist (Daniels's credits include Dylan's *Nashville Skyline*), five Top 40 albums; Georgia's Atlanta Rhythm Section, also with five Top 40 LPs; and the L.A.-based Black Oak Arkansas.

CORPORATE ROCK

Mergers and Megahits

By the time the 1970s rolled around, rock had become the dominant music format of the mainstream culture, a fact that was reflected in the explosive sales growth of records and tapes. In 1973, music was a $2 billion a year industry; by 1978, sales had grown to $4 billion. As rock was becoming big business, the industry began to consolidate, as large corporations started to merge with and acquire major record labels, small independent labels and other music-related businesses. By the end of the 1970s, 80 percent of all record and tape sales were controlled by six of these conglomerates: Columbia/CBS, RCA Victor,

United Artists-MGM, Capitol-EMI, MCA, and Warner Communications. In this new climate of lawyers, accountants, and corporate control, it became imperative to turn a profit, and record labels responded by minimizing their risk whenever possible. Often this meant relying on well-established artists to produce records designed to have the greatest sales potential. These artists became the beneficiaries of massive advertising campaigns and huge contracts as the major labels poured their resources behind them, often with impressive results. Several albums from the 1970s are among the best selling of all time, including (all figures for U.S. only) the Eagles' *Eagles/Their Greatest Hits 1971–1975* (29 million), Fleetwood Mac's *Rumours* (19 million) *Saturday Night Fever* and Pink Floyd's *The Dark Side of the Moon* (15 million each) and Carole King's *Tapestry* (ten million). One of the most bankable stars was Elton John, who held the #1 album spot for a combined total of 39 weeks with seven of his 18 Top 40 LP's during the decade. Other groups, including Air Supply, Paul McCartney and Wings, Journey, Chicago and Foreigner fell back on predictable but stale pop formulas to sell a lot of records that were less than inspiring on a creative level.

The end result of all the fast money being made was that the 1970s marked the beginning of an era of greed, corporate hubris and personal lust for power in the industry that would last for nearly 30 years. Billions of dollars would be made during this time, not only by the labels and their artists, but also by fast talking industry moguls. Men such as David Geffen of Asylum (who, with shrewd investments in the record and movie industries is now estimated to have a personal fortune of more than six billion dollars), Walter Yetnikoff of CBS/Columbia, Neil Bogart of Casablanca and Tommy Mattola of Sony made behind the scenes deals and decisions that shaped this business ethos, often driven by nothing more than personal gain. Investigative books such as Fredric Dannen's *Hit Men* and Steve Knopper's *Appetite for Self-Destruction* offer fascinating and sometimes juvenile accounts of maneuvering, backstabbing and vindictiveness that these and other industry operatives would engage in from time to time just to make a buck, and often just to even a score or exact revenge on a rival. With the accumulation of such staggering amounts of money also came lavish lifestyles, expensive homes and cars, and excessive usage of cocaine.

Ultimately this corporate climate would create a bloated and inefficient business model that could not adapt to the fast-changing technology that the Internet would bring in the new millennium. These changes will be discussed at length in Chapter 13. In the meantime, two bands that perhaps best represent the ethos of corporate rock in the 1970s, the Eagles and Fleetwood Mac, will be discussed at this time.

The Eagles

With 16 albums achieving platinum or multi-platinum status, the Eagles are one the most commercially successful rock bands in history. In spite of this they have attracted their share of criticism as symbolizing the manufactured corporate rock of the 1970s and the self-indulgent California lifestyle. Ironically, none of the original members were from the Golden State: bassist Randy Meisner hailed from Scottsbluff, Nebraska; guitarist Bernie Leadon from Minneapolis; drummer Don Henley from Texas; and guitarist Glenn Frey from Detroit. The group came about as the four worked their way through a variety of influential bands after moving to Los Angeles in the mid 1960s. Meisner was a founding member of Poco and worked briefly in Rick Nelson's Stone Canyon Band. Leadon had briefly been a member of the Flying Burrito Brothers, while Frey had worked with Bob Seger and J. D. Souther. In 1971, after they found themselves working together on a Linda Ronstadt album, the four decided to start a new band—not just any band, but a wildly successful one. "We'd watched bands like Poco and the Burrito Brothers lose their initial momentum, and we were determined not to make the same mistakes," recalled Frey. "Everybody had to look good, sing good, and write good. We wanted it all. Peer respect. AM and FM success. No. 1 singles and albums, great music, and a lot of money." After David Geffen signed them to Asylum and sent them off to an Aspen, Colorado club to tighten their sound, work commenced on their first album. Propelled by three Top 40 singles, *The Eagles* went gold within a year and a half.

In early 1973 the group returned to the studio to record their second album, *Desperado,* which also went gold and contained the hit "Tequila Sunrise." By this time the Eagles were slowly abandoning the country flavor that characterized their early releases in favor of a more mainstream rock sound. The next two albums, *On the Border* and *One of These Nights* (both 1974) hit the Top 10, with the latter being the first of their five #1 LPs. In spite of their success, the shift away from country alienated Leadon, who quit the group in late 1975 and was replaced by Joe Walsh of the James Gang (another guitarist, Don Felder had also joined for On the Border). In 1976 they released of the blockbuster ***Eagles/Their Greatest Hits 1971–1975***, which became the first certified platinum album and today has the distinction of being the third best-selling album in U.S. history with 29 million copies sold, and sales of 42 million worldwide. The next album, *Hotel California,* was released in December 1976 and went platinum within one week. Using California as a metaphor, Henley's lyrics paint

MUSIC CUT 40

"TAKE IT EASY" (JACKSON BROWNE, GLENN FREY)— THE EAGLES

Personnel: Glenn Frey: lead vocals, acoustic guitar; Don Henley: drums, backup vocals; Bernie Leadon: lead guitar, banjo, backup vocals; Randy Meisner: bass, backup vocals. Recorded 1972 at Olympic Sound Studios, London; produced by Glyn Johns. Released May 1, 1972 on Asylum; 11 weeks on the charts, peaking at #12.

"Take It Easy" was the first single ever released by the Eagles, and the leadoff track on Side A of their debut album, *Eagles.* The song's creation begins with singer/songwriter Jackson Browne, who began working on it for his own debut album, but couldn't quite finish it. He played what he had for Glen Frey, a neighbor at the time, who liked it so much he offered to finish it. "And after a couple of times when I declined to have him finish my song, I said, 'alright'," Browne later said. "I finally thought, 'this is ridiculous. Go ahead and finish it. Do it.' And he finished it in spectacular fashion. And, what's more, arranged it in a way that was far superior to what I had written." The song is pure Eagles, in that it is music that perfectly reflects the laid back mood of the post-1960s and pre-Watergate years. On the other hand, it also reflects what many critics disliked about the Eagles. As Robert Christgau wrote, their music was, "suave and synthetic—brilliant, but false. And not always all the brilliant, either."

a dark picture of excesses that yield unsatisfying pleasure. Eventually the album sold an estimated 32 million copies worldwide, and contained the #1 singles "New Kid in Town" and "Hotel California." The albums title track was the group's fourth #1, and their tenth Top 40 single. Although their next album took nearly three years to complete, *The Long Run* (1979) hit #1 and contained three more Top 10 singles, including the #1 "Heartache Tonight." However, by this time diminishing creative energies and inner tensions were beginning to take their toll, and after Frey began work on a solo album, the Eagles broke up in 1980. The group reunited in 1994 and continues to record and tour. In 2007 they released *Long Road Out of Eden* which, with sales of over seven million copies, proved that the band is still immensely popular. The final sales tally for the Eagles: more than 150 million albums sold (U.S.), three diamond LPs, five #1 singles and five Grammies.

Fleetwood Mac

Fleetwood Mac helped define the sound of 1970s rock with its mega-hit LP *Rumours,* which is today the ninth best selling album in U.S. history. The band was formed out of London's blues scene in 1967, fronted in the beginning by former Bluesbreakers guitarist Peter Green, with a rhythm section of Mick Fleetwood on drums and John McVie on bass. Although their first three blues-oriented albums sold well in the UK, commercial success across the pond was non-existent. In 1970 Green had a spiritual crisis, and decided that all band profits should be donated to charities. Fleetwood and McVie balked at the idea, so Green left the band and subsequently gave away nearly all his money. Around this same time, McVie's new wife Christine joined the band on keyboards and vocals, and the band moved toward a more pop-friendly sound. Still, success in America proved elusive, in part because of poorly produced albums and a virtual revolving door of musicians going in and out of the band. However, fortunes began to change in the early 1970s. First the band moved to Los Angeles to increase their visibility in the city. Next, new producers were brought in, most notably Ken Caillat and Richard Dashut. Finally, long-time guitarist/vocalist/primary songwriter Bob Welch quit, which led to the hiring of two Californians, guitarist/vocalist/songwriter Lindsey Buckingham and his girlfriend/musical collaborator, vocalist Stevie Nicks. Now with two women in the band, Fleetwood Mac had a unique sound and stage presence, with Christine McVie's sultry alto voice contrasting Nicks' little girl sweetness and "space cadet/sexpot" persona.

In 1975, the new lineup—Fleetwood, the McVies, Buckingham and Nicks—released *Fleetwood Mac,* sometimes called "The White Album" because of its cover. Although the album was slow to catch on, it finally peaked at #1 more than a year after its release and eventually went 5× platinum. It also contained the band's first Top 20 singles, "Over My Head," "Rhiannon," and "Say You Love Me." The next album was the blockbuster *Rumours.* Containing four Top 10 singles ("Go Your Own Way," "Don't Stop," "You Make Loving Fun," and the #1 "Dreams"), the LP stayed at the #1 spot for 31 weeks in 1977 and 1978 and won the Album of the Year Grammy. It went gold within two weeks of its release, platinum within a month, and eventually sold an estimated 40 million copies. It was the band's creative apotheosis, in spite of the fact that the two inter-band relationships were falling apart during production (the McVie's divorced and the Buckingham/Nicks romance ended following the *Rumours* tour). The next album, *Tusk,* was an experimental endeavor that included, among other things, African Burundi drumming and the USC Trojan Marching Band; although it sold four million copies, it was deemed a failure. In the late 1970s and early 1980s Fleetwood Mac underwent more personnel changes, and in 1983 took a sabbatical so the members could pursue solo projects. They disbanded in 1995, but have reunited from time to time since then for tours.

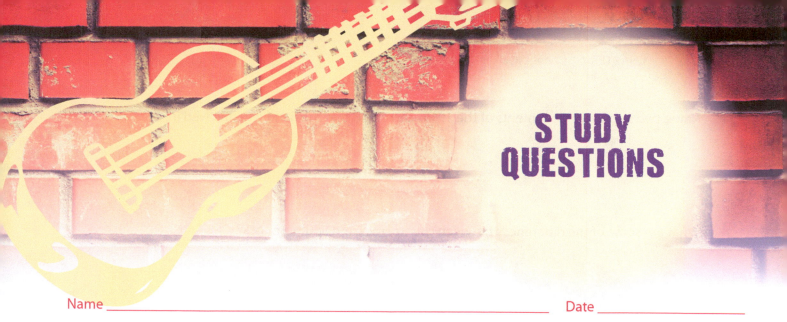

Name _____   Date _____

1. What were some of the reasons that rock began to fragment in the 1970s?

2. Describe the significance of Laurel Canyon and other landmarks of the L.A. scene in the late 1960s and early 1970s.

3. What were the three style phases of the Byrds and the important contributors to each?

4. Name three important characteristics of Crosby, Stills, Nash & Young.

5. What are some of the common characteristics of the music of the singer/songwriters that emerged in the 1970s?

6. Name two important documents of the 1960s and 1970s that the Band was involved in.

7. What are some of the differences between country rock and Southern rock?

8. The Allman Brothers were not the prototypical Southern rock band. What made them different?

9. Describe the culture of the record industry in the 1970s.

10. What was unique about the relationships of the members of Fleetwood Mac, and how did this affect their album *Rumours?*

HISTORICAL INTERLUDE: 1970s

An Experiment in Excess

The counterculture of the 1960s became the norm of the 1970s. Hippie influences in politics, fashion, and entertainment became part of the pop culture. The excesses of political thinking, fashion, drug use, and pop culture reached a peak by the middle of the 1970s and begin to be reeled in by a more conservative attitude that would define much of the 1980s. Sick of the protests and riots, many Americans became part of a "Silent Majority," a philosophical pushback that redefined the normalcy missing from the late 1960s and early 1970s.

The Vietnam War continued through the first half of the decade with the United States withdrawing most of its troops by the end of 1973. Although it was declared a success at the time, most people believe Vietnam was the first war the United States had ever lost. Vietnam continued to be a strongly divisive subject in the mind of the American public throughout the decade.

President Nixon would resign the presidency in August of 1974 due to the Watergate scandal, which was the result of a break in at the Democratic National Head quarters in 1972. This resulted in even less trust of government among many Americans.

Although there was no official economic depression, the economy struggled throughout the 1970s. This struggle was exacerbated by oil shortages in 1973 and 1979. These shortages were due to interruptions in exports from the Middle East. Unrest in the Middle East would also lead to conflict, including the political revolution in Iran in which American hostages were taken. All of these issues would foreshadow the unrest in the Middle East, which continues today.

9

THE HARDER EDGE OF ROCK IN THE SEVENTIES

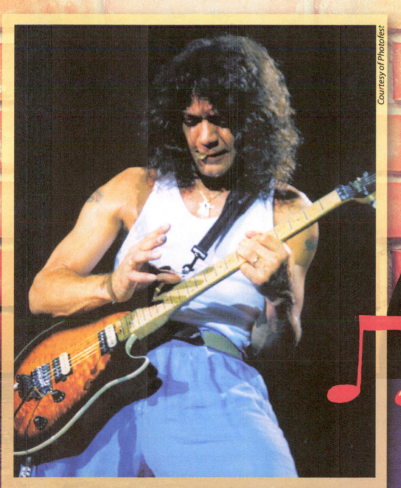

Courtesy of Photofest

"To learn music is like going to school to be a lawyer. But you have to enjoy it. If you don't enjoy it, it's a waste."

—Eddie Van Halen

KEY TERMS

Heavy metal	Art rock	Mini-Moog
Fret board tapping	Mellotron	Glam rock

KEY FIGURES

Black Sabbath	KISS	Alice Cooper
Led Zeppelin	Van Halen	Marc Bolan
Deep Purple	Pink Floyd	David Bowie
Judas Priest	King Crimson	Ziggy Stardust
Queen	Robert Fripp	Elton John
Aerosmith	Yes	

KEY ALBUMS

Paranoid—Black Sabbath	*Toys in the Attic*—Aerosmith	*In the Court of the Crimson King*—King Crimson
Led Zeppelin IV (Zoso)—Led Zeppelin	*Days of Future Passed*—the Moody Blues	*The Rise and Fall of Ziggy Stardust and the Spiders from Mars*—David Bowie
Concerto for Group and Orchestra—Deep Purple	*The Dark Side of the Moon*—Pink Floyd	
A Night at the Opera—Queen		

THE BIRTH OF HEAVY METAL

The Industrial Roots

Heavy metal was born in the dismal, grimy industrial cities of England—places like Birmingham, Aston, and Hertford, where people labored at arduous factory jobs that barely kept food on the table. They were resilient people who had survived the bombings during World War II and went about rebuilding their lives in the years after, persevering and making do as best they could. Nevertheless, it was a dark and troubling world in which their children grew up in the 1950s. The rock that evolved from this time and place was more intense, powerful, angry, aggressive, and louder than any that had come before it. Said heavy-metal protagonist Ozzy Osbourne: "We got sick and tired of all the bullshit, love your brother and flower power forever. We brought things down to reality."

Like the British hard rock bands that came before them (the Yardbirds, Cream, the Jimi Hendrix Experience, etc.), **heavy metal** is deeply rooted in the blues. Hard rock's focus was on the virtuosity and showmanship of the guitarists like Jeff Beck, Jimmy Page, Eric Clapton, and Hendrix, who essentially redefined how the instrument was going to be used in a rock setting. Heavy metal continued this preoccupation with flashy displays of technical prowess, and produced some of the most skilled guitarists in history. Other prominent features of heavy-metal guitar include extreme volume, distortion, and power chords. The use of distortion by guitar players was nothing new to rock by the 1960s: many of the early recordings from Sun Studios, including the 1951 landmark "Rocket 88" utilized the effect. In 1954, North Carolina guitarist Link Wray recorded "Rumble," a tune based around a distorted guitar riff that sold over a million copies and reached #16 in 1958. From this point on and into the 1960s, the most innovative new songs using distortion and power chords came primarily from England.

One of the first British bands to utilize distorted power chords was the Kinks, whose mid-1960s Top 10 hits "You Really Got Me" and "All Day and All of the Night" were both based on repeating power chord riffs. The year 1965 also saw the release of several influential British singles that utilized distorted guitar riffs and power chords, most notably the Who's "I Can't Explain," the Rolling Stones' "(I Can't Get No) Satisfaction," and the Yardbirds' "For Your Love." By 1967, when both Cream and the Jimi Hendrix Experience had formed and codified the blues-based hard rock style, heavy metal was one evolutionary step away. Although the term heavy metal comes to us from the world of chemistry, its first usage in popular culture came from beat writer William Burroughs, who first made reference to Uranian Willy, the Heavy Metal Kid in his 1962 novel *The Soft Parade,* and further developed him as a character in his 1964 novel *Nova Express.* However, the phrase had no musical connection until 1968, when songwriter Mars Bonfire used it in the lyrics to his song "Born to Be Wild," which became a hit for Steppenwolf and was used in the biker cult film *Easy Rider.* Later that year Barry Clifford used the term in a record review of an Electric Flag album in *Rolling Stone;* by the time rock critic Lester Bangs began using the phrase in the early 1970s, the name—a perfect description of the music—had stuck.

So what is the difference between hard rock and heavy metal? Perhaps the most obvious is metal's preoccupation with lyrical themes of darkness, death, and evil that gives no resolution or positive outcome, as is common in the blues. There are also frequent references to the occult, mythology, satanic worship, and witchcraft. These lyrical themes combined with the staging, album artwork, menacing attitudes, and clothes worn by the performers create a dark, foreboding fantasy world for fans to immerse themselves in. Heavy metal often uses influences from classical music, most often in the form of elaborate and intricate passages that are reminiscent of the Baroque period (1600–1750) and composers such as J. S. Bach. There is also an over-the-top display of swagger and machismo posturing in heavy metal, to the point of being theatrical. Vocalists often use screams and yells to evoke a sense of urgency and power. Finally, heavy metal is simply more extreme in every way than hard rock: it's louder, faster, more intense, and—*heavier.*

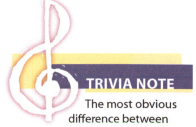

TRIVIA NOTE

The most obvious difference between hard rock and heavy metal is metal's preoccupation with lyrical themes of darkness, death, and evil that gives no resolution or positive outcome, as is common in the blues.

Characteristics of Heavy Metal

1. Louder, more extreme, aggressive, and intense than hard rock
2. Feedback, distortion, power chords; focus on virtuosity of lead guitarist
3. Lyrical themes of evil, death, darkness, the occult, satanic worship, etc.
4. Like hard rock, extensive use of blues riffs, often played in unison by bass and guitar
5. Influence from Baroque era of classical music
6. Typical instrumentation: electric guitar, bass, drums, vocalist

HEAVY METAL

Key Early Heavy Metal Recordings

- "Whole Lotta Love"—Led Zeppelin, 1969
- *Paranoid*—Black Sabbath, 1970
- *Led Zeppelin IV*—Led Zeppelin, 1971
- "Eruption"—Van Halen, 1978

Heavy metal became popular primarily because of its power and volume, and its rebellious and aggressive attitude, all of which struck a chord with its core audience—white, disenfranchised teenage males. It also represented for many rock fans an extreme rejection of the 1970s commercial pop and soft rock styles described in Chapter 8. For these and other reasons, it was widely dismissed by rock critics, who considered it amateurish and simple-minded. It wasn't until the 1990s, when many of the Seattle grunge bands acknowledged its influence that heavy metal began to shake some of the disrespect that had been heaped on it by critics over the years.

THE EARLIEST HEAVY METAL BANDS

Black Sabbath

So who was the first heavy metal band? Many point to the seminal American hard rock bands such as Iron Butterfly and Vanilla Fudge, both of which were formed in 1966, or Britain's Deep Purple. However, the first band to clearly define the conventions of early heavy metal was Black Sabbath from Birmingham, England. From the beginning, Black Sabbath was fixated on the occult, low sonorities, distortion, and bone-crunching volume. They were one of the first bands to use lower tunings on their guitars, which gave their power chords more depth and intensity. Visually, the band looked menacing, wearing steel crucifixes, black clothes, and long hair, while their live shows often included burning crosses and other images of devil worship. Singer Ozzy Osbourne's plaintive wailing was a departure from previous rock singing, and was highly influential to later metal bands.

The members of Black Sabbath, guitarist Tony Iommi, bassist Terry "Geezer" Butler, drummer Bill Ward, and Ozzy Osbourne (1948–) were schoolmates who all grew up within a mile of each other in the working-class city of Aston, just outside of Birmingham, England's second largest city. By the time they began jamming together in 1967, they had encountered their share of tough times: Osbourne had been in jail for six weeks for burglary, while Iommi had lost the tips of two fingers of his right hand while working in a metal press factory. At first they called themselves Polka Tulk, then Earth, but ultimately took the name Black Sabbath from a novel of the same name by occult writer Dennis Wheatley. After being rejected by 14 record labels, they signed with the small Vertigo label and released their self-titled debut album in January 1970.

To everyone's surprise, *Black Sabbath* was well received, peaking at #8 in Britain, #23 in the U.S., and eventually sold more than a million copies. In September 1970, their second album ***Paranoid*** was released, and buoyed by the

BLACK SABBATH
- Tony Iommi
- Terry "Geezer" Butler
- Bill Ward
- Ozzy Osbourne

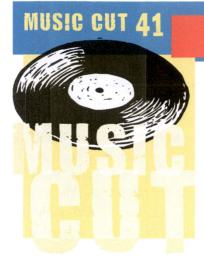

MUSIC CUT 41

"IRON MAN" (OSBOURNE/IOMMI/BUTLER/WARD)— BLACK SABBATH

Personnel: Ozzy Osbourne: vocals; Tony Iommi: guitar; Geezer Butler: bass; Bill Ward: drums. Recorded 1970 at Regent Sound Studios, London; produced by Roger Bain. Released February 1971 on Vertigo/Warner; ten weeks on the charts, peaking at #52.

With one of the most diabolical metal riffs of all time, Black Sabbath's "Iron Man" is one of the defining songs of early heavy metal. Guitarist Tony Iommi's distinctive and influential guitar style resulted in part from an industrial accident at age 17 in which he lost the tips of his middle and ring finger on his right hand (which because he is left-handed is his fretting hand). Although "Iron Man" the single never cracked the Top 40, its LP, *Paranoid* achieved gold status almost immediately and is now certified 4× platinum.

single release of the title track (#4 UK), it went to #12 in the U.S. and sold four million copies. This was accomplished despite the fact that the band was getting virtually no airplay and bad reviews from critics. With a hectic touring schedule of both England and the U.S., Black Sabbath was able to nurture a strong fan base that enabled all of their first five albums to be certified gold. Even the critics began to fall in line with good reviews for 1973's *Sabbath Bloody Sabbath*, a departure from previous efforts with its use of strings, synthesizers and more complex songs. Problems with drug and alcohol abuse began to surface after the release of 1978's *Never Say Die!* which ultimately led to Osbourne's dismissal from the group in 1979. The band has remained together to the present day, albeit with a revolving door of personnel changes. Ozzy's career was reinvigorated in 2002 with his family's popular MTV reality series *The Osbournes*.

Led Zeppelin

Although Led Zeppelin was hardly the prototypical heavy metal band, it was nonetheless one of the most important and influential rock bands of all time. From their founding in late 1968 (putting them chronologically just after Black Sabbath) to the death of John Bonham in 1980, Led Zeppelin out-metaled every other band of its era, but at the same time incorporated influences from the blues, traditional rural American hillbilly music, acoustic folk, classical, funk and reggae. In spite of such a wide and diverse musical base, Zeppelin was able to put their own distinctive stamp on everything they did. Today they stand as the reference point by which all metal bands are judged, and their music is still fresh and compelling to experience. They have sold more than 111 million albums (RIAA figures for U.S. sales only), can claim five diamond certified albums, and

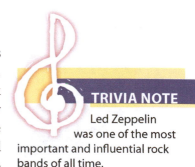

TRIVIA NOTE

Led Zeppelin was one of the most important and influential rock bands of all time.

- Jimmy Page
- John Paul Jones
- Robert Plant
- John Bonham

LED ZEPPELIN

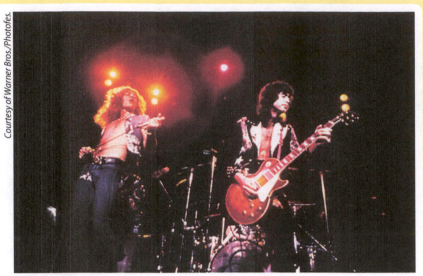

Courtesy of Warner Bros./Photofes.

Robert Plant and Jimmy Page of Led Zeppelin.

with *Led Zeppelin IV*, the third largest selling album of all time.

Led Zeppelin evolved out of the Yardbirds, which Jimmy Page (1944–) joined as the bassist in June 1966. Page had carved out a career as a respected studio guitarist in London, having played on hundreds of recordings including the Kinks "You Really Got Me" and "All Day and All of the Night" and the Who's "I Can't Explain." Although he eventually became the Yardbirds lead guitarist and took control of the band after the volatile Jeff Beck was forced out, Page could not stop the internal bickering that eventually broke up the band in mid-1968. Forced to fulfill a series of contractual obligations in Scandinavia, Page went about putting together a replacement group for the tour. He first asked the Who's John Entwistle and Keith Moon, who briefly toyed with the idea before deciding that the new band would sink "like a lead balloon," according to Moon. Undeterred, over the next few months Page brought together John Paul Jones (1946–), a producer and bass player who, like Page was a veteran of the London studio scene; Robert Plant (1948–), the singer in a Birmingham band called Hobbstweedle; and John Bonham (1948–1980), a powerhouse drummer also from Birmingham. The electricity of their first rehearsal was palpable. "The room just exploded," Jones later remarked. "And we said, 'Right, we're on, this is it, this is gonna work!'"

MUSIC CUT 42

"WHOLE LOTTA LOVE" (WILLIE DIXON/LED ZEPPELIN)— LED ZEPPELIN *(NOTE: THIS CUT IS NOT ON RHAPSODY)*

Personnel: Robert Plant: vocals; Jimmy Page: guitar, backup vocals; John Paul Jones: bass; John Bonham: drums. Recorded May 1969 at Olympic Studios, London; produced by Jimmy Page. Released October 1969 on Atlantic; 15 weeks on the charts, peaking at #4.

The signature song from *Led Zeppelin II,* "Whole Lotta Love" combines one of the most distinctive riffs in heavy metal with an experimental middle section that is a wonder to listen to even today, more than forty years later. The song's riff and lyrics are loosely based on Chicago blues legend Willie Dixon's tune "You Need Love," which Muddy Waters recorded in 1962. Dixon was a major resource for the band in its early days—they also covered "You Shook Me," "I Can't Quit You Baby" and "Bring It on Home" on its first two albums. In 1985 Dixon filed a copyright infringement suit against Zeppelin, which was settled out of court in his favor. Band members acknowledged "borrowing" from their idol; said Plant: "Page's riff was Page's riff. I just thought, 'Well, what am I going to sing?' That was it, a nick. Now happily paid for." Page also weighed in with "Usually my riffs are pretty damn original. What can I say?" The single peaked at #4 and achieved gold status.

After completing the tour of Scandinavia as the New Yardbirds, the band recorded their self-titled debut album in 30 hours without a record contract. Renaming themselves Led Zeppelin (inspired by Moon's comment, with the first word purposely misspelled to avoid mispronunciation), they toured America in early 1969 as the opening act for Vanilla Fudge. Meanwhile, manager Peter Grant had secured an unheard of $200,000 advance from Atlantic Records for the album, which shot to #10 almost immediately after its January release. *Led Zeppelin* contains six originals as well as two songs written by Chicago bluesman Willie Dixon. Promoting themselves with an exhaustive touring schedule, Zeppelin developed a devoted following that took each of the next eight albums to platinum status and either #1 or #2 on the charts. In November 1969, *Led Zeppelin II* was released, which stayed at #1 for seven weeks and included the #4 hit "Whole Lotta Love." *Led Zeppelin III,* released in October 1970, revealed a more diverse musical direction with the introduction of folk elements, and again hit #1. Although the unnamed fourth album, released in November 1971 and alternately referred to by fans as **Led Zeppelin IV** and **ZoSo**, only went as far as #2, it was the band's biggest selling album, with eventual sales of over 23 million copies (U.S.).

ZoSo is noteworthy for its complete lack of identifying marks on the cover. On the album label, each band member chose a symbol with which to identify—Page's symbol appeared to read "ZoSo." Evidence of the band's preoccupation with the occult was also present on the album cover design. (Page in particular was fascinated with the writings of renowned Satanist Aleister Crowley, whose former home Boleskine House he purchased in 1970.) *Led Zeppelin IV* also included the band's signature piece, "Stairway to Heaven," a song that became one of the most played songs in radio history despite the fact that it was not released as a single and was over eight minutes long. Starting off quietly on acoustic guitar with overtones of Celtic Renaissance music, "Stairway" is an epic piece that slowly builds a storm of volume and distortion into a tumultuous climax.

Following tours in 1973 and 1975 in which the band broke numerous box office records (many of which had been set by the Beatles), Led Zeppelin became the biggest act in rock. Their album releases from this period, *Houses of the Holy* (1973) and *Physical Graffiti* (1975) both went gold almost immediately (and have since been certified diamond). By this time the band had redefined the nature of touring by choosing to play only in large cities, forcing many fans to travel hundreds of miles to see them. They also began handling all aspects of promotion and logistics in exchange for a 90 percent cut of the gate (previously, it was customary for the promoter and band to split the proceeds 50/50). They were also becoming notorious for their off-stage behavior, which included the usual hotel room trashing as well as depraved and sometimes bizarre sexual escapades with the many groupies that were in constant supply. One such incident in Seattle involving a live shark and a naked girl became legendary after it inspired Frank Zappa to write his song "The Mud Shark."

Led Zeppelin by this time had developed an us-against-the-world attitude, due largely to their relationship with the rock press. Rock magazines such as *Rolling Stone, Creem,* and England's *Melody Maker* had all taken hits at the band, as had newspapers on both sides of the Atlantic. Many derided the band for

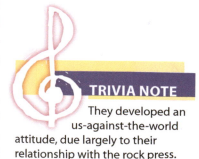

the exhibitionism and pretentiousness of its live shows; others complained that their audience was almost exclusively immature, doped-up white teenage boys, which somehow made the music irrelevant. Throughout the 1970s, interviews with the members of Led Zeppelin were hard to come by.

A series of misfortunes hit the band starting in 1975, when Plant and his family were involved in an auto accident that nearly killed his wife Maureen. A year later, his son Karac died from a respiratory virus. Then, on September 25, 1980, as they were preparing for an upcoming U.S. tour, Bonham died at Page's home in Windsor after an all-night drinking binge. He was 32 years old. Three months later, Page and Jones released a statement saying that Led Zeppelin was disbanding. All three remaining members continued on with solo careers, including a reuniting of Page and Plant in 1984 with the all-star band the Honeydrippers. On December 10, 2007, Led Zeppelin, with John Bonham's son Jason on drums, played a benefit concert at the O_2 Arena in London.

OTHER IMPORTANT HEAVY METAL BANDS FROM THE SEVENTIES

Deep Purple

Formed in 1968 in Hertford, England, Deep Purple was a hard rock band that turned heavy metal, and one of the first bands to fuse influences from classical music together with the other staples of both genres: the blues, distortion, and high volume. After a series of early personnel changes, a stable lineup was set with Ritchie Blackmore on guitar, Jon Lord on Hammond B-3 organ, Ian Paice on drums, Roger Glover on bass, and singer Ian Gillan. The group achieved success almost immediately with covers of Joe South's "Hush" (#4) and Neil Diamond's "Kentucky Woman" (#38), both in 1968. In 1969 the group recorded the ambitious concept album *Concerto for Group and Orchestra*, a multi-movement orchestral work (one of the first albums of this nature made by a rock band) written by Lord. With the album generating poor sales, the group turned its attention to Blackmore's guitar-oriented hard rock material and rebounded with 1970's million-selling *Deep Purple in Rock*. Perhaps their finest album was 1972's multi-platinum *Machine Head,* which includes the metal classics "Smoke on the Water" and "Highway Star." "Smoke on the Water," built on one of the most memorable riffs in rock history, documents the burning of the Montreux Casino in Switzerland during a 1971 Frank Zappa concert. After some internal squabbling and personnel changes, Deep Purple disbanded in 1976. However, they have since reunited from time to time, still performing with some of the original members.

DEEP PURPLE
- Ritchie Blackmore
- Jon Lord
- Ian Paice
- Roger Glover
- Ian Gillan

Judas Priest

Judas Priest was another band that grew up out of the shadows of the steel mills in Birmingham. Formed in 1969, they struggled early on with a revolving lineup, but by 1974 the lineup was set: K. K. Downing on guitar, Ian Hill on bass, Glenn Tipton on guitar, Rob Halford on vocals, and Alan Moore on drums. Their 1974 debut album *Rocka Rolla* received almost no attention; in fact it wasn't until the closeted gay Halford started to adopt a leather-and-studs look from underground S&M stores in 1977 that the band began to take off. That year's *Sin After Sin* received positive reviews, while the following year's *Stained Class* put them on the map as a major force in the metal world. While on tour to promote the 1979 album *Hell Bent for Leather,* Halford would often ride a Harley Davidson on stage, which led to an endorsement deal with the motorcycle company. In 1980 Judas Priest finally cracked the American Top 40 with *British Steel,* and hit the charts with seven more albums during the decade. The band's 1982 LP *Screaming for Vengeance* has been certified 2× platinum, making it the bands biggest seller.

- K. K. Downing
- Ian Hill
- Glenn Tipton
- Rob Halford
- Alan Moore

JUDAS PRIEST

Queen

Queen's roots go back to 1967, when guitarist Brian May and drummer Roger Taylor joined a group called Smile. After several years of struggle, singer Freddie Mercury (Frederick Bulsara) and bassist John Deacon joined the group, which by now had been renamed Queen. Forsaking live performances for two years while the four were enrolled in college, they released three albums in 1973 and 1974: *Queen I, Queen II,* and *Sheer Heart Attack,* the last of which broke through in the American charts at #12. The band's live act focused on May's astonishing chops and Mercury's Liza Minnelli-influenced flamboyant preening. In the studio, their music was highly produced, using heavy doses of overdubbing on vocals to create a unique and highly identifiable sound. Their breakthrough came in 1975 with ***A Night at the Opera*** (#4 U.S., #1 UK), which contained the opera spoof "Bohemian Rhapsody" that reportedly used as many as 180 overdubs of Mercury's voice. The song was such a smash that it stayed at #1 in

- Brian May
- Roger Taylor
- Freddie Mercury
- John Deacon

QUEEN

England for a record-breaking nine weeks. The band also recorded two stadium rock anthems, 1977's "We Will Rock You," and 1980's "Another One Bites the Dust" (#1). Although Mercury and the group never publicly revealed the singer's homosexuality, by the late 1980s rumors were flying that he was ill with AIDS. Finally, on November 22, 1991, he released a statement confirming his illness; he died two days later. "Bohemian Rhapsody" hit the charts again in 1992 after its inclusion in the film *Wayne's World*.

Aerosmith

America was also getting into heavy metal, as it too had its share of disaffected youth who were sick of the peace and love generation. One of the most popular American metal bands of the 1970s was Aerosmith, who despite enduring attacks from critics as a cheap imitation of the Rolling Stones and lingering drug problems have maintained a solid fan base and have sold more than 66 million albums (U.S.). The band formed in 1970 in Sunapee, New Hampshire, as a power trio with drummer/vocalist Steve Tyler, guitarist Joe Perry, and bassist Tom Hamilton. By the end of the year, the group added Brad Whitford on guitar and Joey Kramer on drums (allowing Tyler to front the band as lead vocalist), and moved to Boston, where they signed with Columbia Records in 1972. Although their self-titled debut album sold poorly, its power ballad single "Dream On" was a minor hit that peaked at #59. The second LP, *Get Your Wings,* did slightly better, benefiting from a hectic tour schedule, but still did not break the Top 40.

The group's commercial breakthrough came with 1975's **Toys in the Attic**, which, helped by the #10 single "Walk This Way," went gold and hit #11 (it has since been cerified platinum). Meanwhile, "Dream On" was re-released and charted again at #6. In spite of their phenomenal success, Aerosmith was falling apart from their drug problems. Perry quit in 1979, Whitford in 1980, and the group floundered until both returned in 1984 and Perry and Tyler completed drug rehabilitation programs. Aerosmith's long road back to the top was bolstered by their appearance on Run-D.M.C.'s 1986 cover of "Walk This Way" and the prominent airplay the song's video received on MTV. Reintroduced to a new younger audience, Aerosmith had three subsequent Top 10 LPs: *Pump* (#5, 1989), *Get a Grip* (#1, 1993), and *Big Ones* (#6, 1994) all of which have since gone multiplatinum. Their song about incest, "Janie's Got a Gun," won the 1990 Grammy Award for Best Rock Performance by a Duo or Group.

AEROSMITH
- Steve Tyler
- Joe Perry
- Tom Hamilton
- Brad Whitford
- Joey Kramer

KISS

Heavily influenced by Alice Cooper, KISS formed in 1970 when guitarist Paul Stanley and bassist Gene Simmons found drummer Peter Criss and guitarist Paul "Ace" Frehley through ads they had taken out in music magazines. Rehearsing in a loft in Manhattan, the band began wearing makeup around their eyes; over time they decided to completely cover their faces with designs that reflected their personalities. In 1973 they were close to a record contract with Warner Brothers, but when the label asked them to abandon their makeup (which they refused to do), the deal fell through and they signed instead with newly formed Casablanca Records. Although critics dismissed them, KISS quickly formed a bond with the "KISS Army," their loyal fan base. In 1975 they scored their first Top 10 LP, *Alive!;* their first Top 10 single "Beth" came the following year. In 1977 Marvel Comics published a KISS comic book that reportedly contained blood from band members in the red ink. It sold more than 400,000 copies. In 1978 a second comic book was released, and NBC broadcast an animated TV special entitled *KISS Meets the Phantom of the Park*. KISS at this time also began to market their albums on TV and radio, do in-store appearances, and offer promotions through their fan club, all of which were unusual at the time but are common today. After their popularity began to wane in the late 1970s, they changed their image in 1983 and appeared without makeup for the first time. To date, the group has sold more than 19 million albums (U.S.).

- Paul Stanley
- Gene Simmons
- Peter Criss
- Paul "Ace" Frehley

KISS

Van Halen

Van Halen emerged from the Sunset Strip bar scene in the late 1970s to become one of the most popular American metal bands in history. Brothers Eddie Van Halen (guitar) and Alex Van Halen (drums) were born in Nijmegen, Holland, where their father Jan was a part-time clarinet player. Both boys received extensive classical piano training in their youth. In 1963, when Eddie was eight and Alex ten, the family moved to Pasadena, California, where the brothers developed a love for rock and roll. In 1973, while playing in a bar band, they came across the flamboyant singer David Lee Roth, who sang in a rival band. Roth and the Van Halens joined forces, added bassist Michael Anthony, and began playing at Gazzari's, the Starwood, and other bars along the Strip. In 1977, Gene

- Eddie Van Halen
- Alex Van Halen
- David Lee Roth
- Michael Anthony

VAN HALEN

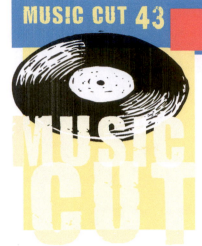

MUSIC CUT 43

"ERUPTION" (EDDIE VAN HALEN)— VAN HALEN

Personnel: Eddie Van Halen: guitar; Michael Anthony: bass; Alex Van Halen: drums. Recorded 1977; produced by Ted Templeman. Released February 10, 1978 on the Warner LP *Van Halen;* not released as a single.

From Van Halen's eponymous debut album, "Eruption" was the shot heard 'round the world for guitar players in 1978. Eddie Van Halen throws his entire repertoire of hammer-ons, pull-offs, fret board tapping, and whammy bar bending into this 1:42 solo display of technical virtuosity and electronic wizardry. It is considered to be one of the most influential guitar solos in history, and helped *Van Halen* achieve diamond status in 1996.

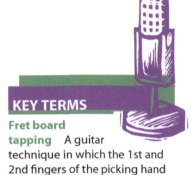

KEY TERMS

Fret board tapping   A guitar technique in which the 1st and 2nd fingers of the picking hand quickly tap in the fret board to produce notes.

Simmons from KISS heard them and financed a demo tape that resulted in a contract from Warner Brothers. Roth's good looks and rock and roll swagger combined with Eddie Van Halen's unbelievable self-taught guitar technique (which includes hammer-ons, pull-offs, and two-hand **fret board tapping**) were irresistible to casual pop fans and serious musicians alike. Since their self-titled debut album from 1978, the group has produced nine straight Top 10 LPs, including three #1s in a row (*5150* from 1986, *OU812* from 1988, and *For Unlawful Carnal Knowledge* from 1991), and the #1 single "Jump" from 1984. In 1985, Roth left to start a successful solo career and was replaced by singer Sammy Hagar.

Other Metal Bands from the Seventies

Other important heavy metal bands from the 1970s include Blue Oyster Cult, Cactus, Ted Nugent and the Amboy Dukes, Uriah Heep, Quiet Riot, and Mountain.

ART ROCK

The Origins of Art Rock

Art rock (or progressive rock) is a designation for a diverse and eclectic mix of rock styles that are bound together more by common philosophy—to incorporate elements of other forms of music generally described as art or high culture into a rock context—than by musical style. These borrowings usually come from European classical music, although they occasionally included American jazz and the musical avant-garde as well. The first stirrings of art rock came from England, where class distinctions and separation of "highbrow" and "lowbrow" art and their audiences were more pronounced than in the U.S. When musicians from the upper classes of English society began developing an interest in rock and roll, they brought a completely different set of social experiences and circumstances to the music than lower- and middle-class musicians, and their music reflected it.

KEY TERMS

Art rock   A diverse and eclectic mix of rock styles that were bound together by the common philosophy to incorporate elements of other forms of music generally described as art or high culture (such as classical and jazz) into a rock context. Also referred to as progressive rock.

ART ROCK

Characteristics of Art Rock

1. Umbrella term to describe the philosophy of incorporating elements of European classical music, American jazz, and the avant-garde into rock
2. Predominant use of keyboards and synthesizers
3. Use of classical forms such as operas, multi-movement suites; concept albums
4. Use of classical instruments such as string orchestras, flutes, oboes, etc.
5. Virtuoso performers with classical music training

Key Art Rock Recordings

- "A Whiter Shade of Pale"—Procol Harum, 1967
- Days of Future Passed—the Moody Blues, 1967
- *Sgt. Pepper's Lonely Hearts Club Band*—the Beatles, 1967
- *Tommy*—the Who, 1969
- *In the Court of the Crimson King*—King Crimson, 1969
- *The Dark Side of the Moon*—Pink Floyd, 1973

Although the Beatles were not from the upper class themselves, their association with the classically trained producer George Martin gave them the opportunity to experiment with influences from classical music. As early as 1965 the band was using classical instruments and influences, including the chamber string ensemble arrangement on "Yesterday" and the baroque-like piano solo on "In My Life," both of which were conceived by Martin. By the time *Sgt. Pepper's* was released in 1967, the Beatles were making extensive use of classical influences, including the album's quasi-opera setting. A few weeks before the release of *Sgt. Pepper's,* London-based Procol Harum released "A Whiter Shade of Pale," whose prominent feature was an organ solo co-opted from Baroque composer J. S. Bach's "Aire on a G String." Also in 1967, Birmingham's Moody Blues released the influential *Days of Future Passed*, which utilized a symphony orchestra as well as the **Mellotron**, an early synthesizer capable of reproducing the sound of violins, cellos, and flutes. With the release of the Who's *Tommy* in 1969, the first rock opera, a number of groups and artists on both sides of the Atlantic were incorporating highbrow art music into rock.

In addition to the use of classical instruments and forms, art rock is also typically characterized by the prominent use of keyboards such as the Mellotron and the **Mini-Moog**, one of the first commercially available portable synthesizers developed by electronic music pioneer Dr. Robert Moog. Many of the musicians who played the music were virtuoso performers with classical music training, which often contributed to excessive displays of showmanship. Concept albums were common, in which songs were thematically or otherwise related and often connected through the use of segues. In some cases, works of classical literature influenced the lyrics of art rock songs as well.

As in the case of heavy metal, critics who felt that rock and roll was supposed to be simple, lowbrow, and rebellious, held art rock in contempt. According to them, art rock was too preoccupied with empty complexity and pretentiousness; it was too clinical. Many young rock musicians felt the same way, and disdain for the music ultimately boiled over in Britain's lower class and

KEY TERMS

Mellotron A keyboard instrument that was capable of playing taped sounds of violins, cellos, flutes and other orchestral instruments.

Mini-Moog One of the first commercially available portable electronic music synthesizers.

disenfranchised youth. The backlash by this faction of society against art rock and other "corporate" rock from the 1970s contributed to the rise of the English punk movement, whose mantra was to return rock and roll to its most rebellious state. Nevertheless, art rock had many fans, and several art rock bands enjoyed high levels of commercial success in the 1970s. Yes scored five Top 10 albums between 1972 and 1979; two Moody Blues albums have reached #1; Pink Floyd's *The Dark Side of the Moon* went to #1 and stayed on the Top 200 album chart for 741 weeks—more than 14 years! With claimed sales of 45 million, it is the second biggest selling album of all time.

IMPORTANT ART ROCK BANDS

Pink Floyd

Perhaps more so than any other band, Pink Floyd was the embodiment of art rock in the 1970s. They were at the vanguard of electronic special effects in their recordings; their music and lyrics took on a grand scale normally associated with classical music or opera; and their concert performances became spectacles of lasers, lights, and props. And it was Pink Floyd that produced the single most significant artifact of the art rock movement, 1973's *The Dark Side of the Moon*. The band was formed in 1965 in London by guitarist Syd Barrett, bassist Roger Waters, drummer Nick Mason, and keyboardist Rick Wright. At first they were a very typical English R&B cover band; in fact, their name was derived from two obscure blues singers from Georgia, Pink Anderson and Floyd Council. However, under the de facto leadership of Barrett, the band soon began to experiment in performance with electronic effects, free-form instrumental breaks, feedback, and psychedelic light shows. By 1967 they had won a devoted following of fans and a record contract from EMI, and their first single "Arnold Layne" made the Top 20. Their debut album, *The Piper at the Gates of Dawn* was an experimental psychedelic epic that some critics put on a par with *Sgt. Pepper's*. Unfortunately Barrett, the group's mastermind, began to exhibit signs of mental instability that ultimately forced him to leave the group in mid-1968.

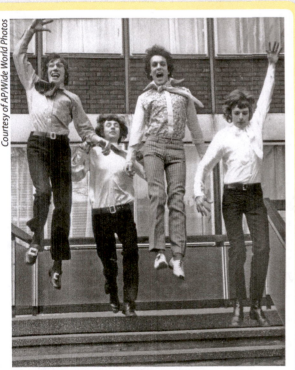

Courtesy of AP/Wide World Photos

Pink Floyd, 1967. From left: Roger Waters, Nick Mason, Syd Barrett, Richard Wright.

PINK FLOYD
- Syd Barrett, 1965–68
- Roger Waters
- Nick Mason
- Rick Wright
- Dave Gilmour, 1968–

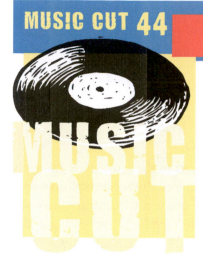

MUSIC CUT 44

"MONEY" (ROGER WATERS)— PINK FLOYD

Personnel: David Gilmour: guitars, vocals; Roger Waters: bass; Richard Wright: Wurlitzer electric piano; Nick Mason: drums; Dick Parry: tenor sax. Recorded June 1972–January 1973 at Abbey Road Studios, London; produced by Pink Floyd. Released June 23, 1973; 9 weeks on the charts, peaking at #13.

It's remarkable that "Money," the one hit from *The Dark Side of the Moon*, even made it into the Top 40, considering its unusual 7/4 time signature and use of cash register and coins sound effects at the beginning of the track. Also unusual is that the signature hook of the song is the distinctive bass line, played by the song's composer, Roger Waters. At 3:59 the song is also long by AM radio standards, and that was after editing it down by more than two minutes from the album version. Guest tenor saxophonist Dick Parry also played on "Us and Them," the track following "Money." Floyd guitarist Dave Gilmour also contributes a rollicking solo on the song.

Just as Barrett was leaving, guitarist Dave Gilmour was brought in, and with the changeover, group leadership shifted to Waters, who reshaped Pink Floyd into a darker, grander, and more experimental unit. Although albums from this period such as *Atom Heart Mother* (#1, UK) were appealing to a growing underground rock audience, Pink Floyd did not have much luck penetrating the American market until the release of **The Dark Side of the Moon**. The album is a state-of-the-art concept album that utilized innovative stereo effects, taped sounds and spoken voices, synthesizers, and dreamy, conceptual pop-oriented songs. By hitting #1 in the U.S. yielding a #13 hit ("Money"), *Dark Side* made Pink Floyd international superstars. Subsequent albums *Wish You Were Here* (dedicated to former leader Barrett, 1975) and *Animals* (1977) continued the themes of isolation and insecurity of modern life first expressed on *The Dark Side of the Moon,* and struck a responsive chord with listeners, going to #1 and #3, respectively.

In 1979 the group released the epic rock opera *The Wall*, an autobiographical double album in which Waters examines the emotional wall that he built up around himself. The album contained a scathing attack on the British educational system in "Another Brick in the Wall, Pt. 2." Tours during this period included animated films, laser light shows, and elaborate staging—*The Wall* tour featured the building of an actual wall that by show's end had completely obscured the audience's view of the band. In spite of their unparalleled successes, the group began to unravel (due in part to Waters's overbearing control), and broke up in 1983 after the release of the LP *The Final Cut*. They reassembled in 1986 without Waters and continued to be nearly as commercially successful as they had in the 1970s, including 1994's #1 LP release, *The Division Bell*.

King Crimson

The brainchild of guitar experimentalist **Robert Fripp** (1946–), King Crimson is one of rock's most far-reaching musical ventures. Incorporating influences from every corner of the musical universe, the sound of King Crimson is perhaps best articulated by Fripp himself when he asked, "What would Hendrix

KING CRIMSON
- Robert Fripp
- Michael Giles
- Ian McDonald
- Greg Lake
- Peter Sinfield

sound like playing Bartok?" During their glory years in the late 1960s and early 1970s, King Crimson's live performances were some of the most explosive ever witnessed, as evidenced by a common refusal of other top bands to share the same stage with them. During these shows, Fripp eschewed the swagger and posturing common to heavy-metal performers, and often sat impassively on a stool while churning out bone-crunching metal. Besides Bartok and Hendrix, Fripp's influences also included composer Gustav Holst (King Crimson often performed "Mars" from Holst's symphonic work *The Planets*), Joni Mitchell, and the Beatles. Fripp was particularly intrigued at how the Beatles could "achieve entertainment on as many levels" as they did, revealing new and interesting things with each repeated listening.

King Crimson began rehearsing in January 1969 with Fripp, Michael Giles on percussion, Ian McDonald on woodwinds and keyboards, Greg Lake on guitar and bass, and lyricist Peter Sinfield. The group's first performance was on July 5 at the Hyde Park concert that was headlined by the first Brian Jones-less Rolling Stones. Soon after, they went to work recording their debut album, *In the Court of the Crimson King*, an epic, symphonic effort that mapped out the future direction of art rock. The album contains diverse elements that range from the orchestral grandeur of the title track, the free-form improvisation of "Moonchild," ethereal melancholy of "I Talk to the Wind," and the distorted, metal chaos of "21st Century Schizoid Man." Sinfield was a master conceptualist whose lyrics were at various times dark, surreal, and tender. Almost immediately after the release of *In the Court of the Crimson King,* Giles, McDonald and Lake left (Lake to become a member of Emerson, Lake and Palmer), setting the stage for the constant personnel changes that would plague the group throughout the 1970s and 1980s. (At last count there were 16 former members of King Crimson.) Notable in their 1970s output were the albums *Lizard* (1970) and *Larks' Tongues in Aspic* (1973). Still performing, now as a quartet that includes guitar wizard Adrian Belew, King Crimson has developed a cult-like following, complete with websites and podcasts that celebrate the group's history and upcoming events.

Yes

As one of the most well-respected art rock bands among musicians, Yes has become legendary for its superior musicianship, high three-part vocal harmonies and intricate and complex compositions. The group has endured a number of personnel changes over the years; the original lineup in 1968 included vocalist Jon Anderson, bassist Chris Squire, drummer Bill Bruford, guitarist Peter Banks, and keyboardist Tony Kaye. Although they achieved instant acclaim in

- Jon Anderson
- Chris Squire
- Bill Bruford
- Peter Banks
- Tony Kaye

FOUNDING MEMBERS OF YES

England, it was not until 1971's *The Yes Album* (#40) that they broke through in the United States. By this time Banks had left and was replaced by guitar virtuoso Steve Howe; shortly thereafter Kaye left and was replaced by keyboard wiz Rick Wakeman. In 1972, Yes released two Top 10 albums, *Fragile* and *Close to the Edge,* that included increasingly adventurous pop-oriented songs, including "Roundabout" (#13). *Close to the Edge* was a paradigm of the progressive rock movement, consisting of three extended pieces, including the four-movement title cut. After its release, Bruford left to join King Crimson, and was replaced by session drummer Alan White.

The band's next two albums, the live *Yessongs* and *Tales from Topographic Oceans* were Wakeman's last; he was replaced in 1974 by Patrick Moraz. *Tales* was another epic that was loved by some critics and ridiculed by others; it was followed by the jazz/rock fusion undertaking *Relayer.* After a world tour, Wakeman rejoined Yes for the remainder of the decade, but the band broke up in 1980. Subsequently the band has reformed and continued touring, achieving their only #1 hit in 1983 with "Owner of a Lonely Heart."

Other Important Art Rock Bands

Other English bands of the era that helped define art rock include Jethro Tull, led by vocalist/flautist Ian Anderson; the innovative organ trio Emerson, Lake and Palmer, led by keyboard virtuoso Keith Emerson; the Moody Blues; Genesis; and Gentle Giant.

SHOCK ROCK: ARENAS, THEATRICS, AND GLAM

As previously mentioned in Chapter 8, rock in the 1970s was undergoing a period of fragmentation for a variety of reasons that were discussed at that time. We have also seen that the business of rock was growing exponentially, the ever-expanding audience was more and more willing to part with their entertainment dollars to see and hear their favorite bands. In addition to selling records, concert appearances were becoming increasingly lucrative for bands as a way to make money. By the 1970s the most popular bands were performing in large outdoor arenas in front of 50,000 or more fans, backed with huge sound and lighting systems. Because video projection systems had not yet been perfected and were not used, some performers began devising different forms of stagecraft to create larger-than-life personas that were visible to even those in the back rows. Although some performers—especially Alice Cooper—were developing outrageous stage acts before they began playing arenas, it was a natural fit that made Cooper, for one, a trendsetter. "David Bowie used to come to our shows in England when he was a folk singer," he recalled. "Elton John was this nice piano player who came to our show at the Hollywood Bowl. The next time I saw him he was in a Donald Duck outfit, wearing huge glasses and doing Dodger Stadium."

Although heavy metal and art rock bands were both early adopters of this trend, the most flamboyant shock tactics were employed by what became known as glam bands and later in the 1980s, hair bands. But before we discuss the glam rockers, we need to give credit where credit is due.

Alice Cooper: Godfather of Gruesome Rock Theatre

Alice Cooper (along with George Clinton, who is discussed in Chapter 10) was a dominant force in the early development of rock as theatre. He was born Vincent Furnier (1948–), and for much of his early life in Detroit and later Phoenix he was a scrawny, sickly kid who dealt with a series of extended illnesses. By the time he was in high school he was healthy enough to run cross-country, and it was with his teammates that he put his first band together, the Earwigs. In the early years the band often practiced in the middle of the desert with a generator hooked up to a telephone pole to power their amps. After a series of personnel and name changes, in 1968 the band became Alice Cooper, a name taken from a 17th century witch found on a Ouija board card. Soon afterward, band members Glen Buxton (guitar), Michael Bruce (keyboards), Dennis Dunaway (bass) and Neal Smith (drums) persuaded Furnier to become the persona of Alice Cooper himself. Armed with a desire to shock their way into the rock world, Furnier and entourage moved to Los Angeles by years end.

Alice Cooper quickly made a reputation for themselves in LA; unfortunately it was for clearing out club patrons faster than a fire alarm. The problem was that the band was just too freaky: in addition to their bizarre original songs, Cooper and his mates had taken to wearing ghoulish mascara and odd clothes that included among other items, see through pants. No self-respecting record label was interested until Frank Zappa signed them to his new Straight Records. After two poorly received album releases, the band was $100,000 in debt. Warner Brothers bought Straight from Zappa in 1970, and released the single "I'm Eighteen," which surprisingly became a national hit at #21. Based on the success of the single, Warner allowed the band to release the LP *Love It to Death,* which Cooper supported with a hectic nonstop touring schedule. The album was a hit, and the band's fortunes changed almost overnight. Subsequent album releases *Killer* (1971), *School's Out* (#2, 1972) and *Billion Dollar Babies* (#1, 1973) all quickly went gold. The single release "School's Out" also went to #7 in 1972.

In the beginning Alice Cooper's stage shows included theatrics as a way to distract the audience from their lack of musicianship. As the years went on, the stage antics took on a gruesome and ghastly tone, incorporating sledgehammers, electric chairs, guillotines and a live boa constrictor that Alice wore around his neck. The shows became legendary and influential to many glam bands of the 1970s as well as more recent bands such as Mötley Crüe and Marilyn Manson.

Furnier eventually tired of being Cooper, and began drinking heavily to cope with the pressures. He left the band in 1975 admitting himself to a psychiatric clinic to treat his alcoholism. He rebounded in the late 1980s with the LP *Trash*, which contained the single "Poison" (#7, 1989). A lifelong baseball fan, he now owns a restaurant in Phoenix appropriately named Cooperstown.

Glam Rock

Glam (a shortening of the word *glamorous*) **rock** was primarily influenced by the pretentious tendencies of art rock and the bluntly audacious qualities of heavy metal. Glam encompassed an eclectic mix of styles; the glue that held the genre together was the use of flamboyant fashions, alter ego stage personalities, and shocking assaults on traditional notions of sexuality, especially male masculinity. Glam rockers learned from Alice Cooper that it was possible to shock and challenge a rock audience by creating a theatrical environment on stage through the use of makeup, staging, and props. Cooper was, after all, an *actor* as much as a musician. By glorifying sexual ambiguity and androgyny, glam was also a backlash of sorts against the sexual revolution of the 1960s. The movement was also characterized by the use of makeup, glitter dust, ostentatious and futuristic costumes, and decadence. Most of all, glam rock was outrageous, glitzy, and campy.

As was the case with several other rock movements, there were parallel scenes in the United States and the United Kingdom. The American scene was centered in New York, where at venues like the Mercer Art Center, groups such as Eric Emerson's Magic Tramps and the New York Dolls performed. The Dolls were performing in drag, lipstick, and makeup as early as 1971, but in spite of using such highly regarded producers as Todd Rundgren and George "Shadow" Morton ("Leader of the Pack"), they were simply too outrageous to achieve anything other than a cult following. The Dolls included Johnny Thunders (later of the punk rock group the Heartbreakers) and David Johansen, who would later have some pop success as Buster Poindexter.

Because London seemed to be more tolerant of men dressing up in women's clothes than New York, it's glam scene flourished. At the forefront was **Marc Bolan**, a veteran of London's mod scene whose pretty looks and fashion sense as the leader of T. Rex set the tone for the burgeoning movement. The groups 1971 release *Electric Warrior* is considered one of the pioneering albums of glam.

Characteristics of Glam Rock

GLAM ROCK

1. An umbrella term encompassing a wide variety of styles held together by the use of flamboyant fashions and assaults on sexual conventions
2. Theatrical presentations: lighting, props, makeup, big hair, and costuming
3. Shock value; glitzy, campy, outrageous

Key Glam Rock Recordings
- *Electric Warrior*—T. Rex, 1971
- *The Rise and Fall of Ziggy Stardust and the Spiders from Mars*—David Bowie 1972
- *All the Young Dudes*—Mott the Hoople, 1972
- *Goodbye Yellow Brick Road*—Elton John, 1973

Bolan disbanded the group in 1975 after 11 British Top 10 and one American hit ("Bang a Gong," #10), and then spent the next two years overindulging himself before dying in an automobile accident in 1977. Other bands that followed in the T. Rex mold were Gary Glitter, Slade, and Sweet. Although Sweet made the biggest impact in America with four Top 10 hits, Glitter had the most enduring song of the era, the sports stadium staple "Rock and Roll Part II" from 1972.

David Bowie

The most influential glam performer was David Bowie (1947–). Born David Robert Jones (he renamed himself after the Bowie knife to avoid confusion with the Monkees' Davy Jones), during the 1960s Bowie released three singles in the mod vein, spent time in a Buddhist monastery, and formed his own mime and experimental art troupes. In 1969 he released the singer/songwriter album *Man of Words, Man of Music* as a way to raise money for his Beckenham Arts Lab. Because the LP and its single release "Space Oddity" (in which he portrayed himself as an extraterrestrial) were hits, Bowie decided to focus his creative energies solely on music. In 1972, Bowie disclosed for the first time in a *Melody Maker* interview that he was gay; around the same time he introduced his new alter ego, the androgynous, bisexual alien rock star **Ziggy Stardust**. Backed by his band the Spiders from Mars, Bowie in late 1972 introduced his new persona in *The Rise and Fall of Ziggy Stardust and the Spiders from Mars*. His extravagantly decorated concerts that followed in London and New York in which he dyed his hair orange and wore women's clothing were smash hits. By the end of 1973, Bowie had released two more LPs, *Aladdin Sane* and *Pin Ups,* produced albums for Lou Reed, the Stooges, and Mott the Hoople, and then unexpectedly retired briefly from live performing.

By this time Bowie had become one of the few glam rockers who would achieve star status in the United States. His vocal style—crooning through clenched jaws in the manner of pub singer Anthony Newley—would in time

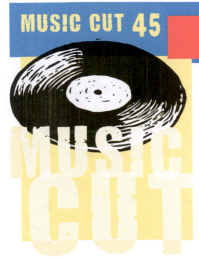

MUSIC CUT 45

"ZIGGY STARDUST" (DAVID BOWIE)—DAVID BOWIE

Personnel: David Bowie: guitar, vocals; Mick Ronson: guitar, piano, vocals; Trevor Bolder: bass; Mick Woodmansey: drums. Recorded November 1971 at Trident Studios, London; produced by Ken Scott and David Bowie. Released June 6, 1972 on the RCA LP *The Rise and Fall of Ziggy Stardust and the Spiders from Mars.* Not released as a single.

"Ziggy Stardust" introduces listeners to the main character of Bowie's album cum stage show *The Rise and Fall of Ziggy Stardust and the Spiders from Mars*. Bowie himself describes the plot: "The time is five years to go before the end of the earth. It has been announced that the world will end because of lack of natural resources. Ziggy is in a position where all the kids have access to things that they thought they wanted. The older people have lost all touch with reality and the kids are left on their own to plunder anything. Ziggy was in a rock-and-roll band and the kids no longer want rock-and-roll." Although the album did not chart well in the U.S., peaking at #75, it was a hit in the UK, where it peaked at #5. It was certified gold by the RIAA in 1974.

prove to be immensely influential. In his American tour of 1974 (after coming out of retirement) Bowie showed a new obsession with soul music, which he repackaged and named "plastic soul." His 1975 album *Young Americans* reflected his new interest, and yielded the #1 single "Fame," cowritten with John Lennon. Bowie would subsequently have one more #1, 1983's "Let's Dance." In 1977 he moved to Berlin where he collaborated with synthesizer pioneer Brian Eno on two innovative electronica-pop albums. By this time he had also launched an acting career, appearing in 1976's *The Man Who Fell to Earth;* later roles included the lead in the Broadway production of *The Elephant Man.*

Other Important Glam Rockers

Far and away the most commercially successful glam rocker has been Reginald Kenneth Dwight, better known as **Elton John** (1947–). Growing up in London, Reginald worked his way into the music scene, working occasionally as a solo pianist in pubs, and at one point forming a band called Bluesology. He also began writing songs, and in 1967 worked with his long time collaborator and lyricist Bernie Taupin for the first time. In 1969 the fledgling singer/songwriter adopted a new stage name borrowed from the names of saxophonist Elton Dean and British R&B singer Long John Baldry, and released his debut album, *Empty Sky.* Since his successful American debut at LA's Troubadour in August 1970, Elton John has been one of the most prolific and enduring recording artists in history. He has released 29 studio and four live albums; 28 have hit the Top 40, 15 have been certified platinum, and seven have hit #1. He has also racked up more than 50 Top 40 singles, including eight #1s. According to the RIAA, he has to date sold 70 million albums in the U.S., and it is estimated that he has sold more than 200 million worldwide. He has also won five Grammies, a Tony Award, an Oscar, and was inducted into both the Songwriters and Rock and Roll Halls of Fame. He also holds a record that most likely will never be broken. On September 6, 1997 John performed a version of his 1973 hit "Candle in the Wind" at the funeral of his friend Princess Diana of England that included lyrics rewritten for the occasion by Taupin. The single release of the song, "Candle in the Wind 1997" subsequently sold nearly 40 million copies worldwide, making it the biggest selling single in history.

Another glam rocker, Rod Stewart, has released 19 Top 40 LPs and 33 Top 40 singles, including four #1s. Roxy Music, formed in 1971 in London, led by keyboardist Bryan Ferry and synthesizer pioneer Brian Eno, and Mott the Hoople, formed in Hereford, England, in 1968 were two other important glam groups that achieved popularity in their native country without making an impact in America.

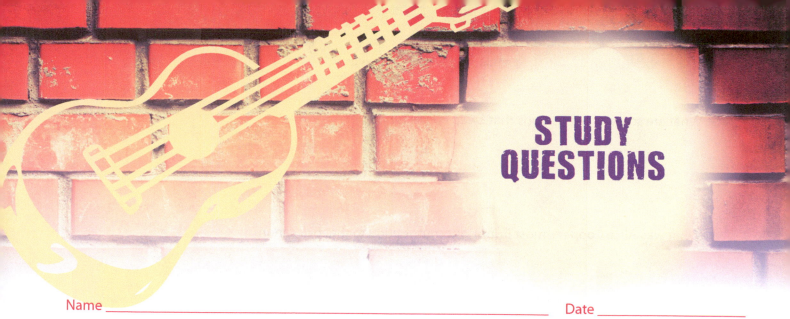

Name _____   Date _____

1. Describe some of the social and musical influences on the birth of heavy metal.

2. What are the main differences between hard rock and heavy metal?

3. Why is Black Sabbath considered to be the first heavy metal band?

4. Name three things (musical or non-musical) that influenced Led Zeppelin.

5. Why is Led Zeppelin not considered to be the prototypical heavy metal band?

6. What are some of the reasons that Deep Purple is unique?

7. What was Alice Cooper's most important contribution to the rock canon?

8. What were some reasons that art rock originated in England instead of America?

9. Describe the evolution of Pink Floyd from its beginnings to the present.

10. Name some common practices used by glam rockers to make themselves outrageous.

10

BEYOND SOUL

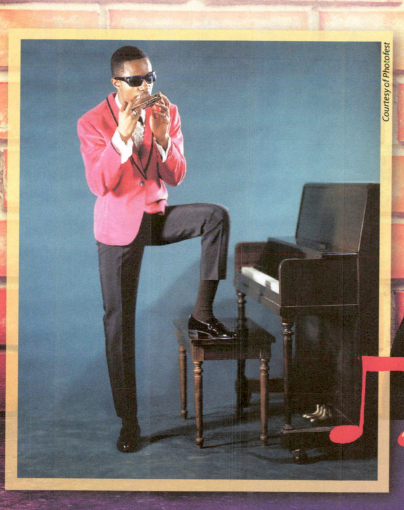

Courtesy of Photofest

"My music actually speaks closer to me than anything I could ever do. If you listen to the songs I've written, or to the songs of others I record, you will hear how I feel. I guess it's the deepest me."

—Stevie Wonder

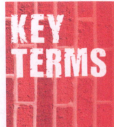

KEY TERMS		
Soft soul (romantic soul)	Riddim	Rap
Philadelphia International Records (PIR)	Rastafarianism	Hip-hop
	Burru	Crew/posse
Disco	Mento	Scratching
Funk	Ska	Back spinning
Slap-bass technique	Rock steady	Punch phrasing
Blaxploitation film	Toasting	Old school rap
Reggae	Island Records	Gangsta rap

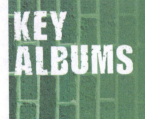

KEY FIGURES		
Dr. Martin Luther King, Jr.	Sly Stone	Beastie Boys
Kenny Gamble	Larry Graham	Public Enemy
Leon Huff	Stevie Wonder	2 Live Crew
Thom Bell	Earth, Wind and Fire	Ice-T
Giorgio Moroder	Chris Blackwell	NWA
Steve Dahl	Bob Marley	Snoop Doggy Dog
George Clinton	The Wailers	Tupac Shakur (2pac)
Parliament/Funkadelic	Grandmaster Flash	Notorious B.I.G.
Sly and the Family Stone	Run-D.M.C.	

KEY ALBUMS		
Saturday Night Fever—soundtrack album featuring the Bee Gees	*Burnin'*—Bob Marley and the Wailers	*Straight Outta Compton*—NWA
Songs in the Key of Life—Stevie Wonder	*Raising Hell*—Run-D.M.C.	*Doggystyle*—Snoop Doggy Dog
Hot Buttered Soul—Isaac Hayes	*It Takes a Nation to Hold Us Back*—Public Enemy	
	As Nasty as They Wanna Be—2 Live Crew	

SOFT SOUL

The Changing Soul Landscape

As we have seen so far in Chapters 8 and 9, the late 1960s and early 1970s saw a number of new music styles emerge as the rock industry began to expand and fragment. In case the reader hadn't noticed, the styles discussed in those chapters (folk rock, heavy metal, singer/songwriters, etc.), were largely performed by white artists for white audiences. But what about black pop in the 1970s? How was soul music, the dominant black pop style of the 1960s, holding up at decade's end? As it turns out, black popular music was undergoing a similar fragmentation process for several reasons. For one, the two biggest soul powerhouses, Motown and Stax, were starting to show the early signs that they were going into decline. Motown's problems started in 1967 when the Holland/Dozier/Holland production team left the company in a dispute over money. It was a harbinger of things to come—Berry Gordy's stingy contracts and royalty agreements were also becoming sticking points for his artists. Although Stevie Wonder and Marvin Gaye renegotiated their contracts and stayed with the company, many would soon leave, including Mary Wells, the Temptations,

Four Tops, Jackson 5, Ashford and Simpson and Martha and the Vandellas. Gordy himself seemed to be losing interest in the constraints of the music business; in 1971 he shut down the company's Detroit operations and moved to Los Angeles to be closer to the Hollywood film industry. In 1982 he signed a distribution agreement with media giant MCA, and in 1988 sold the company outright for $61 million. Ever the shrewd businessman, Gordy held onto Jobete Music, the hugely profitable publishing firm that holds the copyrights for virtually all the hits from the Motown catalogue.

Unfortunately for the owners of Stax, things did not turn out nearly so well. When **Dr. Martin Luther King, Jr.** was assassinated at the Lorraine Motel on April 4, 1968 just a few blocks from the Stax studios, tensions increased between black and white employees. Sadly, the casual atmosphere of racial harmony that the company had enjoyed since its inception began to unravel. Around the same time, owners Jim Stewart and Estelle Axton became aware of the fact that in the fine print of their distribution contract with Atlantic Records, they had inadvertently sold the rights to the master tapes of records that Atlantic distributed. Realizing that they had been tricked into essentially giving away the store, Stewart and Axton promptly ended their association with Atlantic's wily Jerry Wexler and eventually sold the company to Gulf and Western for just under $3 million, far less than what it was worth. Under it's new owners, Stax floundered; questionable business and accounting practices led to a 1973 IRS investigation and its eventual bankruptcy in January 1976.

THE REBIRTH OF STAX

After Stax closed, federal marshals seized the theatre at 926 East McLemore Ave and Union Planters Bank (ironically where Stax former co-owner Estelle Axton used to work), and sold the building to a church for $10 in 1980. Eight years later it was torn down. However, like a phoenix rising up from a deserted vacant lot, the Stax Foundation, spearheaded by former employee Deanie Parker has built an exact replica of the theatre (including the famous marquee) at its former location as a museum and civic landmark. It is called the Stax Museum of American Soul Music.

King's assassination was in many ways the Altamont of the civil rights movement. In spite of the many gains that had been made, the turbulence of assassinations and race riots did not sit well with what was becoming a generally quieter mood of the country. Soul music had always been inescapably linked with the movement, and they both seemed to be running out of steam by the early 1970s. On the other hand, with radio networks and record companies adapting to the growing and changing pop market, it was only inevitable that soul music would change as well. Radio programmers were reluctant to play music that was confrontational, or even reminiscent of the conflicts of the 1960s, and were only too glad to play anything new that wasn't. Some record labels responded by shifting their attention away from black artists to white acts. Exhibit A on this point was Atlantic, which despite its well-earned reputation as one of the finest jazz, R&B and soul labels in the 1950s and early 1960s began to focus more of their attention on signing white acts such as Led Zeppelin, Cream, and Crosby, Stills, Nash and Young by the 1970s.

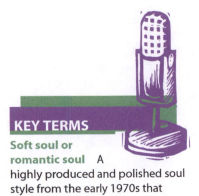

Black pop was nonetheless expanding and fragmenting into nearly as many styles in the 1970s as white pop, and this chapter will take a closer look at those styles.

The Sound of Philadelphia

One of the most popular new black pop styles became known as soft soul, or romantic soul. It is, as its name suggests, a smoother, more sophisticated style than 1960s soul, designed to be danceable and listener friendly, with non-confrontational romantic lyrics. Soft soul records were often orchestrated with lush strings and horns, extra percussion, and rich vocal harmonies. The style was the logical extension of the Motown sound, as and the predecessor to disco, it represented a move toward a more important role of the producer. Because the most important soft soul producers lived in Philadelphia, soft soul records are sometimes referred to as reflecting a "Philadelphia Sound." It was a fitting return to prominence in pop music for the City of Brotherly Love, the birthplace of *American Bandstand* and so many dance and novelty records in the early 1960s.

The architects of soft soul were the songwriting/producing team of **Kenny Gamble** and **Leon Huff**, and independent producer **Thom Bell**. Gamble had apprenticed with Leiber and Stoller in New York before returning to his hometown where he teamed up with Huff. The two began working as independent producers, and scored a #4 hit in 1967 with their song "Expressway (to Your Heart)" by the white group Soul Survivors. In the wake of that success, they began assembling acts for their own Excel, Gamble, and Neptune labels, before forming **Philadelphia International Records (PIR)** in 1971. Over a five-year period beginning in 1968, Gamble and Huff produced 30 records that went gold. The most important artists at PIR were Harold Melvin and the Blue Notes ("If You Don't Know Me By Now," #3, 1972), the O'Jays ("Love Train," #1, 1973), MFSB (an acronym for Mother Father Sister Brother, a band consisting of the studio musicians at Philadelphia's Sigma Sound Studios where Gamble and Huff worked), and the Three Degrees ("When Will I See You Again," #2, 1974).

Bell's rise to fame paralleled Gamble and Huff's, with his first hit coming in 1968 with the Delfonic's "La La Means I Love You," which went to #4. Among his biggest acts were the Stylistics ("Betcha by Golly, Wow," #3,

SOFT SOUL

Characteristics of Soft Soul

1. Highly produced and orchestrated; smooth vocals
2. Medium tempo dance tunes; slow, torchy romantic ballads
3. Predecessor to disco and more recent romantic soul styles
4. Center of development: Philadelphia
5. Great commercial and crossover appeal

Key Soft Soul Recordings

- "If You Don't Know Me By Now"—Harold Melvin and the Blue Notes, 1972
- "Then Came You"—the Spinners ,1974
- "For the Love of Money"—the O'Jays, 1974

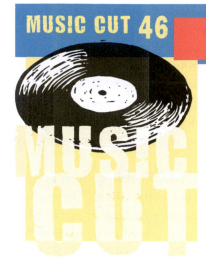

MUSIC CUT 46

"COULD IT BE I'M FALLING IN LOVE" (MELVIN STEALS/MERVIN STEALS)—THE SPINNERS

Personnel: Bobby Smith, Philippé Wynne: lead vocals; Pervis Jackson, Henry Fambrough, Billy Henderson, Linda Creed, Bobby Smith, Philippé Wynne: backup vocals; Sigma Sweethearts (Barbara Ingram, Carla Benson, Yvette Benton): additional backup vocals; MFSB: instrumentals. Recorded at Sigma Sound Studios, Philadelphia, PA; produced by Thom Bell. Released December 1972 on Atlantic; 12 weeks on the charts, peaking at #4.

The group that eventually became the Spinners in 1961 was first formed in Detroit in the mid-1950s. The group put out their first record in August 1961, and "That's What Girls Are Made For" was a #27 hit. Future successes were few and far between for the group throughout the 1960s, but by the 1970s they were a constant presence on the radio, with 13 Top Forty singles (including 1974's #1 "Then Came You") and 10 album releases. "Could It Be I'm Falling in Love" was produced by legendary Philadelphia producer Thom Bell, and recorded at Sigma Sound Studios, where many of the romantic soul hits were made.

1972), the Spinners ("Then Came You," #1, 1974 and six other Top 10 hits between 1972 and 1980.) Other soft soul artists who rose to fame in the wake of the success of soft soul included Al Green ("Let's Stay Together," #1, 1971), Billy Paul ("Me and Mrs. Jones," #1, 1972), Roberta Flack ("Feel Like Makin' Love," 1974, one of her three #1 hits in the 1970s), and Barry White ("Can't Get Enough of Your Love, Babe," #1, 1974).

Disco—The Underground Revolution

Soft soul was just a warm up for what would become the biggest trend in pop music history in terms of record sales. In fact, from 1976 to 1979, **disco** became such an enormous cultural phenomenon that it transcended music in a way that mirrored the swing era of the 1930s and 1940s. Disco's most important feature was that it was intended—like swing—to be dance music, and nothing more. Its musical ancestors included the minimalism of James Brown; lush string and horn orchestrations from Motown and Philadelphia International Records; percolating percussion from Latin music; and vocal chants and honking saxophones

KEY TERMS

Disco Dance oriented pop that incorporates synthesizers, drum machines, and lush orchestrations that emerged in the late 1970s.

Characteristics of Disco

1. Pop oriented dance music whose most important characteristic is the relentless pounding emphasis on every beat
2. Produced in the studio using synthesizers, drum machines
3. Lush strings orchestrations, predominant use of percussion instruments, vocal chants

DISCO

Key Disco Recordings

- "Love to Love You Baby"—Donna Summer, 1975
- *Saturday Night Fever Soundtrack*—the Bee Gees/Tramps, 1977

from rhythm and blues. It also incorporated new technology, making extensive use of synthesizers and drum machines. Disco emerged at a time when much of rock had seemingly become too artsy (art rock), too pretentious (heavy metal), or too self absorbed (singer/songwriters) to care about dancers any more. By the mid-1970s, public dancing as a popular activity was seemingly a distant memory from the early 1960s. In reconnecting pop music to dancing, disco paved the way for the dance-oriented MTV Generation of the 1980s and its superstars Michael Jackson, Madonna, and Prince. Disco also was an important influence on new wave, rap and hip-hop culture.

Disco's origins were in the European and East Coast dance clubs known as discotheques that first became popular during the early 1960s. These clubs generally employed DJ's to play records rather than hire live bands out of economic necessity. By the early 1970s, discos had fallen out of favor with rock's mainstream audience and went underground, catering primarily to the black, Hispanic and gay subcultures. Around 1973 their popularity started to rebound, a trend that was due in part to the ever-increasing skills of DJ's to seamlessly merge one song into the next, using two turntables while keeping the beat constant (disco records often had the beats per minute—bpm—marked on the label). This technique enabled dancers (who were often worked into a frenzy by ingesting cocaine and other uppers) to stay on the dance floor for extended periods of time. Discos initially did not impose dress codes, but it became fashionable for patrons to dress to the nines, enabling them to fantasize that they were the featured performers while they did their best dance moves. As a result of this environment, disco's cultural ethos was able to turn the tables on the established rock culture and let the DJ's, producers, and dancers become the stars instead of the rock singers and instrumentalists.

Disco Conquers the Airwaves

Disco records were initially ignored by radio, but around 1974 began to get extensive airplay. It was in that year that the first bona fide disco hits emerged, "Rock the Boat" by the Hues Corporation and George McCrae's "Rock Your Baby." Both entered the Top 40 on June 15th; on July 6th "Rock the Boat" hit #1 and was replaced the following week by "Rock Your Baby," which stayed there for two weeks. By the following year disco hits were popping up with regularity, with Van McCoy's "The Hustle," Elton John's "Philadelphia Freedom" and KC and the Sunshine Band's "Get Down Tonight" and "That's the Way (I Like It)" all hitting #1. Late in 1975 Donna Summer, the 'queen of disco' emerged for the first time with the hit "Love to Love You Baby" (#2). Produced by European producer **Georgio Moroder**, who created a symphony of synthesized sounds over a drum machine beat, "Love to Love You Baby" featured Summer repeating the title over and over in fake orgasmic ecstasy. She later went on to hold the #1 spot for a cumulative 13 weeks in a one year stretch in 1978 and 1979 with four #1 hits, including "Bad Girls," which stayed at the top for five weeks in the summer of 1979. Summer later became a born-again Christian and renounced her disco heritage.

By 1976, disco ruled the airwaves, as everybody and everything in pop culture came under its influence. Among the #1 hits of the year were Walter

Murphy's adaptation of Beethoven's *Fifth Symphony,* "A Fifth of Beethoven;" Johnny Taylor's "Disco Lady;" and LA DJ Rick Dees' "Disco Duck." Even Paul McCartney got into disco mode with "Silly Love Songs" (#1) with his group Wings. 1976 was also the year that the established-but-floundering English group the Bee Gees introduced their new revamped disco sound with "You Should Be Dancing," also a #1 hit. The song proved to be merely a warm-up for the group, who the following year appeared on the soundtrack LP to the disco movie **Saturday Night Fever** starring John Travolta, which eventually sold an estimated 40 million copies worldwide. The Bee Gees had three #1 singles from the album—"How Deep Is Your Love," "Stayin' Alive" and "Night Fever"—and had three more #1's the following year. The movie itself grossed a stunning $140 million. Throughout 1978 and 1979, disco dominated films, TV, radio, and advertising. There were all-disco radio stations; remakes of Beatles, Beach Boys and classical music set to disco beats were common; even the Rolling Stones couldn't escape disco fever, and profited handsomely with 1978's #1, "Miss You." For a brief moment at the start of 1979, the most popular band in America was the gay-novelty disco group the Village People.

The Backlash

However, it didn't take long before a disco backlash began, and "Death To Disco" and "Disco Sucks" T-shirts and buttons began popping up around the country. It all seemed harmless enough at first, but on the night of July 12, 1979, one of the most surreal events in the history of pop culture revealed just how hated the music had become. When Chicago DJ **Steve Dahl** first came up with the idea for a "Disco Demolition Night" during a nighttime double header at the White Sox' Comiskey Park, it was more of a gimmick than anything. Dahl, after all, was one of the disco haters, and he let his listeners on WLUP know it daily. But even he was shocked when 59,000 other disco haters showed up (the White Sox were averaging 16,000 fans at home games), wearing Led Zeppelin and Black Sabbath T-shirts, shouting, "*disco sucks!*" and throwing empty bottles and records around. When the first crate of disco records was dynamited between games, it ignited a riot as thousands of fans stormed the field, tearing up turf and causing so much chaos and destruction that the second game had to be cancelled. From that moment on, disco just seemed to lose its cool. Before long, Casablanca Records, the leading disco label, was in serious financial trouble and Studio 54, New York's hippest discotheque, closed. By 1980, disco was dead.

Surely the anti-disco backlash was caused in part by the music's overwhelming popularity and the inevitable pendulum swing away from it. There was also the natural dislike of the music by those fans that held the musical virtuosity of real performers in high regard, since disco was created largely in the studio using synthesizers and overdubbing technology. But there was also an uglier side to the backlash as well, fueled by homophobic and racist sentiments. Because disco was perceived by many as gay or black music, it was an easy target for the invective from many of the young white males who made up the base of the heavy metal audience. But the death of disco was a shock system for the music business, which experienced an 11 percent drop in sales in 1979 after a decade of unprecedented growth.

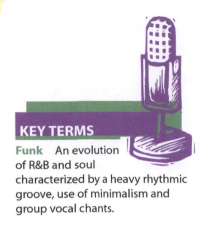

FUNK

Funk Defined

Even as soft soul and disco was smoothing out the grittiness of soul, a more primal form of black pop was emerging that became known as **funk**. The most important element in funk is the groove, formed by layers of syncopated patterns that form a tightly woven rhythmic fabric. Minimalism—simple one and two-bar repeating phrases that create a trance-like effect—is often used. Funk is also loosely structured, with extended jams, long improvisations, and stream of consciousness lyrics common. Funk singers employ all kinds of vocal tricks, from shrieks and screams, guttural noises and grunts, sometimes locked in rhythmically to the band, sometimes floating above it out of rhythm. Group vocal chants are also common. Funk was the most intense and powerful form of black pop music to date, and yet artists such as Sly Stone and Stevie Wonder experienced great crossover success. It was also highly influential to jazz/rock fusion, hip-hop and rap, as well as to a number of alternative rock bands in the 1980s and 1990s.

KEY TERMS

Funk   An evolution of R&B and soul characterized by a heavy rhythmic groove, use of minimalism and group vocal chants.

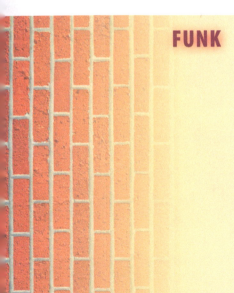

FUNK

Characteristics of Funk

1. Most important element: the rhythmic groove, especially between the bass and drums
2. Typical instrumentation: bass, drums, guitar, electric keyboards, horns
3. Minimalism: simple two- and four-bar repeating phrases that create a trance-like effect
4. The rawest and earthiest form of black pop to date
5. Vocalists employ shrieks, screams, grunts, etc.; group vocal chants common

Key Funk Recordings

- "Get Up (I Feel Like Being a) Sex Machine"—James Brown, 1970
- "Thank You (Falettinme Be Mice Elf Agin)"—Sly and the Family Stone, 1970
- *Shaft*—Isaac Hayes, 1971
- *Talking Book, Innervisions*—Stevie Wonder, 1973
- "Tear the Roof Off the Sucker (Give Up the Funk)"—Parliament, 1976

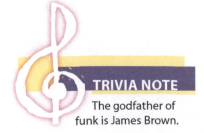

TRIVIA NOTE

The godfather of funk is James Brown.

The godfather of funk is James Brown. His work in the mid-1960s codified the style, especially 1965's "Papa's Got a Brand New Bag" and 1967's "Cold Sweat." Some scholars view his 1970 recording of "Get Up (I Feel Like Being a) Sex Machine" as the single defining recording of the style. These recordings paved the way for other artists to also make innovative contributions to the genre. Besides James Brown (see Chapter 4), the two most prominent funk pioneers were George Clinton and Sly Stone.

George Clinton

George Clinton (1940–) is one of the most eccentric and colorful musicians of all time. Leading a loose aggregation of musicians known at various times as **Parliament**, **Funkadelic**, the P-Funk All Stars, and the Mothership Connection, Clinton produced some of the most adventurous recordings of the 1960s and 1970s. Growing up in Plainfield, New Jersey, he founded a vocal group called the Parliaments at age 15; 12 years later, Clinton was working as a staff writer at Motown when the group had their first hit with "(I Wanna) Testify" (#20). After leaving Motown, Clinton began recording a blend of funk rock and psychedelic music on the Westbound label with two different bands, Funkadelic and Parliament (dropping the 's' in 'Parliaments' after a legal dispute with Motown over the name).

Throughout the 1970s, Clinton built up a cult following through innovative concept albums and dazzling concert experiences. Performances would often include Clinton, dressed in elaborate costumes (rivaling those of David Bowie), jumping out of a coffin while other band members at various times wore diapers, smoked marijuana, and simulated sex acts. A giant flying saucer named the Mothership descended from a huge denim cap. It was an African American parody of cartoon and science fiction. Musically, Clinton mixed influences from psychedelia, funk, R&B, and jazz; lyrically he created cosmic and imaginary worlds with characters such as the Cro-Nasal Sapiens, the Thumpasorus People, and Dr. Funkenstein, all of whom engaged in a sort of primeval struggle for existence. One critic described all this as either James Brown on acid or a black Frank Zappa. As you might imagine, Clinton had a limited crossover appeal to white audiences, although two Parliament albums from the 1970s, *Mothership Connection* and *Funkentelechy vs. the Placebo Syndrome* peaked at #13 and are certified platinum. Clinton's highest charting single came in 1976 with Parliament's "Tear the Roof Off the Sucker (Give Up the Funk)" (from *Mothership Connection*), which peaked at #15. His groups over the years have included such heavyweight musicians as former James Brown band members Bootsy Collins, Maceo Parker and Fred Wesley. His musical motto is "Free your mind and your ass will follow."

Sly and the Family Stone

Like George Clinton's groups, **Sly and the Family Stone** created a hybrid of soul, R&B, psychedelic rock and jazz, but were able to do it with a much greater degree of crossover success with 11 singles hitting the Top 40 between 1968 and 1974, three of which hit #1. The group was led by Sylvester Stewart (aka **Sly Stone**, 1944–), who started his career in the Bay Area as a DJ on soul station KSOL and record producer for Autumn Records. In 1966 he formed the Family Stone with his brother Freddie on guitar, sister Rose on vocals and

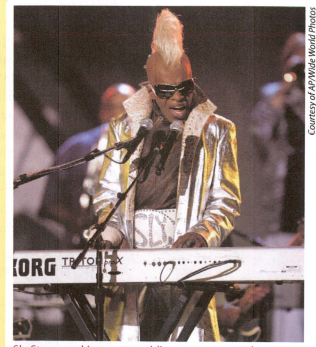

Sly Stone, making a rare public appearance at the Grammy Awards on February 8, 2006, in Los Angeles.

Courtesy of AP/Wide World Photos

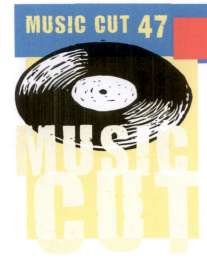

"THANK YOU (FALLETIN ME BE MICE ELF AGIN)" (SLY STONE)— SLY AND THE FAMILY STONE

Personnel: Sly Stone: guitar, vocals; Freddie Stone: guitar, vocals; Rose Stone: vocals; Jerry Martini: tenor sax; Cynthia Robinson: trumpet; Larry Graham: bass, vocals; Greg Errico: drums. Recorded 1969; produced by Sly Stone. Released December 1969 on Epic; 12 weeks on the charts, peaking at #1.

"In late 1969, Sly and the Family Stone were on a roll, propelled by their breakthrough performance at Woodstock in August, four single releases and a #13 album release (*Stand!*) during the year. Their last single release of the year was "Thank You (Falletin Me Be Mice Elf Agin)," which quickly rose up the charts and hit #1 on February 14, 1970 where it stayed for two weeks. The song is the very definition of 1970s funk, with it's hard-baked groove, group vocal chants, horn pops, and soulful minimalism. But the one element that puts the song over the top is Larry Graham's bass popping and thumping, which virtually reinvented bass playing forever and influenced every bass guitar player since. This record is on everyone's top five list of funkiest songs ever.

keyboards, **Larry Graham** on bass, Gregg Errico on drums, Jerry Martini on sax and Cynthia Robinson on trumpet. The group's members created a unique multi-gender, multi-ethnic chemistry with two women and two white musicians (Errico and Martini). Their first national hit came in 1968 with the #8 "Dance to the Music." Within two years, the band had two #1's ("Everyday People" and "Thank You [Falettinme Be Mice Elf Agin]"), a #2 ("Hot Fun in the Summertime"), and had performed at the 1969 Newport Jazz Festival and Woodstock. A third #1 single came in 1971 with "Family Affair."

Sly's success was due to his ability to combine irresistible sing-along hooks, infectious dance rhythms, a unique blend of different styles (who knew that soul could be psychedelic?), and lyrics that generally preached of love, peace and understanding. Occasionally Sly engaged in harsh social commentary, as evidenced by his singles "Don't Call Me Nigger, Whitey," "Sex Machine" and "Stand," and the 1971 album *There's a Riot Going On,* the groups only #1 LP. One of the key elements to the sound of the Family Stone was the bass playing of Graham, the creator of an innovative **slap-bass technique** that has become a staple of all subsequent funk and jazz/rock fusion. Graham left the group in 1972 to start Graham Central Station. Around this time, Sly was becoming notorious for no-shows at concerts, and as rumors of drug addiction flourished, the Family Stone began to unravel. By the mid 1970s, they disbanded. Recent years have found many of the Family Stone's most memorable hits being used for high-profile national advertising campaigns.

Other Important Funk Bands

Other funk artists also achieved enormous crossover success during the 1970s. **Stevie Wonder** reinvented himself as a singer/songwriter/synthesizer conceptualist with an amazing creative streak between 1972 and 1976 in which he had four Top 5 albums (*Talking Book, Innervisions, Fulfillingness' First Finale,* and *Songs in the Key of Life*), eight Top 40 singles—five of which hit #1—and won 11 Grammy Awards. Among the funk classics that Wonder penned during this period were "Superstition," "I Wish," "Higher Ground," and "Living for the City," as well as the pop-friendly "You Are the Sunshine of My Life." **Earth, Wind and Fire**, formed in 1969, used Latin rhythms, jazzy horn lines and an interest in Egyptology to achieve 14 Top 40 hits (including the #1 "Shining Star" in 1975) and eight platinum albums between 1974 and 1979. Other popular funk groups include Kool and the Gang, with 22 Top 40 hits in the 1970s and 1980s, including "Funky Stuff" and "Jungle Boogie," the Ohio Players ("Funky Worm," 1973), the Commodores ("Brick House," #5, 1977) and the Isley Brothers ("It's Your Thing," #2, 1969).

Two other artists, Isaac Hayes and Curtis Mayfield achieved pop success scoring music for what became known as the **blaxploitation films**, movies made by black directors and actors that had inner-city themes of drug deals and ghetto shootings. Hayes, the former Stax writer who broke out onto his own with the landmark LP *Hot Buttered Soul* in 1969, became the first black composer to win an Academy Award for Best Score for 1971's *Shaft* soundtrack LP. Mayfield scored the highly successful *SuperFly* in 1972, emphasizing his high, falsetto vocals and a smooth, pop oriented brand of funk.

REGGAE

What Is Reggae?

Reggae is an indigenous Jamaican music that evolved in the late 1960s from native folk music, American R&B and traditional Afro-Caribbean music. Soon after its emergence on the island, Jamaican reggae recordings began to make a presence in the U.S., and in 1969 two, Desmond Dekker's "Israelites" and Jimmy Cliff's "Wonderful World, Beautiful People" hit the American Top 40. By the early 1970s, rock musicians such as Johnny Nash and Paul Simon were co-opting reggae rhythms into their own music. Nash had a #1 hit with his "I Can See Clearly Now" and a #12 hit with his cover of Bob Marley's "Stir It Up"; Simon hit #4 with "Mother and Child Reunion," recorded in the Jamaican capital city of Kingston. In 1973 the Jamaican film *The Harder They Come* was released, introducing American audiences to the music and its star, Jimmy Cliff. In Boston, a city with a large student population, the film was so popular that one theatre ran it for more than seven years without interruption. In 1974, Eric Clapton's cover of Marley's "I Shot the Sheriff" became the most popular reggae song in American pop history when it went to #1. Throughout the 1970s and 1980s, other artists and bands, including the Clash, Elvis Costello and the Police recorded reggae-inspired music. Reggae in the 1970s became the latest form of black music to become trendy in England, following the trad jazz-skiffle-R&B-blues lineage. Two Birmingham groups, the English Beat and UB40, were among the many that formed in the UK in response to the popularity of the Jamaican music.

The primary rhythmic feature of reggae is the **riddim**, or the intertwined patterns played by the bass and drums. Each instrument in the band has a clearly defined role to play: while the guitar provides choppy, "up stroke" strumming on beats two and four, the bass and drums are locked into a syncopated

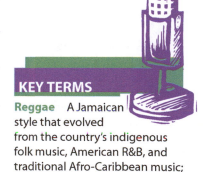

KEY TERMS

Reggae   A Jamaican style that evolved from the country's indigenous folk music, American R&B, and traditional Afro-Caribbean music; it is associated with the Rastafarian movement.

Riddim   The intertwined patterns played by the bass, guitar, and drums that is a characteristic of reggae.

REGGAE

Characteristics of Reggae

1. Combines influences from Jamaican folk (mento), American R&B, Afro-Caribbean music
2. Intertwined patterns played by the bass, drums, and guitar known as "riddim"
3. Lyrics often refer to social injustices, political dissent, racism
4. Identification with Rastafarian movement

Key Reggae Recordings

- "Israelites"—Desmond Dekker and the Aces, 1969
- *Burnin'*—Bob Marley and the Wailers, 1973
- "I Shot the Sheriff"—Eric Clapton, 1974

beat that often de-emphasizes the downbeat of each measure. Most reggae is played slowly, allowing the resulting polyrhythms and lyrics to be clearly heard. Because reggae came from the oppressed lower class in the ghettos of the capital city of Kingston, its lyrics often convey themes of political protest, social injustices, racial equality, and the Rastafarian movement.

Rastafari Culture

Reggae is closely tied to Rastafarian culture. **Rastafarianism** is a religious movement whose followers believe they will be repatriated to their African homeland and escape Babylon (a metaphor for their oppressors in the New World). It was inspired by the writings of Marcus Garvey, a writer and political activist who wrote of the "crowning of a black king" who will "be the redeemer." In 1916 he moved to Harlem and started a "Back to Africa" movement before eventually moving to the continent himself. When Ras Tafari Makonnen was crowned king of the African nation Ethiopia in 1930 and took the name Haile Selassie, many clergymen in Jamaica saw this as a sign that Garvey's predictions had come true. (The word "Ras" is a title that loosely translates to prince or duke.) Rastafarians reinterpreted the Bible to suit their needs, and in time developed their own cultural values that included songs of social and political protest, the smoking of ganja (marijuana) as a sacramental herb, and wearing the hair in dreadlocks. As the movement spread throughout Jamaica, Rastafarian songs were slowed down and mixed with an African influenced drumming style known as **burru**. At this point in time, roughly the mid-1960s, the Rastafarian culture began to intermingle with the popular music of Jamaica to provide the basis for reggae.

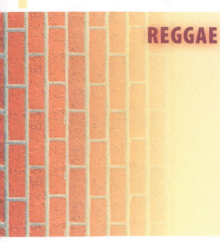

KEY TERMS

Rastafarianism A religious movement originating in Jamaica espousing African repatriation; characterized by songs of political protest, smoking of ganja and wearing of dreadlocks.

Burru A drumming style adopted by and associated with Rastafarian musicians.

Mento The indigenous folk music of rural Jamaica dating back to the 19th century; an ancestor of reggae.

Historical Background to Reggae

Reggae's roots go back to the indigenous folk music of Jamaica known as **mento**, which first appeared in rural areas in the 19th century. Mento's popularity began to fade in the 1940s, when American swing bands such as those of Benny Goodman and Count Basie rose to popularity in the urban dancehalls of Kingston. To emulate them, local musicians formed road bands that played their version of swing music at public dances. By the late 1950s Jamaican youth began copying the R&B records of Fats Domino and Louis Jordan they were hearing on radio broadcasts from New Orleans, Miami, and Memphis, and developed their own variation of the music known as **ska**. Ska (an onomatopoeic word originating from the sound of the strong, sharp offbeat accents) is an up tempo music that combines an R&B-influenced walking bass with accents on the offbeats from mento. It was extremely popular on the island in the early 1960s, and one ska record, Millie Small's "My Boy Lollipop" even hit #4 on the American charts in 1964. The most popular ska band in Jamaica at this time was the Skatalites, led by trombonist Don Drummond.

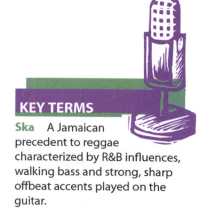

KEY TERMS

Ska   A Jamaican precedent to reggae characterized by R&B influences, walking bass and strong, sharp offbeat accents played on the guitar.

In the summer of 1966, temperatures soared on the island, making ska too fast to play or dance to, and a slower, updated version emerged known as **rock steady**. More relaxed and looser rhythmically than its predecessor, rock steady simplified the bass and drum syncopations of ska, but retained the offbeat accents. Rock steady appealed to the Jamaican lower-class youth known as the Rude Boys, urban hooligans that were generally against the system who sometimes engaged in civil disobedience. Whereas ska lyrics, like those of American R&B, concerned themselves with love and sex, the influence of the Rude Boys and Rastafarian culture into rock steady resulted in songs with themes of social and political protest.

The Dancehall Culture

Another factor that had an impact on the evolving music styles in Jamaica during the 1950s and 1960s was the dancehall culture. The many dancehalls throughout Kingston increasingly became safe houses where the lower class could gather and listen to and dance to music, often provided by portable sound systems that played records. In an attempt to liven up their shows, the DJs who operated these sound systems began to deliver spontaneous commentary on the proceedings, usually in some creative way that involved rhyming, interesting verbal sounds, the use of different dialects, and nonsense syllables. This practice became known as **toasting**. In addition, DJs began to mix interesting sections of different songs together to create even more excitement, and often toasted over the top of the dub. Eventually these styles made their way into recording studios, resulting in hit songs from artists such as King Stitt and U Roy. In the 1970s, Caribbean expatriates such as Kool Herc and Grandmaster Flash took the techniques of dub music and toasting to the Bronx where they played important roles in the incubation of hip-hop culture.

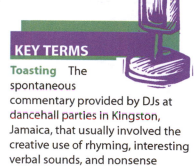

KEY TERMS

Toasting   The spontaneous commentary provided by DJs at dancehall parties in Kingston, Jamaica, that usually involved the creative use of rhyming, interesting verbal sounds, and nonsense syllables.

By 1968 the evolution from rock steady to reggae was complete: the music had slowed down even further, while becoming more intense and driving. The word reggae comes from the local slang term "raggay," or raggedy. Central to the rise in popularity of reggae worldwide was **Chris Blackwell**, the heir to a British fortune who spent much of his youth living in Jamaica. In 1961 Blackwell founded **Island Records**, the driving force behind Millie Small's "My Boy Lollipop." In 1964, Blackwell met and signed Jamaican singer Jimmy Cliff to Island, launching his career with a series of records that became hits in Europe. Cliff eventually had an American hit ("Wonderful World, Beautiful People") and was the star of the influential film *The Harder They Come*. Blackwell also signed Desmond Dekker who released "Honour Thy Father and Mother," a #1 hit on the island in 1963. Dekker later went on to have the 1969 hit "Israelites," which went to #1 in the United Kingdom and #9 in the United States. In the late 1960s, Blackwell turned his attention to rock acts such as Traffic, Jethro Tull, and Emerson, Lake and Palmer, but in 1972 signed the reggae artist who was destined to be the music's biggest star: Bob Marley.

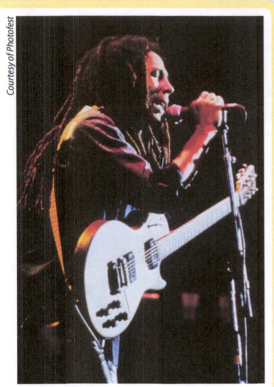

Courtesy of Photofest

Bob Marley

Bob Marley and the Wailers

By the time he died of cancer at the age of 36, **Bob Marley** (1945–1981) had not only become the most famous reggae musician on earth, but a national hero to his fellow Jamaicans. After moving to the shantytown slums of Kingston from rural Jamaica at age 14, Marley began playing guitar and writing songs. At 17, he recorded several lackluster singles with the help of producer Leslie Kong; the next year he formed the Teenagers, later renamed the Wailing Rudeboys, and then simply the Wailers. The original lineup included singers Peter Tosh and Bunny Livingstone. In spite of occasional singles that were hits on the island, the Wailers endured years of financial hardship—Marley even worked in a factory in Delaware for a period. In 1969, they signed with producer Lee "Scratch" Perry, who beefed up the band with the addition of brothers Aston and Carlton Barrett on bass and drums. Over the next three years the Wailers became enormously popular in Jamaica, and were signed to Island in 1972. Their first Island LP, *Catch a Fire*, received favorable international acclaim; their second, ***Burnin'*** included two of Marley's most famous compositions, "I Shot the Sheriff" and "Get Up, Stand Up." Both songs address issues of importance to Jamaicans: "Sheriff" relates a misunderstanding and violent altercation with law enforcement, while "Get Up" addresses fundamental Rastafarian beliefs. When Eric Clapton's cover of "I Shot the Sheriff," went to #1 in both England and America, Marley was poised for worldwide stardom. Around this time both Tosh and Livingstone quit the group to pursue solo careers, but Marley brought in the I-Threes vocal group (which included his wife Rita) for their successful international tour in 1974, their first outside of Jamaica. Leading the wave of reggae's international popularity, the Wailers went on to record six gold albums for Island, including *Rastaman Vibration* in 1976, which went to #8 on the U.S. charts.

Marley used his growing fame to expound upon his political viewpoints, which included social activism, rebellion against the system, and his belief in Rastafarianism. His reverential stature in his native country climbed to levels normally reserved for popular religious leaders or heads of state, and as a result, was wounded in an assassination attempt in December 1976 that forced him into exile for more than a year. In 1980, after collapsing while jogging in New York's Central Park, Marley discovered that he had cancer in his brain, liver, and lungs. His final album *Uprising* was released shortly before he died on May 11, 1981. In his short time in the spotlight, Bob Marley defined the music and politics of reggae for the worldwide rock community.

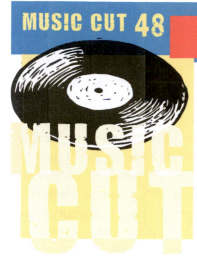

MUSIC CUT 48

"I SHOT THE SHERIFF" (BOB MARLEY)— THE WAILERS

Personnel: Bob Marley: guitar, vocals; Peter Tosh: guitar, vocals, keyboards; Earl Lindo: keyboards; Bunny Livingston: percussion, vocals; Aston "Family Man" Barrett: bass, guitar; Carlton "Carlie" Barrett: drums. Recorded April 1973 at Harry J. Studios, Kinston, Jamaica; produced by Chris Blackwell and the Wailers. Released 1973 on Island; did not chart.

"I Shot the Sheriff," from the Wailers second album *Burnin'*, is one of Bob Marley's most famous and beloved songs. With songs like "Sheriff," "Get Up, Stand Up," "Burnin' and Lootin'," and "Small Axe," the album is a call to action for lower class revolution. According to harmonica player Lee Jaffe, "I Shot the Sheriff" was written one day when Jaffe and Marley were jamming at Jamaica's Hellshire Beach when Bob suddenly threw out the line, 'I Shot the Sheriff,' to which Jaffe replied, 'But you didn't get the deputy.' The song developed from there. Marley's lyrics are a warning to those who attack the poor that at some point the poor will no longer take it and fight back. Gerald Hausman, in his book *The Future is the Beginning: The Words and Wisdom of Bob Marley,* quotes Marley: "'I Shot the Sheriff' is like: I shot wickedness. That's not really a sheriff; it's just the elements of wickedness, you know. How wickedness can happen . . . people have been judging you, and you can't stand it no more, and you explode. So it really carry a message, you know." When Eric Clapton covered the song in 1974, it shot to #1 worldwide and helped create Marley to superstar status as not just a musician and songwriter, but as a political provocateur as well.

Other Reggae Artists

Other influential Jamaican ska, rock steady, and reggae artists to emerge in the 1960s and 1970s were Toots Hibbert, leader of Toots and the Maytals, Peter MacIntosh, going by the name Peter Tosh, Prince Buster, Judge Dread, and the above-mentioned Desmond Dekker and Jimmy Cliff.

RAP

The Origins of Hip-Hop

Rap music is one part (along with break-dancing and graffiti art) of a cultural form known as **hip-hop** that emerged in the South Bronx neighborhoods of New York City in the late 1970s. It is the latest extension of the blues-jazz-R&B-soul lineage of musical expressions that have emerged from the black cultural experience in America. Its most obvious musical connection to previous rock styles are funk (especially James Brown's) and disco; however, rap is an entirely different animal altogether that continues to evolve and assimilate other musical influences. Because of the violent and graphic nature of the lyrics in much of contemporary rap, the genre and its purveyors have been at the center of an enormous amount of controversy, perhaps more than any other style in pop music history. But a closer look at the origins of rap and its motivations reveals that perhaps not all of the anger and outrage directed toward it is warranted.

Hip-hop has been described as the most sweeping American cultural movement of the late 20th Century, and it is through rap music that its message has been transmitted to the American mainstream audience. In the years leading up

KEY TERMS

Rap A style characterized by the use of spoken word (rather than singing) with funk oriented rhythm accompaniment, often using sampled sounds and minimalism; one element of hip hop culture.

Hip hop A cultural form of expression consisting of rap music, graffiti art, and break-dancing that emerged in the South Bronx and other inner city neighborhoods in the late 1970s.

to the emergence of rap, black youth culture was nearly invisible to the rest of the country, the exceptions consisting primarily of athletes and crime reports. However, before the 1960s, black athletes for the most part lived in a conservative sports climate, without a true cultural identity of their own, and often did not identify with the black youth of the streets. One important catalyst that connected sports, black culture, and ultimately music was heavyweight boxing champion Muhammad Ali, who burst into the national spotlight in 1964 as the brash young challenger to Sonny Listen. Ali taunted Listen (and upset him in a TKO after six rounds) with poetic boasts of "I am the Greatest" and "I float like a butterfly, sting like a bee" that set a tone that would ultimately be common to both contemporary rap and professional sports. As ESPN's Chuck Klosterman has written, Ali's "overt self-promotion, indifference toward authority, and confidence that hemorrhages into arrogance" have been emulated by many contemporary rap artists as well as athletes. Or as noted by *The Examiner's* Eric Montgomery, "Ali wasn't a traditional sense that we've come to recognize, but his attitude and 'flow' are predecessors of what would come in the late '70s."

Once this provocative prose and attitude was set into the context of hip-hop and rap music, a new black cultural presence emerged. As Bakari Kitwana states in his authoritative book *The Hip Hop Generation:* "Because of rap, the voices, images, style, attitude, and language of young Blacks have become central in American culture, transcending geographical, social, and economic boundaries." Today, because of rap, hip-hop is omnipresent in national TV ads, fashion, movies and movie stars, and professional sports, particularly basketball. Rap lyrics have also articulated the issues that confront many young blacks, such as police brutality, unemployment, drugs, and gangs. Of course civil rights leaders from previous generations had also addressed these issues, but not in such a confrontational manner.

Hip-hop emerged in the mid to late 1970s as a form of self-expression for the largely black and Hispanic communities of the South Bronx in New York City, in an attempt to negotiate with their oppressive and dismal living conditions. Facing an economic crisis, New York City narrowly avoided bankruptcy in 1975, the same year that President Gerald Ford announced that he would veto any congressional bill that included a bailout for the city (resulting in the famous *New York Daily News* headline "Ford to City: Drop Dead"). During this period the Bronx had been devastated by the ravages of reduced federal funding, shifting and disappearing job opportunities, and the diminished availability of affordable housing. To further complicate matters, the borough had been literally cut in half in the 1960s by the construction of the Cross Bronx Expressway, which destroyed more than 60,000 homes in stable neighborhoods and effectively isolated the southern half of the borough. The resulting infestation of slumlords and toxic waste dumps, increase of violent crime, and the loss of city services created an urban crisis that left the South Bronx in squalor. When a two-day citywide power outage occurred on July 13 and 14, 1977, hundreds of stores in the area were looted and vandalized, resulting in hundreds of millions of dollars in damage. After President Jimmy Carter made a highly publicized tour of the destruction, the South Bronx was characterized as a war zone in the media and through sensationalized films like *Fort Apache, The Bronx*.

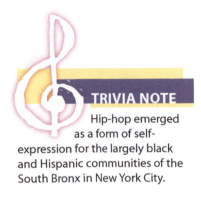

TRIVIA NOTE

Hip-hop emerged as a form of self-expression for the largely black and Hispanic communities of the South Bronx in New York City.

The Beginnings of Rap

In response to these sordid living conditions and the destruction of traditional institutions such as neighborhood associations and community centers, residents of the area began to fashion their own cultural values and identities. By the late 1970s, informal neighborhood groups called **crews** or **posses** began forming as a means of providing identity and support for their members. (This kind of group identity remains deeply rooted in hip-hop culture, and references to crews or posses are frequent in rap recordings.) At parties and other social gatherings, it became fashionable for crews to display graffiti art, break-dancing moves and play records as a way to gain notoriety and celebrity. In the earliest stages of rap's development (around 1977), DJs such as Bronx native Afrika Bambaataa (Kevin Donovan) and two Caribbean expatriates, Kool Herc (Clive Campbell) and Grandmaster Flash (Joseph Saddler), would spin records in innovative ways to create excitement. Kool Herc in particular was instrumental in developing the art of mixing smooth transitions between two turntables to feature the break, or the most danceable, instrumental sections of records. Kool Herc also began to recite rhymes to accompany his mixing, a technique he inherited from his native Jamaica, where it was called toasting. **Grandmaster Flash** is given credit for perfecting the practice of **scratching**, **back spinning**, and **punch phrasing**. He is also credited for creating the crossfader to seamlessly switch between records, and essential tool for JFs ever since. At this early stage of rap's existence, it was the DJs and their turntable prowess that commanded the audience's attention at live shows. Eventually however, MCs (master of ceremonies) were added to take over most of the rhyming and vocal interactions, and they began to attract the most attention from audiences. These were the earliest rappers.

KEY TERMS

Crew/Posse An informal inner city neighborhood group formed as a means of providing identity and support for its members.

Scratching Moving a record back and forth quickly to create a scratching sound.

Back spinning Using the same record on two turntables, a DJ can extend the break of a song by alternating back and forth between records.

Punch phrasing Rhythmically punching in short musical segments (such as a horn hit) from one record onto the beat from another record.

Old school rap The first generation of rap, characterized by party themes and the use of turntables to achieve scratching and back spinning effects.

MUSIC CUT 49

"THE MESSAGE" (ED "DUKE BOOTEE" FLETCHER/GRANDMASTER MELLE MEL/SYLVIA ROBINSON)—GRANDMASTER FLASH AND THE FURIOUS FIVE

Personnel: Grandmaster Melle Mel, Ed "Duke Bootee" Fletcher: vocals; Ed "Duke Bootee" Fletcher: instrumental track. Recorded 1982; produced by Ed "Duke Bootee" Fletcher, Clifton "Jiggs" Chase, and Sylvia Robinson. Released July 1, 1982 on Sugar Hill Records; did not break into the Top Forty, peaking at #62.

Even though "The Message" is credited to Grandmaster Flash and the Furious Five, only two of the group's members—and not Flash himself—appear on the record. The group got their start playing at street parties in the South Bronx in the late 1970s. In 1979 they released their first single "Superappin'," a party record typical of most early rap efforts. "The Message" however, is something altogether different, arguably the first rap record to detail the harsh realities of life in the ghetto. Before this, rap was comprised of feel good party/dance songs. The song was created by combining an instrumental track by Duke Bootee called "The Jungle" with Grandmaster Melle Mel's (Melvin Glover) lyrics. "The Message" is considered to be a pivotal record in the early development of rap.

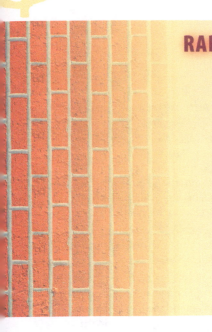

RAP

Characteristics of Rap

1. Rhythmic and rhyming spoken lyrics with rhythmic accompaniment heavily influenced by funk and disco
2. Use of sampled sounds and pieces of existing songs that are repeated to create a minimalist, hypnotic effect
3. Early rap (old school) included the use of scratching and back spinning of turntables to create percussive effects
4. Often has a shuffle or swing beat, with heavy accent on the backbeat (beats two and four)

Key Rap Recordings

- "Rapper's Delight"—the Sugar Hill Gang, 1979
- "The Message"—Grandmaster Flash and the Furious Five, 1982
- *Raising Hell*—Run-D.M.C., 1986
- *As Nasty as They Wanna Be*—2 Live Crew, 1989

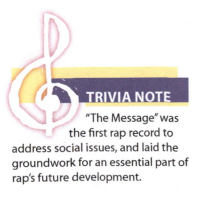

TRIVIA NOTE

"The Message" was the first rap record to address social issues, and laid the groundwork for an essential part of rap's future development.

Throughout this stage of development, rap was still pretty much contained to the Bronx, Harlem, and a few other neighborhoods in New York City. In September 1979, the outside world got its first glimpse of the new style when "Rapper's Delight" by the Sugar Hill Gang of Sugar Hill Records hit #36 on the pop chart and eventually sold over a million copies. Sugar Hill Records was owned by Sylvia Robinson, a former R&B singer ("Pillow Talk," #3, 1973) who had noticed how street MC's that added lyrics and chants to funk and disco records were becoming popular in New York City. To capitalize on the fad, in September 1979 she put together three New Jersey teens who recorded a rap over a rhythm track derived from Chic's early summer #1 hit "Good Times." Not only did the song popularize the word *rap,* but "Rapper's Delight" also alerted MCs and DJs to the commercial potential of the new style. Within the next few years, more rap singles—all on small, independent labels such as Sugar Hill—became big sellers, including "The Breaks" by Kurtis Blow, and Afrika Bambaataa and the Soul Sonic Force's "Planet Rock." This first generation of rappers performed what has become known as **old school rap**, most of which had themes of fun and partying. However, one record from this era that signaled a significant change of direction was Grandmaster Flash and the Furious Five's "The Message" from 1982. A graphic (and controversial) description of the harsh realities of ghetto life in the South Bronx, "The Message" was the first rap record to address social issues, and laid the groundwork for an essential part of rap's future development.

East Coast Rap

Throughout the early 1980s, rap expanded further into the pop charts, and its influence began to extend outside of the Bronx and into other urban areas such as Roxbury in Boston, the Fifth Ward in Houston, Overtown in Miami, and Watts and Compton in Los Angeles. In 1986 rap albums by two New York groups reached multi-platinum status, *Raising Hell* (#3) by **Run-D.M.C.** and

- Run, aka Joseph Simmons
- DMC, aka Darryl McDaniels
- Jam Master Jay, aka Jason Mizell

RUN-D.M.C

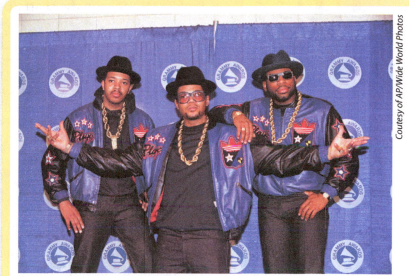

Courtesy of AP/Wide World Photos

Run-D.M.C. at the Grammy Awards in 1988. From left: Joseph "Run" Simmons, Darryl "DMC" McDaniels, and Jason Mizell "Jam Master Jay."

Licensed to Ill (#1) by the **Beastie Boys**, signaling a new level of commercial appeal of the music. Both albums went platinum almost immediately. Run-D.M.C., consisting of three middle-class and college-educated rappers (Run, aka Joseph Simmons; D.M.C., aka Darryl McDaniels; and Jam Master Jay, aka Jason Mizell) had already achieved the first gold rap album with 1984's *Run-D.M.C. Raising Hell* was propelled by an ingenious piece of marketing, a rap remake of Aerosmith's 1976 hit "Walk This Way," recorded with that band's Steve Tyler and Joe Perry. "Walk This Way" hit #4 and sold over a million records to fans of both rap and metal, and its innovative video was the first of the genre to receive airplay on MTV. Run-D.M.C. had a harder edge than earlier rap groups, and featured an innovative vocal technique: Simmons and McDaniels would often finish each other's lines instead of trading verses. The Beastie Boys, the first important white rap group, had a #7 hit with "You've Got to Fight for Your Right to Party" from *Licensed to Ill.*

Other East Coast rappers also emerged during this time, including Public Enemy, L.L. Cool J. (Ladies Love Cool James), the female trio Salt-n-Pepa, Queen Latifa, and Miami's 2 Live Crew. By this time rap was becoming more militant, aggressive, contentious, and controversial. One of the pioneers of what would eventually become known as gangsta rap was Philadelphia's Schoolly D (Jesse Weaver), whose 1986 narrative about a Philadelphia gang, "PSK—What Does It Mean?" is widely credited with inventing the style. In 1987, the Bronx's Boogie Down Productions (KRS-One and DJ Scott LaRock) released the classic *Criminal Minded,* an album that was also influential in gangsta rap's development. LaRock was shot to death later in the year in an eerie foreshadowing of rap's future violence.

- Run-D.M.C.
- Beastie Boys
- Public Enemy
- L.L. Cool J.
- Salt-n-Pepa
- Queen Latifa
- 2 Live Crew

EAST COAST RAPPERS

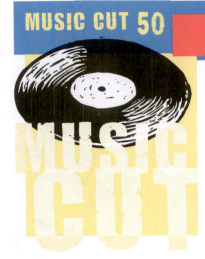

MUSIC CUT 50

"WALK THIS WAY" (STEVEN TYLER/JOE PERRY)— RUN-D.M.C.

Personnel: "DJ Run": vocals; Darryl "D.M.C." McDaniels: vocals; Jason "Jam Master Jay" Mizell: turntable; Steve Tyler: vocals; Joe Perry: guitar. Recorded 1986; produced by Rick Rubin and Russell Simmons. Released July 1986 on Profile; 16 weeks on the charts, peaking at #4.

Run D.M.C.'s innovative reinterpretation of Aerosmith's "Walk This Way" was a milestone in the development of rap. Not only did it appeal to fans of both metal and rap music, it was instrumental in showing that the two music styles were not incompatible and paved the way for other rock and pop artists to begin incorporating rap and hip-hop elements into their own music. In addition, the music video of the song, which shows Run D.M.C. and Aerosmith's Steve Tyler and Joe Perry dueling on opposite ends of a revolving stage, was itself an innovation and the first hybrid rap video played in heavy rotation on MTV. This recording of the song was included on Run D.M.C.'s 1986 LP *Raising Hell,* which went platinum the day it was released.

CNN for Black Culture

In 1988, **Public Enemy**, led by rapper Chuck D, his sidekick Flavor Flav and the Bomb Squad production team, released the controversial LP *It Takes a Nation to Hold Us Back*, which stepped up the rhetoric of black anger to levels above and beyond Schoolly D and BDP. Calling themselves the "prophets of rage," PE combined the politically charged rhymes of Chuck D with the Bomb Squad's heavily layered avant-garde rhythm tracks. Chuck D was also critical of the white-controlled media (as related in 1988's "Don't Believe the Hype"), and called rap "CNN for black culture." PE has encountered more than its share of controversy, from 1988's volatile "Bring the Noise," to the statement by Professor Griff, the group's "minister of information," that Jews are responsible for "the majority of wickedness that goes on across the globe."

The 1989 LP *As Nasty as They Wanna Be* by **2 Live Crew** became the first recording ever to be declared obscene by an American court, even though the group included a warning label on the cover and simultaneously released an edited version called *As Clean as They Wanna Be*. Led by founder Luther Campbell, the group's #26 hit "Me So Horny" created a moral outrage that prompted evangelical Christian attorney Jack Thompson of Miami to file suit against Campbell. In 1990 a Broward County judge declared the album to be legally obscene, making it illegal to sell, and in short order record retailers in Ft. Lauderdale and Huntsville, Alabama, were arrested for selling it (both were prosecuted but acquitted). The band was also arrested for performing the songs in a Hollywood, Florida, nightclub. Eventually Nasty sold more than two million copies (eight times as many as the clean version), a jury cleared 2 Live Crew after 13 minutes of deliberation, and in 1992 the 11th U.S. Circuit Court of Appeals reversed the obscenity ruling. However, by that time 2 Live Crew had disbanded.

West Coast and Gangsta Rap

Meanwhile, California was becoming a hotbed of rap development. Oakland's M.C. Hammer (Stanley Burrell) released the pop-accessible LP *Please Hammer Don't Hurt 'Em* in 1990 (containing the #8 hit "U Can't Touch This" and two other Top 10 singles), which stayed at #1 for 21 weeks and sold ten million copies, making it one of the bestselling rap albums of all time. But other West Coast rappers, particularly those from the ghettos of Los Angeles, were turning up the threatening and menacing tone of gangsta rap to the boiling point. The West Coast gangsta rap that emerged in the 1990s is among the most controversial music ever produced. The main point of contention was the use of the first-person accounting of vivid descriptions of violence, rage, and sexist degradation rather than the more passive third person used in previous rap narratives such as "The Message." One of the first instances of the style on the West Coast came from **Ice-T** (Tracy Morrow), who assumed the persona of a hardened Los Angeles criminal in his 1986 record "6 'n the Mornin'." This and subsequent other Ice-T recordings were criticized as glorifying violence, when in reality the songs usually sent a not-so-subtle message that crime and violence doesn't pay. His newly formed group Body Count received national notoriety with the release of its self-titled debut album in 1992, which contained the track "Cop Killer." The song was denounced by police departments all over the country, as well as President George H. W. Bush, Vice President Dan Quayle, and the Parents Music Resource Center, and was ultimately dropped from the album by Time Warner, owner of Sire Records. In response, Ice-T left the label.

The controversy over gangsta rap escalated further with 1989's double platinum *Straight Outta Compton* by **NWA** (Niggaz with Attitude), a Los Angeles-based group led by Ice Cube (O'Shea Jackson) and Dr. Dre (Andre Young). Although the album went multi-platinum, it incensed rap's detractors with its narratives of gang violence, drive-by shootings, and drug dealings in songs like "Gangsta Gangsta" and the title cut. The most offensive song, "Fuck tha Police," caused the FBI to send a warning letter to the group's label, Priority. Unlike Ice-T's earlier recordings, the songs on *Straight Outta Compton* offer no social commentaries, but instead are vicious tirades directed toward women, the police, and the group's adversaries. Although NWA began to unravel in the early 1990s, they had another smash hit with 1991's *Efil4zaggin* (*Niggaz 4 Life* spelled backwards), which hit #1 two weeks after its release and went platinum.

In 1992 Dr. Dre, along with producer Marion "Suge" Knight started the independent label Death Row, which released Dre's landmark debut LP *The Chronic* in 1993. The album went triple platinum, hit #3 on the charts, spawned two Top 10 singles, and introduced Dre's understudy, **Snoop Doggy Dog** (Calvin Broadus). Reviews of Snoop and his lazy drawl style of rapping were enthusiastic, which fueled excitement about his own forthcoming debut LP.

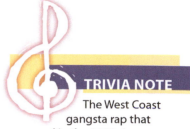

TRIVIA NOTE

The West Coast gangsta rap that emerged in the 1990s is among the most controversial music ever produced.

- M.C. Hammer
- Ice-T
- NWA
- Ice Cube
- Dr. Dre
- Snoop Doggy Dog

WEST COAST RAPPERS

GANGSTA RAP

Characteristics of Gangsta Rap

1. Lyrics use first-person accounting of gang-related themes that include violence, rage, and sexual degradation
2. Hard-hitting, angry vocal delivery
3. Guns, sirens, and other urban sound effects often used

Key Gangsta Rap Recordings

- *Straight Outta Compton*—NWA, 1989
- "Cop Killer"—Body Count, 1992
- *The Chronic*—Dr. Dre, 1993
- "Hit 'Em Up"—Tupac Shakur, 1996

However, while recording the album in August, Snoop and his bodyguard were arrested for the murder of a man they claimed was a stalker. When **Doggystyle** was finally released in November, the pent-up anticipation resulted in it becoming the first debut album in history to enter the *Billboard* pop chart at #1 (it eventually went quadruple platinum). After a lengthy trial in late 1995 and early 1996, Snoop was cleared of all charges. His second album, *The Doggfather,* was released later that year. Snoop has since become a celebrity beyond the scope of rap, with his numerous movie and TV roles.

The East Coast-West Coast Rivalry

In the mid-1990s, an ugly East Coast-West Coast rivalry developed from an ongoing feud between **Tupac Shakur (2pac)** (1971–1996) and the **Notorious B.I.G.** (Christopher Wallace, aka Biggie Smalls) (1972–1997) that ended with the brutal murders of both artists. The feud started after 2pac was shot and robbed outside a New York recording studio in November 1994. 2pac implicated B.I.G. for the attack, and after some back and forth bickering between the two camps released the single "Hit 'Em Up," a malicious attack that boasted of sleeping with B.I.G.'s estranged wife, Faith Evans. Shakur was murdered in a drive-by shooting on September 7, 1996; B.I.G. was also subsequently murdered in a similar shooting on March 9, 1997. Although conspiracy theorists believed that B.I.G.'s death was retribution for 2pac's and amid reports of LAPD corruption, neither case has been solved. The Notorious B.I.G.'s final album *Life After Death* was released within days of his murder, and sold 700,000 copies in the first week and went diamond in less than two years. It also spawned two #1 singles that were both certified platinum, making B.I.G. the first entertainer in history to have two posthumous #1 hits. Like B.I.G., 2pac has achieved a degree of immortality: his death has prompted somewhere in the vicinity of 15 compilations and reissues. In 2002, filmmaker Nick Broomfield made a documentary of the tragic story of these two artists entitled *Biggie and Tupac.*

With so much common talent and perspective to share, the murders of Tupac and the Notorious B.I.G. were tragic and unnecessary. While their music was difficult for many middle Americans to listen to, it is important to

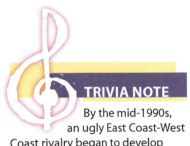

TRIVIA NOTE

By the mid-1990s, an ugly East Coast-West Coast rivalry began to develop that consumed the attention of the entire rap community and in the end turned violent and tragically lethal.

The Notorious B.I.G. was the first entertainer in history to have two posthumous #1 hits.

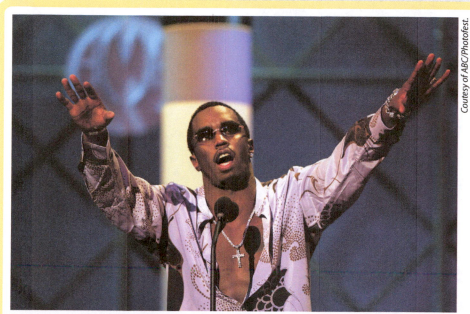

Rapper, producer, and fashion designer Sean Combs, who has also been known as Puff Daddy, P. Diddy, and Diddy earlier in his career.

Courtesy of ABC/Photofest.

remember that the stories that Tupac, B.I.G., NWA, and others related were not fictional ones. These artists did not invent the miserable conditions in the ghetto, or the gang-related warfare, or drive-by shootings. Like the first blues singers from the Mississippi Delta who came nearly 100 years before them, rappers are their generation's voice of the downtrodden and oppressed, of people who otherwise aren't being heard. When miserable living conditions exist for some Americans, like they did in the South Bronx in the 1970s and still do in many urban areas, the results can have far-reaching effects. As rock critic Mikal Gilmore states: "The America that we are making for others is ultimately the America we will make for ourselves. It will not be on the other side of town. It will be right outside our front door."

STUDY QUESTIONS

Name _____ Date _____

1. What were some important differences between soft soul and funk?

2. Name three reasons why there was a backlash against disco.

3. In what ways did James Brown influence funk?

4. Name three differences between the music, bands, and careers of George Clinton and Sly Stone.

5. How did American music and Jamaican reggae cross influence each other?

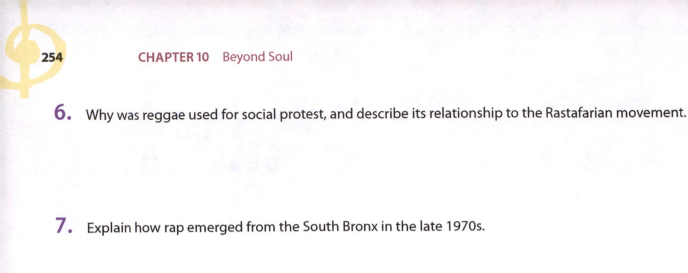

6. Why was reggae used for social protest, and describe its relationship to the Rastafarian movement.

7. Explain how rap emerged from the South Bronx in the late 1970s.

8. What is the importance of Run-D.M.C.'s "Walk This Way"?

9. How specifically did gangsta rap differ from previous rap styles?

10. In what ways did the East Coast-West Coast rivalry escalate?

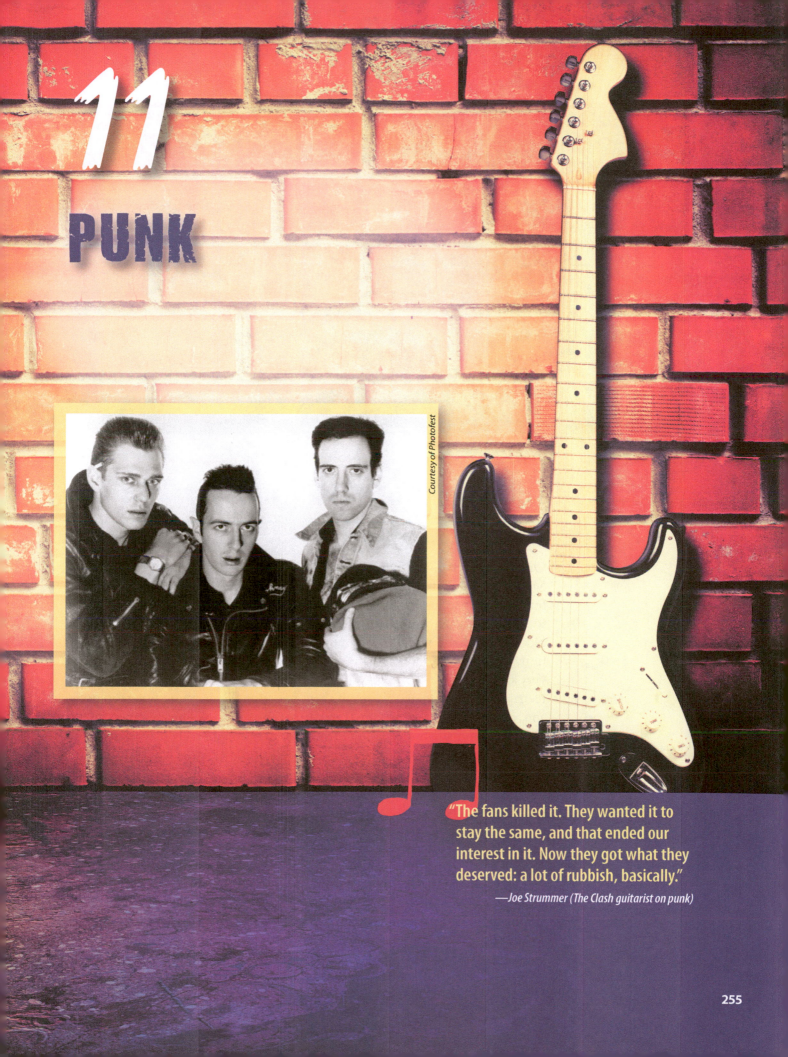

11

PUNK

Courtesy of Photofest

"The fans killed it. They wanted it to stay the same, and that ended our interest in it. Now they got what they deserved: a lot of rubbish, basically."

—*Joe Strummer (The Clash guitarist on punk)*

KEY TERMS	Punk Pogo Garage band	Exploding Plastic Inevitable CBGB Pub rock circuit	New wave Hardcore
KEY FIGURES	The MC5 The Stooges Iggy Pop Andy Warhol The Velvet Underground New York Dolls	Patti Smith The Ramones The Sex Pistols Malcolm McLaren The Clash	Blondie Talking Heads Elvis Costello The Police Black Flag

KEY ALBUMS	*The Velvet Underground
	and Nico*—the Velvet
	Underground
	The Ramones—the
	    Ramones
		*Never Mind the Bollocks,
		Here's the Sex Pistols*—
		    the Sex Pistols
		Fear of Music—Talking
		    Heads
			Damaged—Black Flag

THE ORIGINS OF PUNK

The Anti-Revolution

On November 6, 1975, a new band played their first show at London's St. Martin's School of Art. Bands had been performing at schools like St. Martin's for years, and so in the days leading up to the performance there was no reason to believe that anything out of the ordinary would happen—just some good old rock and roll played by an unknown group looking for a little recognition. However, it soon became apparent that this was indeed going to be a very different type of show. Within minutes, the band members—all scrawny teenagers—began to angrily insult their audience. Their music was raw, noisy, and offensive—that is, if you wanted to call it music. The members of the band made no attempt to hide the fact that they could barely play their instruments. The performance was a combination of noise, anger, invective, chaos, and rebellion. It was also short—after ten minutes the school's social programmer pulled the plug and cut off their power. But in those ten minutes the world got its first glimpse of the Sex Pistols.

The Sex Pistols were not the first punk rock band, but they certainly were the most notorious. **Punk** emerged in the mid-1970s as a backlash reaction against nearly everything that rock had brought to the decade: the conservative and self-indulgent tendencies of folk rock and the singer/songwriters; the pretentiousness of art rock and heavy metal; the slick studio production of funk; and the control and manipulation of the marketplace by the rock establishment. To punks, rock at age twenty was middle-aged, soft, and irrelevant. To their eyes, there were too many pampered millionaire rock stars, and too many flashy guitar and keyboard solos that served no purpose other than to let the performers show off. More and more, rock had become the music of the mainstream

KEY TERMS

Punk A style emerging simultaneously in New York and London in the late 1970s that is characterized by an angry, nihilistic do-it-yourself attitude; also refers to the culture that sprang up around the music.

rather than the music of the outsiders; it had become safe rather than dangerous; and worst of all, it had lost the rebellious attitude that had been its birthright. Punk brought rock back to the streets, back to its primeval days, and in doing so, it dramatically influenced its future evolution.

Punk Culture

Punk was more than just a musical trend, however—it was a culture, defined by its rejection of any and all conventional norms of society. Its mantra was simple: to shock, disrespect, disrupt, offend, and destroy anything in its path, using whatever means possible. But because these nihilistic tendencies were so passionate and universal, punk culture was also full of contradictions. For instance, punks rejected traditional pop fashion trendiness, but turned right around and created their own fashion statement of torn jeans, spiked hair, dog collars, and safety pins. Some punks embraced progressive social issues while others adopted racist and fascist stances. And ultimately punk became attractive enough to the rock establishment that major labels began signing groups like the Sex Pistols, in effect making them a part rather than a rejection of the status quo. When this happened, the punk movement suddenly lost its credibility.

Even though punk's moment on earth was brief—roughly from 1975 to 1978—it has inspired more journalistic efforts than any other subject in rock (with the possible exception of the Beatles). And rightfully so: punk was one of the most fascinating trends in modern pop culture. Punk's lifetime also roughly paralleled that of disco, and many writers have pointed out the contrasts between the two movements. Disco's origins were in black music, punks in white (the "whitest music ever" according to historian Jim Curtis). Disco was smooth and sensual; punk jagged and dissonant. Disco was constructed in the studio using sophisticated studio technology; punk was the ultimate anyone-can-do-it music. Disco dancing was coordinated and stylish; in punk, dancing (if you want to call it that) was a pushing, jostling, shoving match called pogo. Disco fashion was leisure suits, dresses, and high heels; punk fashion was leather and safety pins. Finally, disco was dismissed by the rock press as escapist, while punk was embraced by many of the same writers as a long-awaited return to the rebellious spirit of rock and roll.

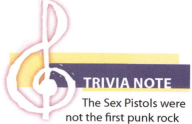

TRIVIA NOTE

The Sex Pistols were not the first punk rock band, but they certainly were the most notorious.

Punk brought rock back to the streets.

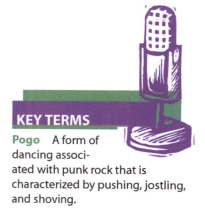

KEY TERMS

Pogo A form of dancing associated with punk rock that is characterized by pushing, jostling, and shoving.

Characteristics of Punk

1. Raw, angry, nihilistic; characterized by a do-it-yourself attitude
2. Typical instrumentation: electric guitars, bass, drums, vocalist
3. Lyrics with themes of nihilism, anger, alienation, desperation, and darkness
4. Counter culture associated with clothing styles, body pins, etc.

PUNK

Key Punk Recordings

- *The Velvet Underground and Nico*—Velvet Underground, 1967
- *Fun House*—the Stooges, 1970
- *Never Mind the Bollocks, Here's the Sex Pistols*—the Sex Pistols, 1977
- *London Calling*—the Clash, 1979

THE EARLIEST PUNK BANDS

Protopunk

By definition, the unruly attitude of punk can be traced back to the beginnings of rock and roll. In the broadest definition of the word, many of the early rock and rollers can be described as punks, especially rebel rousers like Jerry Lee Lewis, Little Richard, and Link Wray. By the 1960s, punk attitude could be found in "My Generation" by the Who ("Why don't you all f-f-f-fade away") and a growing number of **garage bands** that were populating the suburban American landscape. Garage bands were typically after-school endeavors put together by friends for fun and to play for an occasional school dance. Every now and then a garage band's self-produced single would become a local hit; sometimes these records would even get regional or national attention. Examples of national hits by what were essentially local garage bands include "Louie, Louie" (1963) by Seattle's the Kingsmen, "Psychotic Reaction" (1966) by San Jose, California's, the Count Five, and "96 Tears" (1966) by the Flint, Michigan-based ? and the Mysterians. The prevailing attitude of the 1960s garage band was that anybody could buy a guitar and an amp, learn three chords, and start a band. This is also fundamental to the principles of punk.

The case can be made that the seeds of the 1970s punk movement germinated in Michigan in the mid-1960s with two now legendary bands. Detroit—the Motor City—has always been a tough blue-collar and industrial city, but even in the heyday of the U.S. auto industry, economic conditions were often harsh and offered little hope for local youth. There were however, a lot of bands for them to play in; this was, after all, the home of Motown and a thriving club scene. The **MC5** (short for Motor City Five) was formed in the city in 1964 with the idea that they would be a white man's version of James Brown. "Our show was based on the dynamic of James's shows," stated guitarist Wayne Kramer. "It was going to start at ten-and-a-half and go up from there." Aligning high-energy music with radical political ranting and sloganeering, the band had a recipe for mischief that earned them a devoted following, and in 1968 a contract with Elektra Records. Unfortunately their debut album *Kick Out the Jams* immediately immersed the band in hot water with the label. As if the opening track "Ramblin' Rose" wasn't controversial enough with its evangelical call for revolution ("Brothers and sisters, I wanna see a sea of hands out there . . ."), the title track opens with the following proclamation: "Right now it's time to . . . *kick out the jams, motherfucker!*" As one might imagine, radio stations, retailers and Elektra were all less than excited to hear this sort of disrespectful language; kids however, thought it was way too cool. After Hudson's, Detroit's largest record store refused to sell the album and shipped their stock back to Elektra, the band took out an ad in a local underground rag that included the following in giant letters: "*FUCK HUDSON'S!*" When Elektra began making plans to re-release a cleaned up version of the LP, the band had what Elektra president Jac Holzman later described as "a hemorrhage." He dropped them soon afterward. Although the MC5 later signed with Atlantic and recorded two more albums, including the highly regarded **High Time**, the label dropped them in 1972 and they fell apart soon after.

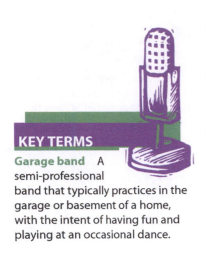

KEY TERMS

Garage band   A semi-professional band that typically practices in the garage or basement of a home, with the intent of having fun and playing at an occasional dance.

The Stooges formed in Ann Arbor, Michigan after guitarist Ron Asheton and bassist Dave Alexander witnessed an electrifying performance by the Who and decided to start their own band. Enlisting Asheton's brother Scott to play drums and James Osterberg to sing lead, the group, (initially calling themselves the Psychedelic Stooges) played their first gig at a Halloween party in 1967. By this time Osterberg, a rough and tumble youth who had been raised in a trailer park in nearby Ypsilanti, began calling himself **Iggy Pop**. Driven by Iggy's outrageous stage antics, which included stage diving, exposing himself, and rubbing meat, peanut butter and shards of glass over his naked torso, Stooges concerts became an onslaught of noise and anarchy. With help from the MC5, the group signed with Elektra in 1968, and over the next two years released *The Stooges* and *Fun House*. Although neither album sold well or were well received by critics, the primal nature of the music and the despairing lyrical themes essentially created the blueprint for punk. *The Stooges'* "1969" takes would become a common punk theme—boredom. On the musical side, "I Wanna Be Your Dog" from the same album is three minutes of the same three heavily distorted notes repeated over and over. "L.A. Blues" from *Fun House* is five minutes of aural nihilism. By the time *Fun House* was released, the group was deep in the throes of the heroin and alcohol addiction that led to their breakup in 1971. They later regrouped as Iggy and the Stooges and released a third and final album, 1973's highly regarded *Raw Power*. The band briefly reunited again in 2003. Today Iggy Pop is often referred to as the Godfather of Punk, and with good reason.

THE NEW YORK SCENE

The Velvet Underground

The Velvet Underground was the first important New York band to adopt the lyric themes of despair, drug addiction, and violence that would later be commonly associated with punk. During their existence they never sold many records—they were too crude for anything more than a cult following. However, their influence was great, and it has often been said that everyone who bought a Velvet's record went out and started a band. Taking their name from an S&M novel, the group was formed in 1965 by two fixtures of New York's avant-garde art scene, poet Lou Reed (vocals, guitar) and composer John Cale (vocals, violin), with the addition of guitarist Sterling Morrison and drummer Maureen Tucker. The band's dissident music quickly earned them a reputation as an outlier to the current state of rock, but a performance at the Café Bizarre

- Lou Reed
- John Cale
- Nico (1966–67)
- Sterling Morrison
- Maureen Tucker

THE VELVET UNDERGROUND

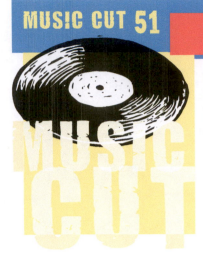

MUSIC CUT 51

"I'M WAITING FOR THE MAN" (LOU REED)— THE VELVET UNDERGROUND

Personnel: Lou Reed: vocals, guitar; John Cale: piano; Sterling Morrison: bass; Maureen Tucker: drums. Recorded May 1966 at T.T.G. Studios, Hollywood, CA; produced by Andy Warhol and Tom Wilson. Released March 1967 on the Verve LP *The Velvet Underground and Nico.* Not released as a single.

Recorded when it seemed the rest of the music world was going psychedelic, the songs on *The Velvet Underground and Nico* often deal with the dark side of life. With the sponsorship of Andy Warhol, the band was able to record an album without the usual interference from record peeps trying to make it more marketable. Today the album stands as one of the most influential of all time, creating a blueprint for future alternative rock music. (*Rolling Stone* ranked it as #13 on its list of 500 Greatest Albums.) "I'm Waiting for the Man" is one of the more depressing songs on the album, with its theme of making a drug purchase and its incessant, hypnotic pounding. There is no flashy playing or production on the song, just straight ahead garage band simplicity, reinforced by Lou Reed's expressionless vocals.

caught the attention of artist **Andy Warhol**, who invited them to take part in his traveling mixed media show the **Exploding Plastic Inevitable** and perform at his art loft the Factory. On Warhol's insistence, European model/singer Nico joined the Velvets, and with her they recorded the Warhol-financed, *The Velvet Underground and Nico*, on MGM/Verve. Containing such plaintive Reed compositions as "I'm Waiting for the Man," a song about a white kid trying to get a heroin fix in Harlem, and "Venus in Furs," a song about sado-masochism, sales of the LP were poor. The now-famous album cover, designed by Warhol, was a simple peel-off sticker of a banana that could be removed to reveal an erotically peeled pink banana. With its lack of success, Warhol and Nico both abandoned the group after the album's release, but the band none-theless followed it up with an even more experimental album, *White Light/White Heat.* Two more albums were eventually released, but internal bickering forced the band to break up in 1970.

With their crude sound, lyrics of alienation, desperation and darkness, and their association with the New York arts community, the Velvet Underground was perhaps the most influential of the pre-punk era bands. From them, the torch would soon be passed to a new crop of New York bands that would create a bona fide punk movement.

CBGB

The New York punk movement was connected to the city's conceptualist art scene known as the New York School. Conceptualist art, such as that created by abstract expressionist painters such as Jackson Pollock (who laid his canvas on the floor and threw paint at it), eschews technique for an "I-did-it-my-way" approach to creativity. Early pre-punk bands in New York used this tie-in with high culture as an excuse for their own lack of musical technique as well as their lack of commercial success (Pollock himself was largely dismissed until after his death in 1956). While the Velvet Uderground were championed by pop artist Andy Warhol, the **New York Dolls** first gained notoriety playing at the Mercer Arts Center on the lower East Side. Formed in 1971, the Dolls combined a glam look (see Chapter 9) with an amateurish approach to performing. For a brief period before they started to fall apart in early 1975, they were managed by Malcolm McLaren, a London clothier who was fascinated with the French situationist's strategy of staging media events for the sole purpose of disrupting everyday life. Before returning to England later that year, McLaren had the Dolls perform in red with a communist flag as a backdrop.

Around this time, a grimy little bar at 315 Bowery in New York's Lower East Side renamed itself **CBGB** and started to book underground rock bands. Within months, CBGB (actually named CBGB and OMFUG for Country, Bluegrass and Blues, and Other Music for Urban Gourmets) became the center of the burgeoning New York punk scene. (The only other major club supporting punk at this time was Max's Kansas City in Greenwich Village.) One of the first groups to play at CBGB was Television, a band that included bassist Richard Myers, who went by the name Richard Hell, and guitarist Tom Miller, who went by the name Tom Verlaine (after the French symbolist poet). Television's influences included avant-garde saxophonists John Coltrane and Albert Ayler, the Rolling Stones, and French impressionistic composer Maurice Ravel. Hell was also influential to punk fashion as the first to wear the ripped clothes and just-fell-out-of-bed hairstyle, and as the writer of the first punk anthem, "Blank Generation," whose lyrics seemed to express the hopelessness that many in the rock underground felt. Hell later went on to play with the Heartbreakers and led the seminal band the Voidoids, which recorded "Blank Generation."

Another early CBGB artist was **Patti Smith** (1946–), a painter, poet, and rock journalist who began experimenting in 1971 with setting her poems to the musical accompaniment of guitarist Lenny Kaye and pianist Richard Sohl. In early 1974, the trio recorded "Hey Joe," backed with Smith's "Piss Factory," a song about her experience working at an assembly line job in New Jersey. With the release of the single, Smith's group began a residency at Max's Kansas City alongside Television, after which both bands moved to CBGB. These successes were instrumental in securing a contract with newly formed Arista Records and the 1975 release of *Horses*. Produced by John Cale, *Horses* is an amalgamation of rock and roll, poetry, and primal experimentation. In spite of this, it was one of the few punk albums of the era that actually charted, going to #47. Smith also made an alternative punk fashion statement of her own with a white button down shirt and men's tie.

The Ramones

The band that is considered by many to be the first true punk band was the Ramones, a group of high school buddies from the Forest Hills section of Queens, New York. The Ramones played rock and roll that was simple (four chords maximum per song), fast (most songs were played at breakneck tempos and were over in less than two and a half minutes), raw, energetic, and fun. Their music was intense and unrelenting (a sort of punk version of Phil Spector's Wall of Sound), while their shows, rarely lasting over twenty minutes, have been called the most powerful in rock history. Taking a surname used by Paul McCartney in his early years, the group was formed in 1974 by Jeffrey Hyman, John Cummings, Doug

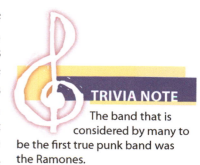

TRIVIA NOTE

The band that is considered by many to be the first true punk band was the Ramones.

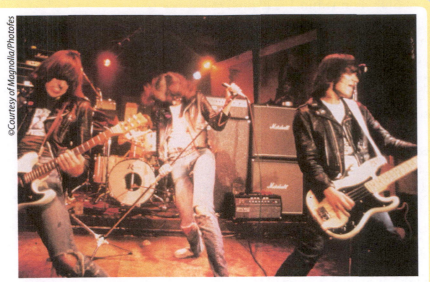

The Ramones

Colvin, and Tom Erdely, who became Joey, Johnny, Dee Dee, and Tommy Ramone, respectively. With a uniform of torn jeans and leather jackets, the Ramones played their first show on March 30, 1974, at New York's Performance Studio. Later that summer, they began a year-long off and on residency at CBGB, which played an important role in developing a small cult following. Near the end of 1975, they signed a contract with Sire Records and in early 1976 recorded their debut album *The Ramones* for just over $6,000.

In the summer of 1976, the Ramones toured England and created a sensation in the rock underground that helped ignite the British punk movement. Later that year they recorded their second album, *Ramones Leave Home,* which had limited success in the United States (like their first LP) but became somewhat of a hit in England. Capitalizing on their newfound celebrity in the United Kingdom, the Ramones released "Sheena Is a Punk Rocker" in early 1977, which became a Top 40 hit there. Key to the success of the Ramones among punks was their amateurish musical abilities and the fact that they only played their own material. The band wrote their own songs not out of an artistic undertaking but because they couldn't learn other people's. As Johnny Ramone admitted in an interview, "We put records on, but we couldn't figure out how to play the songs, so we decided to start writing songs that were within our capabilities." Their lyrics, often containing biting sarcasm and mindless humor, also held great appeal to punkers. Songs such as "I Don't Care," "I'm Against It," "I Wanna Be Sedated," and "Teenage Lobotomy" offered welcome relief from the soul-searching confessionals of the singer/songwriters and other types of narcissistic 1970s rock.

THE RAMONES
- Jeffrey Hyman, Joey
- John Cummings, Johnny
- Doug Colvin, Dee Dee
- Tom Erdely, Tommy

THE LONDON SCENE

No Future

While New York punk was linked to the city's art scene, the British punk movement was driven primarily by the country's poor economy. In 1975, with unemployment at more than one million and inflation at a record 18 percent,

MUSIC CUT 52

"SHEENA IS A PUNK ROCKER" (JOEY RAMONE)— THE RAMONES

Personnel: Johnny Ramone: guitar; Joey Ramone: vocals; Dee Dee Ramone: bass; Tommy Ramone: drums. Recorded 1977 at Media Sound, NYC; produced by Tony Bongiovi and T. Erdelyi. Released May 1977 on the Sire LP *Rocket to Russia;* 13 weeks on the charts, peaking at #81.

"Sheena Is a Punk Rocker" from *Rocket to Russia* is a great example of the distinctive punk cum bubblegum sound of the Ramones, meaning it is two and a half minutes of mindless fun. Composer and Ramones lead singer Joey Ramone later said, "I combined Sheena, Queen of the Jungle with the primalness of punk rock. It was funny, because all the girls in New York seemed to change their names to Sheena after that." Although "Sheena Is a Punk Rocker" never cracked the Top 40 (*Rocket to Russia* also sold poorly), it is a classic recording by one of punk's most influential bands.

many British kids had no future to look forward to when they finished school. Many went on "the dole" (welfare) and there was a general mood of cynicism, despair, and boredom. From these grievances, punk emerged as a legitimate social protest. But dissatisfaction went beyond the economy. There was also a tremendous amount of resentment directed toward the record industry, which was enduring hard times of its own. In 1976, sales of singles leveled off and album sales actually declined in England for the first time in years. To be sure, part of the problem was that kids had less disposable income, but there was also a growing dissatisfaction with the continued promotion of aging British Invasion stars ("boring old farts" as they were called), whose best work was years behind them. When sales started to sag, many in the industry, mindful of how the Beatles had revitalized the entire industry back in the early 1960s, began looking for the "next big thing," the "new Beatles" that could rev things up again. As industry A&R men and talent scouts started to snoop around, many turned their attention to the small but flourishing pub rock scene.

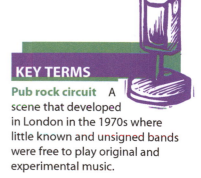

KEY TERMS

Pub rock circuit   A scene that developed in London in the 1970s where little known and unsigned bands were free to play original and experimental music.

London's **pub rock circuit** was the 1970s version of the city's 1960s R&B scene, where little known and unsigned bands were free to experiment with new music in an intimate club environment. Among the popular pubs in the scene were the Nashville, the Tally Ho, the Hope, and the Anchor. By focusing on live performances rather than the more controlled environment of the studio, pub bands were more exciting and energetic than many established recording bands. Although their repertoire often included R&B covers, many pub bands began to put an emphasis on original material, and the scene became a training ground of sorts for new songwriters. The essence of pub rock was from the beginning a back-to-basics, stripped-down guitar-oriented music. Over time,

- Nashville
- Tally Ho
- Hope
- Anchor

PUBS FROM LONDON'S PUB ROCK CIRCUIT

pub bands started to adopt a more aggressive stage attitude, the music got faster and louder, and the beginnings of British punk began to emerge.

Among the more popular pub bands were Brinsley Schwarz (featuring songwriter Nick Lowe), Dr. Feelgood, Bees Make Honey, Eddie and the Hot Rods, City, and the 101ers. 101ers guitarist Joe Strummer left the band in 1976 to start his band the Clash soon after hearing the Sex Pistols in concert. New wave artist Elvis Costello also got his start in the pub scene. There were also a number of small independent record labels that sprang up for pub bands and the burgeoning punk movement, the most important of which were Stiff and Rough Trade. As is usually the case, the major labels were resistant to taking a risk on the new music.

However, as pub rock evolved into punk, it was only a matter of time before one band would emerge that would be so offensive and so disruptive that the majors could no longer afford to ignore them. That band was the Sex Pistols.

The Sex Pistols

The Sex Pistols were either the perfect antidote for everything that was wrong with rock or a clever act of fraud played on the record industry, the media, and the establishment. In a period of slightly more than two years, they managed to outrage the British press, offend the Royal Family, confound the radio and record industries, and take punk beyond the limits of anyone's sensibilities. And most importantly, they had a deep impact on the future course of rock music. The Pistols were the brainchild of London clothier **Malcolm McLaren**, who got his first taste of band management with a short-lived stint with the New York Dolls in early 1975. After the Dolls broke up, McLaren returned to London and his Kings Road boutique Let It Rock, which at the time sold neo-teddy boy clothing. Anticipating a new trend, McLaren changed the name of the store to **Sex** and began selling leather and metal S&M fashions. Among the frequent store patrons were drummer Paul Cook, guitarist Steve Jones, and bassist Glen Matlock of a band called the Strand. At some point the three approached McLaren to manage them and to find a suitable (as in, having the right look and attitude) vocalist. In one of McLaren's many strokes of genius, he found the perfect fit in John Lydon (1956–), an out-of-work janitor whose teeth were green from neglect and who had such a nasty attitude that the others began calling him Johnny Rotten. It is also worth noting that Lydon had never

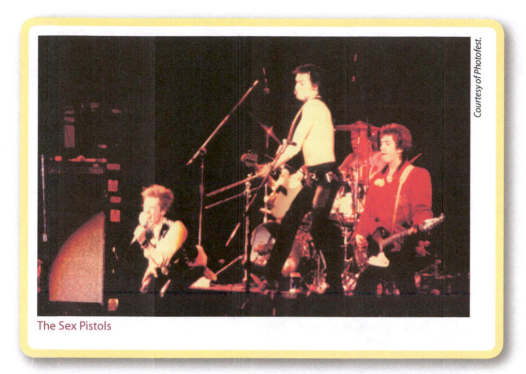

Courtesy of Photofest.

The Sex Pistols

sung before. At first, McLaren saw the band as a means to advertise his store (hence, the name Sex Pistols), but he soon saw the potential in using them as mercenaries in his own nihilistic agenda.

After their first gig in November 1975, the Pistols began playing college campuses in England and writing their own material. One of their first songs, "Anarchy in the UK" is a three and a half minute diatribe that begins with "I am an antichrist" and ends with "Get pissed, destroy." It was also a rallying cry that effectively put the Sex Pistols at the vanguard of Britain's punk movement. In September 1976, McLaren staged the Punk Rock Festival at London's 100 Club as a showcase for the Pistols and other punk bands, including the Clash, the Buzzcocks, and the Vibrators. The strategy worked: in October the Pistols signed with EMI and received a £50,000 advance; in November they released "Anarchy in the UK" as a single. In December 1976, the group encountered their first scandal when they appeared live on the nationally broadcast *Today* TV program. Host Bill Grundy seemed intent on provoking the band; they in turn seemed bent on causing trouble. The fun started when Rotten muttered the word "shit" under his breath; Grundy responded by asking Steve Jones to "say something outrageous." Then, this exchange followed (remember, this is being broadcast live on the state-run BBC):

JONES: You dirty bastard.
GRUNDY: Go on again.
JONES: You dirty fucker!
GRUNDY: What a clever boy.
JONES: You fucking rotter!

The uproar that followed caused EMI to drop the Pistols in January 1977, thereby forfeiting their advance to the band. In March the Pistols were signed by A&M, and given another £50,000 advance; one week later they were fired

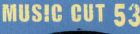

MUSIC CUT 53

"GOD SAVE THE QUEEN" (PAUL COOK/STEVE JONES/GLEN MATLOCK/JOHN LYDON)—THE SEX PISTOLS

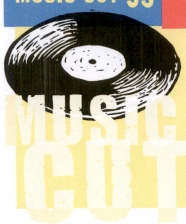

Personnel: John Lydon (Johnny Rotten): vocals; Steve Jones: guitar, vocals; Glen Matlock: bass; Paul Cook: drums. Recorded 1976/77 at Wessex Sound Studios, London; produced by Chris Thomas and Bill Price. Released May 1977 on Virgin; peaked at #2 (UK).

With "God Save the Queen," the Sex Pistols managed to offend just about every facet of polite English society during the year celebrating the Queen's 25th anniversary on the throne. With a title mocking the British national anthem, lyrics accusing the Queen of running a "fascist regime" that left the underclass with "no future" and a sleeve picturing Her Majesty's eyes and mouth obscured with cutout letters, the BBC banned the song for "gross bad taste." In spite of the banishment (or perhaps *because* of it), the song rose to the top of the charts. But the Pistols were destined to get their just deserts. On June 7, 1977 during the celebration of the Silver Jubilee, they attempted to play the song from a boat on the River Thames outside the Palace of Westminster. Authorities thwarted the stunt. Said lead vocalist Johnny Rotten, "Watching her on telly, as far as I'm concerned, she ain't no human being. She's a piece of cardboard they drag around on a trolley." The song also appears on the LP *Never Mind the Bollocks, Here's the Sex Pistols*.

and given £25,000 more as a buyout fee. Around this time, bassist Matlock decided to quit the group; his replacement was John Ritchie (1957–1979), a friend of Rotten's who went by the name Sid Vicious. The band signed with Virgin in May and released their second single "God Save the Queen," a malicious attack on the monarchy that came just as the country was gearing up for the queen's Silver Jubilee in June, marking Elizabeth's 25th year on the throne. In spite of being banned from the BBC and the refusal of many stores to sell it, "God Save the Queen" quickly sold 200,000 copies and became the #1 single in Britain, although the BBC would not play it and the title was covered with a black bar on the official printed chart. By the end of the year the Pistols released their only LP, ***Never Mind the Bollocks, Here's the Sex Pistols*** on Virgin in the UK and on Warner in the U.S.

In January 1978 the Sex Pistols undertook a disastrous 14-day tour of the southern and western United States. After the last concert in San Francisco, Rotten quit (or was fired, depending on who you talk to), and the group broke up. Sid Vicious, a heroin addict, was charged in October with the stabbing death of girlfriend Nancy Spungen in their room at New York's Chelsea Hotel. Although he was released on bail, he died of a heroin overdose in February 1979 before he was brought to trial. After dismissing the Sex Pistols as a farce, John Lydon in 1978 formed the group Public Image, Ltd. Whether or not they were indeed a farce is still being debated; however, there is universal agreement that as the most notorious and outrageous British punk band the Sex Pistols had a major impact on the future of rock and roll.

The Clash

The Clash have always occupied a secondary role to the Sex Pistols in the annals of British punk (and after all, who could top the Pistols?), but in fact they took punk beyond its early narrow focus and outlived the Pistols by nearly ten years.

- John Mellor, aka Joe Strummer
- Mick Jones
- Paul Simonon
- Terry Chimes, aka Tory Crimes, 1976–77
- Topper Headon, 1977–86

THE CLASH

The Clash were also the most political of the English punk bands (working for change rather than just destruction), and incorporated a broad base of musical styles into their recordings. The group formed in 1976 when guitarist/vocalist John Mellor, aka Joe Strummer, left his band the 101ers to join forces with guitarist Mick Jones and bassist Paul Simonon of the London SS. The 101ers were a pub band whose name was taken from the torture room number in George Orwell's novel 1984. The name for the new band was chosen from a commonly used newspaper term for racial and class conflicts. Also included in the initial lineup was drummer Terry Chimes, aka Tory Crimes, and 101ers guitarist Keith Levene, who left shortly after their first show. Managed by Malcolm McLaren associate Bernard Rhodes, the Clash opened for the Sex Pistols in their 1976 summer tour of England, which led to a contract with British CBS in February 1977. After securing a $200,000 advance, the group released its eponymous debut album, after which Chimes left and was replaced by Topper Headon.

Although the Clash by this time were becoming popular in Britain, they were virtual unknowns in the United States. However, in 1979, buoyed by their Pearl Harbor Tour of America and the release of their third album *London Calling* (which went to #27), they began to make inroads into the American market. That same year they appeared in the semi-documentary film *Rude Boy,* which featured extensive footage of their live shows. In 1980 the triple album *Sandinista!* was released, an experimental mix of styles that drew mixed reviews (although it was named album of the year by the *Village Voice*). The Clash were not afraid to tackle political and social issues in their music, including racism ("Police and Thieves"), rebellion ("White Riot"), unemployment ("Career Opportunities"), and class consciousness ("What's My Name"). Their music incorporated influences that were beyond the scope of most punk bands, including reggae, gospel, Euro-pop, funk, jazz, R&B, and rap. The fact that they were influenced at all by black American music set them worlds apart from the Sex Pistols and most other punk bands. The Clash also managed to find some commercial success, most notably with 1982's *Combat Rock* (#7), which included the #8 single "Rock the Casbah." Another song from *Combat Rock,* "Should I Stay or Should I Go" was re-released in 1991 after it was featured in a Levi's TV commercial and went to #1 in the UK. The band broke up in 1986.

Other Important Punk Bands

The Sex Pistols and the Clash inspired hundreds of other punk bands to form in England and America in the late 1970s. Among the most important were the Damned, the Vibrators, the Buzzcocks, Joy Division, Generation X, and Siouxsie and the Banshees.

THE PUNK AFTERMATH

New Wave

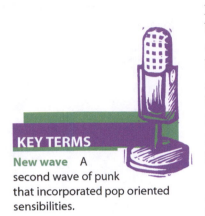

KEY TERMS

New wave   A second wave of punk that incorporated pop oriented sensibilities.

Even before the record industry could recover from the initial wave of punk bands, a second or "new wave" of artists began to appear that took elements of punk and fused them with a more pop oriented sensibility. **New wave** bands also began to incorporate other stylistic strains into their music, including American R&B, reggae and even synthesizer based techno-pop. Two American bands that were early adopters of this strategy were Blondie and the Talking Heads. Blondie, led by bleached blonde singer and former Playboy bunny Deborah Harry, made their debut at CBGB in August 1974, and became regulars there for the next several years. After recording two albums for Chrysalis in 1976 and 1977, the band had made impressive inroads into the European and Australian markets, but were pretty much unknown in the U.S. They finally broke through in their native country with 1978's *Parallel Lines,* which peaked at #6 and yielded their first #1 single, the disco-infused "Heart of Glass" in 1979. Over the next two years they had seven more Top 40 singles, including three #1s. They broke up in 1982.

Talking Heads first came together in 1973 as the Artistics, in homage to the Rhode Island School of Design, where David Byrne (guitar, vocals), Chris Frantz (drums) and Tina Weymouth (bass) were students. After the band broke up in 1974, the three moved to New York and made their debut at CBGB as the Talking Heads in May 1975, where they became regulars over the next few years. In 1976 the group added keyboardist Jerry Harrison, and eventually signed with Sire Records in 1977. Later that year they released their debut album *Talking Heads '77,* which yielded the single "Psycho Killer," inspired by the Norman Bates character from Alfred Hitchcock's film *Psycho.* In the song Byrne sings in a clipped, almost stuttering sing/speak that in a strange sense fit his stage persona. The Talking Heads were one of the most unusual bands to come out of the CBGB scene in the late 1970s, and for good reason. Their 1979 release ***Fear of Music*** is often called their best, with its innovative production and use of rhythm. All had attended college, which no doubt had an influence on their more sophisticated look and sound. All were accomplished musicians, and drew influences from such disparate sources as punk, R&B, and New York minimalist composers Philip Glass and Terry Riley. They also rejected the leather and jeans punk dress code and wore slacks and sweaters, giving them a nerdy-smart college student image. Lead singer Byrne's on-stage moves were also out of the ordinary, and were described by one rock critic this way: "Imagine an out-of-it kid practicing Buddy Holly moves in front of a mirror." In time, Byrne's self-conscious awkwardness became fashionably cool. The band continued recording until their breakup in late 1991.

NEW WAVE BANDS

- Blondie
- Talking Heads
- Cars
- Pretenders
- Devo
- Romantics
- Elvis Costello
- The Police

Characteristics of New Wave

1. A post-punk style with commercial pop sensibilities
2. Utilizes influences from R&B, reggae, techno-pop
3. Synthesizers frequently used

Key New Wave Recordings

- *My Aim Is True*—Elvis Costello, 1978
- *Fear of Music*—Talking Heads 1979
- "Whip It"—Devo, 1980
- *Synchronicity*—the Police, 1983

From Boston, the Cars emerged as a major commercial success, with eight Top 40 albums and four Top 10 singles before their breakup in 1988. Akron, Ohio born songwriter/singer/guitarist Chrissie Hynde hooked up with three Londoners to form the Pretenders, which had five Top 40 LPs in the 1980s. Also coming from Akron was Devo (short for de-evolution), who combined a futuristic robotic image with techno-pop sensibilities. Devo's 1986 LP *Freedom of Choice* yielded the #14 hit "Whip It," which was made into a innovative music video in which the members wore pots on their heads. Another band that relied heavily on image was Athens, Georgia's the B52's, whose two female vocalists wore bouffant hairdos. Their biggest hit was 1990's "Love Shack" (#3). From Detroit, the Romantics contributed one of the 1980s more memorable anthems, "What I Like About You."

The English new wave movement was just as strong as its American counterpart. In addition to the Pretenders, the most important artists in the British scene were Elvis Costello and the Police. In 1975, **Elvis Costello** (DeClan Patrick McManus) (1954–) was married and worked as a computer programmer when he suddenly quit his job to work as a roadie for Brinsley Schwartz. After

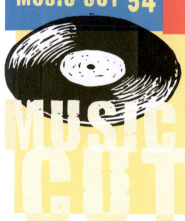

MUSIC CUT 54

"BURNING DOWN THE HOUSE" (DAVID BYRNE/CHRIS FRANTZ/ JERRY HARRISON/TINA WEYMOUTH)—TALKING HEADS

Personnel: David Byrne: guitar, keyboards, percussion, lead vocals; Jerry Harrison: keyboards, guitar, backup vocals; Tina Weymouth: bass, backup vocals; Chris Frantz: drums, backup vocals; Bernie Worrell: clavinet. Recorded 1982 at Sigma Sound, Philadelphia; produced by Talking Heads. Released 1983 on Sire; 11 weeks on the charts, peaking at #9.

The leadoff track to Talking Heads fifth studio album *Speaking in Tongues*, "Burning Down the House" became the bands only single to crack the Top Ten. The song started out as an instrumental jam by husband and wife band members Chris Frantz and Tina Weymouth. After some crafting by the entire band into a more song-like form, vocalist David Byrne began chanting nonsense syllables to fit the phrasing of the music. Later, he wrote words to fit the phrasing. Chris Frantz has commented that the title of the song (and perhaps the group vocals) were inspired by a George Clinton performance he attended in 1979. And in fact, Clinton's keyboard player Bernie Worrell plays the clavinet on this recording.

submitting demos of his own songs, he secured a contract with Stiff Records in 1976, and eventually released his debut LP *My Aim Is True* in 1978. It was a hit (#32 in the U.S.) and won critical raves. Since then Costello's musical focus has been remarkably eclectic, with influences ranging from jazz, R&B, reggae, punk and lounge music. His intelligent, witty and sometimes hostile lyrics owe a debt to Dylan. Since his debut, 12 albums and two singles have hit the Top 40, making him one of the most commercially successful post-punk artists.

The Police were formed in 1977 by bassist Gordon Sumner, aka Sting, drummer Stewart Copeland and guitarist Andy Summers. The group name is thematically related to a number of other Stewart family concerns: his father at one time worked for the CIA, and his brother owned a small record label, Illegal Records Syndicate (I.R.S.) and a talent agency, Frontier Booking, International (FBI). After forming in 1977, the Police's first self-produced single sold 70,000 copies in Britain. After signing a lucrative contract with A&M Records, the group toured small clubs in America in a rented van and developed a strong grass roots following. By mixing strong pop melodies, reggae influenced dance music and blond good looks, over the next ten years the group scored six albums and nine singles in the Top 40. The high point of their popularity came in the summer of 1983, when "Every Breath You Take," from the LP *Synchronicity* stayed at #1 for eight weeks. The album eventually went 8x platinum and stayed at the #1 spot for 17 weeks.

Hardcore

At the same time that new wave was exploring a more pop-friendly side of punk, a harder-edged offshoot was also emerging. **Hardcore** incubated in Los Angeles, although another important albeit smaller scene also developed in Washington, DC. Hardcore music, like punk, reflected a culture of angry and frustrated white teenagers who "began devising an ultra-punk—undiluted, unglamorous, and uncompromising—that no corporation would ever touch," states Michael Azerrad. Hardcore is darker, angrier, faster and louder than punk, and was accompanied by a fashion ethos of tattoos, buzz cut haircuts and Army boots. Audience members often engaged in moshing, in which participants would form pits in front of the stage and smash into each other. Diving into the mosh pit from the stage was also common. Hardcore concerts often erupted in chaos and violence, often at the incitement of the bands.

HARDCORE   **Characteristics of Hardcore**

1. A harder edged, darker and angrier evolution of punk
2. Counter culture associations with fashion, slam dancing, mosh pits
3. Scene centered in Los Angeles

Key Hardcore Recordings

- *Fresh Fruit for Rotting Vegetables*—the Dead Kennedys, 1980
- *Damaged*—Black Flag, 1981

Important Hardcore Bands

Azerrad describes **Black Flag** as "the flagship band of American hardcore itself," and "required listening for anyone who was interested in underground music." Founded in 1977 in Hermosa Beach, California by guitarist Greg Ginn and vocalist Keith Morris, the band originally called themselves Panic before changing to Black Flag after discovering another band named Panic. Since they initially has trouble finding a reliable bass player, Ginn devised a distinctive playing style that was rhythmic and emphasized lower pitches. Because the band initially had trouble finding a label to release they're recordings, Ginn started SST Records in 1979, which in time became the most important independent hardcore label. Morris left that year, and further personnel changes over the next two years led to a permanent Black Flag lineup of Ginn, Chuck Dukowski on bass, Dez Cadena on rhythm guitar, Roberto Valverde, going by the name Robo on drums, and Henry Garfield, who assumed the name Henry Rollins on vocals. Black Flag shows had always incited trouble between fans and police, but Rollins's skinhead, tattoos and angry stage presence added a whole new level of disorder. One critic labeled him "a cross between Jim Morrison and Ted Nugent"; another called the Rollins-led band "a gruesome and intimidating display of rock aggression and frustration," that "like a high-speed car crash, you couldn't keep your eyes—or ears—off." The sound and fury of Black Flag was best captured in their 1981 LP *Damaged*, which is today considered one of the defining hardcore albums. Despite their influence and renown among the hardcore faithful, Black Flag never was able to make anything resembling even a meager income, and eventually broke up in 1986.

Minor Threat is often called the definitive hardcore band. They were formed in Washington, DC in 1980 by vocalist Ian MacKaye, drummer Jeff Nelson, bassist Brian Baker and guitarist Lyle Pressler. Initially calling themselves the Teen Idles, they were inspired by the established local hardcore band Bad Brains, who not only played punk at incredibly fast speeds but "were the

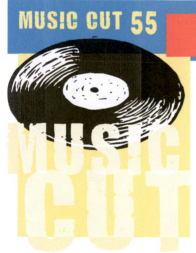

MUSIC CUT 55

"RISE ABOVE" (GREG GINN)— BLACK FLAG

Personnel: Henry Rollins: lead vocals; Greg Ginn: lead guitar, backup vocals; Dez Cadena: rhythm guitar, backup vocals; Chuck Dukowski: bass, backup vocals; Roberto Valverde (Robo): drums, backup vocals. Recorded August 1981 at Unicorn Studios, Los Angeles; produced by Spot, Black Flag. Released December 1981 on the SST LP *Damaged;* not released as a single.

Damaged, Black Flag's debut album on SST Records, has been called "a key hardcore document, perhaps *the* hardcore document" by writer Michael Aserrad (*Our Band Could Be Your Life*). "It boiled over with rage on several fronts: police harassment, materialism, alcohol abuse," and, "the stultifying effects of consumer culture." The band had made two previous attempts to record material for a first album with singers Ron Reyes and Dez Cedena, but were unhappy with the results. It wasn't until the addition of vocalist Henry Rollins, who managed to channel the pent up rage from an unhappy childhood, that Black Flag found their muse. The refrain to "Rise Above" pretty much sums up the sentiments of the album—and hardcore, for that matter: "We are tired of your abuse/Try to stop us, it's no use!"

coolest-looking, most heavy-looking dudes," according to MacKaye. Around the time they changed their name to Minor Threat, MacKaye and Nelson—in true hardcore spirit--decided to start their own label, which they called Dischord Records. The label's first release was the eight-song EP *Minor Disturbance* from the Teen Idles that comprised all of ten minutes of music. As Minor Threat, the band released two EPs and one LP. 1983's *Out of Step,* which turned out to be their last release. The band broke up that year over personal disagreements.

Other hardcore bands included LA's X, the Circle Jerks, and the Minutemen; Washington, DC's Bad Brains and Fugazi; Hüsker Dü from Minneapolis, the Minutemen from San Pedro, California, and San Francisco's the Dead Kennedys, led by political activist Jello Biafra.

STUDY QUESTIONS

Name _____ Date _____

1. Who were some of the people and bands that were influential to the creation of punk, and what were their contributions?

2. Why was punk so influential to rock, and why did it lose its credibility?

3. What were some important differences between the New York and London punk scenes?

4. Describe how the Velvet Underground were unique for their time and why they were influential to later punk bands.

5. Why did New York punk musicians feel it was not necessary to be virtuoso performers on their instruments?

6. Describe a show by the Ramones.

7. How was London's pub rock scene instrumental in the development of the city's punk scene?

8. In what ways did the Sex Pistols manipulate the music industry and how did they contribute to the end of the punk era?

9. In what ways were the Clash unique among punk bands of the era?

10. In what ways were the Talking Heads an out of the ordinary band for the CBGB scene in the late 1970s?

HISTORICAL INTERLUDE: 1980s

A Return to the Conservative

The idea of conservatism came to be the new policy for many Americans in the 1980s. Tired of the counterculture excesses, political scandals, tumultuous war, and unrest in the Middle East, many Americans embraced social, political, and economic conservatism. Ronald Reagan, a leader of the conservative attitude, became president in 1980.

The Cold War, which had been ongoing with the Soviet Union since the end of World War II, reached a peak in the early 1980s. Ronald Reagan pushed for an arms race intended to outspend the Soviet Union, therefore crippling them economically. This strategy worked and a new leader of the Soviet Union, Mikhail Gorbachev, took over in 1985. He helped lead the dissolution of the USSR by 1991.

During the 1980s, more than 150,000 people were diagnosed with AIDS. Ninety thousand deaths related to AIDS occurred from 1981-1999, which created an increased awareness of sexually transmitted diseases. By the 1990s, household names who had contracted HIV including Freddy Mercury of the band Queen (who would die of AIDS in 1991) and the NBA basketball superstar, Magic Johnson. New attention about safe sex and STDs would headline discussions of the late 1980s and early 1990s.

Money and how to make more of it would become a major theme of the 1980s. The term "yuppie" was often used to describe a well-educated baby boomer who was self-centered and often into material goods. Credit card debit increased exponentially for many young adults throughout the decade.

The high tech industry advanced impressively throughout the decade and included the development of the personal computer. Computers could now be purchased for the home, and the high tech industry would continue to grow into the 1990s.

Cable television would grow in popularity throughout 1980s. Cable had been created in the 1970s to bring television signals to areas of the country that could not get good reception such as mountainous regions of the West and wide-open spaces in the Midwest. From its beginnings at the start of the decade, cable and programming such as CNN, ESPN, and MTV became the new necessity in the world of entertainment to millions of households by 1989.

12

THE EIGHTIES

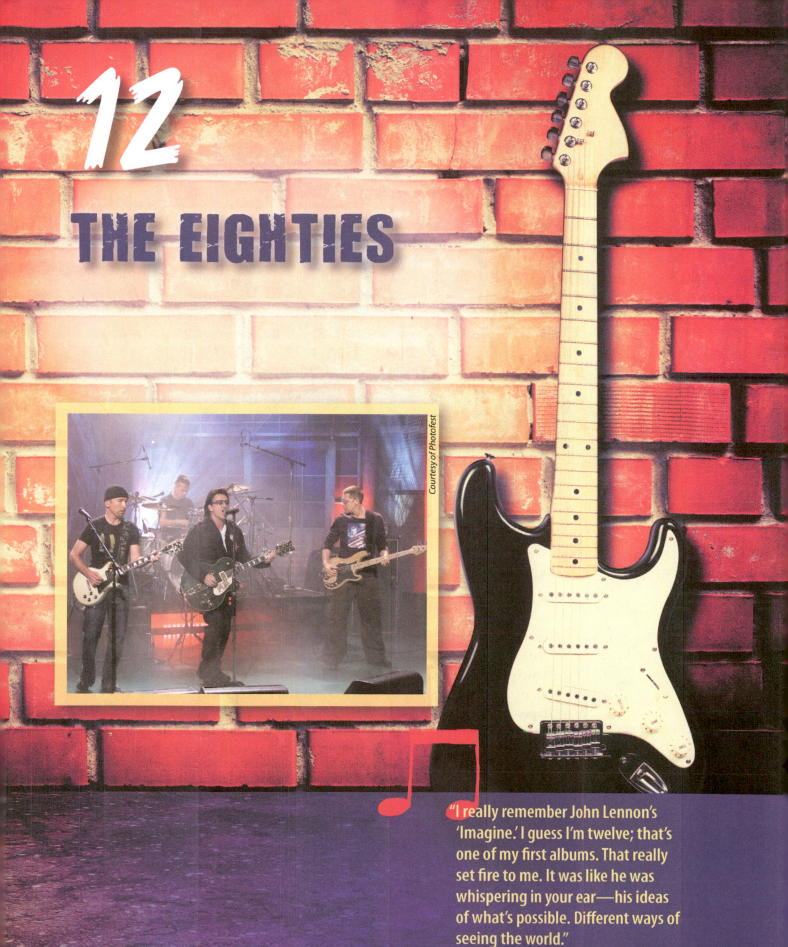

Courtesy of Photofest

"I really remember John Lennon's 'Imagine.' I guess I'm twelve; that's one of my first albums. That really set fire to me. It was like he was whispering in your ear—his ideas of what's possible. Different ways of seeing the world."

—*Bono*

<table>
<tr>
<td rowspan="2">

KEY TERMS

</td>
<td>

Cassette tape
Compact disc
MIDI
Digital samplers
DAT

</td>
<td>

MTV
Alternative rock
New Wave of British
  Heavy Metal
Industrial

</td>
<td>

PMRC
Live Aid/Farm Aid

</td>
</tr>
</table>

<table>
<tr>
<td rowspan="2">

KEY FIGURES

</td>
<td>

Michael Jackson
Quincy Jones
Madonna
Prince
The Revolution
Bruce Springsteen

</td>
<td>

E Street Band
U2
Bono
Whitney Houston
R.E.M.
Sonic Youth

</td>
<td>

Metallica
Bon Jovi
Guns N' Roses
AC/DC
Nine Inch Nails

</td>
</tr>
</table>

<table>
<tr>
<td rowspan="2">

KEY ALBUMS

</td>
<td>

Thriller— Michael Jackson
Purple Rain—Prince
Nebraska—Bruce
  Springsteen
Born in the U.S.A—Bruce
  Springsteen

</td>
<td>

The Joshua Tree—U2
Whitney Houston—
  Whitney Houston
Murmur—R.E.M.
Daydream Nation—Sonic
  Youth

</td>
<td>

Metallica—Metallica
The Downward Spiral—
  Nine Inch Nails
Double Fantasy—John
  Lennon and Yoko Ono

</td>
</tr>
</table>

TECHNOLOGY RULES

Changing Consumer Technologies

As rock entered the 1980s, it seemed clear that the music industry was about to undergo some significant changes. Although the punk *movement* was dead, the back to basics attitude of the music had engendered a sort of wiping-the-slate-clean effect, and already a number of new post-punk styles were emerging. Disco was also dead, and with its death came the end of the salad days of soaring record sales. According to *Billboard* and the RIAA, yearly sales of records and tapes tripled between 1970 and 1978, peaking at $4 billion; by 1982 they had dropped to $3.5 billion. Casablanca Records, which had bet the farm on disco, imploded; in 1982 CBS records fired 300 employees and closed nine of its 19 sales offices around the country. Although disco's death had contributed to the industry woes, other factors were also at play. Sales of 8-track tapes, nearly $1 billion in 1978, had almost disappeared by 1982, while album sales were down 20 percent. At the same time however, sales of pre-recorded cassette tapes tripled. Cassettes seemed to be a bright spot; although the audio fidelity was not as good as LPs, they were portable, didn't scratch or warp, and were resistant to jostling, making them ideal for car stereos. After Sony introduced the Walkman portable cassette player in the U.S. in 1980, cassette sales exploded and actually exceeded album sales for the first time in 1984. By 1988 they were outselling albums by more than four to one.

Unfortunately for record labels, pre-recorded cassettes were cheaper than albums and yielded smaller profit margins. Then there was the issue of blank cassettes, on which consumers could record copies of their friend's albums,

KEY TERMS

Cassette tape   A tape storage media introduced in the 1960s in which the tape is enclosed in a small plastic molding, or cassette.

music off the radio, or make their own customized playlists. Obviously, when a consumer buys a blank cassette and tapes someone else's album to listen to in their car, the label is effectively cut out of the transaction and doesn't make a dime. Home taping became such a concern for the music industry that a "Home Taping is Killing Music" campaign was kicked off with a skull and crossbones logo. Producer Quincy Jones told a congressional committee looking into the matter in April 1982 that unless something was done about home taping, "there would never be another hit album that would sell as many as five million units." (Congress did nothing; ironically, nine months later Michael Jackson released the Jones-produced *Thriller* album, which went on to sell more than 100 million copies.) Consumers loved the versatility and convenience of cassettes, and the trends of the early 1980s suggested that it was a format that was here to stay.

As we all know however, the cassette tape was *not* here to stay. In 1982 engineers at Sony and Dutch electronics giant Philips introduced the **compact disc** (CD), a digital music format with just as much portability and dramatically better sound quality than the cassette. CDs were non-linear (meaning that jumping from one song to another was instantaneous), they were lightweight, and handled jostling well. Like albums, they were a playback-only media, so home taping was not an issue. Although record labels and retailers were hostile to them at first (after all, building new pressing plants and installing new store fixtures was going to be expensive), they eventually realized that the CD presented a golden opportunity to resell consumers their entire record collection all over again—at a higher price. *Brilliant!* In 1982 Sony simultaneously introduced the first CD player, the CDP-101, and the first album released on CD, Billy Joel's *52nd Street*. Consumers responded positively, and sales of CD's exploded, going from $16.7 million in 1983, to $100 million in 1984, $378 million in 1985, and $900 million in 1986. Cassette sales hung in there for a while, but by 1991 CD sales overtook them for good. By then albums were all but gone, and overall industry sales had soared to $7.6 billion—and were still climbing!

MIDI and Digital Tape Recording

Technological advances from the 1980s also dramatically changed the way that music was going to be created in the future. When the **MIDI** (musical instrument digital interface) protocol was agreed upon by musical instrument manufacturers in 1983, the way was cleared for the creation of keyboards, **digital samplers**, drum machines, and other digital instruments that could "talk" to each other and interconnect with computers. When a MIDI controller such as a keyboard or drum pad is played, it sends out a digital signal containing such information as what note was played, how hard it was struck, and whether more pressure was applied after the initial strike, and so on. This information can then be recorded on computer sequencing software, where it can be edited in powerful ways and played back on any other MIDI instrument. In this way, one person can easily play all the synthesized instruments on a recording, and can quickly change a guitar part to a piano part, or change the piece's key to accommodate a singer. Producers and do-it-yourselfers could now use MIDI technology in the same way that tape recorders were used. The 1980s saw a dramatic

KEY TERMS

Compact disc A digital storage media introduced in 1982 by Sony and Philips.

MIDI An acronym for musical instrument digital interface, a computer protocol that enables digital instruments and computer software to communicate with each other.

Digital samplers Synthesizers that digitally record (sample) sounds that can be played back and manipulated from a MIDI instrument.

MIDI   MIDI, an acronym for the Musical Instrument Digital Interface protocol, has transformed the world of music production since it was introduced to consumers in 1984. As commercially produced music synthesizers were becoming increasingly digital in the late 1970s and early 1980s, the limitation of their interconnectivity was becoming painfully apparent. In the early 1980s, engineers from manufacturers Sequential Circuits, Roland and Oberheim began work on a standard that would allow digital instruments to be controlled remotely. The MIDI 1.0 Standard, which was first published in 1983, was an instant success and has become an industry standard that is used by professionals and part-time enthusiasts alike.

increase in the number of small, home-based studios that could produce music much quicker and less expensively than the large commercial studios, many of which went out of business. Over the years the technology has improved and the software has become much more user-friendly; today, MIDI is a ubiquitous production tool in the music industry.

The 1980s also saw advancements in digital audio recording technology. Digital multi-track tape recorders, although extremely expensive, allowed never before heard of sonic quality and clarity. Because recorded information stored on digital tape required less space than it did using analog technology, more tracks became available to record on—as many as 48 in some cases. The introduction of Digital Audio Tape (**DAT**) recording technology in the late 1970s allowed for a low-cost solution to stereo (two-track) digital recording on tiny tapes that could store up to two hours of material. Throughout the 1980s and early 1990s, most music recording studios were busy replacing their analog tape recorders with digital ones. By the end of the 1990s, digital tape itself began to get phased out in favor of hard disc recording.

MTV

One of the most significant developments in the music business in the 1980s came ironically from an old technology: television. On August 1, 1981, Music Television (MTV) began broadcasting on cable, and almost overnight changed everything about how music was packaged, sold, and consumed. Marketed to the largest record-buying demographic—ages 12 to 34—MTV became the fastest-growing cable channel in history when its subscription went from 2.5 million to 17 million within two years, despite the fact that only 40 percent of the country was wired for cable. When it premiered, MTV was essentially a visual version of radio, with non-stop broadcasting of music videos hosted by VJs (video jockeys). At first, music videos from Britain dominated MTV's programming because many British bands had already been experimenting with the genre throughout the 1970s. (The very first music video shown on the station was the appropriately named "Video Killed the Radio Star" by the British group the Buggles.) The popularity of other British bands such as Duran Duran (with five platinum LPs between 1983 and 1986), Human League, Eurythmics, and Flock of Seagulls in the early 1980s can be directly attributed to their exposure on MTV.

TRIVIA NOTE

One of the most significant developments in the music business in the 1980s came ironically from an old technology: television. On August 1, 1981, Music Television (MTV) began broadcasting on cable, and almost overnight changed everything about how music was packaged, sold, and consumed.

The consequence of MTV as a new pop music medium is that the music video essentially became an advertisement for the record, the band, and the record label. Simply stated, a catchy and memorable video that people liked to watch sold records. American labels that had previously looked at music videos as an intangible expense now viewed them as marketing necessities. Although the nonmusical attributes of artists—how they looked, what clothes they wore, how well they danced—had always been important in pop music, they suddenly took on even greater significance, and became perhaps even more important than the artist's talent. MTV rapidly became the most powerful player in the industry, since their programmers decided which videos to play and which not to play. In the first few years those choices were overwhelmingly white: a mid-1983 survey by *Billboard* found that of the 100 videos in heavy or medium rotation the week of July 16, none were of black artists. MTV, under heavy criticism from just about everyone, feebly tried to defend their programming as the result of extensive market research. But they could not explain how an artist like Rick James, whose most recent album *Street Songs* had sold nearly four million copies couldn't get his video for "Super Freak" shown on their network. MTV was "taking black people back 400 years," said James.

It wasn't until the incredible success of Michael Jackson's *Thriller* album and the three videos that accompanied it that the network was forced to change its programming. Although the songs "Beat It," "Billie Jean" and "Thriller" all became Top 10 hits and their videos set new standards for production quality, it wasn't until Columbia Records president Walter Yetnikoff threatened to yank all of the label's videos off the network that MTV capitulated and put "Billie Jean" into heavy rotation. It has since become known as the 'video that broke the color barrier'. This story may be apocryphal, as there have been several different tellings of it. But wherever the truth lies, MTV played a small but significant role in the rise of an artist that did nothing less than dominate pop music in the early 1980s and in the process revitalized a sagging industry. As Steve Knopper writes in *Appetite for Self-Destruction:* "In late 1982, Michael Jackson almost magically restored the music industry's superstar clout by releasing one record."

MICHAEL, MADONNA, AND PRINCE: POST-DISCO DANCE DOMINANCE

The King of Pop

Michael Jackson (1958–2009) was the second youngest of the Jackson brood of five boys and three girls (sister Janet is the youngest). Hailing from Gary, Indiana, Michael and his brothers (Tito, Jermaine, Jackie and Marlon) began performing together in the early 1960s under their father Joe's tutelage. Joe Jackson was a former part-time musician whose relentless rehearsal of the boys bordered on abuse; nonetheless they developed quickly into a dynamic act playing the chitlin' circuit and winning regional music contests such as the famous Apollo Theatre Amateur Night in August 1967. In 1968 they auditioned for Motown Records and were signed in 1969. Once in his stable, Motown president Berry

Gordy put them through the usual developmental process, and decided to mold the group as an updated version of Frankie Lymon and the Teenagers. At this point in time Michael was only 11 years old, but it was already becoming apparent that he was a superstar in the making. The Jackson 5's first single, "I Want You Back" was released in November 1969, and it, along with the next three singles "ABC," "The Love You Save" and "I'll Be There" all went to #1, the first time in history such a feat had been accomplished. Although he officially stayed with the group until the early 1980s, Michael began his solo career in 1972 with the release of his album *Got to Be There,* whose title cut went to #4 on the charts. The title cut from his second LP *Ben* gave Michael his first #1 single in 1972. In 1975 Michael and his brothers left Motown and signed with CBS, and all future recordings by both the group (now calling themselves the Jacksons) and Michael were released on Columbia's Epic label.

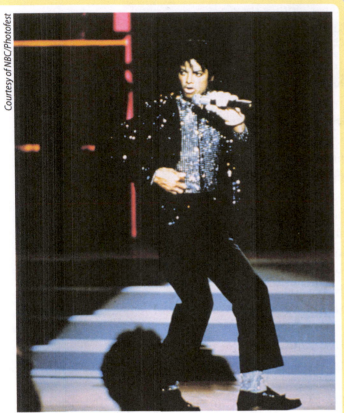

Michael Jackson

Courtesy of NBC/Photofest

Michael released two more albums in the mid-1970s, but it wasn't until 1979, when the 21-year-old singer teamed up with veteran producer **Quincy Jones** that he began his meteoric rise to the top. Their first collaboration, *Off the Wall* is a well-crafted fusing of funk, post-disco pop and soul that sold seven million copies and produced four Top 10 hits, two of which, "Don't Stop 'Til You Get Enough" and "Rock with You" hit #1. The next Jackson/Jones collaboration was the blockbuster of all blockbusters. *Thriller*, released in 1982, became the album that made Michael Jackson an international superstar. All in all, it won eight Grammy Awards (not including the four that Quincy Jones won as producer), yielded an unprecedented seven Top 10 singles out of its nine songs (including two #1's, "Billie Jean" and "Beat It") and stayed on the charts for 91 weeks, 37 at #1. The three videos from the album elevated the genre to new levels, and were so popular that Jackson produced a documentary entitled *The Making of Michael Jackson's Thriller* that sold nearly half a million copies. Michael-mania had arrived.

Thriller was groundbreaking on several levels. The music is superbly produced, arranged and impeccably recorded with state of the art digital technology. There are a remarkable variety of songs, from heavy funk grooves ("Thriller") to heavy metal ("Beat It") to light pop ("The Girl Is Mine"). Jackson also brought in a strong supporting cast of guest artists, including Eddie Van Halen, who played a scorching solo on "Beat It;" Paul McCartney, who sang in duet with Michael on "The Girl Is Mine," (a song McCartney co-wrote); and horror movie veteran Vincent Price, who did a semi-comical rap on the title cut. Jackson's vocals are also perfect, ranging from breathless and high energy to fragile and poignant. Jackson did such a good job of connecting to nearly every

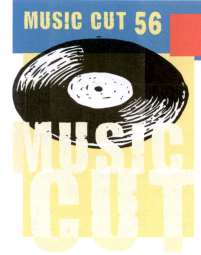

MUSIC CUT 56

"BILLIE JEAN" (MICHAEL JACKSON)— MICHAEL JACKSON

Personnel: Michael Jackson: vocals; Greg Smith, Bill Wolfer: synthesizers; Greg Phillinganes: electric piano, synthesizer; David Williams: guitar; Louis Johnson: bass; Ndugu Chancler: drums; Michael Boddicker: Emulator; Tom Scott: lyricon; Michael Jackson: vocal, rhythm and synthesizer arrangement; Jerry Hey: string arrangement. Recorded 1982 at Westlake Recording Studios, Los Angeles, CA; produced by Quincy Jones. Released January 2, 1983 on Epic; 17 weeks on the charts, peaking at #1.

"Billie Jean" was one of two #1 hits (along with "Beat It") from Michael Jackson's blockbuster album *Thriller,* and the winner of 1984 Grammy Awards for Best R&B Song and Best R&B Male Vocal. "I knew it was going to be big while I was writing it," Jackson later said. "I was really absorbed in writing it." The storyline for "Beat It," about a fabricated paternity case, was reportedly inspired by Jackson's own experience with overzealous female fans, both on his own and with his older brothers from the Jackson 5 days. Jackson nailed his vocal track in one take. The song spent seven weeks at #1, 17 weeks in all on the Top 40, and is one of seven songs from *Thriller* to hit the Top 10. To say that Michael Jackson was hot in 1983 is understating the case—he even snuck a non-*Thriller* single in, "Say Say Say" (with Paul McCartney) and it became his third #1 of the year. In all, Jackson held the top spot on the charts in 1983 for 16 weeks. Of course, perhaps the most remarkable—certainly the most historic—aspect of "Billie Jean" is the music video, which is often referred to as "the video that broke the color barrier" on MTV.

segment of the record buying public that it became the first album in history to simultaneously top the singles and album charts in both the R&B and pop categories. The music videos that accompanied "Beat It," "Billie Jean" and "Thriller" more or less revolutionized the genre, as Jackson made each of them into epic mini-dramas of Hollywood proportions. The "Thriller" video, in which Jackson leads a troupe of ghoulish dancers in late night choreography, is often rated as the best music video of all time.

Thriller's success was bolstered by the aura that surrounded Michael throughout most of 1983, which he created through his innovative music videos and an incredible performance on the national TV special *Motown 25: Yesterday, Today, Forever.* During his solo appearance on the NBC program, which aired on May 16, 1983, Michael sang and danced his way through "Billie Jean" with a variety of unbelievable break-dance moves and introduced his now famous moonwalk, all while wearing a black fedora and one white sequined glove. Up to this point in time, many Americans had not yet heard *Thriller,* and many still had a vision of Michael as an 11-year-old phenom. After that night, Jackson became a pop legend, and sales of *Thriller* went through the roof.

Thriller is today listed as the best selling album in history, with estimated sales somewhere between 51 and 65 million copies worldwide and 29 million in the U.S. Although it was the apex of Michael Jackson's career, he was still able to conjure up two #1 multi-platinum albums, 1987's *Bad* and 1991's *Dangerous,* and seven more #1 singles before 1995. By the late 1980s however, his personal life increasingly became the focal point of his career. In 1988 he bought a ranch outside Santa Ynez, California and for 17 million dollars built an amusement park he called Neverland where he invited busloads of children to come play. He underwent several cosmetic surgeries to reshape and thin his nose. He was accused by some in the black community of undergoing treatments to lighten his skin, although he claimed that he had a disorder known as vitiligo, which destroys skin pigmentation. An alarming weight loss made some speculate that he suffered from anorexia nervosa. Most troubling were the 1993 accusations of molesting a 13-year-old boy that had been a frequent overnight visitor to Neverland, which resulted in an out of court settlement reported to be nearly 20 million dollars. In 2003 Jackson was charged with seven counts of child molestation with another 13-year-old boy, but was acquitted of all charges after a five-month trial in 2005. Amidst all the weirdness, he had two short-lived marriages, the first to Elvis Presley's daughter, Lisa Marie, and the second to Debbie Rowe, an unknown nurse. Michael also fathered three children.

The last years of Michael Jackson's life were spent in a financial free fall with dramatically worsening health problems. Although he had made many astute business decisions, including the 1988 purchase of the Northern Songs catalog containing nearly all of John Lennon and Paul McCartney's Beatles songs, Jackson was also a habitual shopaholic who sometimes spent hundreds of thousands of dollars in a single shopping spree. His worsening financial situation caused him to give up the Neverland Ranch in 2008 and struggle to hold on to the Northern Songs holdings. It is believed that the 50 concert tour that he was scheduled to perform in the summer of 2009 was planned more as a way to pay off past bills than to reinvigorate his career. Jackson was also becoming increasingly dependent on prescription pain medication, reportedly Deprivan, Demerol, Oxycodone and a wide assortment of others. Some have speculated that his drug use began after his scalp caught on fire during the filming of a Pepsi commercial in 1984; the progressive affects of vitiligo and lupus, another disease he was known to be suffering from, have also been mentioned as possible causes.

As we now know, Jackson's final tour never happened. On June 25, 2009 he was found not breathing in the bedroom of his rented Los Angeles home, and although CPR was performed and he was transferred to the UCLA Medical Center, Jackson, 50, was pronounced dead at 2:26 P.M. from cardiac arrest. The shock was immediate and felt around the world; many fans will long remember where they were when they heard the news. In the week that followed, 422,000 Jackson albums were sold, including 101,000 copies of *Thriller*. 2.3 million digital downloads of his single tracks were also purchased, the first time in history that any artist has had more than one million within a week. The song "Thriller" alone had 167,000 downloads, "Billie Jean" 158,000. It was the final act in a career that was larger than life and at times seemed to be scripted and staged by the pop gods. As *Newsweek's* David Gates so aptly said in one of the many Jackson eulogies: "In retrospect, so much of what Jackson achieved seems baldly symbolic. This was the black kid from Gary, Ind., who ended up marrying Elvis's daughter, setting up Neverland in place of Graceland, and buying the Beatles' song catalog—bold acts of appropriation and mastery, if not outright aggression." Long live the King of Pop.

The Material Girl

Like Michael Jackson, **Madonna** (Madonna Ciccone, 1958–) combined innovative dancing and choreography, dramatic visual artistry and strong post-disco dance grooves to become a pop sensation. Since her self-titled debut album in 1983, more than 30 of her singles have reached the Top 40, with 11 #1's and five more hitting #2. Every one of her 13 albums has gone platinum, with five of them hitting #1. Madonna has also elicited strong negative reactions to her at times brazen eroticism and sexuality, making her one of the most controversial pop figures since Elvis Presley. She has managed to keep herself in the public eye for more than 20 years through an unwavering ambition and an iron fisted control over her career. After starting out as a dancer in her native Detroit, Madonna moved to New York in 1977 and slowly began to make an impression in the city's trendy club scene as a singer. In 1982 she signed with Sire Records (owned by Warner Entertainment) and the following year released *Madonna,* which included

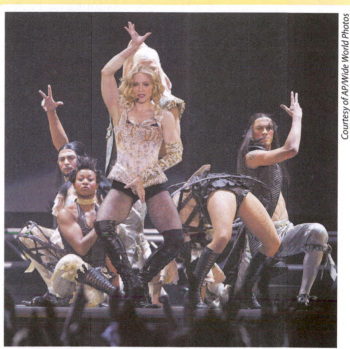

Madonna performs at the Forum in Los Angeles on May 24, 2004.

the #10 hit "Borderline." Her next two albums, *Like a Virgin* and *True Blue* both went to #1 and yielded nine more Top 10 singles. In 1985 she appeared in the film *Desperately Seeking Susan,* and continued to pursue acting roles in other films such as *Shanghai Surprise* (with then husband Sean Penn), *Dick Tracy* (with then boyfriend Warren Beatty) and Andrew Lloyd Webber's *Evita* in 1996, for

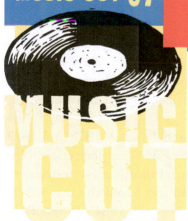

MUSIC CUT 57

"PAPA DON'T PREACH" (BRIAN ELLIOT/MADONNA)— MADONNA

Personnel: Madonna: vocals; David Williams, Bruce Gaitsch, John Putnam: guitars; Fred Zarr: keyboards; Stephen Bray: drums, keyboards; Johnathan Moffett: percussion; Siedah Garrett, Edie Lehmann: backup vocals. Recorded 1985/1986; produced by Madonna and Stephen Bray. Released June 11, 1986 on Sire/ Warner; 13 weeks on the charts, peaking at #1.

"Papa Don't Preach" is certainly the most controversial of the five Top 5 and three #1 singles from Madonna's 1986 album *True Blue.* The subject matter: a young unwed woman becomes pregnant and must tell her father, with whom she has a very close relationship, that she is keeping the baby. Coming right in the thick of the conservative Reagan years, the song created a firestorm of debate between those on both sides of the abortion issue, with pro-lifers generally siding with Madonna and others contending that the song condoned teenage pregnancy. The song is interesting in musical ways as well, in that it combines a heavily synthesized dance-pop beat with a tinge of classical baroque-ness. In the video made to accompany the song Madonna appears as a tomboy with short hair, and Hollywood actor Danny Aiello plays her father. "Papa Don't Preach" eventually achieved gold status, and *True Blue* went 7× platinum.

which her starring role as Evita Peron won a Golden Globe Award for Best Actress (Musical or Comedy).

Madonna has been adept at pushing the controversy button throughout her career, beginning with her first hit "Borderline," which explored the topic of inter-racial love. Her 1985 #1 hit "Like a Virgin" was sometimes performed while simulating masturbation. In her 1986 single "Papa Don't Preach," a young unwed pregnant woman defiantly decides to keep her baby, against her father's wishes. In her video to "Open Your Heart" she is shown scantily clad on display at a peepshow before a crowd of men. In 1989, the music video of "Like a Prayer" featured burning crosses and an erotic black Jesus figure, which prompted Pepsi to cancel her lucrative endorsement deal and the Vatican to censure her. In 1991 she produced an X-rated documentary film entitled *Truth or Dare,* and in 1992 she published the coffee table book *Sex,* which featured nude and S&M clothed photos of herself. In 1994 she engaged in a profanity-laden shouting match with the host on *The Late Show with David Letterman.* Her 2003 LP *American Life* received mixed reviews, in part because Madonna for the first time rapped on record and in part for the sometimes confessional and sometimes political nature of the songs. However the reviews did not keep the album from hitting #1 and going 4× platinum. Her most recent studio albums are 2008's *Hard Candy,* which reached #1 and is certified gold and 2012's *MDNA.* Her career so far has garnered nine Grammy Awards, 37 Top 10 singles, 25 of which achieved gold status, 12 multi-platinum LPs with total album sales of 63 million (U.S.).

The Artist Formerly Known As . . .

Prince (Prince Rogers Nelson, 1958–) has also invoked controversy during his career, most noticeably for his decision in 1993 to change his name to an unpronounceable symbol, prompting many to call him simply "The Artist Formerly Known As Prince" (TAFKAP). But he is undeniably one of the most talented and commercially successful pop musicians of the 1980s, producing ten platinum albums and 30 Top 40 singles, including five that hit #1. He has been amazingly prolific, averaging roughly an album a year through the 1980s and 1990s. He also reportedly has hundreds of songs that have never been released in his vaults. Perhaps most remarkably, he has maintained complete artistic control of his career and achieved success on his own terms with his own studio and record label (both located in his hometown Minneapolis), and writing his own music, playing many of the instruments on his self-produced recordings, and self-directing his music videos.

After releasing his first two albums *For You* and *Prince* in 1978 and 1979, Prince in 1980 released his first masterpiece, *Dirty Mind,* an eclectic mix of funk, R&B, new wave and pop in which he played nearly every instrument. His fifth album, 1983's *1999* went triple platinum and paved the way for the album that would take Prince to the top of the pop world. 1984's **Purple Rain,** recorded with his touring band **the Revolution,** was the soundtrack LP to the feature length film of the same name. It sold 11 million copies and stayed at #1 for 24 weeks. Prince not only starred in the semi-autobiographical movie, he wrote and produced all the songs, five of which hit the Top 25 with two, "When Doves Cry" and "Let's Go Crazy" hitting #1.

Prince's music has absorbed a variety of influences, from funk, jazz, R&B, punk, hard rock, and disco. He followed *Purple Rain* with another #1 album, the bizarre *Around the World in a Day,* but did not have another #1 until 1989's *Batman,* the soundtrack to Tim Burton's film. During the 1990s he released ten LPs, all of which went either gold or platinum. During this time he also had ten singles hit the Top 40, including 1991's #1 "Cream." Prince has also been active as a talent promoter in the careers of many up-and-coming artists, including percussionist Sheila E, Carmen Electra, the Time, and the female vocal trio Vanity 6.

THE BOSS, BONO, AND THE REST: BACK TO BASICS

The Boss

Bruce Springsteen (1949–) is the latest version of rock and roll's working-class hero. A prolific writer of songs that tell romanticized stories of the underprivileged, downtrodden, and those who are somehow missing out on the American Dream, Springsteen has been compared to Bob Dylan and Woody Guthrie, and hailed as the savior of rock and roll. By casting himself as hard-working, small town, and blue collar, Springsteen in many ways was the antithesis of the 1980s superstar, although that is exactly what he became. However, by continuing to write relevant music that perfectly reflects our times and putting on lengthy, high-energy concerts, he has remained a vital and important rock and roll artist.

Born in Freehold, New Jersey, to a bus driver and a secretary, Springsteen worked his way through a variety of local bands and as an aspiring folksinger in Greenwich Village before successfully auditioning for Columbia Records' legendary John Hammond in 1972. Springsteen released his debut album *Greetings from Asbury Park, N.J.* in 1973, which contained a combination of folk and R&B influences and had modest sales. Later that year he released his second LP, *The Wild, the Innocent, and the E Street Shuffle,* which garnered rave reviews but little interest from buyers. Then, in 1974 while playing at a club in Cambridge, Massachusetts, critic Jon Landau (his future manager) heard him, and wrote in the local rag *The Real Paper:* "I saw rock & roll's future and its name is Bruce Springsteen." Springsteen responded with his harder-edged third album in the fall of 1975, *Born to Run,* which hit #3, included his first Top 40 hit (the title track, #23) and garnered cover stories from both *Time* and *Newsweek* magazines. Although his star dimmed somewhat for a few years in the wake of the punk, new wave, and disco crazes, Springsteen released two noteworthy albums that eventually went platinum, *Darkness on the Edge of Town* (1978) and *The River* (1980). In 1982, he released the dark and stripped-down **Nebraska,** a collection of demos that he recorded with his four-track cassette recorder. Even though the songs on *Nebraska* typically told well-developed stories, the album was demanding for his established audience to listen to, and a somewhat risky career move.

Springsteen finally rose to superstar status in 1984 with the release of ***Born in the U.S.A.,*** which has sold 15 million copies (U.S.) and yielded seven Top

TRIVIA NOTE

Springsteen rose to superstar status in 1984 with the release of *Born in the U.S.A.,* which has sold 15 million copies and yielded seven Top 10 hits from its 12 songs, including the platinum-selling "Dancing in the Dark." Springsteen has been hailed as the savior of rock and roll.

MUSIC CUT 58

"BORN IN THE U.S.A." (BRUCE SPRINGSTEEN)— BRUCE SPRINGSTEEN

Personnel: Bruce Springsteen: guitar, vocals; Steve Van Zandt: guitar, vocals; Roy Bitten: piano; Danny Federici: organ, piano; Garry W. Tallent: bass; Max Weinberg: drums. Recorded May 1982 at The Power Station, New York, NY; produced by Bruce Springsteen, Jon Landau, Chuck Plotkin and Steve Van Zandt. Released October 30, 1984 on the Columbia LP *Born in the U.S.A.;* 17 weeks on the charts, peaking at #9.

"Born in the U.S.A." is Bruce Springsteen's heartfelt story of a working class youth's induction into the army, service in Vietnam, and disillusioned return home with "nowhere to run, ain't got nowhere to go." Springsteen empathized with the dilemma faced by embittered returning vets, and was inspired to write the song after reading Vietnam veteran Ron Kovic's memoir *Born on the Fourth of July* and filmmaker Paul Schrader's movie script entitled *Born in the U.S.A.* Originally the song was envisioned as an acoustic piece to be included in the *Nebraska* LP, but eventually Springsteen brought it to a recording session where the E Street Band quickly rendered the version on the album. "We played it two times, and our second take is the record," Springsteen said. "That thing in the end with all the drums, that just kinda happened." "Born in the U.S.A." was the third of seven Top 10 songs from *Born in the U.S.A.* the album, peaking at #9. The single is certified gold, while the album is certified 15× platinum.

10 hits from its 12 songs, including the platinum-selling "Dancing in the Dark" (#2). The album's title cut is a pained story of a Vietnam veteran who is unable to find a job or rebuild his life on returning home from war. Ironically, Ronald Reagan's 1984 presidential campaign used the song as a patriotic rallying cry, apparently unaware of the song's real message and focusing only on the anthem-like sing-along hook, *"Born in the U.S.A!"* Springsteen wisely distanced himself from such boosterism. His next album was the intensely personal *Tunnel of Love* (1987), which went triple platinum within months despite its *Nebraska*-like stark and pessimistic tone. While his most political album, 1995's *The Ghost of Tom Joad,* condemned the growing divide between America's rich and poor, perhaps his most poignant was 2002's *The Rising,* a timely reflection on life written in the aftermath of the September 11, 2001, attacks on the World Trade Center.

Springsteen's music is riveted to rock's past. His band, the **E Street Band**, which he used exclusively in the studio and on tours from 1974 through 1989, is your basic 1960s garage band styled guitar-bass-drums-Hammond organ combo, with a nod to 1950s R&B with the addition of the honking tenor saxophone of Clarence Clemons. Springsteen's lyric writing is clearly indebted to Bob Dylan and the 1960s folk ethos. At times even his arrangements have an unmistakable Dylanesque quality, with gruff vocals and country-ish harmonica playing. Although record sales have slowed for Springsteen in recent years,

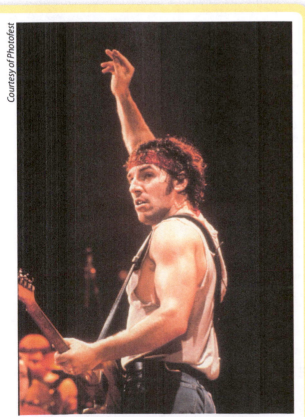

Courtesy of Photofest

Bruce Springsteen: rock & roll working class hero.

his popularity cuts across generational lines and he remains a top concert attraction. In July 2003 he kicked off a yearlong "Rising" tour that included a ten-night sold-out run at New Jersey's 55,000 Giants Stadium, which grossed $79 million and set a record for the most tickets ever sold in a concert series at one venue—more than half a million.

U2

Dublin, Ireland's U2 made their mark in the pop world in the 1980s with a unique sound that blended sweeping operatic-like instrumentals, searing guitar work, and passionate vocals with socially conscious lyrics. The band formed in 1976, and after the usual sorting out period they settled on a personnel lineup of Paul Hewson (**Bono**) on vocals and guitar, David Evans (The Edge) on guitar, keyboards and vocals, Adam Clayton on bass and Larry Mullen on drums. In the beginning they were all students at Dublin's Mount Temple High School, and none of the four were particularly proficient on their instruments, but learning in a self-taught fashion slowly began to pay off with innovative results. In 1980 they signed with Island Records and released their debut album *Boy*, which explored themes of adolescence. 1981's *October* examined issues of faith, as Bono, the Edge and Mullen were all practicing Christians. 1983's *War* saw U2 tackle the conflict in Northern Ireland, best addressed on the single "Sunday Bloody Sunday," and the album's #12 U.S. chart position was evidence that the group was finally breaking into the American market. The next two releases from 1984 and 1985, *The Unforgettable Fire* and *Wide Awake in America* (a four song EP) were the first of several collaborations with producers Brian Eno and Daniel Lanois, and yielded their first U.S. hit single, "Pride (In the Name of Love)." The group also made appearances at Live Aid and the Conspiracy of Hope Tour benefiting Amnesty International

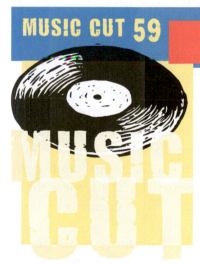

MUSIC CUT 59

"I STILL HAVEN'T FOUND WHAT I'M LOOKING FOR" (BONO)—U2

Personnel: Bono: vocals, harmonica; The Edge: guitar, keyboards, vocals; Adam Clayton: bass; Larry Mullen Jr.: drums, percussion. Recorded at Windmill Lane Studios, Dublin, Ireland; produced by Brian Eno, Daniel Lanois. Released March 9, 1987 on Island; 17 weeks on the charts, peaking at #1.

The anthemic "I Still Haven't Found What I'm Looking For" was one of two #1 singles (along with "With or Without You") from U2's multi-platinum *The Joshua Tree*. The album was the second and last produced for the group by Brian Eno and Daniel Lanois, and became their most commercially successful, hitting #1 in the spring of 1987 and staying there for two months. It eventually went on to sell ten million copies in the U.S., and (according to virginmedia.com), 25 million copies worldwide. The album also won Grammy Awards for Album of the Year and Best Rock Performance by a Duo or Group with Vocal. Although lead vocalist Bono is listed as the composer of "I Still Haven't Found What I'm Looking For," producer Daniel Lanois claims some credit. "I remember humming a traditional melody in Bono's ear," Lanois later recalled. "He said, 'That's it! Don't sing any more!'—and went off and wrote the melody as we know it."

U2's next album put them into the pop mainstream. 1987s' **The Joshua Tree** quickly went platinum (and eventually diamond in 1995), produced two #1 singles ("With or Without You," "I Still Haven't Found What I'm Looking For") and stayed in the Top 40 for more a year. The album was another Eno/Lanois production, and won two Grammy Awards. At this point, U2 had become one of the most popular bands in the world. Of their seven albums released since *The Joshua Tree,* six have hit #1 in the U.S., and six are certified platinum or multi-platinum. Bono has also become one of the foremost humanitarians on the world stage, lending his visibility and support to Amnesty International, AIDS relief efforts, world economic forums, disaster, hunger and disease relief, Product Red, and African aid organizations. For his efforts, he has been nominated for the Nobel Peace Prize and was granted honorary knighthood by Queen Elizabeth II of England.

Whitney Houston

Whitney Houston (1963–2012) exploded onto the scene in 1985 with the most successful debut album ever by a female artist, and has since gone on to sell nearly 200 million albums worldwide, chart 11 #1 singles and win seven Grammy Awards. The cousin of Dionne Warwick and the daughter of Cissy Houston (a former backup singer for Aretha Franklin), she signed with Arista Records in 1983 after company president Clive Davis heard her sing at New York's Sweetwaters supper club. At the time, Houston was somewhat of a work in progress, but under Davis' guidance, she progressed quickly, and as she neared completion of her debut album, hopes rose that it might sell 150,000 copies at best. However, buoyed by the success of three #1 singles ("Saving All My Love for You," "How Will I Know" and "Greatest Love of All") **Whitney Houston** went on to sell approximately 25 million copies worldwide after staying on the charts for an amazing 162 weeks, with 14 at #1. Her second album *Whitney* from 1987 did nearly as well with sales of 20 million, and her next three studio albums have each been certified multi-platinum as well. Houston's biggest selling album came in 1992 with *The Bodyguard,* the soundtrack album from the film of the same name, which she also starred in opposite Kevin Costner. To date it has estimated sales of 40 million worldwide, and an RIAA certified 17 million in the U.S. Houston's singles output was as impressive as her album sales, with 11 #1's, 23 Top 10's and 30 Top 40 hits. Her accidental death at the Beverly Hilton Hotel on February 11, 2012 was a shock to the world, although she had been experiencing personal problems for a number of years.

Other artists that achieved extraordinary success in the 1980s include singer/songwriter/pianist Billy Joel, who had 20 Top 40 hits in the decade including nine Top 10's and two #1's; former Genesis drummer Phil Collins, whose 1985 LP *No Jacket Required* (#1, seven million copies, two

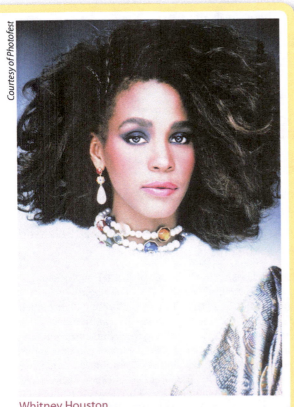

Courtesy of Photofest

Whitney Houston

#1 singles) won the Album of the Year Grammy. Also among the tops in 1980s pop were Americans Huey Lewis and the News (12 Top 10 hits, including three #1's and three platinum selling albums); and future *American Idol* judge Paula Abdul (six #1 singles between 1988 and 1991 and the seven million selling *Forever Your Girl* from 1989).

EIGHTIES ALTERNATIVE

The Cultural Underground Railroad

As we have seen throughout this chapter, the music business was alive and well during the 1980s. The introduction of the compact disc, MTV and Michael Jackson's blockbuster LP *Thriller* all helped to bring the industry out of its post-disco doldrums; in addition, the number of multi-platinum albums from the decade is so large that it is hard to imagine by today's standards. But there was another side to rock music in the 1980s that was virtually invisible to the mainstream pop fan, and whose own fan base was so intensely devoted to the cause as to adopt a near religious fervor. **Alternative rock** (or simply alternative), as author Michael Azerrad describes in the definitive text *Our Band Could Be Your Life,* was music that spawned a "cultural underground railroad," a network of "fanzines, underground and college radio stations, local cable access shows, mom-and-pop record stores, independent distributors and record labels, tip sheets, nightclubs and alternative venues, booking agents, bands and fans" that flourished under the radar screen throughout the decade. Alternative was more than just music however; it was the ideology of DIY (do-it-yourself), of seeking your own path, of investigating what was out there rather than buying into what corporate powers that be were feeding you. It was about taking control.

If this sounds a bit like the cultural revolution of the 1960s, well it was, kinda. Obviously there was no war going on in the 1980s and the civil rights movement was over, but since Alternative Nation was the offspring of the peace/love/flower power generation, they obviously had grown up with its culture to some extent. Politically the 1980s were in many ways like the 1950s—conservative and Republican—and that in itself was enough to organize many to go

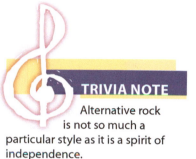

TRIVIA NOTE

Alternative rock is not so much a particular style as it is a spirit of independence.

Characteristics of Eighties Alternative

1. Umbrella term encompassing a wide variety of stylistic approaches with a decidedly DIY (do-it-yourself) independent attitude
2. Influences from punk, psychedelia, folk and hard rock
3. Lyrics are often angst-ridden or reflecting punk attitudes

Key Eighties Alternative Recordings

- *Murmur*—R.E.M., 1983
- *Let It Be*—the Replacements, 1984
- *Daydream Nation*—Sonic Youth, 1988

ALTERNATIVE ROCK

in an opposite direction. And like the 1950s, the key players in the alternative scene were the independent labels and renegade radio stations: just like corporate rock, alternative rock needed to be documented and distributed, heard and promoted to keep its ecosystem nourished. The Suns and Chess's of the 1980s were SST and Sub Pop; the Alan Freeds and Dewey Phillips' were university students working at campus stations in Athens, Georgia, Boston and Austin, Texas and other college towns.

Alternative rock is not so much a particular style as it is a spirit of independence from the major labels and mainstream styles. Alternative groups favored a garage band approach that incorporated influences from punk, psychedelic music, folk rock and hard rock.

Important Alternative Bands

When **R.E.M.** released their debut album *Murmur* in 1983, they instantly rose from obscurity to become "America's Hippest Band" and win *Rolling Stone's* awards for Band of the Year, Best New Artist and Album of the Year. Formed in Athens, Georgia by University of Georgia student Michael Stipe (vocals), record store manager Peter Buck (guitar), and Macon, Georgia natives and boyhood friends Mike Mills (bass) and Bill Berry (drums), the band played their first gig at a birthday party in 1980 as the Twisted Kites. Within a year they had changed their name, nurtured a jangly, Byrds-like sound, and made their first recording of an original song called "Radio Free Europe." The record quickly became a staple of college radio stations, and the band's exhaustive touring schedule in their run-down van helped develop a cult-like albeit underground following. When the president of I.R.S. Records heard them in New Orleans, he signed them to the label, and in 1983 they released **Murmur**, which included a re-recorded version of "Radio Free Europe." *Murmur* spent 30 weeks on the charts and led to tours warming up for the Police and an appearance on *The David Letterman Show*. Four more albums between 1984 and 1987, including the platinum *Document* allowed the band to sign a $10 million, five-record deal with Warner in 1988. Between 1991 and 1994 R.E.M. released three multi-platinum albums (*Out of Time, Automatic for the People* and *Monster*) and had two Top 10 hits, "Losing My Religion" and "Shiny Happy People." The band has continued to tour and record, with their most recent LP release coming in 2008 with *Accelerate*. As the first 1980s alternative rock band to breakthrough to superstardom, they played a crucial role in the genre's development.

More than any other alternative band from the 1980s, **Sonic Youth** incorporated the energy of New York's downtown music scene, as manifested in the works of Philip Glass, Steve Reich and Glenn Branca, and in the process produced some of alternative's most innovative and textured music. The band's

ALTERNATIVE BANDS
- R.E.M.
- Sonic Youth
- Replacements
- Red Hot Chili Peppers
- The Cure
- The Violent Femmes
- The Pixies
- The Feelies

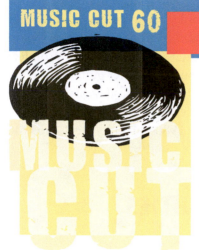

MUSIC CUT 60

"RADIO FREE EUROPE" (MICHAEL STIPE/PETER BUCK/MIKE MILLS/ BILL BERRY)—R.E.M

Personnel: Michael Stipe: vocals; Peter Buck: guitar; Mike Mills: bass; Bill Berry: drums. Recorded January 6– February 23, 1983 at Reflection Studio, Charlotte, NC; produced by Mitch Easter and Don Dixon. Released July 1983 on I.R.S.; 5 weeks on the charts, peaking at #78.

"Radio Free Europe" was one of the first songs R.E.M. ever recorded, but the version that ended up on the 1983 album *Murmur* is actually its second recording. The first was made in tiny Drive-In Studios in Winston-Salem, North Carolina in 1981 and was released on the indie Hib-Tone label. Unhappy with the recording, the band rerecorded the song after signing with I.R.S. Records in 1982 and included it as the opening track on their debut album. With its jangly guitars from Peter Buck and muffled vocals from Michael Stipe, "Radio Free Europe" is exemplar of the R.E.M. sound that made them one of the most influential alternative bands of the 1980s.

beginnings date to 1981 when college dropout Thurston Moore (guitar, vocals) became friends with art student Lee Renaldo (guitar, vocals) and artist/bassist Kim Gordon (who married Moore in 1985). Although the three were in different bands, their common interest in the music of Glenn Branca's experimental guitar ensemble, which explored unique tunings and high volume to create sonically intense music, led them to join forces. Between 1981 and 1984 they went through several drummers before Steve Shelley joined in 1985 as the permanent drummer. By the time the band made their CBGB debut in 1982, they were combining the energy of punk with the experimental leanings of the Branca ensemble, which led them to using alternative guitar tunings that were sometimes achieved wedging screwdrivers or drumsticks between the strings and fret board. In the early 1980s they made several recordings with tiny indie labels and toured extensively while they further developed their innovative sound through trial and error. In 1986 they signed with the alternative label SST, and released *EVOL* (1986), *Sister* (1987), which along with **Daydream Nation** (1988, Enigma) became enormously influential alternative rock documents. By the late 1980s as their music became progressively more pop friendly, Sonic Youth had developed a larger audience and positive reviews, and in 1990 they signed with major label Geffen. Since then they have released ten albums and achieved a place of prominence among the alternative community. Says bassist Gordon: "We were influential in showing people that you can make any kind of music you want."

The Replacements formed in 1980 in Minneapolis and fronted by Paul Westerberg, were critically lauded but received little in the way of commercial success. In spite of a well-deserved reputation for drunk and disorderly conduct on stage ("Getting fucked up is what rock bands did, right?" said Westerberg), the band delivered one of alternative's defining albums with 1984's *Let It Be*. They broke up in 1991. The Red Hot Chili Peppers have managed to capture the essence of punk while incorporating funk influences from the likes of George Clinton and Sly and the Family Stone, and have won seven Grammies since their inception in 1983. Their self-named first album was released in 1984 to mixed reviews. In 1985 they released the Clinton produced *Freaky Styley*, which bassist Flea described in the liner notes as, "More than any other record we ever made it falls into the category of 'too funky for white radio, too punk rockin' for black'." With the release of 1989's *Mother's Milk,* the Peppers were receiving airplay on MTV for their videos of their cover of Stevie Wonders "Higher Ground" and "Knock Me Down," a tribute to former guitarist Slovak, who died from a heroin overdose in 1988. Their 1991 LP *Blood Sugar Sex Magik* is considered by many to be their best, and has been certified 7× platinum.

Other influential alternative bands from the 1980s include the Cure, the Violent Femmes, the Pixies, and the Feelies.

THE EDGIER SIDE OF THE EIGHTIES

1980s Metal

Metal continued to become more popular in the 1980s as a second generation of bands began to emerge to take the place of early stalwarts such as Led Zeppelin and Black Sabbath. Once again it was the Brits that led the way in this renewal, with what became known as the **New Wave of British Heavy Metal** (NWOBHM). According to Allmusic.com, "The NWOBHM kicked out all of the blues, sped up the tempo, and toughened up the sound, leaving just a mean, tough, fast, hard metallic core." Among the new metal bands that rode in with this wave were Iron Maiden, Motörhead, Def Leppard, and Grim Reaper. Even though these and other NWOBHM bands proved to be popular with metalheads, the most popular and enduring metal bands from the 1980s came from America, and in one case, Australia.

Metallica was formed in Los Angeles in 1981, when guitarist James Hetfield answered an ad posted in a local paper by drummer Lars Ulrich, who was looking for metal musicians to jam with. The band came together over the next couple of years, which also saw them move to the San Francisco Bay Area. After signing with Megaforce Records, they released their debut album *Kill 'Em All* in 1983, which went—like all future Metallica albums—multi-platinum. The band's best selling effort was 1991's *Metallica*, which ranks as the best selling album of the Soundscan Era (see chapter 13) with 16 million copies sold (US). It was also the first of five consecutive albums to debut at #1 on the *Billboard* charts, a feat that no other band has accomplished. Metallica gained some negative notoriety in 2000 when they filed suit against Napster for copyright infringement. The beginnings of **Bon Jovi** go back to 1982, when singer/songwriter Jon Bon Jovi (John Bongiovi, Jr.) began recording song demos at Power Station Studios in New York where he worked. In 1983, after one of the songs, "Runaway," started to get airplay by a few radio stations, Jon Bon Jovi began assembling a band, which eventually included Richie Sambora on guitar. The success of "Runaway," which hit #39 led to the band signing with Mercury in 1984. Bon Jovi released four albums and 16 singles in the 1980s, including 1986's 28 million selling album *Slippery When Wet.* Four of the singles hit #1. The band has remained popular, with total album sales in the 1990s and 2000s of nearly 100 million.

Guns N' Roses formed in 1985 in Los Angeles. Led by vocalist Axel Rose and guitarist Slash (Saul Hudson), the band was signed by Geffen in 1986 and released their debut album in 1987. That album, *Appetite for Destruction,* has to date worldwide sales of 35 million copies, the largest selling debut album of all time. Except for 1993's *The Spaghetti Incident* (6 million), the next five albums all sold a minimum of 15 million copies. They also spawned three Top Ten hits, including "Welcome to the Jungle." Beginning in 1993, internal conflicts in the band led to a number of personnel changes and no new studio albums until 2008's *Chinese Democracy,* which, at a cost of $13 million, is reportedly the most expensive rock album ever produced. Formed in Australia in 1973 by brothers Angus and Malcolm Young, **AC/DC** released a remarkable eight albums between 1975 and 1978, although because four of them were released in their home country only, they did not have much impact on the US market. That all changed in 1979 with the release of *Highway to Hell,* which hit #17 on the charts. However, their real breakthrough came with 1980's *Back in Black,* which with sales to date of 40 million copies worldwide is the fourth highest selling album of all time. The band began work on the album just two days after the death of singer Bon Scott as a form of therapy to get over the tragedy. Brian Johnson replaced Scott. To date, AC/DC has released 18 studio albums and 46 singles, and has sold more than 200 million albums worldwide.

Industrial

Industrial emerged in the later 1970s as yet another way for post-punk musicians to express themselves. Its main tenet is the use of non-traditional sounds from synthesizers, avant-garde electronics and mechanical sources to infuse the sounds and ethos of modern industrial life into the music. Industrial is usually abrasive and aggressive, suggestive of a factory or heavy machinery. Many of the earliest industrial bands were European, such as England's Cabaret Voltaire and Throbbing Gristle, Germany's Einstürzende Neubauten (English translation: collapsing new buildings), and Belgium's Front 242. The leading American industrial band is **Nine Inch Nails**, the one-man band of writer/arranger/producer/performer Trent Reznor. The band's origins go back to 1988, when Reznor recorded a demo at a local Cleveland studio where he worked as an engineer, playing all the instruments himself except the drums. (This recording/production method would become the standard for nearly all future Nine

Characteristics of Industrial

INDUSTRIAL

1. Abrasive and relentlessly mechanical; pounding jackhammer beat
2. Use of digital samples, avant-garde electronics, taped music and white noise
3. Use of industrial materials (power tools, etc) in performance
4. Lyrical themes of alienation, despair and dehumanization

Key Industrial Recordings

- *Halber Mensch*—Einstürzende Neubauten, 1985
- *Mind Is a Terrible Thing to Taste*—Ministry, 1989
- *Pretty Hate Machine*—Nine Inch Nails, 1989
- *Last Rights*—Skinny Puppy, 1991

Inch Nails recordings.) His first full-length album release, *Pretty Hate Machine*, came in 1989. NIN's breakthrough LP was 1994's **The Downward Spiral**, which Reznor produced while living in the home where the Manson Family murdered actress Sharon Tate. He has also written scores for film, including *Lara Croft: Tomb Raider* and Oliver Stone's *Natural Born Killers*. In all, NIN has released eight albums.

OTHER EIGHTIES GOINGS ON

The 1980s started off with one of the saddest events in the history of pop music: the murder of John Lennon outside his New York City apartment on December 8, 1980. Lennon had more or less retired from music in 1976 but had returned to recording new material with his wife Yoko Ono in the summer of 1980. The resulting album, *Double Fantasy* had entered the charts on December 6; its single release "(Just Like) Starting Over" had entered in early November at #38. As he and Yoko walked home from a late night recording session, Lennon was gunned down by deranged fan Mark David Chapman. In the wake of his death, a worldwide ten-minute silent vigil was held on December 14 at 2:00 PM EST; on December 27, both *Double Fantasy* and "(Just Like) Starting Over" hit #1 (where they stayed for eight and five weeks, respectively). For many, Lennon's death, along with the fallout from disco and punk, represented an ending of sorts to a confusing time, while leaving a great amount of uncertainty about the future of rock music.

As America experienced a period of political conservatism marked by the presidency of Ronald Reagan (1981–1989), the watchdog group known as the Parents Music Resource Center (**PMRC**) was born in May 1985 to "to educate and inform parents of this alarming new trend . . . towards lyrics that are sexually explicit." The group also claimed that rock music glorified violence, drug use, suicide, and criminal activity. Formed by a group of "Washington Wives" that included Susan Baker (wife of Secretary of the Treasury James Baker), Tipper Gore (at the time, the wife of then Senator Al Gore of Tennessee), Peatsy Hollings (wife of Senator Ernest Hollings of South Carolina), the PMRC immediately garnered considerable influence in the nation's capital and the backing of many religious and conservative political groups. On September 19, only four months after the PMRC's founding, the Senate Commerce, Technology and Transportation Committee began hearings to investigate the pornographic content of rock music.

The PMRC advocated the use of warning labels to inform parents as to the graphic nature of the lyrics contained in a record that were similar to the movie rating system: X for sexually explicit material, O for occult, V for violence, and so on. Among those who testified against the idea were Frank Zappa, Dee Snider of Twisted Sister and country singer John Denver. Zappa was particularly articulate in his opening remarks, calling the warning labels, "an ill-conceived piece of nonsense which fails to deliver any real benefits to children, infringes the civil liberties of people who are not children, and promises to keep the courts busy for years." In spite of his testimony, the mere threat of government intervention prompted the RIAA (Recording Industry Association of America) to ask its members on November 1, 1985 to either affix a warning label or actually print the lyrics on the sleeve of the objectionable records. Over the next three years, 49 new albums (out of 7500 released by RIAA members) displayed a warning label. The PMRC has remained in existence, although it has lost considerable clout in recent years. But the warning labels still exist.

There was also a flurry of charity events staged during the decade, ranging from "We Are the World," Live Aid, Sun City and tours supporting Amnesty International. Modeled after the successful single "Do They Know It's Christmas" to assist famine relief in Ethiopia by the British group Band Aid, "We Are the World" was written by Michael Jackson and Lionel Ritchie to benefit the relief agency U.S.A. for Africa. A group of 45 artists were assembled at A&M Studios in Hollywood on the night of January 28, 1985 under the supervision of producer Quincy Jones, who insisted that they "check their egos at the door." The song hit #1 three weeks after its release and went multi-platinum. Some of the singers who participated in the recording included Michael Jackson, Lionel Ritchie, Stevie Wonder, Paul Simon, Bruce Springsteen, Tina Turner, Dionne Warwick, Bob Dylan, Diana Ross, Cyndi Lauper, Ray Charles, Willie Nelson, Billy Joel, Smokey Robinson, and Harry Belafonte.

Live Aid, the simultaneous concerts held at London's Wembley Stadium and Philadelphia's JFK Stadium on July 13, 1985 was the largest staged event in history. Conceived by promoter Bob Geldorf (the brainchild behind Band Aid) to again assist famine relief in Ethiopia, the concerts lasted 14 hours and featured a host of stars, including Paul McCartney, Eric Clapton, Elton John and Mick Jagger, and were broadcast by 14 satellites to 160 countries. Phil Collins performed twice—first in London, then in Philadelphia after hopping a Concorde for the trans-Atlantic flight. Ultimately the effort raised over $100 million. Live Aid spawned a number of music benefit telethons, including the **Farm Aid** concerts spearheaded by Willie Nelson to benefit and draw attention to American farmers caught up in difficult economic times. The first Farm Aid concert was held in Champaign, Illinois on September 22, 1985 and featured Bob Dylan, Billy Joel, B.B. King, Loretta Lynn, Roy Orbison, Tom Petty and others. Subsequent concerts have been held yearly at stadiums around the country.

STUDY QUESTIONS

Name _____ Date _____

1. Name four significant changes in technology in the music business in the 1980s.

2. Describe the programming on MTV in its early years and some of the controversies surrounding it.

3. Describe some reasons why *Thriller* became the best selling album of all time.

4. Name four instances in which Madonna pushed herself into a position of controversy.

5. Name four ways in which Prince has carved out a unique and successful career.

6. Describe the influences on Bruce Springsteen's songwriting and E Street Band.

7. Name one unique characteristic of three of the members of U2 and how it has possibly affected Bono's non-musical contributions to the world.

8. Describe the sound and culture of 1980s alternative music.

9. What was the PMRC and what was its effect on rock?

10. Name two important music related news events from the 1980s.

HISTORICAL INTERLUDE: 1990s

You Can't Touch This

Positivity abounded at the beginning of the 1990s with the fall of the Berlin wall and the conclusion of the Cold War, and extended to the economic growth throughout the decade. The Internet and cable television created an environment of alternative mass media, which continued to be a major influence into the 2000s.

The high tech industry began in the 1980s, but exploded in the 1990s. Many CEOs of these companies, including Bill Gates, the co-founder of Microsoft and Steve Case, the co-founder of America Online, took on rock star status and became household names. Money flowed into the high tech industry with everyone wanting to purchase the newest and fastest technology.

Although positivity seemed to prevail at the start of the decade, many negative events brought reality back to the forethought of the country. Racial tensions erupted in 1992 when four white police officers in Los Angeles stopped Rodney King, black man, and beat him with their police clubs. The event was caught on videotape and broadcast around the country. The four officers were acquitted on nearly all of the changes and protest riots erupted in Los Angeles.

In 1999, Columbine High School became the center of attention when two teenagers killed classmates, teachers, and finally themselves during the school day. Many parents blamed the influence of grunge music, gothic clothing, violent video games and violent movies as contributing to this horrific event. National discussions about the entertainment industry, depression, and bullying were raised and have now become a central part of many schools' objectives.

13

THE NINETIES AND BEYOND

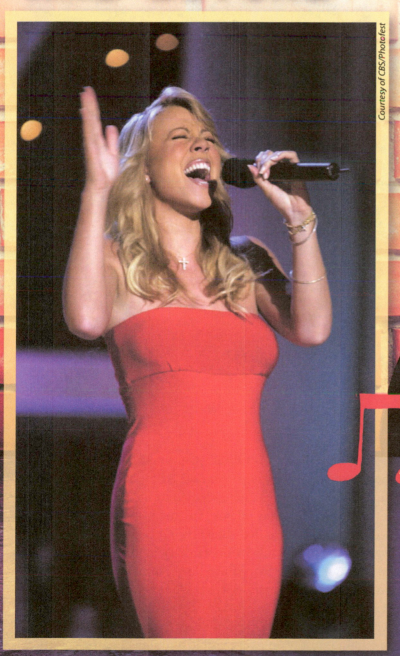

"I think one of the reasons I pushed myself so hard and worked so hard is because I never felt special. Like, the one thing that made me feel special was my music."

—*Mariah Carey*

KEY TERMS

Grunge	Napster	Music streaming
Soundscan	Mp3	
Boy bands	iTunes Music Store	

KEY FIGURES

Nirvana	Britney Spears	Twain
Kurt Cobain	Eminem	Dixie Chics
Pearl Jam	Jay-Z	Taylor Swift
Phish	Kanye West	Lady Antebellum
Radiohead	Beyoncé	Wilco
Dave Matthews Band	Justin Timberlake	Bright Eyes
Beck	Justin Bieber	Death Cab for Cutie
Weezer	Nickelback	The White Stripes
New Kids on the Block	Coldplay	Creed
Boyz II Men	Maroon 5	Linkin Park
Backstreet Boys	Lady Gaga	Foo Fighters
'NSync	Adele	Shawn Fanning
TLC	Garth Brooks	
Mariah Carey	Shania	

KEY ALBUMS

Nevermind—Nirvana	*Reasonable Doubt*—Jay-Z	*Wide Open Spaces*—the
Ten—Pearl Jam	*The College Dropout*—	Dixie Chicks
OK Computer—Radiohead	Kanye West	*Icky Thump*—the White
Pinkerton—Weezer	*I Am . . . Sasha*	Stripes
Daydream—Mariah Carey	*Fierce*—Beyoncé	*Human Clay*—Creed
. . . Baby One More Time—	*Born This Way*—Lady Gaga	*Hybrid Theory*—Linkin
Britney Spears	*21*—Adele	Park
The Marshall Mathers	*Come On Over*—Shania	
LP— Eminem	Twain	

THE 1990s: THE TRIUMPH OF ALTERNATIVE NATION

Nirvana

On January 11, 1992, Michael Jackson's multi-platinum album *Dangerous* was knocked out of the #1 spot on the *Billboard* charts by an album released by a relatively unknown band from Seattle. There seemed to be some sort of cosmic significance to the moment: the King of Pop, his sequined glove and highly produced post-disco dance music was dethroned by a group wearing torn jeans and T-shirts who were uncomfortable with stardom, and played music that eschewed glitz and glamour and embraced the do-it-yourself attitude of post-punk alternative rock. Although Nirvana's *Nevermind* would end up spending only two weeks at #1, it effectively sent a clear message to the music industry: the 1980s were over. As discussed in Chapter 12, Alternative Nation was alive and growing in the 1980s, it just wasn't very visible to the major labels. With the success of *Nevermind,* the gulf between "what people said was hip to listen to" and "the kind of stuff which we all really listened to" had finally been bridged, according to Nirvana guitarist Kurt Cobain. In many ways it was the perfect album to come along at the perfect time to wipe the slate clean once and for all of the dominance of Michael, Madonna, and Prince and let Alternative Nation finally emerge.

Nirvana's beginnings go back to 1987 and the tiny town of Aberdeen, Washington, 100 miles southwest of Seattle, where guitarist/vocalist/songwriter **Kurt Cobain** (1967–1994) grew up. Cobain's early years could easily be described as miserable. At age eight, his parents divorced, forcing him to move back and forth from one set of relatives to another. Growing older, he grew increasingly sullen, resentful and withdrawn. As an artistic youth who did not fit in with most people in the red-neck logging town, Cobain was often beat up by other kids just because he was "different," including once for befriending an openly gay fellow student. But he found solace in music: first the Beatles, then metal, and finally punk. In 1987, around the time he turned 20, Cobain and fellow Aberdonian Krist Novoselic (bass) formed what would eventually become Nirvana, moving to nearby Olympia to work the Olympia-Tacoma-Seattle bar circuit. While working its way through a series of drummers, the band signed with local independent label Sub Pop and in spring 1989 recorded its debut LP *Bleach* at a cost of $606.17. Containing 12 Cobain original songs, *Bleach* received favorable reviews from the underground rock press, and sold an impressive 35,000 copies. Along with a number of other Seattle bands that included Mudhoney and Soundgarden, Nirvana was defining a style that journalists were beginning to identify with the city's music scene and call grunge. Shortly after recording *Bleach,* Nirvana finalized their lineup with the addition of drummer Dave Grohl.

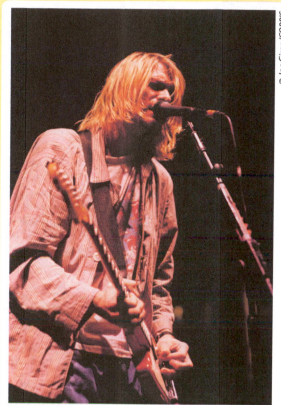

The late Kurt Cobain, guitarist and lead vocalist for Nirvana.

During the summer of 1989, Nirvana recorded several song demos with producer Butch Vig, with the intention of shopping them around to major labels. After eventually signing with Geffen imprint DGC for $287,000, they recorded **Nevermind** in the summer of 1991 and released it in September. Propelled by Cobain's brilliant, generational songwriting and the powerful, dynamic playing of Grohl and Novoselic, *Nevermind* quickly sold out its initial printing of 50,000 copies and hit the charts in early November, where it stayed for the next 50 weeks. Propelling the album was the Gen X anthem "Smells Like Teen Spirit," which peaked on the charts at #6 on its way to a platinum certification. In the heady months that followed the album's release, the band toured heavily, released three more singles, and appeared on *Saturday Night Live,* giving the program its highest ratings in months.

In February 1992, Cobain married singer Courtney Love, with whom he fathered a daughter. The relationship was turbulent, and with persistent rumors of heavy drug usage, became the focus of a relentless paparazzi harassment that put the couple in constant media spotlight. Cobain had at this point become the de facto spokesman for Alternative Nation, a role he loathed and was ill

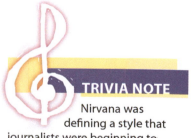

TRIVIA NOTE

Nirvana was defining a style that journalists were beginning to identify with Seattles music scene and call grunge.

Kurt Cobain has become one of the most commercially successful songwriters in pop music history.

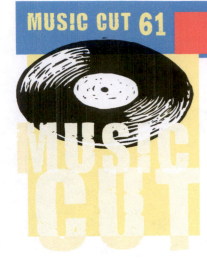

MUSIC CUT 61

"SMELLS LIKE TEEN SPIRIT" (KURT COBAIN/DAVID GROHL/ KRIST NOVOSELIC)—NIRVANA

Personnel: Kurt Cobain: vocals, guitar; David Grohl: drums, vocals; Krist Novoselic: bass, vocals. Recorded May 1991 at Sound City Studio, Van Nuys, CA; produced by Butch Vig. Released September 10, 1991 on DGC; 20 weeks on the charts, peaking at #6.

The opening track and biggest hit from Nirvana's monster LP *Nevermind.* Kurt Cobain wrote the basic four-chord riff, but the song didn't come together until the group jammed on it for nearly an hour, tinkering with dynamics and the arrangement. Cobain's main influence was the Boston-based alternative band the Pixies, who often used stop-start dynamics in their songs. "This really sounds like the Pixies," bassist Krist Novoselic commented after hearing the playback in the studio. "People are really going to nail us for it." "I was trying to write the ultimate pop song," Cobain later told *Rolling Stone.* "I was basically trying to rip off the Pixies. I have to admit it. When I heard the Pixies for the first time, I connected with that band so heavily that I should have been in that band—or at least a Pixies cover band. We used their sense of dynamics, being soft and quiet and then loud and hard." Much has also been made of the song's lyrics, which are indecipherable enough as to cause rock journalist Dave Marsh to call it "the 'Louie Louie' of the nineties." What is plainly heard is the repeating plaintive cry, "Here we are, now entertain us," which are widely interpreted to be a call for Generation X revolution, a "My Generation" for the nineties. It certainly became an anthem for many X-ers, as it very quickly sold a million copies and helped propel Nirvana to superstardom.

prepared to assume, and this pressure no doubt contributed to his early death. In the last year of his life, there were no less than five incidents that were either suicide attempts or could be perceived as such, including three drug overdoses. The last of these occurred on March 4, 1994 while the band was on tour in Europe; after a short hospitalization, Cobain returned to the U.S. and checked into the Exodus Recovery Clinic in Los Angeles. On April 1, after telling security he was going out for some cigarettes, Cobain escaped from the clinic and disappeared. After several days of frantic searching by family and police, his body was discovered in a small room above the garage of his Seattle home. The cause of death was a self-inflicted gunshot wound to the head, estimated to have occurred on April 5. Although a suicide note was found, speculation that he was murdered has persisted to this day. As the primary composer for a group that has now sold more than 50 million records worldwide, Kurt Cobain became one of the most commercially successful songwriters in pop music history. His death was mourned by millions of fans, and he was eulogized by numerous tributes on radio and MTV in the weeks and months that followed.

Grunge and the Seattle Scene

In spite of Cobain's personal traumas, Nirvana had managed to finish their fourth album, *In Utero* in the summer of 1993, and posthumously released *MTV Unplugged in New York,* recorded from the TV special taped the previous year. Both LPs hit #1 and went multi-platinum, and Unplugged won the 1995 Alternative Music Grammy Award. By this time Nirvana had succeeded in almost single-handedly returning the rock mainstream to a punk esthetic with an updated style that became known as **grunge**. Grunge eschewed the virtuosic artistry and pretentiousness of metal; songs were often slow and plodding,

KEY TERMS

Grunge A style associated with Seattle in the 1990s that incorporates elements of punk and heavy metal; also associated with a fashion statement of flannel shirts and ripped jeans, etc.

Characteristics of Grunge

GRUNGE

1. Punk influences, both in music and in attitude
2. Slow, plodding tempos
3. Simple chord progressions
4. Avoidance of virtuosity, pretension or posturing
5. Start-stop dynamics
6. Lyrics are often of dark and murky themes, sung in a plaintive, lamenting manner
7. Accompanying fashion included plaid flannel shirts, ripped jeans, stocking caps and mountain boots.

Key Grunge Recordings

- *Deep Six*—C/Z Records, 1986
- *Nevermind*—Nirvana, 1991
- *Ten*—Pearl Jam, 1991

and usually contain very little in the way of chord progressions. Choruses often are set apart from verses simply by start-stop dynamic contrasts. The style had evolved in the mid- to late-1980s in Seattle's thriving underground rock scene, with support from local radio stations, a prospering underground rock press and the indie label Sub Pop. Other Seattle bands signed to Sub Pop included Soundgarden, Mud Honey, Screaming Trees and Alice in Chains. Pearl Jam, another Seattle band formed in 1990, was able to benefit from the growing interest in the city's music scene and sign with major label Epic. Their debut LP *Ten* was certified 13× platinum and stayed on the charts for 100 weeks.

Other Nineties Alternative Rock

The success of the Seattle bands gave a huge boost to the already existing alternative rock scene that had flown mostly under the radar during the 1980s. Among the more creative and inspired alternative artists from the 1990s are **Phish**, Radiohead, the Dave Matthews Band, and Beck. Phish could be described as a Grateful Dead redux, with it's eclectic mix of bluegrass, country, folk, and rock and roll, all tied together with a whimsical sensibility and improvisational spirit. The group formed in late 1983 while its four members, guitarists Trey Anastasio and Jeff Holdsworth, bassist Mike Gordon and drummer Jon Fishman, were students at the University of Vermont. Early on, keyboardist Page McConnell joined the band and Holdsworth left, giving the group its permanent lineup. Over the next several years, Phish toured extensively, and cultivated a devoted fan base by interacting with them during performances and becoming one of the first rock bands to create an Internet Usenet newsgroup in 1991. In the late 1980s the group released three self-produced albums, including *The Man Who Stepped into Yesterday*, which was based on Anastasio's senior thesis. In 1991 they signed with Elektra Records, and have since been one of the most prolific recording bands ever, releasing 14 studio albums, seven conventional live albums, and CDs of 27 live concerts; they have also released six videos on DVD.

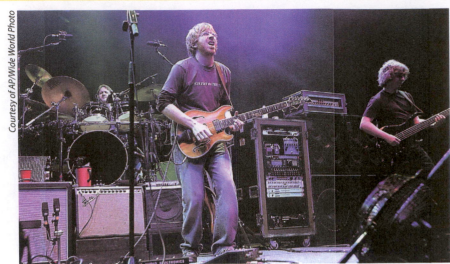

Courtesy of AP/Wide World Photo

Phish perform at Madison Square Garden on December 31, 2002.
From left: Jon Fishman, Trey Anastasio, Mike Gordon.

The group also has a website, livephish.com that allows fans to download many of their recent concerts in mp3 or FLAC format. However, like the Grateful Dead, Phish has always put their primary focus on their live shows, and have developed a fan-based community similar to the Dead's "Deadheads" that often follow the band faithfully from one show to the next.

The band that eventually became **Radiohead** first came together at prep school in Oxford, England, calling themselves On a Friday because it was the only day of the week they could all practice. From the beginning the members have been Thom Yorke on guitar and vocals, Ed O'Brien on guitar, Jonny Greenwood on lead guitar and his brother Colin Greenwood on bass, and Phil Selway on drums. In 1989 the group broke up while each member went off to college but reunited in 1991. Later that year a self-produced demo caught the attention of EMI, who signed the band. Around this time they also changed their name to Radiohead, a name that was inspired by a song on a Talking Heads album. After the release of the EP *Drill,* the group released their album debut *Pablo Honey,* which yielded their only American hit single, the #34 "Creep." Heavy touring hampered the bands efforts to return to the studio, but in 1995 they released *The Bends,* which together with a European tour warming up for R.E.M. brought Radiohead more acclaim. The breakthrough came in 1997 with the release of their third album, the multi-platinum ***OK Computer***. The album won praise for its unconventional tendencies in combining the best

KEY NINETIES ALTERNATIVE RECORDINGS

- *Under the Table and Dreaming*—Dave Matthews Band, 1994
- *Pinkerton*—Weezer, 1996
- *Odelay*—Beck, 1996
- *OK Computer*—Radiohead, 1997

MUSIC CUT 62

"PARANOID ANDROID" (THOM YORKE/JONNY GREENWOOD/ED O'BRIEN/COLIN GREENWOOD/PHIL SELWAY)—RADIOHEAD

Personnel: Thom Yorke: vocals; Jonny Greenwood: guitar; Ed O'Brien: guitar; Colin Greenwood: bass; Phil Selway: drums. Recorded September 1996 at St. Catherine's Court, Bath, England; produced by Nigel Godrich. Released May 26, 1997 on Capitol; peaked at #3 (UK), did not chart in U.S.

"Paranoid Android" is the most ambitious song on Radiohead's profound and disturbing 1997 LP *OK Computer*. Its basic construction was inspired by John Lennon's "Happiness Is a Warm Gun," which moves from tenderness to primal scream to doo-wop parody and somehow works. Said vocalist Thom Yorke: "Walked into the rehearsal room one day, 'Well, you know "Happiness Is a Warm Gun," you know how that's like three songs put together? Let's do that.' And I didn't obviously think it was going to work, until we put it together finally, which was a fucking shock." "Paranoid's" construction with three basic parts gives it somewhat of an art rock quality. The Fender Rhodes electric piano is also used in the song, a tribute to one of jazz trumpeter Miles Davis' seminal works. "We're just obsessed by *Bitches Brew*," remarked Yorke, "or anything even vaguely like it. That's a record for the end of the world." "Paranoid Android" was recorded in actress Jane Seymour's 15th-century manor house near Bath, England, which Yorke believes is haunted.

values of alternative rock (angst-ridden lyrics, post-punk attitudes, etc.) with an ear toward creating unusual and experimental electronic textures. Influences to the album include jazz trumpeter Miles Davis' *Bitches Brew* LP, the works of film composer Ennio Morricone, and 20th century avant-garde classical composer Krzysztof Penderecki. It has been called the *Sgt. Pepper's* of alternative music. Since releasing *OK Computer*, Radiohead has released four more highly regarded albums. They have also won three Grammy Awards, for *OK Computer*, 2001's *Kid A*, and 2009's *In Rainbows*.

The Dave Matthews Band, led by the transplanted South African guitarist/vocalist, has become one of rocks most popular alternative bands since their inception in the early 1990s. Like many alternative bands, their initial success came by connecting with college audiences through non-stop touring. After self-releasing *Remember Two Things* in 1993, the band was able to sign with RCA and release *Under the Table and Dreaming* the following year. Helped in part by the #9 hit single "What Would You Say" and the popular "Ants Marching," the album went quadruple platinum. In 1996, their single "So Much to Say" was awarded a Grammy for Best Rock Performance by a Duo or Group with Vocal, and since 1998 the band has released three #1 albums and no less than six live LP's. The sound of the DMB combines pop oriented world beat and loose jam-band sensibilities with touches of country and folk.

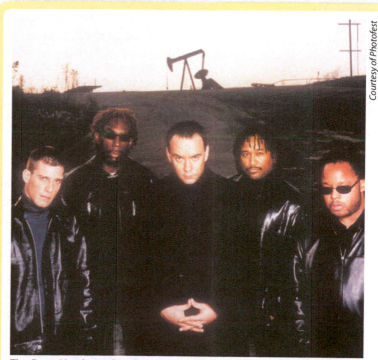

Courtesy of Photofest

The Dave Matthews Band

One of the most inventive and original musicians in the 1990s was Beck Hansen, who goes by the name **Beck**. He is the son of Bibbe Hansen, a part of Andy Warhol's Factory scene in the 1960s and the grandson of Al Hansen, an important figure in the New York art scene who is best known for helping launch the career of Yoko Ono. After trying his hand at acoustic blues, folk and poetry, Beck made his first recordings in 1992; by 1994 he signed a lucrative contract with Geffen and released *Mellow Gold,* a #13 hit. Geffen also re-released the underground smash "Loser," which became a Hot 100 #10 hit. "Loser" captures the essence of Beck's ability to create his own musical universe, combining bottleneck blues guitar, a hip-hop beat, rap lyrics and an infectious sing along hook. Subsequent albums *Odelay* (1996) and *Mutations* (1998) received Alternative Music Grammy Awards.

Another alternative band from the mid-1990s was **Weezer**, formed in Los Angeles in 1992. Emerging in the post-Nirvana grunge world of working-class angst, Weezer was something altogether different. Their sound has become characterized as a primary example of Emo, an oft misunderstood and hated term. Emo's beginnings date back to the mid-1980s in Washington, DC and a scene where bands combined a hardcore punk musical esthetic, poetic and self-indulgent lyrics, and a go-for-it live performance style. Weezer is led by lead singer/guitarist and primary songwriter Rivers Cuomo, whom author Andy Greenwald (*Nothing Feels Good: Punk Rock, Teenagers and Emo*) describes as: "a fully formed nerd singing about what he knew best: vintage clothes, random trivia, and trouble with girls." After signing with Geffen, the band released their debut album Weezer, which won fans and yielded two popular singles, "Undone—The Sweater Song," and "Buddy Holly." When the second album, the darker and less fan-friendly **Pinkerton** was negatively received by critics and fans, Cuomo retreated into seclusion. When Weezer finally resumed touring in 2000, to their surprise they found a new fan base that had discovered *Pinkerton* in their absence. Initially deemed a failure, it became the defining Emo album of the 1990s.

POP IN THE 1990s

Soundscan

Before we go further, let's take a quick look at how the industry has been keeping track of record sales since the early 1990s. In 1991, *Billboard* magazine began using a new sales tracking system to compile their charts. **Nielsen Soundscan** proved to be a much more precise method than previously used, phone surveys conducted with record store employees (basically, "Hey, what's selling this week?"). Because Soundscan compiles data from UPC and ISRC codes read into cash registers at the point of purchase, it was much more accurate and proved that there were a number of misconceptions in the traditional tracking method. For instance, genres like country and gospel were selling many more records than previously thought. It was also believed that it was rare for records to debut at #1, but Soundscan showed that in fact it was quite routine. Because sales figures changed so much, the 1991-present period is often referred to as the

"Soundscan Era." While Soundscan figures are used by *Billboard,* the R.I.A.A. (Recording Industry Association of America) tracks record sales by counting record shipments made minus records returned. As a result, there is often some discrepancy between the two methods. So, in reading further, keep in mind that if you see a gold, platinum, or diamond designation used, it is from the R.I.A.A.; a *Billboard* reference means that Soundscan was used. It should also be noted that Soundscan and the R.I.A.A track U.S. sales only; worldwide sales figures are tracked by the International Federation of the Phonographic Industry (IFPI) and other national associations.

TEEN POP

The Boy Bands

One of the biggest trends in recent pop history came in the form of teenage vocal groups and solo singers. Teen pop was nothing new—the industry had been pushing them since the late 1950s with the Teen Idols (Chapter 3); early examples of teenage boy bands include the Monkees, the Osmonds, and the early Jackson 5. However, the teen pop of the late 1990s and early 2000s was a record sales juggernaut that dwarfed all previous eras. Consider these facts: the Backstreet Boys set an all-time record for first week album sales when 1999's *Millennium* sold 1.13 million copies. Britney Spears topped that in May 2000 when *Oops!. . . I Did It Again* sold 1.3 million in its first week; unfortunately she had already been outdone two months earlier when 'NSync's *No Strings Attached* sold 2.4 million copies. Three albums, three weeks, nearly five million albums of teen pop sold. The first boy band to really take off in the 1990s was **New Kids on the Block**, which formed in Boston in 1984. Their breakthrough came with their second LP *Hangin' Tough,* which contained two #1 and one #2 singles. Their next album, 1990's *Step by Step* hit #1, went triple platinum and with the title cut yielded their biggest hit single. During their heydays the New Kids made $200 million in concert sales and $800 million in merchandise revenues. Quick on their heels were **Boyz II Men**, who made their breakthrough in 1991 with two Top 5 singles; their third album, 1992's *II* went diamond in just over a year and yielded two #1 and one #2 singles. According to their website they have sold more than 60 million albums; their singles include "One Sweet Day," a 1995 collaboration with Mariah Carey that is the biggest hit in *Billboard* history.

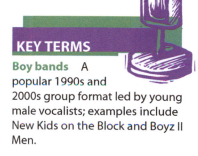

KEY TERMS

Boy bands   A popular 1990s and 2000s group format led by young male vocalists; examples include New Kids on the Block and Boyz II Men.

■ New Kids on the Block
■ Boyz II Men
■ 'NSync
■ Backstreet Boys

BOY BANDS

For a two-year run at the end of the millennium the hottest acts in the pop world were The Backstreet Boys and 'NSync. Both bands were the brainchildren of Lou Pearlman, who had the instincts to know that boy bands would sell once the grunge mania subsided, and put both groups together with Monkees-style auditions in the early 1990s. First to break were the **Backstreet Boys**, who in 1996 and 1997 released two albums, *Backstreet Boys* and *Backstreet's Back* that together sold roughly 50 million copies worldwide. 1999s *Millennium* sold nearly that many. All told, they have sold an estimated 200 million albums. **'NSync** was formed in Orlando in 1995, and under Pearlman's direction toured extensively overseas before breaking into the U.S. market (Pearlman earlier used the same strategy with the Backstreet Boys). Their self-titled debut album was released in the U.S. in March 1998; within two years it was certified diamond, pushed by two Top 10 hits. The group disbanded in 2002 after Justin Timberlake left to start a highly successful solo career. After becoming successful, both the Backstreet Boys and 'NSync sued Lou Pearlman for defrauding them of millions of dollars and won their cases. Pearlman is now serving time in a federal penitentiary for a host of crimes including money laundering.

The Girls Respond

Boys weren't the only ones getting in on the teen pop gravy train. **TLC**, the female counterpart to Boyz II Men broke big in 1994 with *CrazySexyCool* achieving diamond status, the first album by a female group to do so. They also racked up four #1 singles between 1994 and 1999. But TLC was just a warm up for **Mariah Carey**, whose amazing career has so far generated 18 #1 singles, 14 platinum or multi-platinum albums (including two that are diamond certified), five Grammy Awards and an estimated 200 million albums sold. Carey was an unknown 18-year-old in 1988 when her demo tape fell into the hands of Columbia Records president Tommy Mottola at a party. Mottola, who had a hunch that Carey was destined for greatness, immediately signed her. Over

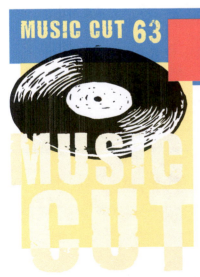

MUSIC CUT 63

"ONE SWEET DAY" (MARIAH CAREY/WALTER AFANASIEFF/ WANYA MORRIS/NATHAN MORRIS/SHAWN STOCKMAN/ MICHAEL MCCARY)—MARIAH CAREY, BOYZ II MEN

Personnel: Mariah Carey: vocals; Boyz II Men: vocals; Walter Afanasieff: synthesizers, programming; Tristan Avakian: guitar; Babyface: keyboards; Terry Burrus: piano; Loris Holland: organ; David Morales: bass; Dan Shea, Gary Cirimelli, Satoshi Tomiie: keyboards, programming. Recorded 1994–1995; produced by Mariah Carey, Walter Afanasieff. Released November 14, 1995 on Columbia; 46 weeks on the charts, peaking at #1.

"One Sweet Day" debuted on the charts at #1 on November 26, 1995, where it stayed for 16 continuous weeks (which means it was #1 throughout the months of December, January, February and half of March!). The song is the #1 hit in *Billboard* history, and just one of Mariah Carey's incredible 18 #1 hits. The song was a collaboration between Carey and Boyz II Men, who were independently working on songs celebrating friends who had recently died. The song is included on Carey's diamond certified album *Daydream*.

the next couple of years, Mottola spent $800,00 producing Carey's self-titled debut album, $500,000 on her first video, and another $1 million dollars in promotion. The two also became romantically involved and married in 1993 (and subsequently divorced in 1997). Carey's first five single releases went to #1, the first artist ever to accomplish the feat. Her two biggest selling albums, 1993's *Music Box* and 1995's **Daydream**, both peaked at #1 and achieved diamond status. Carey left Columbia in 2001 and signed with Virgin, but was dropped from the label after an emotional breakdown. She has since signed with Island and had another multi-platinum album in 2005 with *The Emancipation of Mimi*.

Carey's emotional problems pale in comparison to those of **Britney Spears**, who has very publicly gone from "schoolgirl to snake-wielding burlesque dancer to Kevin Federline's wife to head-shaving mom to MTV awards show bust to suicide risk," as author Steve Knopper humorously notes. She signed with Jive Records in 1997 as a 15-year-old former Mouseketeer on Disney's The *New Mickey Mouse Club*. Her first album, 1999's **. . . Baby One More Time** debuted at #1 and yielded the smash #1 hit of the same name. Her next three albums also debuted at #1, making her the first female artist to accomplish the feat. Spears has also included Madonna-influenced tightly choreographed dance routines into her shows that include fist jabbing, pounding feet and provocative hip movements. Although her personal life went through some turbulent times in the early 2000s, she became a pop icon that as *Rolling Stone* declared "cultivated a mixture of innocence and experience that broke the bank."

ROCK IN THE NEW MILLENNIUM

One good sign of the health of pop/rock music in the 2000s is that it has become so fragmented and diverse that today it is nearly impossible to even come up with classifications to describe the music. As Bruce Springsteen said in his 2012 South by Southwest Keynote address, "Pop has become . . . a series of new languages, cultural forces, and social movements. There are so many subgenres and factions: two-tone, acid rock, alternative dance, alternative metal, alternative rock, art punk, avant-garde metal, black metal," he said, continuing on with several dozen more styles before concluding with ". . . garage rock, blues rock, death and roll, lo fi, jangle pop . . . folk music!" He then wrapped up by saying, "Just add neo- and post- to everything I said and mention them all again." While Springsteen got a couple of good laughs from the crowd, he spoke the truth. And never before has it been easier to make music, either on your own or collaboratively, and make it available to anyone, anywhere at any time. That is not to say everything is hunky dory, because the 2000s have been a time of turbulence for the music business. We will address some of the troubling issues facing the industry later in this chapter.

With so many styles, and by extension, artists out there, it becomes prohibitive to try to cover everything in a history text such as this. Instead, we will take a look at some of the performers representing five of the most important contemporary categories: Rap/Soul/Hip Hop, Pop/Rock, Country, Indie/Alternative, and Contemporary Hard Rock/Metal.

Rap/Soul/Hip Hop

When rap first emerged in the late 1970s, many observers believed that it would be a short-lived fad. Instead, rap, and its broader classification of hip hop, has grown into a dominant force in popular music and culture today. In addition to continuing the tradition of bringing other styles into the rap fold (the first of which being the 1986 Run-D.M.C./Aerosmith rap/metal mashup "Walk This Way"), hip hop artists today are experimenting with innovative production techniques, alternative rapping styles, and new marketing strategies. Some, most notably Jay-Z and Kanye West, have used their fame to build impressive business empires. Gangsta rap continues to be popular, albeit less controversial, and today coexists with more commercially oriented styles. And hip hop has also branched out from the New York–L.A. domination of the 1990s to develop other new regional styles, including Southern and Midwestern rap.

At the turn of the millennium, raps newest lightening rod for controversy was white rapper **Eminem** (Marshall Mathers III) (b. 1972). With lyrics that include graphic depictions of violence and bizarre sexual exploits, misogyny and homophobia, Eminem has drawn some of the harshest criticism of any artist in recent history. Mathers endured an impoverished and troubled childhood, took up rapping at age 14, and by his early 20s first developed his alter ego Slim Shady, through whom he began to comment on his own troubled personal life. After catching the attention of producer Dr. Dre, the two began collaborating in the studio, leading to Eminem's major label debut *The Slim Shady LP,* released in 1999. The album, fueled by the success of the hit single "My Name Is," was a breakthrough effort that turned the rapper into an international star, with worldwide sales of 15 million and praise from the critics. In 2000 he released his next album, ***The Marshall Mathers LP***, which became the fastest selling rap album in history, selling nearly two million copies in its first week alone and eventually selling 27 million worldwide. 2002's *The Eminem Show* did nearly as well, selling 25 million copies worldwide. Although Eminem's creative output waned mid-decade, he came back in 2009 and 2010 with two albums that have

MUSIC CUT 64

"STAN" (MARSHALL MATHERS, DIDO ARMSTRONG, PAUL HERMAN)—EMINEM

Personnel: Eminem: vocals; Dido: vocals; John Bigham: guitar; Mike Elizondo: bass. Recorded 1999–2000 at The Record Plant; produced by Eminem and The 45 King. Released May 23, 2000 on Aftermath/Interscope; 15 weeks on the charts, peaking at #51.

"Stan," from Eminem's *The Marshall Mathers LP,* is the scary tale of an obsessed fan that writes a series of letters to Eminem that get increasingly frustrated, angry, and finally rage-filled over the star's lack of response. By the third verse, Stan is speeding down the freeway, speaking into a tape recorder while "on a thousand downers" with his pregnant girlfriend screaming and locked in the trunk. In the final verse, Eminem finally responds, only to realize that it is too late. "He's crazy for real, and he thinks I'm crazy, but I try to help him at the end of the song," said Eminem about the fictional Stan. "It kinda shows the real side of me." "Stan" also cleverly mixes in a hook from Dido's song "Thank You," which is heard at the beginning of the song and between each verse.

sold a combined 16 million so far. He has also announced plans to release his eighth album later in 2013.

While Eminem has focused on controversy to stay relevant, **Jay-Z** has parlayed his musical successes into a business empire that is today estimated to be worth $500 million. Shawn Carter (b. 1969) grew up poor and fatherless in the projects of Brooklyn, but began working his way up the musical food chain with cameo appearances on recordings and shows produced by local rappers, including his mentor, Jaz-O. When Jay-Z (a stage name adopted in part as homage to Jaz-O) began producing his own recordings, he was unable to land a deal with a major label, so in 1995 he created his own, Roc-A-Fella Records. His debut album *Reasonable Doubt* was released in 1996, and is today considered a rap landmark, helping to create the genre known as Mafioso Rap, characterized by imagery of rappers with lavish lifestyles and expensive tastes. A 1997 distribution deal with Def Jam (where he later became CEO) helped turn Jay-Z into a superstar: his next 13 albums charted no lower than #3, with 11 of them hitting the top spot—the record for most by a solo artist. His latest release, *Magna Carta . . . Holy Grail* was released on July 4, 2013. Jay-Z has to date sold approximately 50 million albums and won 17 Grammy Awards. Jay-Z's business interests include Roc-A-Fella Records, the entertainment agency Roc Nation, and the full service sports management company Roc Nation Sports. He also co-owns the sports bar chain 40/40 Club, is co-founder of the clothing designer Rocawear, and has a minority interest in the NBA's Brooklyn Nets. In 2008 he married Beyoncé Knowles, and together they have a daughter, Blue Ivy Carter.

Kanye West (b. 1977) was born in Atlanta but spent most of his youth in Chicago. He began rapping in the third grade, and by his early teens was selling original songs to local rappers. He eventually formed a close friendship with producer DJ No I.D., who became his mentor. Although West aspired to become a rapper, his first success came as a producer for a number of Chicago area rap artists. In 2000 he began working for Roc-A-Fella Records, and first gained wide recognition for his production work on Jay-Z's 2001 album *The Blueprint*. His first taste of fame as a performer came in 2003 when he appeared along with Jamie Foxx on rapper Twista's single "Slow Jamz," which hit #1. West had by this time signed an artist contract with Roc-A-Fella, and released his debut album on the label, *The College Dropout* in early 2004. *TCD* was an instant success, debuting at #2 on the charts, yielding five charting singles, and winning the 2005 Grammy for Best Rap Album. The album also featured Kanye's patented "chipmunk soul" technique of using sped-up vocal loops (as in the track "Through the Wire"). West has since released six more albums (including 2013's *Yeezus*), and while sales figures do not compare to Eminem or Jay-Z, all have gone platinum. He has also released an astonishing 93 singles and 87 music videos. His business ventures include his own record label GOOD Music, and the women's fashion label DK Kanye West. West is in a relationship with the celebrity Kim Kardashian, with whom he has a daughter.

Beyoncé Knowles (b. 1981) has largely eschewed rap to focus her career on a more traditional R&B style, and has in the process become one of the most successful recording artists of all time. Her first successes came as a member of Destiny's Child, a group originally called Girl's Tyme that she put together in 1990 when she was 9 years old. Changing their name to Destiny's Child in

1993, the group, comprised of Beyoncé, Kelly Rowland, and Michelle Williams, released four studio albums and 23 singles (four hitting #1) and sold approximately 60 million records before breaking up in 2005. Beyoncé released her debut album *Dangerously in Love* in 2003, which went on to sell 11 million copies worldwide. Her third album *I Am . . . Sasha Fierce* introduced her alter ego Sasha Fierce and won five Grammy Awards. In all, Beyoncé has released four studio albums (all hitting #1), four live albums, and 38 singles (five #1s), with total record sales exceeding 100 million copies. Her stage performances feature highly choreographed dance moves that have drawn much critical praise. She has also released 38 music videos, and starred in seven Hollywood films, including playing the role of Etta James in 2008's *Cadillac Records*. 2008 was also the year that she married rap mogul Jay-Z.

Pop/Rock

For the purposes of this book, we will define pop/rock as the most mainstream form of popular music, making it by definition the most commercially successful as well. Pop music in the 2000s embraces everything from oldies acts such as the Eagles and Rolling Stones to new sensations including Katy Perry, Bruno Mars, Ke$ha, Rihanna, Will.i.am, and Robin Thicke. Oh yeah, in-betweeners like Michael Jackson and Mariah Carey continue to sell lots of records as well.

After starting his solo career in 2002, former 'NSync member **Justin Timberlake** (b. 1981) has released three platinum certified albums and 32 singles, all while nurturing a successful acting career. Timberlake was also involved in one of the most famous (infamous/bizarre?) recent music-related incidents when he tore off part of Janet Jackson's costume at the end of their performance at the halftime of the 2004 Super Bowl. The "wardrobe malfunction" (as Timberlake called it) was seen live by more than 140 million TV viewers worldwide. In the wake of the controversy that ensued, Timberlake issued an apology. Another Justin, **Justin Bieber** (b. 1994) is the latest Teen Idol to set the world of young pubescent girls on fire. Bieber was discovered in 2008 after his future agent Scooter Braun accidentally ran across the videos his mother had been posting on YouTube. Bieber signed with Island Records in 2009, and released his debut album *My World 2.0* in 2010. The album sold 5 million copies worldwide and contained six Top Twenty singles. Bieber has released three albums to date, all charting at #1, 19 singles, and 24 music videos. Although he has yet to win a Grammy, he has been nominated twice, and has won a number of American Music, *Billboard,* and other awards.

A number of pop/rock groups have enjoyed commercial success in the 2000s. **Nickelback** was formed in Canada in 1995, and has released seven studio albums since 1996 that cumulatively have sold more than 50 million copies. This despite the fact that the group is often the target of criticism from the music press for what is referred to as an uninspiring, formulaic sound. **Coldplay** formed in London in 1996 and have released five studio albums since their debut in 2000, with total sales of nearly 60 million copies worldwide. 2002's *A Rush of Blood to the Head* has sold 16 million copies on its own. Los Angeles's **Maroon 5** was formed in 2001 when the four original members of the recently broken up Kara's Flowers regrouped and added Lincoln, Nebraska native James

Valentine on guitar. Their debut album *Songs About Jane* was released the following year, and propelled by three charting singles, went 4× platinum. The band won the Grammy Award for Best New Artist in 2005. Three subsequent studio albums have all charted at no lower than #2, and three of their 17 singles have reached #1, including 2011's "Moves Like Jagger." Lead vocalist Adam Levine was also a judge on the reality TV show *The Voice*.

Unquestionably the most interesting storyline for any new major pop artist belongs to Stefani Germanotta, aka **Lady Gaga**. Germanotta was born in New York City in 1986, where early on she became involved with a number of music related activities in and out of school. After attending NYU for two years, she quit to focus on her music career. A series of demo tapes created with producer Rob Fusari (who gave her the moniker "Lady Gaga" inspired by the Queen song "Radio Ga Ga") led to a short-lived contract with Def Jam Records. In 2007 she was signed by Streamline Records, which led to a music publishing deal with Sony/ATV, where she wrote songs for among others, Britney Spears and Fergie. Gaga released her debut album *The Fame* in 2008, and supported its release with club performances with a carefully crafted act that was a stylized updating of burlesque, performance art, and general insanity. By 2009, two singles from the album had become huge #1 hits, "Just Dance" and "Poker Face," which helped the album sell 15 million copies worldwide. "Poker Face" won the Grammy Award for Best Dance Recording in 2010 and has gone on to become one of the best selling singles in history with more than 12 million copies sold. In 2011 Gaga released her second album ***Born This Way***, which spawned four Top Ten singles, including the #1 title track. But record sales alone are not what Lady Gaga is about. She has in her own way redefined the essence of pop culture. Her music, according to pop writer James Parker, is, "top-quality revenge-of-the-machines dance-stomp with beefy, unforgettable choruses," but the Gaga phenomena is more about what he calls "Gaga-dom." "Gaga-dom is the thing: a persona, something like the incarnation of

MUSIC CUT 65

"POKER FACE" (STEFANI GERMANOTTA/NADIR KHAYAT)— LADY GAGA

Personnel: Lady Gaga: lead and background vocals; RedOne: production. Recorded 2008 at the Record Plant Studios, Los Angeles, CA; produced by RedOne. Released September 23, 2008 on Streamline, Kon Live, Cherrytree, Interscope; peaked at #1 for one week on April 11, 2009.

One of two singles from her debut album *The Fame* that went to #1, "Poker Face" was a huge international hit that sold 12 million copies and won the 2010 Grammy Award for Best Dance Recording. The song was written by Gaga and Nadir Khayat, who goes by the name RedOne. Originally from Morocco, RedOne first achieved fame in Sweden, where he worked on music for Britney Spears, Shakira, and Wyclef Jean among others. After moving to New York in 2007 he was introduced to Lady Gaga, and they soon began writing songs together. Although Gaga has given a variety of interpretations of the song, we'll go with the one given England's *Daily Star* in 2009: "I've dated a lot of guys that are really into sex and booze and gambling so I wanted to write a record that my boyfriends would like," Gaga added. "But something I don't really talk about is if you listen to the chorus, it's got an undertone of confusion about love and sex . . ."

Pop stardom itself, that she has foisted upon the world. In wigs and avant-garde getups she appears, strange-eyed, her large, high-bridged nose giving a hiero-glyphic otherness to her face. On red carpets the presence manifests, where Gaga, like a dome of many-colored glass, refracts the white radiance of Pop. And who will be post-Gaga? Nobody. She's finishing it off, each of her produc-tions gleefully laying waste to another area of possibility. So let's just say it: she's the last Pop star. Après Gaga, the void." Gaga announced in July 2013 that her new album *ARTPOP* would be released November 11th, and will be accom-panied by an app that is "a musical and visual engineering system that combines music, art, fashion and technology."

Pop's latest super diva is England's **Adele** Adkins (b. 1988). Adele began singing at age four, wrote her first song when she was 16, and was signed to the XL label in 2006 at age 18. By this time her singing had evolved in to an R&B/Blue Eyed Soul style that was heavily influenced by jazz singer Ella Fitzgerald, R&B legend Etta James, and contemporary pop singers such as Beyoncé, the Spice Girls, and Pink. Her debut album *19* (named for her age at the time) was an immediate hit that hit #1 in the UK and eventually sold more than six mil-lion copies worldwide. Her most recent album *21*, from 2011, was a genuine blockbuster, with sales of 26 million and five charting hits, including the #1s "Rolling in the Deep," "Someone Like You," and "Set Fire to the Rain." All three songs hit the top of the singles chart while *21* was at #1 on the album chart, making Adele the first artist in history to accomplish such a feat. *21* also won six Grammy Awards in 2012. Being a plus size, Adele has been criticized for her weight, which she has defended as a response to the sexualization of the pop industry. "I would only lose weight if it affected my health or sex life, which it doesn't."

Country

Country music has retained wide popularity in the new millennium in part because, "Its appeal is deeply rooted and directly relevant," according to the Country Music Association. Country artists have also learned that the more they incorporate pop elements into their music, the more records they will sell. This is nothing new of course—the "Nashville Sound" was created in the late 1950s by producers Chet Atkins of RCA, Owen Bradley of Decca, and Don Law of Columbia to do just that, and before long artists like Glen Campbell, John Denver, Kenny Rogers, and Dolly Parton were scoring huge hits that crossed over onto the pop charts. The 1980s saw a huge spike in country's popularity, helped in no small measure by the 1980 movie *Urban Cowboy* and its #3 charting soundtrack album. But it was the 1990s that saw country explode into the realm of pop bring a new wave of superstars to the music, including LeAnn Rimes, Reba McEntire, Faith Hill, Martina McBride, Tim McGraw, and Kenny Chesney.

In the 1990s, two names stood above all others in country music. **Garth Brooks** (b. 1962) began his music career in 1984 after graduating from Oklahoma State University, which he attended on a track scholarship. His eponymous first album, released in 1989, was an immediate smash, going diamond (US sales of

10 million) and containing two country #1 hits. The next seven albums sold a total of over 100 million copies (US), and contained 77 single releases, 19 of which went to #1 on the country charts. His biggest selling album was 1991's *Ropin' the Wind,* which debuted at #1 and has sold 17 million copies worldwide. It is estimated that he has sold 200 million records worldwide, making him one of the best selling recording artists in history. Brooks is also the top selling artist of the Soundscan Era (1991–); the Beatles are in second place. **Shania Twain** (b. 1965) first rose to fame in 1995 with her second album *The Woman in Me,* which went to #1 on the country charts and eventually sold 20 million copies worldwide. Her next album, 1997s **Come On Over** put her into superstar status with sales of more than 40 million worldwide, making it the best selling country album in history and the best selling studio album by a female artist in any category. Twain released 12 of the album's 16 songs as singles, with eight hitting the Top Ten. Today she is known as The Queen of Country Pop, has five Grammy Awards under her belt, and has her own TV show on the Oprah Winfrey Network.

Propelled by the success of Brooks and Twain, by the late 1990s a new group of country stars began to emerge. The **Dixie Chicks** formed in 1989 in Dallas and recorded three well-received albums in the early 1990s. With the addition of new lead vocalist Natalie Maines in 1995, the group established a more contemporary pop/country sound. The first album with Maines, 1998's **Wide Open Spaces**, proved to be their breakthrough, selling 14 million copies worldwide and winning two Grammy Awards, including Best Country Album. The next album Fly went to #1 and won two more Grammies. *Home,* from 2002, debuted at #1 on the pop charts, and won four more Grammies. Clearly the Dixie Chicks were on a roll! Then, on March 10, 2003, on the eve of the Iraq War, Maines told an audience in London, "Just so you know, we're on the good side with y'all. We do not want this war, this violence, and we're ashamed that the President of the United States is from Texas." Although she later apologized for her comments, the negative reaction was intense and record sales suffered, with several radio stations staging boycotts of their CDs.

Taylor Swift (b. 1989) made her first trip to Nashville at age 11 when her mother drove her there to drop off some demo tapes Taylor had made. In 2003 the entire family packed up and moved to the city to help facilitate the 14-year-old's musical ambitions. In 2005 (at age 16) Taylor signed to Big Machine Records and began working on her first album *Taylor Swift,* which after its release in 2006 sold 5 million copies. To date she has released four studio albums, 33 singles, and has sold more than 26 million albums worldwide. Her 2007 single "Our Song" made Swift at age 18 the youngest person to solely write and sing a #1 country song. She has won seven Grammies, including Album of the Year for her second album *Fearless.* **Lady Antebellum** formed in Nashville in 2006, and forged a unique multi-genre vocal sound with the harmonies of band members Hillary Scott, Charles Kelley, and Dave Haywood. They have released six studio albums, three of which have hit #1 on the pop charts, and 13 singles. Their second album *Need You Now* debuted at #1 on the pop charts and won five Grammies, including Best Country Album and Song of the Year and Record of the Year for the title track.

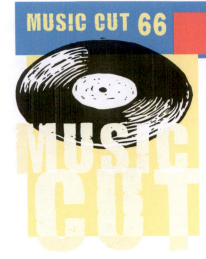

MUSIC CUT 66

"NEED YOU NOW" (HILLARY SCOTT/CHARLES KELLEY/DAVE HAYWOOD/ JOSH KEAR)—LADY ANTEBELLUM

Personnel: Hillary Scott, Charles Kelley: lead vocals; Dave Haywood: acoustic guitar, backup vocals; Jason "Slim" Gambill: electric guitar; Rob McNelley: electric guitar solo; Paul Worley: acoustic, electric guitar; Michael Rojas: piano, synthesizer; Craig Young: bass guitar; Chad Cromwell: drums. Recorded 2009 at Warner Music Studios, Nashville, TN; produced by Lady Antebellum and Paul Worley. Released August 24, 2009 on Capitol Nashville; peaked at #2 pop, #1 country.

"Need You Now" was the fourth single release by Nashville-based Antebellum, and the first and title track from their second album. The song hit #1 on the country charts on November 28, 2009, and stayed there for five weeks. To say that the song and the album achieved commercial and critical success would be an understatement; the single has sold more than six million copies, while the album became the #2 selling album in 2010. The song won four awards at the 2011 Grammies, for Record of the Year, Song of the Year, Best Country Performance by a Duo or Group with Vocals, and Best Country Song. It is also the most downloaded country song in history. The song came together quickly when the group met for the first time with songwriter Josh Kear for the first time. "Actually, it was the second song we wrote that day," said Kear. "We were only together for 2½ hours. We finished the first one in the first 45 minutes. Charles had a guitar thing and an opening line for a song and we wrote 'Need You Now' really fast and went, 'great, that was fun.' It was the first day I'd ever spent with them." What's the song about? Hillary Scott gives us the scoop: "All three of us know what it's like to get to that point where you feel lonely enough that you make a late night phone call that you very well could regret the next day. But you do it anyway because it's the only thing that's going to give you any relief in that moment."

Indie/Alternative

We first identified the term "Alternative" back in chapter 12 in reference to the fiercely independent, DYI underground scene that emerged in the 1980s that included such bands as R.E.M., Sonic Youth, and the Replacements. We have also seen that in the 1990s Alternative emerged from the underground with the popularity of the Seattle grunge scene and the spectacular success of Nirvana. And just like every other genre, in the 2000s, Alternative, or Indie, or Post-Punk—whatever you want to call it—has become increasingly diverse in sound. As described in chapter 12, Alternative music is hard to categorize, but one underlying characteristic is still the DIY, 1960s garage band esthetic.

Formed in Chicago in 1994, **Wilco** has carried on the alternative tradition with a willingness to experiment with avant-garde sounds and combine diverse musical influences. The band is led by Jeff Tweedy on vocals and bassist John Stirratt on bass (the only original members), with Tweedy the primary songwriter. The group has released eight studio albums between 1995–2011, with their last four breaking into the Top Ten. One of their most interesting albums was a 1998 collaboration with singer/songwriter Billy Bragg called *Mermaid Avenue,* which consists of previously unrecorded Woody Guthrie lyrics set to music by Bragg and Wilco. **Bright Eyes** is the name given to the musical endeavor of Omaha guitarist/singer/songwriter Conor Oberst (b. 1980). Oberst began his music career by releasing self-produced cassettes of original songs at age 13 and forming a variety of short-lived bands to play his music. He formed

Bright Eyes in 1995 with Mike Mogis on guitar, and Nate Walcott on keyboards and trumpet. Soon after, the band signed with Omaha indie label Saddle Creek Records and released their first album, *A Collection of Songs Written and Recorded 1995-1997*. It had generally poor reviews. However, their 2002 album *Lifted or The Story Is in the Soil, Keep Your Ear to the Ground* received very positive reviews in *Rolling Stone* and several other publications, and brought the group national attention. Conor Oberst was suddenly an alternative celebrity. Bright Eyes was further pushed into the spotlight when they toured with R.E.M. and Bruce Springsteen in 2004's Vote for Change tour.

Death Cab for Cutie is a four-piece group that formed in 1997 in Bellingham, Washington. The band was originally a solo project for guitarist/vocalist Ben Gibbard, who decided to expand into a group format after securing a contract with the small Seattle-based indie label Barsuk Records. The group released their debut *Something About Airplanes* in 1998, the first of four on Barsuk. DCFC burst into the mainstream after signing Atlantic in 2004, with their last three albums charting no lower than #4 on the pop charts. Their 2008 album *Narrow Stairs* hit #1 and was generally very received by the music press. **The White Stripes** were formed in Detroit in 1997 by husband and wife Jack and Meg White, and have been one of the new century's most interesting and influential bands. What's interesting about them? For starters, the only primary instruments are drums (played by Meg) and guitar (played by Jack). In addition, the Whites divorced in 2000 but continued to record and tour together until disbanding in 2011. The band's music is rooted in the blues and punk, and they are fully committed to a "lo-fi" production style. There is also a serious fascination with red, white, and black (Google "White Stripes images" and you'll get the idea!). Their eponymous debut album, released in 1999, was dedicated to Mississippi Delta bluesman Son House, one of Jack White's primary musical influences. The band went on to record five more albums, the last being 2007's *Icky Thump*, which won a Grammy for Best Alternative Music Album.

MUSIC CUT 67

"THE BIG THREE KILLED MY BABY" (JACK WHITE)— THE WHITE STRIPES

Personnel: Jack White: guitar, vocals, production; Meg White: drums. Recorded January 1999 at Ghetto Recorders and Third Man Studios, Detroit, MI; produced by Jack White, Jim Diamond. Released March 1999 on XL Recordings; did not chart.

"The Big Three Killed My Baby" was the third single release by the White Stripes, and the only one from their eponymous debut album. The "big three" referenced in the song title and lyrics are the Big Three automakers from Detroit—GM, Ford, and Chrysler. The song is a rant against the carmaker's lack of innovative yet expensive products, coziness with big oil, and planned obsolescence. The song's production is a great example of the White Stripes "lo-fi" production technique, and was recorded at Detroit's Ghetto Recorders, which bills itself as having "All the Amenities of Prison." The album was co-produced by studio owner Jim Diamond.

Contemporary Hard Rock/Metal

Another enduring genre with a large stylistic umbrella, hard rock/metal continues to be a part of the genetic code of pop music in the 2000s. Established metal bands such as AC/DC, Metallica (whose 1991 album *Metallica* is the top selling album of the Soundscan era), and Bon Jovi (whose 11 2000s era albums have sold well over 30 million copies worldwide) continue to be very popular, while new bands have continued to evolve the style. Formed in 1995 in Tallahassee, Florida, **Creed** released four studio albums between 1997–2009 that have collectively sold over 24 million copies. The band is led by Scott Stapp on vocals and Mark Tremonti on guitar, former Tallahassee high school classmates who also are the primary songwriters. After the self-produced album *My Own Prison* became popular in their home state, Creed was signed by Wind-Up Records, who re-mixed and re-released the album and four singles from it. The singles all hit #1 on the Hot Mainstream Rock Tracks chart, and *My Own Prison* went 6× platinum. The next album, **Human Clay**, did even better, with sales of nearly 12 million (US), and the track "With Arms Wide Open" reaching #1 on the pop charts and winning a Grammy. The band dissolved in 2004, but reunited in 2009 with a new album release.

Linkin Park was formed in 1996 in Agoura Hills, California by high school classmates Mike Shinoda, Brad Delson, and Rob Bourdon. In the early years, the band went through several personnel changes before adding three more members. They also had a series of name changes, going from Xero to Hybrid Theory to finally Linkin Park, a spelling play on Santa Monica's Lincoln Park. After much struggle, the band signed with Warner Bros. in 1999 and released their debut **Hybrid Theory** in 2000. Astonishingly, the album was one of the most successful debuts in history, becoming the biggest selling album of 2001 and eventually selling 24 million copies worldwide. Linkin Park has to date released five studio albums with sales of 60 million worldwide, and released 24 singles. **Foo Fighters** were founded in 1994 as the one-man project band of former Nirvana drummer Dave Grohl after the April 5, 1994 death of Nirvana front man Kurt Cobain. The band's 1995 self-named debut album featured songs composed by Grohl, who, with the exception of one guitar part and a few backup vocals, played all the instruments and sang all the vocal parts. The album debuted at #23 on the pop charts and received generally good reviews. Upon its release, Grohl put together a four-piece band to play the music live. Six more studio albums were forthcoming between 1997–2011, all of which have hit the Top Ten. The band became a five-piece unit in 2010 when original member Pat Smear rejoined. Foo Fighters have won 11 Grammy Awards, including Best Rock Album for 2001's *There Is Nothing Left to Lose*, 2004's *One by One*, 2008's *Echoes, Silence, Patience & Grace*, and 2012's *Wasting Light*. In 2013 Grohl produced and directed the documentary film *Sound City*, about the legendary San Fernando Valley studio where Nirvana's *Nevermind* and many other legendary albums were recorded.

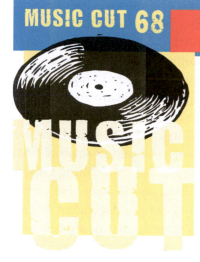

MUSIC CUT 68

"ROPE" (FOO FIGHTERS)— FOO FIGHTERS

Personnel: Dave Grohl: lead vocals, rhythm guitar; Chris Shiflett: lead guitar, backup vocals; Pat Smear: rhythm guitar; Nate Mendel: bass guitar; Taylor Hawkins: drums, backup vocals; Rami Jaffee: keyboards; Drew Hester: cowbell. Recorded September 6–December 21, 2010 in Dave Grohl's garage, Encino, CA; produced by Butch Vig. Released on March 1, 2011 on RCA as a digital download and on vinyl, peaking at #68.

"Rope" is the first single release from Foo Fighters seventh album *Wasting Light*. The album was noteworthy for a couple of reasons; it reunited leader Dave Grohl with producer Bitch Vig (producer of Nirvana's 1991 album, on which Grohl played drums), and it was recorded old school with analog equipment in Grohl's garage. Grohl has long been a critic of how digital recording makes it possible to "fix" studio performances with sophisticated software. "You have the ability to completely manipulate and change the performance with the digital stuff. You don't really have that with analog . . . [but] I don't want to even know I can do that. I don't want to know I can tune my voice, because I want to sound like me," Grohl said. "It all came together as one big idea. Let's work with Butch, but let's not use computers, let's only use tape. Let's not do it at 606 (Grohl's professional studio), let's do it in my garage. And let's make a movie that tells the history of the band as we're making the new album, so that somehow it all makes sense together in the grand scheme of things. What we're doing here is in some ways making sense of everything we've done for the last 15 years." The movie, *Foo Fighters Back and Forth* debuted March 15, 2011 at the SXSW festival in Austin, Texas. At the 2012 Grammies, the film won the award for Best Long Form Music Video.

THE MUSIC INDUSTRY IN THE EIGHTIES AND NINETIES: LIVING LARGE IN L.A.

The Majors Rule

As we discussed back in Chapter 12, the music industry—and in particular the major labels—had experienced tremendous growth in the 1970s, only to suffer a debilitating post-disco crash that sent sales figures plummeting. As painful as that medicine was, to say the record business rebounded nicely would be a gross understatement. The 1980s and 1990s were the best of times for the major labels, a time when new sales records were constantly being set, new technologies emerging, and new stars were being made, sometimes overnight. Consider this: of the Top 100 Albums compiled by the RIAA, 61 were released in the 1980s or 1990s. By comparison, a grand total of only 11 have come from the 2000s, the highest ranked being *Up!* by Shania Twain, which sits at #54. For the major labels, the 1980s and 1990s was a time for getting fat and living large.

Industry wide, sales figures for records, tapes and CDs jumped from $3.5 billion to nearly $13.5 billion between 1982 and 2000. Growth like that naturally caught the attention of Wall Street investors, who jumped in with a series of mergers and corporate takeovers that ultimately put the industry into the hands of a small number of large multi-national conglomerates. Although consolidation of the music industry had been going on since the beginning of the rock era, by the late 1970s six super-major labels had emerged that controlled

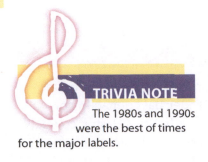

the lion's share of record sales and distribution. Four of those six, CBS, Warner, RCA and MCA were American owned; of the other two, PolyGram was owned by German and Dutch interests while Capitol-EMI was British. Further consolidation in the 1980s and 1990s reduced the number of majors to five when the German owned BMG bought RCA, Sony bought CBS, and PolyGram and MCA were bought by the Canadian owned Seagram Company and renamed Universal Music Group. The latest round of consolidation occurred 2008 when Sony bought BMG, creating the "Big Four," and in 2011 when EMI was cut up and sold off to Sony and Universal. In 2012 Universal sold its share of EMI to Warners. As a result, today there is a "Big Three": Universal Music Group, which has a 39% share of the market, Sony with 30%, and Warner, 19%. (The rest of the market—approximately 11%—is from sales by independent labels.) To even refer to these companies as record labels is somewhat of a misnomer, as they are actually huge multinational umbrella corporations that have made investments in companies that make records.

What did consolidation mean for artists and consumers? Fredric Dannen, author of the 1990 industry exposé *Hit Men* described the majors at that time as the "sovereign states" of pop music. "Today, there is virtually no American pop singer or rock band of national stature that a major does not, in one way or another, have a piece of. The days are gone in which a pint-sized company can launch [a national act] with independent distribution." By the mid-1990s, artists had fewer places to go to get a contract signed, the independent labels that still existed were essentially shut out of distribution networks, and consumers were left with fewer choices as to what to buy. After years of battling with independent labels and fickle consumers, it seemed as if the major labels had finally achieved permanent market dominance.

Hubris

But we must not underestimate the power of hubris, in this case the pop music industry's collective ability to screw up a good thing. Let's start with the drug-induced decadence that came with the good times in the 1980s and 1990s, because many executives seemed hell bent on outdoing their artists in living the rock and roll lifestyle. Exhibit A was Casablanca Records president Neil Bogart. Bogart had the company offices palatially designed to match Rick's Café in the movie *Casablanca* (get it: Humphrey *Bogart—Neil Bogart?*), had music blare from giant speakers, and made drugs—and lots of them—available at all times. Casablanca, which was heavily invested in disco artists, crashed in the early 1980s and Bogart died of cancer soon after. The industry also made a number of strategic mistakes that seemed like good ideas at the time but in fact weren't. One was the mid-1990s decision to stop selling singles. Once the single was killed off in 1998, consumers had no choice but to buy a $17 CD if they wanted to buy their favorite song. Initially this was great for business, but eventually buyers became embittered and felt they were getting ripped off. "If you only sold hand lotion in five-gallon bottles, pretty soon people would be tired of it," says producer Albhy Galuten. "You can't go around forcing people to buy something they don't want."

Another major blunder the industry made was to allow the killing off of the mom and pop record store. Brick and mortar record stores had traditionally fostered a sense of community as a hangout for music lovers, musicians, and other hipsters; in addition, they were the only place where records could be purchased. However, that all changed in the 1990s when big box stores like Walmart and Best Buy began selling records at deeply discounted prices that the small stores could not match. Consumers flocked to the boxes, which before long accounted for 65% of CDs sold. The first casualties of the box store bargains were the small locally owned record stores, but eventually even the large chains like Tower and Musicland (Sam Goody) went out of business. With their newfound clout the big boxes began to dictate the terms of what they would and wouldn't sell, which meant that labels sometimes had to airbrush over risqué album covers or produce clean versions of CDs with explicit lyrics. Once Walmart and Best Buy decided to reduce the shelf space in their record sections, consumers were left with soullessly sterile purchasing environments with a limited selection of only the biggest selling pop CDs.

THE MAJORS MEET THEIR MATCH

Napster

The cumulative effect of the drugs, decadence, arrogance, corporate consolidation and bad business decisions left the music industry completely unaware of the fact that they were in a very vulnerable situation by the end of the 1990s. This vulnerability was soon exposed. In 1998, Northeastern University student **Shawn Fanning** created Napster, a file-sharing website that allowed users to log on and see a display of the music titles on the hard drives of everyone else who was currently logged on. Then, using the program's search engine, they could easily find a specific piece of music by artist or title, and download it to their own computer. Napster worked because it used highly compressed **mp3** files, a music file format developed in the early 1990s. And because the record store had suddenly been neatly excised from the transaction, the music was *free!* Once someone bought a CD, stored the music from it on his or her computer as mp3 files and logged on to Napster, that CD was now available to anyone anywhere that was currently logged on. The ramifications of this new way of obtaining music were enormous, and could possibly bring down the entire music industry as it currently existed.

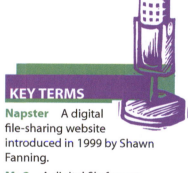

Now, it is important to keep in mind that at this time record industry executives were so out of touch with things outside of their world that most didn't even know what an mp3 file was. Once the R.I.A.A. started figuring out what was going on, they became alarmed—in fact, very alarmed. After all, consumers were stealing their product! By October 1999 there were already 150,000 Napster registered users sharing 3.5 million files, and it was expanding at an astonishing rate. After demands by the R.I.A.A. for Napster to remove all their signed artists were ignored, the R.I.A.A. filed suit on December 6, 1999, claiming the site was guilty of "contributory and vicarious copyright infringement." Napster countered by claiming it was not unlike manufacturers of copying machines or VCRs, who were not held responsible for the potential illegal use by the owners of their products. The one-day trial was held on July 26, 2000, with Judge Marilyn Hall Patel of the Federal Court in San Francisco ruling that Napster was in fact violating copyright laws. Although appeals would drag the case on for another year, in the end Napster was shut down. In the meantime, Shawn Fanning became a generational folk hero as the kid who single-handedly "stuck it to the man." As Steve Knopper writes in *Appetite for Self-Destruction,* Fanning became "a symbol, a rebellious David-vs.-Goliath type who invented the coolest slingshot ever."

But by this time other file-sharing sites had sprung up like weeds, and no self-respecting college student was going to go back to paying $17 for a CD when he or she could get the music online for free, albeit illegally. New statistics showed that sales of CDs, albums and tapes in 2000 fell by nearly 10% from the previous year, the first downturn since 1982. At the same time, blank CDs outsold prerecorded ones for the first time ever. It seemed pretty clear to music executives that instead of buying CDs, consumers were downloading music illegally and burning their own custom CDs. It was also clear that shutting down Napster had not solved the digital piracy problem. Meanwhile, record labels began laying off hundreds of employees and severing the contracts of many artists to cut costs. The R.I.A.A. returned to the courtroom to shut down new file-sharing sites like Grokster, LimeWire, and Morpheus. In 2003 they also began serving subpoenas to hundreds of suspected copyright violators, with the threat of fines of up to $150,000 per illegally copied song on their computers. To actually bring lawsuits against the very consumers they were trying to turn into customers was an extreme step to take, but one the RIAA felt they had no choice in doing. "We didn't want to be suing, but there weren't a lot of alternatives," said one industry source. "It's one thing when you're looking from the outside and saying how stupid this is, but it's another thing when you're seeing half your company laid off." It was a public relations mess, but the lawsuits continued on until late 2008, by which time more than 35,000 had been filed, with an average settlement of $3,500.

The iTunes Music Store and Beyond

The fact that the RIAA started suing customers in 2003 was only partly due to the fact that the industry struggled to come to grips with online piracy and to figure out a plan of attack. But the bottom line was that until Apple Computer launched the **iTunes Music Store**, consumers had no convenient, inexpensive and legal option to buy music online. The iTunes software was first made available for Macintosh computers in 2001 to interconnect with the Apple iPod mp3 player. After wrangling out complicated licensing agreements with the major labels, Apple CEO Steve Jobs introduced the iTunes store on April 28, 2001 as a site where consumers could conveniently buy legal mp3 files for 99¢ a song and typically $9.90 per album. On that day 200,000 songs were available from nearly every major artist (major exceptions included Led Zeppelin and the Beatles, both of whom have since come on board), and it was an instant smash hit. Today there are more than 26 million songs available on iTunes, and as of February 2013, 26 billion songs have been downloaded from the site, which currently accounts for 64% of all online legal digital music sales worldwide.

Of course, the iTunes Music Store did not immediately stop the illegal downloading, although at first it was difficult to gauge how much piracy was still going on. But it was pretty clear that the genie had been let out of the bottle. Record sales immediately started to fall: in 2000 there were 730 million CDs sold; by 2012, 198 million. But increasingly, consumers did in fact start buying music legally online. In 2004 (the first year they were tracked), 141 million single tracks were purchased and downloaded; by 2012 the number was at 1.336 billion, an increase of nearly 1000%. With Amazon, Xbox Music and others getting into the online music store business, it is easier than ever to buy music legally online. But—the growth in digital downloads appears to be slowing down, indicating that there is something else going on. And there is: it's becoming increasingly clear that the new business model is for consumers to not actually buy music in any form at all but instead to stream it directly to their computer, tablet device, or smartphone. Streaming services such as Rhapsody offer millions of songs available for a monthly subscription fee. Internet "radio stations" such as Pandora, Spotify, and Rdio offer endless streaming of free music in the form of listener customizable "stations" based on a specific artist, genre, or song. Currently Pandora is the largest player in this market, although they are currently in litigation with ASCAP, BMI, and other music licensing agencies for the very low royalty rates they pay out to artists. If you are a creative musician, this is where the turf war is being fought today to determine your ability to make a living from your recorded music.[1]

THE FUTURE

The End of the World as We Know It?

So, where does the digital age leave the music industry? Well, you could ask the newspaper, publishing, and radio industries the same thing. The short answer is, because we are in a time when tremendous economic changes are occurring because of the Internet, we simply don't know yet. We do know that the CD is dying, as consumers have clearly shown a preference for having convenient access to their music, whether in the form of an mp3 or having it streamed. And while the album is not dead, its relevance as a creative document seems to be, as consumers have also shown that they prefer buying singles "cafeteria style" rather than albums. One could also make the assumption that sales in the 1990s—when consumers *had* to buy $17 albums—were artificially high and were bound to fall eventually. A similar sales downturn occurred in the early 1980s, but the industry had the trifecta of *Thriller,* MTV and the introduction of the CD to pull it out of that slump. The coming of the digital age revealed an industry that was woefully inefficient and ill prepared to respond to the changes

[1] Ironically, the only sales category besides digital downloads to increase in recent years is vinyl records. Yes, vinyl . . . you know—*records*. Vinyl had sales in 2007 of 990,000, 4.5 million in 2012. The big sellers are youth-oriented groups like Daft Punk, the Transplants, and Dessa. However, with a lack of turntables being made for the consumer market, it is unclear whether young people are buying vinyl records to listen to or instead to look at and display their cover artwork. Apparently the kids and boomers agree on one thing: nothing has come along to beat the old-fashioned 12" album cover with liner notes on the back. Even the most diehard digital fan must admit to that!

afoot, and one that was extremely slow to respond to those changes. When the music industry finally did get around to addressing online piracy, it was astonishingly off target. "They left billions and billions of dollars on the table by suing Napster—that was the moment the labels killed themselves," says Jeff Kwatinetz, CEO of The Firm, a management company. "The record business had an unbelievable opportunity there. They [consumers] were all using the same service [Napster]. It was as if everybody was listening to the same radio station. Then Napster shut down, and all those thirty or forty million people went to other [file sharing services]." However, one industry insider says there were pressures from other sources as well. "A lot of people say, 'the labels were dinosaurs and idiots, and what was the matter with them?'" said Hilary Rosen, who was CEO of the RIAA at the time. "But they had retailers telling them, 'You better not sell anything online cheaper than in a store,' and they had artists saying, 'Don't screw up my Wal-Mart sales.'"

But enough about the labels and the business; what about the music itself? What lies ahead for rock and pop music? There's a lot of complaining going on today about the quality of pop music, so perhaps the case could be made that it is the music itself, and not the industry, that is in trouble. Some say there is nothing good anymore; others say that it's all derivative of something from the past; while still others complain that there is no new movement or style, no rap, punk or grunge to unite the field and lead the way. In reality, all these things are true to one extent or another, but a larger truth is that the term pop music itself may be oxymoronic in today's world. With the gatekeepers (the major labels) out of the way, consumers are free to control exactly what they want to be entertained with, how to search for it, and how to be kept abreast of any new developments in it. And they can move on to something else whenever they want. "Pop music is the music that the most people are listening to most of the time," writes Helium.com contributor Gordon Ashley. "But the sheer volume of content that can be sifted from the mind-boggling expanse of the Internet will make that idea obsolete. And without the money-makers tightly holding the strings and manipulating what the most people are digging on most often, the idea of a definable pop culture will disappear."

And with the Internet and the technology available today, more people than ever are making music. Digital Audio Workstations (DAW) such as ProTools, Apple Logic Pro, and Digital Performer are becoming less expensive, more comprehensive and easier to use. Getting your music "out there" is also simpler than ever with YouTube and other sites. And when it is out there, who knows who is going to hear it and what they're going to do with it. "Music now has the possibility of having a much larger gene pool," says Robert Thompson, professor of pop culture at Syracuse University. "There are more mutations out there than before simply because there are more opportunities for something to actually get into the distribution system." And as we have seen, the new distribution system is radically different than the old one where CDs were sold in record stores. Today it is possible for an artist to "easily bypass the traditional infrastructure—going into the studio, sending singles to radio stations—and make songs available for download almost as soon as they're written," according to Dan Brown of CBC News Online. It is even possible for stars to be made by bypassing the traditional radio route. Just ask Justin Bieber, who became famous on YouTube, or Kelly Clarkson, whose first album sold more than two million copies after she won *American Idol* in 2005.

Whether all of this is a good thing or just going to lead to the creation of a clutter of crappy music is yet to be seen. A similar revolution has already taken place in the video world, where inexpensive, easy to use technology has allowed almost anyone to make and edit movies. (You only have to look as far as YouTube to see whether or not that has produced anything interesting.) However, as Chris Anderson writes in *The Long Tail: Why the Future of Business is Selling Less of More,* "Talent is not universal, but it's widely spread: give enough people the capacity to create, and inevitably gems will emerge." Perhaps the future of rock and pop music is best summed up by Peter Rojas, founder of Engadget and co-founder of RCRD LBL, a free, online-only music label launched by Downtown Records. "I don't pretend to know what the industry will look like in ten years, but the funny thing about all of this is that music itself is healthier than ever. The Internet, combined with low-cost (or even no-cost) digital tools, has led to an explosion of creativity, with millions of amateurs making music for every conceivable genre, sub-genre, and micro-genre, and then sharing their creations online. We have an infinite number of choices available to us, and when content is infinitely abundant, the only scarce commodities are convenience, taste, and trust. The music companies that are successfully shaping the Internet era are recognizing that the real value is in making it easier to buy music than to steal it, helping consumers find other people who share their music tastes, and serving as a trusted source for discovering new music."

As one wise and prescient man first said back in 1963, "The times they are a-changin'." Indeed they are.

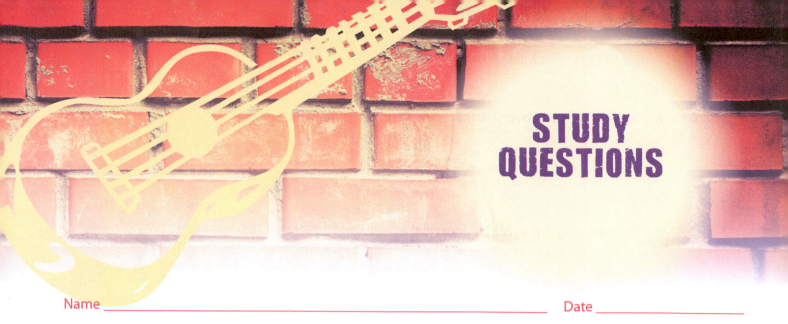

Name _____   Date _____

1. Why was Nirvana's album *Nevermind* hitting #1 in 1992 so significant?

2. What are some of the reasons that Seattle was important to grunge?

3. Which album proved to be the commercial breakthrough for Radiohead, and what were some of the influences on its music?

4. Describe emo and how it came about.

5. Describe how Mariah Carey was discovered and some of her successes and failures.

6. What are some of the controversies that Eminem has embroiled himself in?

7. Describe the culture of the music business in the 1980s and 1990s.

8. Describe exactly what MPEG Audio Layer III is and its role in changing the record business in the late 1990s and early 2000s.

9. Who is Shawn Fanning and why did he play such an important role in the evolution of the record business?

10. Describe some of the ways that the music industry is changing. Give your thoughts on what the future holds.

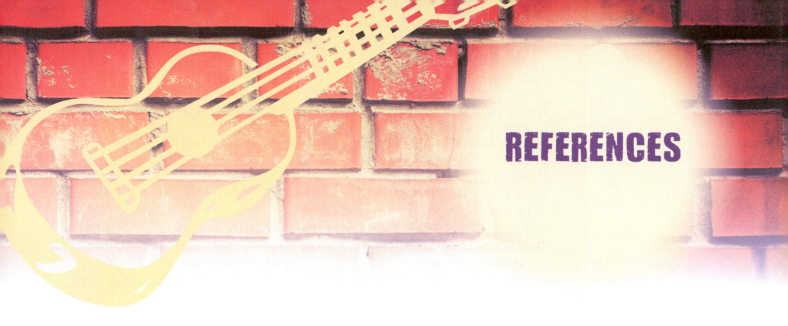

REFERENCES

Altschuler, Glenn C.: *All Shook Up: How Rock and Roll Changed America;* Oxford University Press, New York, 2003

AMG: All Music Guide

Azerrad, Michael: *Our Band Could Be Your Life: Scenes from the American Indie Underground 1981–1991;* Back Bay Books, New York, 2001

Barkley, Elizabeth F.: *Crossroads: Popular Music in America;* Prentice Hall, Inc, Upper Saddle River, NJ, 2003

Bianco, David, editor: *Parents Aren't Supposed to Like It: Rock & Other Pop Musicians of the 1990s;* UXL, Detroit, MI, 1998

Bronson, Fred: *The Billboard Book of Number One Hits;* Billboard Publications, New York, 1992

Browne, David: *Fire and Rain: The Beatles, Simon and Garfunkel, James Taylor, CSNY, and the Lost Story of 1970;* DaCapo Press, NY, 2012

Brown, Mick: *Tearing Down the Wall of Sound: The Rise and Fall of Phil Spector;* Vintage Books, New York, 2007

Christgau, Robert: *Any Way You Choose It: Rock and Other Pop Music 1967–1973;* Penguin Books, Baltimore, MD, 1973

Clapton, Eric: Clapton: *The Autobiography;* Broadway Books, New York, 2007

Cogan, Brian: *The Encyclopedia of Punk;* Sterling, New York, 2006

Cogan, Jim and Clark, William: *Temples of Sound: Inside the Great Recording Studios;* Chronicle Books, San Francisco, CA, 2003

Cohodas, Nadine: *Spinning Blues Into Gold: The Chess Brothers and the Legendary Chess Records;* St. Martin's Press, New York, 2000

Cross, Charles R.: *Room Full of Mirrors: A Biography of Jimi Hendrix;* Hyperion Books, New York, 2005

Curtis, Jim: Rock Eras: *Interpretations of Music and Society, 1954–1984;* Bowling Green State University Press, Bowling Green, OH, 1987

Dannen, Fredric: *Hit Men;* Vintage Books, New York, 1991

Davis, Francis: *The History of the Blues;* Hyperion Books, New York, 1995

Davis, Stephen: *Hammer of the Gods: The Led Zeppelin Saga;* Ballantine Books, New York, 1985

Davis, Stephen: *Jim Morrison: Life, Death, Legend;* Gotham Books, New York, 2004

Doggett, Peter: *Are You Ready For The Country: Elvis, Dylan, Parsons and the Roots of Country Rock;* Penguin Books, New York, 2000

Emerick, Geoff: *Here, There and Everywhere: My Life Recording the Music of the Beatles;* Gotham Books, New York, 2006

Escott, Colin with Hawkins, Martin: *Good Rockin' Tonight: Sun Records and the Birth of Rock 'n' Roll;* St. Martins Press, New York, 1991

Farley, Christopher John: *Before the Legend: The Rise of Bob Marley;* Amistad, NY, 2006

Fletcher, Tony: *Moon;* HarperCollins, New York, 1999

Fong-Torres, Ben: *The Hits Just Keep on Coming: The History of Top 40 Radio;* Miller Freeman Books, San Francisco, CA, 1998

Friedlander, Paul: *Rock & Roll: A Social History;* Westview Press, Boulder, CO, 1996

Gaines, Steven: *Heroes and Villains: The True Story of the Beach Boys;* Da Capo Press, New York, 1995

Garofalo, Reebee: *Rockin' Out: Popular Music in the USA;* Prentice Hall, Inc, Upper Saddle River, NJ, 2002

Gillett, Charlie: *The Sound of the City: The Rise of Rock and Roll;* Outerbridge & Dienstfrey, New York, 1970

Gilmore, Mikal: *Night Beat: A Shadow History of Rock and Roll;* Doubleday, New York, 1998

Goodman, Fred: *The Mansion on the Hill: Dylan, Young, Springsteen, and the Head-On Collision of Rock and Commerce;* Vintage Books, New York, 1997

Greenwald, Andy: *Nothing Feels Good: Punk Rock, Teenagers, and Emo;* St. Martin's Griffin, New York, 2003

Guralnick, Peter: *Last Train to Memphis: The Rise and Fall of Elvis Presley;* Little, Brown and Company, Boston, MA, 1994

Guralnick, Peter: *Sweet Soul Music: Rhythm and Blues and the Southern Dream of Freedom;* Back Bay Books, Boston, MA, 1986

Halberstam, David: *The Fifties;* Fawcett Books, New York, 1993

Harry, Bill: *The Ultimate Beatles Encyclopedia;* MJF Books, New York, 1992

Hermes, Will and Michel, Sia, editors: *20 Years of Alternative Music: Original Writing on Rock, Hip-hop, Techno and Beyond;* Three Rivers Press, New York, 2005

Hertsgaard, Mark: *A Day in the Life: The Music and Artistry of the Beatles;* Delacorte Press, New York, 1995

Heylin, Clinton: *From the Velvets to the Voidoids: The Birth of American Punk Rock;* A Cappella Books, Chicago, IL, 1993

Holm-Hudson, Kevin: *Progressive Rock Reconsidered;* Routledge, New York, 2002

Hoskyns, Barney: *Waiting for the Sun: Strange Days, Weird Scenes and the Sound of Los Angeles;* St. Martin's Press, New York, 1996

Isis Productions: *The Grateful Dead: Anthem to Beauty;* Eagle Rock Entertainment, New York, 2005

Joplin, Laura: *Love, Janis;* HarperCollins, New York, 1992

Kitwana, Bakari: *The Hip Hop Generation: Young Blacks and the Crisis in African-American Culture;* Basic Civitas Books, New York, 2002

Klosterman, Chuck: Did Ali Invent Rap; ESPN.com, 2006

Knopper, Steve: *Appetite for Self-Destruction: The Spectacular Crash of the Record Industry in the Digital Age;* Free Press, New York, 2009

Konow, David: *Bang Your Head: The Rise and Fall of Heavy Metal;* Three Rivers Press, New York, 2002

Kostelanetz, Richard: *The Frank Zappa Companion: Four Decades of Commentary;* Schirmer Books, New York, 1997

Laing, Dave: *One Chord Wonders: Power and Meaning in Punk Rock;* Open University Press, Milton Keynes, UK, 1985

Lang, Michael: *The Road to Woodstock;* HarperCollins, New York, 2009

Lang, Michael: *The Road to Woodstock;* Ecco Books, New York, 2010

Lomax, Alan: *The Land Where the Blues Began;* New Press, New York, 1993

Marcus, Griel: *The Doors: A Lifetime of Listening to Five Mean Years;* Public Affairs, New York, 2011

Markoff, John: *What the Dormouse Said: How the 60s Counterculture Shaped the Personal Computing Industry;* Viking, New York, 2005

Marmorstein, Gary: *The Label: The Story of Columbia Records;* Thunder's Mouth Press, New York, 2007

Marsh, Dave: *The Heart of Rock & Roll: The 1001 Greatest Singles Ever Made;* Plume Books, New York, 1989

McNally, Dennis: *A Long Strange Trip: The Inside History of the Grateful Dead;* Broadway Books, New York, 2002

Miles, Barry: *Zappa;* Grove Press, New York, 2004

Montgomery, Eric: *Float Life a Butterfly, Rap Like Jay-Z? Muhammad Ali's Rap Legacy; The Examiner,* 1/17/2012

Norman, Philip: *Shout, The Beatles in Their Generation;* Fireside Books, New York, 1981

Norman, Phillip: *Rave On: The Biography of Buddy Holly;* Fireside Books, New York, 1996

Palmer, Robert: *Dancing in the Street: A Rock and Roll History;* BBC Books, London, 1996

Phinney, Kevin: *Souled American: How Black Music Transformed White Culture;* Billboard Books, New York, 2005

Perry, Charles: *The Haight-Ashbury: A History;* Wenner Books, New York, 2005

Richards, Keith: *Life;* Little, Brown and Co.; Boston, MA, 2010

Rolling Stone Magazine: *50 Moments That Changed the History of Rock and Roll;* Issue 951, June 24, 2004

Romanowski, Patricia and George-Warren, Holly: *The New Rolling Stone Encyclopedia of Rock & Roll;* Fireside, New York, 1995

Rose, Tricia: *Black Noise: Rap Music and Black Culture in Contemporary America;* Wesleyan University Press, Hanover, NH, 1994

Rotolo, Suze: *A Freewheelin' Time: A Memoir of Greenwich Village in the Sixties;* Broadway, New York, 2008

Schaefer, G. W. Sandy, Smith, Donald S., Shellans, Michael J.: *Here to Stay: Rock and Roll through the '70s;* GILA Publishing Co. 2001

Scorsese, Martin: *Bob Dylan—No Direction Home;* Paramount Pictures, Los Angeles, CA, 2005

Shelton, Robert: *No Direction Home: The Life and Music of Bob Dylan;* Ballantine Books, New York, 1986

Simons, David: *Studio Stories: How the Great New York Records Were Made: From Miles to Madonna, Sinatra to the Ramones;* Backbeat Books, New York, 2004

Smith, RJ: *The One: The Life and Music of James Brown;* Gotham Books, New York, 2012

Snyder, Randall: *An Outline History of Rock and Roll;* Kendall/Hunt, Dubuque, IA, 2001

Sounes, Howard: *Down the Highway: The Life of Bob Dylan;* Grove Press, New York, 2001

Starr, Larry and Waterman, Christopher: *American Popular Music: From Minstrelsy to MTV;* Oxford University Press, New York, 2003

Stuessy, Joe and Lipscomb, Scott: *Rock and Roll, Its History and Stylistic Development;* Prentice Hall, Inc, Upper Saddle River, NJ, 2003

Sullivan, James: *The Hardest Working Man: How James Brown Save the Soul of America;* Gotham Books, New York, 2008

Thompson, Dave: *Never Fade Away: The Kurt Cobain Story;* St. Martin's, New York, 1994

Thompson, Dave: *Alternative Rock;* Miller Freeman Books, San Francisco, CA, 2000

Walker, Michael: *Laurel Canyon: The Inside Story of Rock and Roll's Legendary Neighborhood;* Faber and Faber, London, 2006

Ward, Ed, Stokes, Geoffrey, and Tucker, Ken: *Rock of Ages: The History of Rock and Roll;* Prentice Hall, Inc, Englewood Cliffs, NJ, 1986

Weller, Sheila: *Girls Like Us: Carol King, Joni Mitchell, Carly Simon—and the Journey of a Generation;* Washington Square Press, New York, 2008

Whitburn, Joel: *The Billboard Book of Top 40 Albums;* Billboard Publications, New York, 1995

Whitburn, Joel: *The Billboard Book of Top 40 Hits;* Billboard Publications, New York, 1996

White, Armond: *Rebel For the Hell of It: The Life of Tupac Shakur;* Thunder's Mouth Press, New York, 1997

Wicke, Peter: *Rock Music: Culture, Aesthetics and Sociology;* Cambridge University Press, New York, 1987

Woliver, Robbie: *Hoot! A 25-Year History of the Greenwich Village Music Scene;* St. Martins Press, New York, 1986

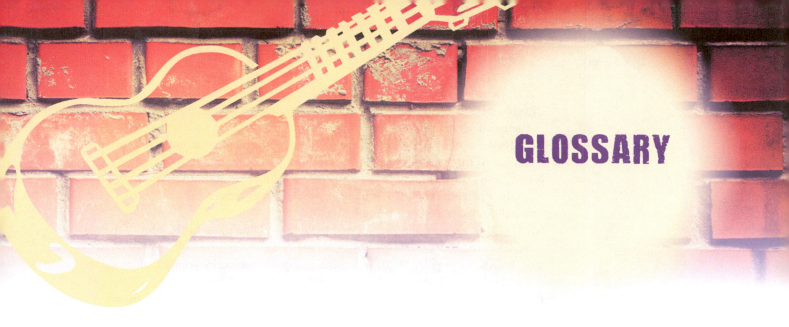

GLOSSARY

AAB lyric form—the lyric form used in blues verses in which there are three lines, the first two being identical.

Abbey Road Studios—the EMI recording studio located on Abbey Road in London where most of the Beatles' recordings were made in the 1960s.

Acid rock—the umbrella term to describe the folk and blues influenced music of the psychedelic era.

Acoustical process—the recording process used before 1925 that used acoustical horns instead of microphones.

Altamont Speedway Free Festival—the music festival held at the Altamont Speedway on December 6, 1969 that became infamous for the murder of a participant by a member of the Hells Angels.

Album—the 33⅓ rpm 12″ LP (long playing) record format introduced by Columbia Records in 1948.

Aldon Music—a songwriting company founded in New York in 1958 by Al Nevins and Don Kirshner.

Alternative rock—an umbrella term describing music from the 1980s with a wide variety of stylistic approaches and a decidedly DIY (do-it-yourself) independent attitude.

American Bandstand—the television show began in 1952 and hosted by Dick Clark from 1956 to 1987 that featured teens dancing to popular hit songs.

Art rock—an umbrella term to describe the philosophy of incorporating elements of European classical music, American jazz and the avant-garde into rock.

Audio Home Recording Act—a law passed by Congress in 1992, which among other things, allowed consumers to make personal copies of copyrighted material.

Basement Tapes—a series of recordings made by Bob Dylan and members of the Band in Woodstock, NY in early 1967.

Beatlemania—the word first coined by the *Daily Mirror* in 1963 to describe the huge popularity of the Beatles.

Beat writers—a name given to authors and poets such as Jack Kerouac, William S. Burroughs and Allen Ginsberg who gained notoriety in the 1950s and espoused a philosophy of existentialism and a rejection of materialism.

Billboard **magazine**—the industry magazine that charts record sales.

Blackboard Jungle—a 1955 fictional film about juvenile delinquency that inadvertently turned Bill Haley's "Rock Around the Clock" into a hit by using it under the opening credits.

Blaxploitation films—movies made by black directors and actors with inner city themes of drug deals and ghetto shootings.

Bluegrass—a fast paced, acoustic music that incorporated virtuoso improvised solos similar to those found in jazz.

Blues, the—the form developed in the Mississippi Delta and other Southern locales in the late 19th century that incorporates a 12-bar verse, AAB lyric form, and tonalities from the blues scale.

Bo Diddley rhythm—a rhythm first used by Bo Diddley in his first hit of the same name.

Boy bands—a popular 1990s and 2000s group format led by young male vocalists; examples include New Kids on the Block and Boyz II Men.

Brill Building Pop—the term to describe the pop songs that emerged from professional songwriters based in and around New York's Brill Building in the late 1950s and early 1960s.

Bristol sessions, the—the first important country music recordings made in Bristol, Tennessee in 1927 by Ralph Peer. Among the artists that Peer recorded were Jimmie Rodgers and the Carter Family.

British folk tradition—the traditional folk music, including ballads, lyric songs and work songs, of the British Isles. British immigrants brought these songs to the New World.

Bubblegum—a short-lived strand of carefully crafted sing along pop songs aimed at pre-teens that was generally produced in the studio by session players.

Calypso—the traditional folk music of Trinidad.

Cassette tape—a tape storage media introduced in the 1960s in which the tape was enclosed in a small plastic molding, or cassette.

Cavern Club—the underground pub in Liverpool, England where the Beatles often performed in the early 1960s.

CBGB—a club located at 315 Bowery in New York's Lower East Side that was the focal point of the city's punk scene.

Chess Records—the Chicago studio and independent label run by brothers Phil and Leonard Chess from 1950 to 1967.

Classic blues—the first recorded blues from the 1920s; characterized by the use of female singers such as Bessie Smith.

Compact disc—a digital storage media introduced in 1982 by Sony and Philips.

Country blues—the first form of the blues.

Country rock—a style that combined influences from country music with rock.

Cover—a new recording of a charting song that seeks to "cover" up the original song.

Cowboy songs—traditional country and hillbilly songs used in Hollywood films that were orchestrated to create a more commercial pop sound.

Crew/posse—informal neighborhood groups formed as a means of providing identity and support for their members.

DAT—an acronym for digital audiotape, a stereo digital tape media introduced in the 1980s.

Deadheads—the ardent followers of the Grateful Dead.

Digital sampler—a synthesizer that digitally records (samples) sounds that can then be played back and manipulated from a MIDI instrument.

Disc jockey (DJ)—a radio announcer who spins records (discs) interspersed with lively banter. The first DJ is believed to have been Al Jarvis of KFWB in Los Angeles, who was injecting his own personality into his show as early as 1932.

Disco—dance oriented pop that incorporates synthesizers, drum machines and lush orchestrations that emerged in the late 1970s.

Doo-wop—a cappella group vocal style that incorporates high falsetto vocal leads, scat singing, rhythmic vocal backings and sometimes lead vocals or spoken verse by the bass singer. Most doo-wop recordings added a rhythm section for more commercial dance appeal.

DRM—digital rights management, the term for any one of several technologies designed to limit the number of digital copies that can be made of a file.

Dub—a technique of mixing interesting sections of different songs together first used by Jamaican DJs.

Electrical process—the recording process used after 1925 that used microphones to transduce sound waves into electrical signals.

Electric ballrooms—older ballrooms in San Francisco such as the Fillmore and Avalon that staged youth dances in the early years of the city's psychedelic movement.

Electric Lady—the Greenwich Village recording studio built by Jimi Hendrix in the late 1960s.

Emo—an umbrella term describing a 1990s music style that combined a hardcore punk musical esthetic, poetic and self-indulgent lyrics, and a go-for-it live performance attitude.

Exploding Plastic Inevitable—a 1960s traveling mixed media show led by Andy Warhol.

Falsetto—a technique where male singers sing in a very high "head" voice that is beyond their natural vocal range.

Fame Studios—the recording studio founded in Muscle Shoals, Alabama in 1959 by Rick Hall. The name is an acronym for Florence Alabama Music Enterprises.

Fifties folk revival—refers to the renewed interest in folk music that occurred in the late 1950s after an earlier anti-Communist furor had pushed it underground.

File sharing—the transferring of digital files, usually mp3, from one computer to another via the Internet.

Folk rock—the pop style characterized by strumming acoustic guitars, rock rhythm sections, vocal harmonies, and lyric story lines.

Fret board tapping—a guitar technique first popularized by Eddie Van Halen.

Funk—the more primal evolution of R&B and soul that emerged in the early 1970s whose most important characteristic is the rhythmic groove.

Gangsta rap—a rap style emerging in the 1990s characterized by lyrics using first person accounting of gang related themes that include violence, rage and sexual degradation.

Girl groups—a genre characterized by young females singing songs of innocent love and devotion to their boyfriends.

Glam rock—an umbrella term encompassing a wide variety of styles held together by the use of flamboyant fashions and assaults on sexual conventions.

Gold, platinum, and diamond records—designations of 500,000, one million and ten million units sold, as certified by the RIAA.

Gold Star Studios—a Los Angeles studio often used by Phil Spector, the Beach Boys and others in the early 1960s.

Gospel—a highly emotional evangelical vocal music made popular by Thomas Dorsey that emerged from spirituals and was highly influential to rhythm and blues.

Grand Ole Opry—the radio program that began broadcasting in 1925 from WSM in Nashville that essentially made that city the center of the country music industry.

Grunge—a 1990s post-punk style that incubated with Seattle bands such as Nirvana, Soundgarden and Mud Honey.

Haight-Ashbury—the district in San Francisco that became ground zero for the city's 1960s youth movement.

Hammond's Folly—the nickname given to Bob Dylan's eponymous debut album, produced by the legendary John Hammond.

Hardcore—a harder edged, darker and angrier evolution of punk that evolved in Los Angeles, and to a lesser degree, Washington, D.C., in the 1980s.

Hard rock—a forerunner style to heavy metal characterized by distorted guitar, blues riffs and power chords.

Heavy metal—a late 1960s evolution of hard rock characterized by intense volume, distortion, and a preoccupation with themes of evil, death, the occult, etc.

Hillbilly music—the traditional old time music of the rural South and Appalachian regions, with origins in English folk music. Hillbilly music is the foundation of modern country music.

Hip-hop—a cultural expression that includes rap music, break-dancing and graffiti art that first emerged in the South Bronx neighborhoods of New York City in the late 1970s.

Hippie—the term first coined by reporter Michael Fellon in 1965 to describe young people who wore long hair, headbands, tie-dyed shirts and bell-bottom pants.

Honky tonk—a country-oriented predecessor to rock and roll that uses a rhythm section, electric guitar and electric pedal steel guitar to create a louder and hard driving sound. Honky tonk lyrics often deal with drinking, cheating, etc.

Hootenanny—a folk jam session where traditional folk songs are sung.

Human Be-In—an event held in Golden Gate Park in San Francisco on January 14, 1967 that featured speakers, poets and live music.

Independent labels—the small startup labels that began emerging in large numbers in the 1940s and 1950s.

Industrial—a 1980s punk style that incorporated non-traditional sounds from synthesizers, avant-garde electronics and mechanical sources to infuse the sounds and ethos of modern industrial life.

Island Records—the record label founded in 1961 by Chris Blackwell that initially became known for its reggae releases.

iTunes Music Store—the online music store introduced in 2003 by Apple Computer.

Jazz—the improvisational art form of individual expression first developed in New Orleans in the first years of the 20th century.

J&M Recording Studio—a studio in New Orleans owned and operated by Cosimo Matassa where many early R&B hits were recorded, including "Tutti Frutti."

Last Waltz, The—the concert film directed by Martin Scorsese that chronicles the last performance of the Band on Thanksgiving Day, 1976.

Laurel Canyon—the mountainous wooded area north of West Hollywood where many rock artists lived in the mid to late 1960s.

Left wing folk song conspiracy—describes the association between folk music and liberal politics throughout much of the early 20th century.

Lifehouse—an ill-fated album and science fiction film conceived by the Who's Pete Townshend.

Live Aid/Farm Aid—two charity rock concert events from the 1980s.

Lizard King—the persona adopted by the Doors' Jim Morrison to ignite audience reaction.

Major labels—the largest corporate record labels.

Melisma—the singing embellishment of a single syllable into several notes.

Mellotron—an early synthesizer capable of reproducing the sound of violins, cellos and flutes on tape loops activated when keys were depressed.

Mento—the indigenous folk music of Jamaica.

Merry Pranksters—the friends and followers of author Ken Kesey, who in 1965 and 1966 held a series of "acid tests," where LSD was distributed.

Mersey Beat—the name given to the snappy, upbeat music of early British Invasion bands. Named for the Mersey River in Liverpool.

MIDI—an acronym for musical instrument digital interface, a digital transfer protocol introduced in 1983.

Minimalism—the use of short repeating musical phrases to create a hypnotic effect.

Mini-Moog—an early portable analog electronic synthesizer developed by Dr. Robert Moog.

Mississippi Delta—the 250-mile-long area of Mississippi stretching from Memphis south to Vicksburg that is widely believed to be the birthplace of the blues.

Mods—a mid-1960s London youth cult that was known for snappy clothes, short hair, scooters and amphetamine consumption.

Monterey International Pop Festival—one of the first large outdoor music festivals, held in Monterey, California in June 1967.

Moondog House Rock and Roll Party, The—the name of Alan Freed's radio program on WJW in Cleveland.

Motown Records—a record label founded in Detroit in 1959 by Berry Gordy that specialized in highly produced soul.

Mp3—a digital file format that compresses sound files to approximately 1/10 normal size with little apparent loss of fidelity.

MTV—Music Television, a TV network introduced in 1981 with programming that focuses on music.

Music streaming—music that is available for listening in streaming (non-downloadable) format.

Newport Folk Festival—an annual folk festival that was first held in 1959 in Newport, Rhode Island.

Napster—a digital file-sharing website introduced in 1999 by Shawn Fanning.

New wave—a second wave of punk that incorporated pop oriented sensibilities.

1968 Democratic Convention—the presidential convention held by the Democratic Party in August 1968 that was marred by clashes between anti-war protesters and police.

Nor Va Jak Studio—the Clovis, New Mexico studio owned and operated by Norman Petty where Buddy Holly made his first hit records.

Old school rap—the first generation of rap music, which usually had themes of fun and partying.

Our World—the first live worldwide TV broadcast, occurring on June 25, 1967, which featured the Beatles performing "All You Need is Love."

Overdubbing—a feature of multi-track tape records that allows the recording of additional parts independently of each other while listening to previously recorded tracks with headphones.

Payola—the practice of DJs accepting cash (known euphemistically in the music business as the "$50 handshake"), favors and other gifts from record companies to play their songs.

Philadelphia International Records (PIR)—the Philadelphia-based label headed by producers Kenny Gamble and Leon Huff.

Pirate radio stations—illegal radio stations that broadcast pop music from ships anchored off the British coast in the early 1960s before the debut of BBC's Radio One.

PMRC—Parent's Music Resource Center, a watchdog group organized in 1985 to "educate and inform parents of this alarming new trend . . . towards lyrics that are sexually explicit."

Pogo—a violent, body-contact style of dancing associated with punk music.

Progressive rock radio—a radio format from the late 1960s and early 1970s characterized by the playing of an eclectic mix of music, particularly long, non-commercial album cuts, usually accompanied by low key, spaced-out DJ conversation. Sometimes called underground radio.

Pub rock circuit—a club scene in 1970s London where little known bands were free to experiment with new music.

Punk—the style emerging from New York, London and other cities in the mid-1970s characterized by an angry, nihilistic, do-it-yourself attitude.

Race music—a catchall term to describe any records or songs by black artists, including the blues and what would later be known as rhythm and blues (R&B).

Rap—the musical expression of hip-hop culture whose most distinguishing characteristic is the use of rhyming, melodic spoken words instead of sung lyrics.

Rapcore—an umbrella term describing bands that combine elements of rap with hardcore, metal or punk.

Rastafarianism—a religious movement whose followers believe they will be repatriated to their African homeland and escape Babylon (a metaphor for their oppressors in the New World).

Record Industry Association of America (RIAA)—the industry trade group that certifies record sales and designates gold, platinum and diamond records.

Reeperbahn—the red light district in Hamburg, Germany where the Beatles often played in the early 1960s.

Reggae—the Jamaican music that evolved from the combination of indigenous folk, American R&B and traditional Afro-Caribbean music.

Rhythm and Blues—an evolution of the blues that was more dance and commercially oriented. R&B bands often included electric instruments such as guitars, bass guitars and organs, vocalists and a horn section, often with a honking tenor saxophone soloist.

Riddim—the intertwined patterns played by the bass and drums in reggae.

Riot on Sunset Strip—a confrontation between youth and police on the night of November 12, 1966 that inspired Stephen Stills to write the Buffalo Springfield hit "For What It's Worth."

Rockabilly—the first style of rock and roll, characterized by merging elements of R&B and country (the word is a contraction of the words rock and hillbilly), slap bass, hiccupping vocals and a fast, nervous beat.

Rock steady—a Jamaican music that is slower and more relaxed than ska and is the immediate predecessor to reggae.

Scratching/back spinning—the technique utilized by DJs of playing a record back and forth quickly to create a scratching sound.

Singer/songwriter—an umbrella term describing solo performers who write and sing original songs that often tackle personal issues and emotional struggles.

Single—the 45 rpm 7" record format introduced in 1949 by RCA Victor.

Ska—an up tempo music (and predecessor to reggae) that combines an R&B influenced walking bass with accents on the offbeats from mento.

Skiffle—an English adaptation of traditional American jug band music.

Slap-bass technique—a technique for playing the electric bass guitar first conceived by Larry Graham.

Snakepit, The—the Motown recording studio, located in the basement of the Detroit headquarters.

Soft soul—a highly produced and polished soul from the early 1970s that emphasized lush string and horn arrangements and smooth vocal harmonies.

Soul music—a more pop oriented version of R&B associated with the 1960s that contains heavy influences from gospel music.

Southern rock—a rock style deeply rooted in country music and the blues that often featured bands with two or more lead guitarists.

Stax Records—a record label founded in Memphis in 1957 as Satellite Records by Jim Stewart. The label changed its name to Stax in 1961.

Stop time—the interruption of a regular beat pattern in the rhythm section.

Sullivan Show, The Ed—the popular TV show running from 1948 to 1971 on which many rock stars, including Elvis Presley and the Beatles appeared.

Sun Records—an independent label started in 1952 by Sam Phillips in Memphis.

Sunset Strip—the stretch of Los Angeles' Sunset Boulevard that was the focal point of the city's club scene in the mid 1960s.

Surf—a driving, high energy and primarily instrumental music style associated with the surfing culture of early 1960s Southern California.

Swing Era—the name given to the period from 1935–1946 when big band jazz was the most popular music in America.

Tape-delay echo—an effect created by feeding a sound source, such as a vocal, into the record head of a separate tape machine and back into the mix after it passes the playback head a split second later.

Teddy boy—the term describing alienated British young men in the late 1950s and early 1960s, who often greased their hair and wore leather jackets.

Teen idols—the clean cut, wholesome singers that the major labels promoted in the late 1950s and early 1960s to counter the success of independent label R&B and rock and roll.

Tin Pan Alley—the term describing the music publishing industry in the first half of the 20th century.

Toasting—spontaneous commentary to music by Jamaican DJs that creatively involved rhyming, interesting verbal sounds, the use of different dialects and nonsense syllables.

Top 40—the radio format in which the 40 top selling songs are played in repetition, first developed by Todd Storz at KOWH in Omaha, Nebraska.

Trad jazz—the British nickname for traditional New Orleans jazz.

Trips Festival—a three-day music festival held at Longshoreman's Hall in San Francisco in January 1966.

Troubadour, the—the preeminent Los Angeles nightclub for folk music in the 1960s.

Underground rock radio—see progressive rock radio.

Wall of Sound (Grateful Dead)—an innovative sound reinforcement system used by the Grateful Dead that consisted of 604 speakers and 26,400 watts of power. Also refers to a production technique used by Phil Spector.

Wall of Sound (Phil Spector)—a production technique developed and popularized by Phil Spector that involved the use of large instrumental groups, liberal doses of reverb, and multi-track overdubbing. Also refers to a sound system used by the Grateful Dead.

Western swing—a form of country music that incorporates jazz swing rhythm and instruments associated with a jazz swing band.

Whisky a Go Go—the preeminent nightclub on Los Angeles' Sunset Strip.

Wobblies—the nickname for the International Workers of the World labor union.

Woodstock Music and Arts Fair—the music festival held in Bethel, New York in August 1969 that drew an estimated audience of 450,000.

Work song, shout, field holler—three song forms of African origin that were widely used on slave camps in the Southern United States.

Wrecking Crew, the—a loose collection of Los Angeles studio musicians often used by Phil Spector and other producers in the early 1960s.

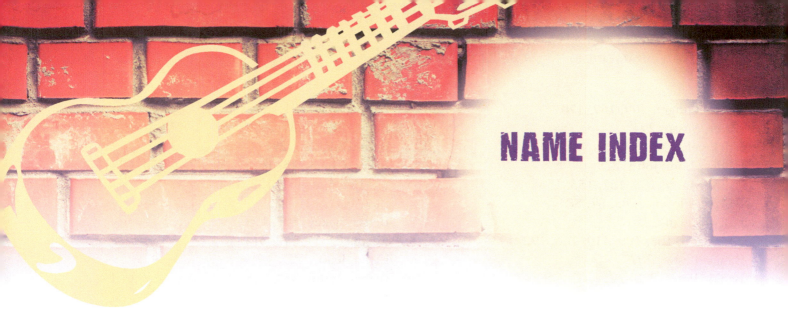

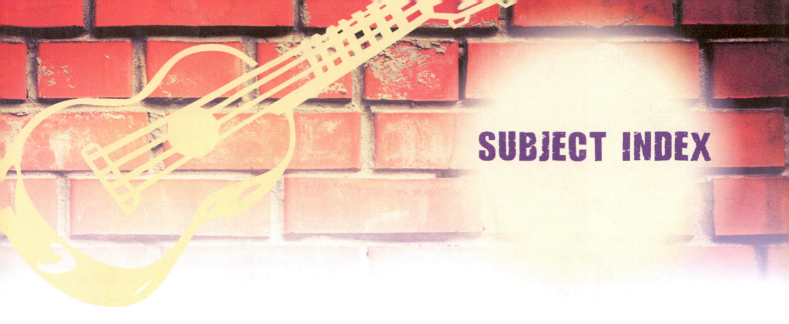

SUBJECT INDEX